Mexico City

timeout.com/mexicocity

Published by Time Out Guides Ltd, a wholly owned subsidiary of Time Out Group Ltd.
Time Out and the Time Out logo are trademarks of Time Out Group Ltd.

© **Time Out Group Ltd 2008**

10 9 8 7 6 5 4 3 2 1

This edition first published in Great Britain in 2008 by Ebury Publishing
A Random House Group Company
20 Vauxhall Bridge Road, London SW1V 2SA

Random House UK Limited Reg. No. 954009

Random House Australia Pty Limited 20 Alfred Street, Milsons Point, Sydney, New South Wales 2061, Australia
Random House New Zealand Limited 18 Poland Road, Glenfield, Auckland 10, New Zealand
Random House South Africa (Pty) Limited Isle of Houghton, Corner Boundary Road & Carse O'Gowrie, Houghton 2198, South Africa

Distributed in the US by Publishers Group West
Distributed in Canada by Publishers Group Canada

For further distribution details, see www.timeout.com

ISBN: 978-1-84670-111-5

A CIP catalogue record for this book is available from the British Library.

Printed and bound by Firmengruppe APPL, aprinta druck, Wemding, Germany.

The Random House Group Limited supports The Forest Stewardship Council (FSC), the leading international forest certification organisation. All our titles that are printed on Greenpeace approved FSC certified paper carry the FSC logo. Our paper procurement policy can be found at www.rbooks.co.uk/environment.

Time Out carbon-offsets all its flights with Trees for Cities (www.treesforcities.org).

Edited and designed by
Time Out Guides Limited
Universal House
251 Tottenham Court Road
London W1T 7AB
Tel + 44 (0)20 7813 3000
Fax + 44 (0)20 7813 6001
Email guides@timeout.com
www.timeout.com

Editorial
Editor Claire Rigby
Managing Editor Mark Rebindaine
Consultant Editors Chris Moss, David Lida
Copy Editors Matt Chesterton, Ros Sales
Proofreader Gabriela Chesterton, Patrick Mulkern
Editorial Assistant Ruth-Ellen Davis
Researchers Emma Clifton, María Dolores Martínez
Listings Checkers Jonathan Jucker, Sue-Ellen Mason
Indexer Jonathan Cox

Managing Director Peter Fiennes
Editorial Director Ruth Jarvis
Series Editor Will Fulford-Jones
Business Manager Dan Allen
Editorial Manager Holly Pick
Assistant Management Accountant Ija Krasnikova

Design
Art Director Buenos Aires Gonzalo Gil
Designer Buenos Aires Javier Beresiarte
Art Director Scott Moore
Art Editor Pinelope Kourmouzoglou
Senior Designer Henry Elphick
Graphic Designers Gemma Doyle, Kei Ishimaru
Advertising Designer Jodi Sher

Advertising
Commercial Director Mark Phillips
International Advertising Manager Kasimir Berger
International Sales Executive Charlie Sokol
Advertising Sales (Mexico City) Simon Burgess
Advertising Assistant Kate Staddon

Marketing
Marketing Manager Yvonne Poon
Sales & Marketing Director, North America Lisa Levinson
Senior Publishing Brand Manager Luthfa Begum
Marketing Designers Anthony Huggins, Nicola Wilson

Production
Group Production Director Mark Lamond
Production Manager Brendan McKeown
Production Controller Damian Bennett
Production Coordinator Julie Pallot

Time Out Group
Chairman Tony Elliott
Group General Manager/Director Nichola Coulthard
Time Out Communications Ltd MD David Pepper
Time Out International Ltd MD Cathy Runciman
Group IT Director Simon Chappell
Head of Marketing Catherine Demajo

Contributors
Introduction Claire Rigby. **History** Richard Grabman, Matt Chesterton (*City of exile* Sarah Gilbert*; Mexico City by numbers* Christiana Ferris). **Mexico City Today** Témoris Grecko (*Superslums and the megacity* Sarah Gilbert). **Aztec Traces** Michael Parker (*Death in Mexico* DBC Pierre). **¡Viva la Lucha!** Chris Moss (*Fight facts* Simone Baird). **Where to Stay** Vanessa Able, Kate Joynes-Burgess, Tara Fitzgerald, Caroline MacKinnon, Michael Parker, Claire Rigby, Vivienne Stanton (*Habita forming* Michael Parker; *Don't stop* Tara Fitzgerald). **Sightseeing** Vanessa Able (*Arriba, arriba* Simone Baird; *Chilango bingo* Claire Rigby; *Pulp art* Vivienne Stanton). **Restaurants, Bars, Cafés & Cantinas** Vanessa Able, Deborah Bonello, Kate Joynes-Burgess, Fátima Escobar, Christiana Ferris, Tara Fitzgerald, Caroline MacKinnon, Michael Parker, Claire Rigby, Vivienne Stanton (*Sugar and spice, Menu decoder, Mexification and Vitamin T* Vivienne Stanton; *Vino vido vici* Fátima Escobar; *Tequila forever* Tara Fitzgerald). **Shops & Services** Kate Joynes-Burgess (*Naco but nice* Tara Fitzgerald). **Festivals & Events** Kate Joynes-Burgess (*Thank God it's Friday* Chris Moss). **Children** Caroline MacKinnon. **Clubs** Sue-Ellen Mason. **Film** Elisabeth Lastschenko (*Mexico City in the movies* Tara Fitzgerald, Nacha Cattan). **Galleries** Caroline MacKinnon (*Painted prayers* Tara Fitzgerald). **Gay & Lesbian** Michael Parker. **Music** Jonathan Jucker (*Cry me a río* Deborah Bonello). **Sports & Fitness** Christiana Ferris (*Three colours chilango* Kate Joynes-Burgess). **Theatre & Dance** Kate Joynes-Burgess (*Dancing in the sunlight* Tara Fitzgerald). **Best of Mexico** Chris Moss, except **Acapulco** Barbara Kastelein; **Riviera Maya** Claire Rigby (*Cavediver* Fiona James). **Directory** Kate Joynes-Burgess. **DF Eye** Sue-Ellen Mason.

Thanks to Daniel Nielson, Fátima Escobar, Hector Barrera, Témoris Grecko, Celeste Bustelo, Jorge Luis Hadad and all the interviewees in the DF Eye series.

Special thanks to Manuel Díaz Cebrián and Lupita Ayala from Mexico Tourism Board for their valuable assistance with this guide.

Maps by Nexo Servicios Gráficos, Luis Sáenz Peña 20, 7B, Buenos Aires (www.nexolaser.com.ar).

Illustrations/graphics by: Melanie Schöllhammer (DF Eye); Federico Gilardi (page 13); Mercedes Juáregui (pages 31, 68, 177); Jessica Abel (page 61); Elizabeth Gleeson (page 139).

Photography by Hector Barrera, except: page 17 Instituto del Derecho de Asilo Museo Casa de León Trotsky; page 15 Hugo Brehme/Casasola Bazar de Fotografía; pages 18, 19 Agustín V Casasola/Casasola Bazar de Fotografía; pages 20, 63, 93, 214 Kate Joynes-Burgess; pages 22, 57, 62 Oscar Ruiz Cardeña; page 26 Comunicación Social del Distrito Federal; pages 27, 30, 56, 85, 86, 95, 98, 161 Vanessa Able; pages 29, 158, 162, 230, 234 Deborah Bonello; pages 32, 34 Lucha Libre London; page 67 courtesy Telmex; pages 51, 79 Claire Rigby; page 134 Adrián García; page 163 Témoris Grecko; pages 167, 168, 170, 171, 172, 182, 188 Jesús León; page 173 courtesy Cámara Carnal Films; page 174 courtesy Alameda Films; pages 210, 229 Mexican Tourist Board, UK; page 211 Chris Moss; pages 221, 223 Barbara Kastelein. The following images were supplied by the featured establishments/artist: pages 36, 39, 40, 45, 47, 50, 96, 113, 125, 130, 173, 178, 180, 184, 195, 233.

Contents

Introduction

Sooner or later, every visitor to Mexico City finds themself in the Zócalo, dwarfed by its dimensions, with the city radiating out in every direction. Once upon a time, you could see the city's sentinel mountains from here, a reminder of its 2,240-metre altitude; and, on a clear day, you still can. But most days, the horizon fades into the endless urban blur of one of the world's original megacities, with all the sharp social inequality that implies. As ancient at its heart, built on Aztec ruins, as it is is futuristic in its epic scale, seen from afar Mexico City can seem threatening, harsh, overwhelming – a too-big city, impossible to get to grips with. Once you're here, you see that you don't have to: you just dive in and start walking. In a vintage cantina or at a kicking art show event; lazing in a park or punting on age-old, manmade waterways; stunned by its archaeological jewels, or lost in music in the hurly-burly of the night, you'll find your DF, as they call it here - the one you take home in your memory.

Secular and progressive on paper – civil partnerships and abortion are legal, and it's an important hub in the American cultural sphere – DF is also a city steeped in religion, evidenced in some of its most colourful spectacles, from the Sonora witches' market to the Passion play performed at Iztapalapa, a million-strong neighbourhood.

Downtown, it's hard to get a sense of the metropolitan area's almost 20 million inhabitants, because there's space here – lots of it. The Centro was, until recently, crammed with vendors and teeming with street life; but Mayor Ebrard's efforts to declutter the streets have made it a far calmer place than you would have found a year ago. Where you might feel the city's jolting magnitude is at Lagunilla market on a Sunday, on the edge of the dicey Tepito neighbourhood. Buy a bag of fruit slices from a street seller, letting them dust it with chilli and salt; then roam on, taking in the pirate goods on some of the stalls: counterfeit books beside fake designer labels; and blockbuster films, but also packed stalls selling knock-off arthouse cinema.

Notorious, maligned and eternally misunderstood, this isn't the prettiest city in the world; but then looks aren't everything, and DF becomes a far more interesting place once you get under its skin and meet its people. Most of Mexico's tourists barely touch down in DF; but if you do, then there's every chance that even as you marvel at Mexico's many and varied charms, it'll be the city that lingers, wishing you back.

ABOUT THE TIME OUT CITY GUIDES

This is the first edition of *Time Out Mexico City*, one of an expanding series of travel guides produced by the people behind London and New York's successful listings magazines. Our guides are written and updated by local experts who have striven to provide you with all the up-to-date information you'll need to explore the city and beyond, whether you're a regular or a first-time visitor.

THE LIE OF THE LAND

Vast Mexico City contains some 400 official *colonias* (neighbourhoods). Focusing on the parts of the city of most interest to visitors and following the informal divisions used locally, we have divided the city into a series of areas, organising the book's content into those areas where possible, and shading them for clarity in the streetmaps at the back of the guide and in the locator maps in our Sightseeing chapters. The names of other neighbourhoods in which venues feature are also marked on the streetmaps, and we give page and grid references for every venue that falls within the scope of our maps. Addresses are given in Spanish to help you tell a taxi driver or ask a local, and the exact location of each hotel, bar and restaurant is given using a numbered dot.

THE LOWDOWN ON THE LISTINGS

Above all, we've tried to make this book as useful as possible. Addresses, telephone numbers, websites, opening times and prices have all been included, as have details of facilities, services and events, all checked and correct as we went to press. However, owners and managers can change their arrangements at any time, and often do, so before you go out of your way, we'd strongly advise you to phone to check opening times and other details. While every effort has been made to ensure the accuracy of the information contained in this guide, the publishers cannot accept responsibility for any errors it may contain.

PRICES AND PAYMENT
The prices given in this guide, which are always listed in pesos (MX$), should be treated as guidelines, not gospel. If prices vary wildly from those we've quoted, please let us know. We aim to give the best and most up-to-date advice possible, so we always want to know when you've been badly treated or overcharged.

In listings, we have noted where the following credit cards are accepted: American Express (AmEx), Diners Club (DC), MasterCard (MC) and Visa (V).

TELEPHONE NUMBERS
Mexico City telephone numbers are given without area code in this guide, as they should be dialled from within the city. Outside the city, dial 55 for Mexico City, and if calling from abroad, dial 52 first – the international dialling code for Mexico. For all numbers in our Best of Mexico section, area codes are given. For more information on telephones and codes, *see p247.*

ESSENTIAL INFORMATION
For all the practical information you might need for visiting Mexico, including visa and customs information, emergency telephone

numbers, transport options, car hire and a list of useful websites, please turn to the Directory chapter at the back of the guide.

MAPS
The maps section of this book includes an overview of the Mexico City area and around, a key to our areas, detailed street maps with a comprehensive street index, and a map showing the Metro and Metrobús systems. Maps start on page 258, with a map of Mexico the country on page 208 as part of the Best of Mexico section.

LET US KNOW WHAT YOU THINK
We hope you enjoy *Time Out Mexico City and the Best of Mexico*, and we'd like to know what you think of it. We welcome tips for places you believe we should include in future editions, and we take note of your criticism of our choices. You can email us at guides@timeout.com.

There is an online version of this book, along with guides to 50 international cities, at **www.timeout.com**.

Advertisers
We would like to stress that no establishment has been included in this guide because it has advertised in any of our publications and no payment of any kind has influenced any review. The opinions given in this book are those of Time Out writers and entirely independent.

Milan
Mumbai & Goa
Naples
New York
Paris
Patagonia
Prague
Rio de Janeiro
Rome
Seville & Andalucía
Shanghai 上海
Singapore
South of France
Provence & the Côte d'Azur
Stockholm
Sydney
Tokyo 東京
Toronto
Turin
HAIGHT
Venice
Vienna
Washington, DC
Amsterdam
Athens
Bangkok
Barcelona
Beijing
Berlin
Brussels
Budapest
Buenos Aires
California
Cape Town
Chicago
Copenhagen
Croatia
Dubai
Edinburgh
Florence
Havana
CUBA
Hong Kong
Istanbul
Las Vegas
Lisbon
London
Mallorca
Marrakech
Miami
Milan
Mumbai & Goa
Naples
New York
Paris
Rio de Janeiro
Rome
San Francisco
HAIGHT
Seville & Andalucía
Shanghai 上海
Singapore
South of France
Provence & the Côte d'Azur
Stockholm
Toronto
Turin
Vancouver
Venice
Vienna
Washington, DC
Amsterdam
Athens
Beijing
Berlin
Boston
Brussels
Stockholm
Budapest
Buenos Aires
California
Copenhagen
Croatia
Dubai
Abu Dhabi & the UAE
Dublin
Edinburgh
Florence
Havana
Hong Kong

www.treesforcities.org

Trees for Cities
Charity registration number 1032154

Travelling creates so
many lasting memories.

Make your trip mean
something for years to
come - not just for you
but for the environment
and for people living in
deprived urban areas.

Anyone can offset their
flights, but when your
plant trees with Trees for
Cities, you'll help create
a green space for an
urban community that
really needs it.

Leave
Your
Mark
Create a green future for cities.

In Context

History of Mexico: The Oppressed Peasantry. Diego Rivera, 1935.

History

Ruin, reconstruction, invasion, revolution: DF has it all.

At first blush, the history of Mexico seems to be a story of ruptures and revolutions; of civilisations arising from nowhere, achieving magnificence, and then disappearing as mysteriously as they emerged; of alien cultures trying to superimpose their languages, customs and religion on an often recalcitrant native population; of lost lives, lost wars and lost territory. If there is a recurring motif in Mexican history – one that links the temples of Teotihuacán with the aftermath of the 1985 earthquake – it is *ruins*.

Look deeper, however, and you'll discover continuities in the country's history that are even more startling than the ruptures: good habits die hard in Mexican society and can survive the destruction of the civilisations that promulgated them. Finally, you may come to understand why Mexicans themselves are so hooked on their country's past. Put simply and to borrow a phrase, it's one of the greatest stories ever told.

THE FIRST MEXICANS

Some time between 40,000 and 30,000 BC, nomadic peoples from the north-east Asian plains began to cross the Bering Straits – then very shallow – and to populate the Americas.

From footprints, human remains and other archaeological evidence, we know that some of these wanderers were living in present-day Mexico from around 10,000 to 8,000 BC. They were hunter-gatherers who used Stone Age weapons to kill big game such as mammoths, camels and wild horses, all of which they hunted to extinction. For further sustenance they gathered and prepared mesquite beans, fruits, pine nuts and prickly pear cacti.

The first Mexican revolution was the discovery of agriculture. Crop cultivation began in around 7,000 BC and transformed the lives of the early inhabitants of Mesoamerica. Family groups merged into large tribes and developed distinct but related languages, cultures and cuisines, and many of the staples of Mexican, and indeed world gastronomy to this day date from that period, around 2,000 BC. Corn-flour dough was rolled out as tortillas and cooked on stone slabs heated by charcoal. The early Mexicans also cultivated the cacao plant, smoked the rolled-up leaves of a native plant called *tabaco*, drank the fermented pulp of the agave plant, and chewed the chicle resin of the chicozapote tree. Such is the flow of history: 4,000 years before the invention of televised sports, Americans were chewing gum and washing down corn-based snacks with beer.

They were also building civilisations and empires. The Olmec, who emerged in the Veracruz coastal lowlands of Mexico, were at their peak as a culture between 1,000 and 400 BC. They built temples and ceremonial centres rather than cities, and carved colossal stone heads, of which more than a dozen are extant, that are believed to be portraits of Olmec leaders. The Maya, who dominated southern Mesoamerica until around 900 AD, developed a progressive and cohesive society in which writing, mathematics and complex architectural structures – constructed without metal tools – were dominant traits. But the largest of the ancient Mesoamerican cities was Teotihuacán in the Anáhuac Valley, as the Aztecs would later call the Valley of Mexico. Its ruins, now known to all as simply 'the Pyramids', are just 40 kilometres from present-day Mexico City. We know very little about Teotihuacán except that it was extremely populous – with perhaps as many as 200,000 inhabitants – and that it fell in around AD 650. Later civilisations to rise and fall in the Mesoamerican region include the Toltec, the Zapotec and the Mixtec.

While discrete, these civilisations had much in common. Their religions were polytheistic: they worshipped the gods of the elements and of the moon and sun. These deities were capricious, and needed to be appeased from time to time with human sacrifices. All of these societies were rigidly hierarchical, with ruling classes consisting of priests and intellectuals. They all produced pottery, statuary and the stepped, truncated pyramids that are their main material legacy. Lacking draft animals, none made the single most important technological advance in human history: the invention of the plough. And as surely as they rose, all of these civilisations collapsed again; though as we have noted, their influence endured.

THE AZTEC ASCENDANCY

The Valley of Mexico, with its rich, volcanic soil and abundant water sources, must have seemed like the promised land to the many nomadic tribes that sought to establish permanent settlements there. The last and most important of them were the Mexica, more commonly known today as the Aztecs. They arrived in the region some time around 1100 AD.

The Náhuatl-speaking Aztecs were just one of many groups struggling to impose their authority in the valley and they were, for several centuries, little more than bit-part players, watching from the wings while others strutted the stage. The turning point came in

the early 1300s, when the Aztecs reached the swampy archipelago of Lake Texcoco. According to legend, the tribe warmed to this unpromising site when they saw an eagle with a snake in its beak perched on a nopal cactus, which they took as a sign from the gods that this was where they should settle. The resultant city was named Tenochtitlán.

By 1500, this obscure island city had become an empire, and most of central and southern Mexico was under its control. Tenochtitlán had grown from a few thatched huts half sunk in a bog to a prodigious metropolis of adobe houses, stone temples, ballcourts, aqueducts, pyramids and *chinampas* – ingenious, highly fertile man-made islands (*see photo, left*). The city's network of canals, dykes and causeways demonstrated a genius for hydraulic technology that would have been the envy of the world, had the world only known about it.

Like most successful imperialists, the Aztecs were ruthless and greedy, but also pragmatic. Conquered city states were allowed to observe their own religious and cultural practices as long as they ceded political sovereignty to Tenochtitlán. They were also expected to give generous tribute in the form of crops, cacao, precious metals and animal skins. The Aztecs' prisoners of war could not expect to treated well: in fact, war was often motivated by the very need for sacrificial victims, who would be ritually slaughtered and their blood offered to the gods, whose thirst for human gore was regarded as unquenchable. Victims were usually dragged to the top of a pyramid and held down by four priests, while another drove

an obsidian dagger into the unfortunate's chest and snatched out his still-beating heart.

By the early 16th century, the Aztecs must have reckoned that none of their Mesoamerican neighbours was a threat to their hegemony, and that only some extraordinary, unforeseen event could topple them. They were right on both counts.

THE CONQUEST

In April 1519, Spanish adventurer Hernán Cortés sailed from Spanish Cuba and landed in present-day Veracruz in eastern Mexico. Cortés had 11 ships, 700 troops, horses, guns, and perhaps most frightening of all, lawyers. The lawyers were required to draw up papers justifying the conquest, since Cortés had been authorised only to explore and trade.

Aided and abetted by tribes in eastern Mexico, who had every reason to hate the Aztecs, Cortés and his forces initially carried all before them. The Aztec emperor, Moctezuma II, decided that the only way to get rid of the invaders was to buy them off. Making a virtue of a necessity, the emperor invited the Spanish to visit Tenochtitlán, and on 8 November 1519, Cortés and his men entered the Aztec capital.

The Aztec ruler had made a tragic miscalculation. Once Cortés's men, most of whom were roughnecks and mercenaries, had seen the magnificent city, no amount of gold and jewels was ever going to be enough to sate their avarice. Indeed, Cortés himself was to melt down the pair of Aztec calendar discs that were Moctezuma's gift to him on their first meeting, one of gold and one of silver, for their material value. Moctezuma was arrested – it is unclear at whose instigation – and the Spanish took control of Tenochtitlán.

'Neither a triumph nor a tragedy, but the birth pangs of the Mexican people.'

Now it was Cortés's turn to overplay his hand. He demanded that the Aztecs close down their temples and replace their gods with the Christian God. The ensuing insurrection forced Cortés to retreat to Tlaxcala, east of the city. Meanwhile, a smallpox epidemic began to exact a terrible toll on the Aztecs. The new worlders had no resistance to old world diseases, and they would eventually succumb in their millions. Moctezuma died on 1 July 1520. No one knows whether he was killed by the Spanish or murdered by his own subjects.

Safe at Tlaxcala, Cortés recruited reinforcements for a fresh attack on the island city. This time there were no hitches. Establishing a beachhead in Tenochtitlán, the Spanish systematically levelled the city block by block, filling canals with rubble as they advanced. Forced into suburban Tlatelolco, the Aztec forces surrendered on 21 August 1521. A monument marks the spot and it reads, in Spanish and Náhuatl: 'This was neither a triumph nor a tragedy, but the birth pangs of the Mexican people.'

NUEVA ESPAÑA

In the European-style city of castles and churches that began to rise from the ruins of Tenochtitlán, native labourers, architects and craftsmen kept their own traditions alive. New buildings had a distinctly Mexican appearance, as did religious services and practices. Lacking bells, churches used native drummers to call the people to services; and dancing, always part of the old religions, continued as part of the new one too. The Church of Rome, which had in previous epochs and far away successfully absorbed and 'repackaged' Celtic, Anglo-Saxon and even Viking customs and rituals, had proved its flexibility once again.

Mexico City was the capital of Nueva España, an empire stretching from Wyoming to the straits of Darién. After 1580, the city was also the administrative capital of the Philippines, and many Chinese merchants representing businesses in the Asian archipelago relocated to Mexico. They weren't the only ones who found it convenient to live in the capital of the vast territory. The wealthy poured money into building churches as well as imposing homes for themselves. Cortés himself founded the Hospital de Jesús, still standing (he is buried in the chapel). Among the institutions founded in this era were the first – and still the largest – university in North America; the first medical school; and the continent's first printing press.

With disease – smallpox and later typhus – decimating the native labour force, the Spanish were forced to import African slaves. African men generally married indigenous women, who, according to Spanish law Catholic doctrine, were free to marry whomever they chose. The shortage of Spanish women meant that most Spanish men also had indigenous wives, and attempts by the Crown to classify people by race in the 1700s were largely ignored. Even among the few 'pure Spaniards' concentrated in Mexico City, there was a growing rift between those from the Old World (*peninsulares*, born in the Iberian peninsula) who held the top administrative and clerical positions, and the *criollos*, the Mexicans of Spanish descent who were legally second in class to the *peninsulares*, and who were barred from occupying high political posts. Even the haughtiest of *criollos* began thinking of the rulers as *gachupines*, a Náhuatl term of abuse for arrogant Spaniards.

FALL OF THE REIGN FROM SPAIN

The Mexican Wars of Independence, which raged sporadically from 1810 to 1821, are only superficially similar to the American and French revolutions that preceded them. Those looking for a Franklin, a Washington, a Jefferson, or even a Robespierre will be disappointed. The old social order was not overthrown; if anything, it was strengthened. High-flown ideas about equality and the rights of man are conspicuous by their absence. Instead, the independence struggle is the story of a colonial possession trying to reinvent itself in the light of the plunging fortunes of its feeble owner, the Spanish monarchy.

In 1808, Napoleon Bonaparte invaded Spain, deposed Charles IV and put his own brother, Joseph, on the throne. Mexican *peninsulares*, protective of their privileges, launched a coup the same year to forestall any move towards independence, and the Spanish viceroy, José de Iturrigay, who had envisioned himself as king of a newly independent Mexico, was replaced by his more pliable compatriot Pedro Garibay.

Enter a turbulent priest. Miguel Hidalgo, a *criollo* from the small town of Dolores who raged against 'French atheists' and 'Spanish puppets', began to conspire against the government. On 16 September 1810 (now celebrated as Mexico's Independence Day), a crowd gathered to hear Hidalgo call for rebellion against the *peninsulares*. His rallying call is known as the Grito de Dolores (Cry of Dolores): 'Long live our Lady of Guadalupe! Death to bad government! Death to the *gachupines*!'

Hidalgo's peasants, carrying images of the Virgin of Guadalupe, faced Spanish regulars and a *criollo* militia. At first, the revolution carried all before it; but when Hidalgo had the chance to occupy Mexico City, he hesitated, perhaps fearing that his forces would sack the city. That pause gave the loyalist army the time it needed to regroup, then to pursue and defeat the rebels. Hidalgo and his lieutenants tried to escape to the north but were captured and executed in Chihuahua on 30 July 1811.

Hidalgo's banner was taken up by José María Morelos Pavón, who, in 1813, convened a congress that met at Chilpancingo to discuss Mexican independence. Delegates drafted a constitution-in-waiting that included radical proposals such as universal male suffrage, the abolition of slavery and even an end to corporal punishment. Without elite backing, though, Morelos had no chance of success, and in 1815 he was captured, defrocked and executed.

The war ended rather tamely in September 1821, when the *criollo* officer Agustín de Iturbide and the revolutionaries led by Vicente Guerrero worked out a *modus vivendi*: the church could

Trams and cars in the Zócalo, 1924.

keep its privileges in Mexico, while the *criollos* would have full political control. Slavery would be abolished in an independent Mexican Empire. Early the next year, Itubide, in conscious imitation of Napoleon Bonaparte, made himself Emperor Augustin I. But Irtubide was no Napoleon, and his empire endured for less than a year. On 1 December 1822, Veracruz garrison commander Santa Anna rose against Iturbide and declared a republic.

REMEMBER THE ALAMO

From a figure of around 160,000 in 1820, the population of Mexico City swelled to approximately 250,000 by 1846. It remained poor, dirty and dangerous, but no more so than most Latin American cities. More importantly, the country's wealth and culture were concentrated in the capital. As British and French trade and business interests began to invest heavily in the region, the military threat from the Old World began to recede. A more clear and present danger loomed in the shape of Mexico's increasingly ambitious northern neighbour, the United States of America.

> **'The 1857 constitution was a sweeping affirmation of core Enlightenment values such as freedom of speech.'**

Having acquired Texas in 1845 after a protracted struggle (which had included the Battle of the Alamo in 1836), the USA, seeking to expand its power towards the Pacific coast, began to eye Mexico's other North American territories. In May 1846, it used a boundary dispute as a pretext to invade California and New Mexico. When its forces became bogged down in this northern theatre, the USA opened a second front, mounting a huge amphibious assault on Veracruz. Meeting little resistance, General Winfield Scott marched on the capital, which he expected to fall without a fight.

Some *chilangos* had other ideas. Its ranks swelled by Irish Catholic deserters from the US invasion force, the Mexican army defended the capital every bit as ferociously as the Texans had defended the Alamo a decade earlier. At the Castillo de Chapultepec (Chapultepec Castle), military cadets, mostly teenagers, inflicted heavy casualties on the US Marines in a last-ditch action. (The 'blood stripe' on the Marine dress uniform pays tribute to the battle.) Choosing death over surrender, the last of the cadets, Juan Escutia, leapt from the walls wrapped in the Mexican flag, thus saving it from capture by US troops. There is a monument celebrating the sacrifice of the

niños heroes – the heroic boys – at the entrance to Bosque de Chapultepec (Chapultepec Park).

The capital was occupied by US troops from 13 September 1847 to July 1848, when the Mexican Congress ceded a massive chunk of territory – the present-day states of New Mexico, Arizona, Nevada, Utah and California – to the USA for some US$15 million. Painfully, bloodily, and rarely of its own volition, modern Mexico was taking shape.

REFORM AND THE SECOND EMPIRE

The loss of a third of the nation's territory and the shame of occupation cost the conservative ruling class its last shred of legitimacy. Liberals, led by Zapotec Indian lawyer Benito Juárez, set out to build a nation free of conservative and church control, and by 1857, they were in control, with Juárez as president. They launched *la reforma*, a programme to strip big landlords of political power and the church of its properties. The constitution of 1857 was drafted in the same spirit, and is a sweeping affirmation of core Enlightenment values such as freedom of speech, freedom of the press and the separation of church and state. It also stated that any slave who set foot on Mexican soil would, *ipso facto*, be free, and thus Mexico became a sanctuary for African American slaves fleeing across the border.

All of this was, of course, anathema to conservatives; and not for the first or last time, Mexico's internal affairs were to be unsettled by a sustained period of foreign intervention. Under the pretext of recovering debt, and with the support of Mexican conservatives, Napoleon III sent an invasion force that landed at Veracruz in October 1861. The French encountered strong resistance from Mexican forces led by General Ignacio Zaragoza, they and were defeated at Puebla on 5 May 1862 (the date is now celebrated as a national holiday). The French regrouped, however, and Mexico City was occupied the following year.

In June 1863, a provisional government was formed. It was dominated by conservatives, most of whom were beholden to Napoleon III. In October, a government delegation offered the crown to Ferdinand Maximilian Joseph von Habsburg of Austria, who accepted. He arrived in Mexico City in June 1864 with his wife, Princess Charlotte of Belgium, thereafter known as Empress Carlota of Mexico, and they set up home at Chapultepec Castle. Their subjects, however, were hopelessly divided: Benito Juaréz refused to recognise Maximilian's authority, and headed north with his loyalist forces.

Maximilian, a well-meaning and – by the admittedly low standards of his dynasty – liberal ruler, was one of those unfortunate

City of exile

Ever since Cortés turned up at Veracruz with his motley crew, several of whom were forcibly converted but still observant Jews, seeking respite from the Spanish Inquisition, Mexico has offered a home to outsiders, exiles and refugees, many of whom have stayed, settled and made their home in the capital over the centuries.

Fidel Castro and Che Guevara holed up in Mexico while they plotted Batista's overthrow; Leon Trotsky found sanctuary there and friendship with Frida Kahlo and Diego Rivera (*pictured with Trotsky*) before he met with an ice-pick-wielding KGB agent; and many artists, including Chilean writer Pablo Neruda, found the creative freedom in Mexico that their home countries denied them.

According to Mónica Palma Moro, a historian at the Instituto Nacional de Antropología e Historia, and author of *From Strange Lands: A Study of Immigration to Mexico, 1950-1990*, the welcome extended to exiles has its roots deep in Mexico's political history.

After the 1810 revolution, the new republic sought to insert itself into the world and find allies among other liberal democratic nations. 'One of the ways of finding legitimacy was through a democratic and open foreign policy,' Moro says.

What first marked Mexico out as an exile-friendly nation was the arrival of some 20,000 Spanish republicans escaping Franco's Spain, who established their government in exile in Mexico City before moving it to Paris after the Nazis' defeat.

During World War II, Austrian, German, Italian and Polish exiles and refugees trickled in; and though Mexico's original crypto-Jews were forced entirely underground when the Spanish Inquisition opened its first colonial office, they were joined centuries later by Sephardic Jews fleeing the collapse of the Ottoman Empire, and eastern European Ashkenazi Jews fleeing Nazism and Stalinism.

Strictly speaking, an exile is someone who claims political asylum through the embassy of a foreign nation, but many people forced to flee their country because of their beliefs or ethnicity consider themselves exiles, though they may be classified as refugees or immigrants. From US writers and activists escaping McCarthyism to the many refugees who fled across Mexico's southern borders during Central America's civil wars, countless people have settled in Mexico as self-described exiles.

During the 1970s, many thousands from South America – Chile, Argentina, Uruguay, Bolivia, Peru and Brazil – sought exile at Mexico's embassies, fleeing violent military dictatorships that crushed free speech and saw political dissidents 'disappear' in extra-judicial kidnappings and killings. Many of these newcomers settled in DF, where their work as journalists, artists and university professors helped enrich the city's intellectual and cultural scene. According to Mora, while the Uruguayan theatre troupe El Galpón turned Mexicans on to Brecht, Argentinian and Chilean academics helped generate an interest in Mexican history, as well as helping to establish contemporary Latin American and development studies.

Nowadays, while Mexico's policy towards refugees and exiles remains as liberal as ever, circumstances make the practice more difficult. Hundreds of illegal immigrants cross the country's borders each day in a desperate effort to reach the USA. Political refugees often get mixed up in the same flow as these economic migrants, using the same clandestine channels and exposing them to the risk of deportation.

Dictator **Porfirio Díaz**, with his wife.

buildings in its capital: thus entire adobe neighbourhoods were obliterated and replaced with 'modern' tenements. Modern cities did not have beggars circulating on the streets: thus beggars were sent to work camps along with political dissenters.

Porfirio's advisors, known as *los científicos* ('the scientists'), looked to Europe for inspiration, and what they could not build from scratch, they would import. Nothing was more important than 'progress'; and 'progress' was whatever Porfirio and his coterie defined it to be.

Porfirio's 31-year (1876 to 1911, with a four-year hiatus from 1880 to 1884 during which he was the de facto if not the de jure leader) regime transformed Mexico, for good and for ill. Technological and industrial modernisation were achieved at the cost of social fragmentation. Most foreigners praised the enhancements (street lamps, policing, indoor plumbing, and so on) and ignored the blemishes (rigged elections and political assassinations). Europeans as dissimilar as Karl Marx, Leon Tolstoi and Kaiser Wilhelm I all trumpeted Díaz as a model leader; and like many successful dictators, Díaz was careful to cultivate a 'democratic' image.

THE 1910 REVOLUTION

Mexican peasants proved harder to fool than Russian novelists. Díaz had undoubtedly succeeded in modernising Mexico, but in doing so, he had left no clause of the 1857 constitution unviolated. Opponents of the regime had been jailed or killed, the clergy had recovered some of its temporal powers, and free speech had been brazenly suppressed.

Díaz won the election in 1910, but only by locking up thousands of opposition activists along with his opponent, Francisco Madero. Madero was eventually released and went into exile in the USA, where he continued to agitate against Díaz. In October 1910, he issued the Plan of San Luis Potosí, in which he urged the Mexican people to rise up on 20 November. Copies of the plan were widely distributed across Mexico, and while the November rising fizzled out quickly, the momentum was now with the growing anti-Díaz faction.

The pace of events now quickened. In January 1911, a large rebellion broke out in the northern state of Chihuahua, led by Francisco 'Pancho' Villa and Pascual Orozco. Similar uprisings took place across the country, including in Morelos, where peasant leader Emiliano Zapata had radicalised hacienda labourers and led them in raids against their erstwhile landlords. Madero declared himself

people who can please none of the people all of the time. The liberals, of course, were implacably opposed to his rule. Far worse for Maximilian was the fact that the conservatives, his natural constituency, were swiftly afflicted with buyer's remorse. By refusing to revoke the Reform Laws, he alienated conservatives; by insisting that Juárez and his followers swear allegiance to the crown, he alienated liberals; and by failing to stabilise the political situation in Mexico, he alienated his sponsor, Napoleon III, who began recalling troops from Mexico. When conservative forces started to switch sides and conspire against Maximilian, his fate was sealed. Juárez resumed his campaign on 19 February 1867, and on 15 May, Maximilian surrendered. He was executed by firing squad on 19 June, a scene immortalised in Édouard Manet's *Execution of the Emperor Maximilian*.

THE PORFIRIATO

In 1876, José de la Cruz Porfirio Diaz Mori (usually known simply as Porifirio Díaz) seized power in a coup. A *mestizo* from Oaxaca and a veteran of 1862's Battle of Puebla, Díaz was determined to drag his nation, kicking and screaming if necessary, into the late Victorian age. A brilliant administrator and a ruthless political operator, Díaz had few scruples and even fewer doubts. A modern nation did not have crooked, dark streets and shabby provisional president and returned from the USA to lead the revolution. Mobs chanting anti-Diaz slogans filled the streets of Mexico City, and on 25 May 1911, the dictator, now an old man of 80, agreed to relinquish power. Almost unnoticed amid the tumult, he slipped out of the capital and sailed to exile in France.

'In the 1920s and 1930s, artists and intellectuals were drawn to Mexico City.'

The 1910 revolution was followed by a decade of civil war, anarchy and schism in which competing revolutionary factions struggled for supremacy. On one side were Zapata, Villa and other peasant leaders; on the other, Venustiano Carranza, Álvaro Obregón and other relative moderates. Villa achieved fame in his own country and notoriety north of the border through his 1916 raids on US border towns. But the most important event in this period is the drafting of the 1917 constitution, presented to Congress by Carranza. This is the present constitution of Mexico, and it renders the howls of rage and frustration that made the 1910 revolution possible into the sober, measured legal clauses that have made its legacy permanent.

NEW ARRIVALS, NEW VOICES
Mexico City suffered from food and power shortages at various periods during the Revolution, but immigrants from Europe and the Middle East, fleeing the greater chaos of

World War I, flooded into the capital. Despite continuing violence in the 1920s – anti-clerical laws led right-wing extremists to organise a rural guerrilla movement and a campaign of assassinations, including that of Álvaro Obregón in 1928 – the capital presented opportunities for small businessmen and manufacturers willing to take risks. A Lebanese immigrant, Yusef Salim Haddad, began buying up property from Porfirio-era millionaires headed into exile. His son, Carlos Slim of telecoms giant Telmex, is now the second richest man in the world.

In the 1920s and 1930s, artists and intellectuals were drawn to Mexico City, fascinated by its witches' brew of deeply rooted tradition and freewheeling modernism. Foreign writers and artists like American novelist Katherine Ann Porter and French photographer Henri Cartier-Bresson found their muses on the streets of the city, while Mexican artists, above all Diego Rivera, David Alfaro Siqueiros and José Clemente Orozco, were supported by the revolutionary leadership as they deconstructed and then reassembled the pre-Columbian past in the artistic language of modernism. The gray years of Franco's fascism made Mexico City, not Madrid, the cultural capital of the Hispanic world, and in the late 1930s and 1940s, people from across Europe found a safe haven here. The city's Jewish community, centred in Polanco, dates from this time, when tolerant Mexico – where even the colonial Inquisition seldom persecuted Jews – welcomed more European Jews than the USA, the British Empire, France and the Soviet Union combined.

THE (ONE) PARTY MUST GO ON
Amid all this upheaval, there was one constant Mexicans could rely on: the identity of the ruling party. Founded by Plutarco Elías Calles in 1929 during the political crisis that followed the 1928 assassination of Álvaro Obregón, the National Revolutionary Party (PNR) was renamed the Party of the Mexican Revolution (PRM) by president Lázaro Cárdenas, and was given its current name – the Institutional Revolutionary Party (PRI) – by President Ávilo Camacho in 1946. The party had been popular under Cárdenas, who had initiated the so-called 'Mexican miracle' in which GDP was to expand sixfold between 1940 and 1970. But the kind of deformities, such as corruption and fraud, that are always inherent in 'one-party' states (the PRI was to enjoy 70 years of uninterrupted rule) began to afflict the Mexican body politic after World War II and were never properly cured.

Still, Mexico was a beacon of tolerance and pluralism compared with most Latin American countries of that era: it was, at least, a nominal democracy. And in 1968, Mexico City grabbed

Francisco Madero votes, 1911.

the global spotlight when it hosted the summer Olympic games, the first to be held outside the 'developed' world. Among the projects built for the games were a ring road around the capital, parks, sports facilities, apartment complexes and the Metro. The city was transformed.

1968 was also a year that saw student – and worker – protests roll around the world. Worried that the Olympics might be interrupted by protesters, police over-reacted to a fight between high school boys after a soccer game. The schoolboy protests were joined by university students, professors, civil servants, middle class professionals, workers, intellectuals and even some of the Catholic clergy, all with their own grievances against the ruling elite. Prevented from marching in the streets, the protesters rallied at Tlatelolco on the night of 2 October 1968. Survivors claim soldiers in civilian clothes opened fire on the crowd, taking their cue from a helicopter. Both rescue crews and the press were kept at bay by armed soldiers, and the number of deaths (possibly in the hundreds) and arrests were never determined, nor would the events of that night be officially acknowledged for nearly 30 years. Many of those arrested were never seen again. The foreign press barely covered the incident. Every year, on 2 October, students and leftist organisations march from the Zócalo to Tlatelolco singing 'never forget October 2nd'.

THE PETRO PESO
When oil prices skyrocketed in the 1970s, crude-exporter Mexico was one of the few beneficiaries. Not that poorer Mexicans noticed. The rich carved out enclaves north of Chapultepec Park, where they could live behind high walls, while the poor scrambled for housing anywhere they could. The shanty town of Nezahualcóyotl grew to a city of over a million in the 1970s and '80s, while for the middle classes, Ciudad Satélite became a popular choice.

The prospect of eternal economic growth caused individuals, corporations and government to speculate, often unwisely. Huge foreign loans paid for hastily constructed new apartment complexes, highways and other projects that were often based on foreign designs and poorly suited to Mexico City's environment. The country was running further and further into debt, but as President Portillo said, 'There are only two kinds of countries: those with oil, and those without. We have oil!'

Oil prices dropped suddenly in the 1980s and the economy nearly collapsed, propped up only by further foreign loans. But it was the least of the city's problems. On 19 September 1985, an earthquake measuring 8.1 on the Richter scale killed up to 20,000 people. It was followed the next day by an 6.5 aftershock. The collapse of new apartments and hospitals was not nearly as shocking as the government's seeming inability to respond to the disaster, and political aftershocks rocked the establishment too. Self-help groups sprang up overnight, and, joined by veterans of the student movement and later by right-wing heirs to the 19th-century conservative and clerical parties, were the seed of new political organisations that forced the system to change.

Rally in favour of Obrador, 26 February 2006, in the run-up to the presidential elections.

Mexico City by numbers

25 tons The weight of the Sun Stone in the Museum of Anthropology.

400 Quetzal feathers in the Museum of Anthropology's replica of Moctezuma's headpiece – the original is in Vienna.

250,000 The population of Tenochtitlán in 1519 when the Spaniards arrived.

30,000 The population in 1521.

37,450 The number of people in the Distrito Federal (DF) in 2000 speaking Náhuatl.

105,000 The city's population in 1700.

105,000 The seating capacity of Aztec Stadium, opened in 1966.

230m The height of the Torre Mayor, Latin America's tallest building.

2,239m Mexico City's elevation.

6-8 inches The depth by which Mexico City is sinking annually due to groundwater extraction.

127,000 tons The weight of the towers of the Metropolitan Cathedral in the Zócalo.

68 The percentage of Mexicans who were overweight in 2008 – a sevenfold increase since 1989.

115 litres The annual per-capita consumption of Coca-Cola, the highest in the world.

40 cubic m The amount of sewage treated per second by the city's treatment plants.

200km The total length of canals in Xochimilco.

200km The total distance of Metro tracks.

10,200,000km The total length of DF's streets.

2,932 The number of marches in 2007, with roughly 12 million total participants.

28,000 The number of minibuses and combis on the streets of Mexico City.

398 parts per billion The highest recorded level of ozone pollution, on 16 March 1992.

90km the total length of cycle lanes in DF. Plans are underway to bring that total to 644km over the next five years.

4,541 The official number of people killed in the 1985 earthquake. Other estimates put the figure well above 60,000.

7 The average number of children per woman in Mexico City before 1970.

2 The average number of children per woman in Mexico City as of 2000.

78.8 The percentage of women of childbearing age using contraception in 2000.

700 The number of mariachi guild members in Plaza Garibaldi.

NEW MEXICO?

The city's physical collapse seemed to be a metaphor for a political one. In 1988, PRI reformers joined leftists to run a viable alternative candidate, and a close (and almost certainly rigged) election put Carlos Salinas de Gortari in power. Salinas, a Harvard-educated technocrat, saw integrated markets as the key to future prosperity in the global economy. His brainchild, the North American Free Trade Agreement (NAFTA), sought to integrate the closed Mexican economy with the capitalist USA and Canada in a common market. In theory, NAFTA should have meant that US and Canadian manufacturers would move their operations to Mexico, as indeed many have; but for Mexican farmers, competition from corporate-owned and government subsidised northern agricultural giants was a disaster, and the promises of higher wages and more consumer goods never quite panned out.

Politically, the post-NAFTA era has had a profound effect on the capital. Andrés Manuel López Obrador was elected mayor in 2000. His attempts to ameliorate some of the economic hardships caused by stagnant wages made the former union organiser the most popular politician in the country. Obrador ran for president in 2006, losing to Felipe Calderón by a narrow margin. He and his supporters claimed not to have lost at all, and months of streets protests ensued which culminated in Obrador being proclaimed 'Legitimate President' by his supporters in a rally in the Zócalo.

Within the city, the leftist administration, now under mayor Marcelo Ebrard, has created new opportunities and is attracting attention. While the creation of an old-age home for retired prostitutes and a raft of free activities for city residents are the sort of initiatives that tend to be admired and derided in equal measure, others are of deeper significance. The introduction of legal abortion, the recognition of gay civil unions, street cleaning brigades and the moving-on of city-centre vendors are all viewed as positive quality of life changes. While overall, Mexico's quality of life is comparable with former Eastern Bloc nations like Slovenia or Bulgaria, Mexico City's is comparable to wealthier nations like Italy or New Zealand. It's small wonder that eastern Europeans are among the most visible of the new immigrants. And as ever – as it has done for centuries – DF soaks them up.

Mexico City Today

Journalist Témoris Grecko on a city changing its spots.

The first thing you might notice when you arrive in Mexico City is that it's far from the dystopian, crime- and pollution-ravaged superslum some might imagine it to be. The second, if you look a little closer, is that this is an exceptionally vibrant, friendly city, studded with archaeological gems, and which, despite its obvious hardships, is far more functional than any metropolis with a population exceeding that of Holland has any right to be.

Linguistically and geographically, Mexico City finds itself right in the centre of the Spanish-speaking world. Above is the USA, with its 35 million Latinos; to the east, Spain; and ranging far into the south, Central and South America. It has the largest concentration of Spanish speakers anywhere, and in terms of business, it's second only to São Paulo as the Latin American city in which deals are done. Architecturally, it's a treat, with a range that spans the ages from pre-Columbian to just last

week. It has more museums than any other city in the world; the fourth greatest number of theatres; and with the inexorable growth of its art scene plus ZONAMACO (*see p159*), the annual contemporary art fair, it's becoming an ever more important stop on the international art circuit. And yet it still gets a bad press.

The world's second largest metropolitan area – or third, depending on which figures you consult – with more than 19 million inhabitants, Mexico City isn't an easy place to live. Whatever its charms, and they are considerable, there's no getting away from the fact that the city struggles with problems of crime, pollution, traffic, corruption, water shortages and poverty – it takes guts to be a *chilango*, as the city's inhabitants are known; but *chilangos* nevertheless, native and adoptive, survive the city and indeed, they thrive in it. So don't be surprised if you arrive worrying about kidnappings, smog and corruption and leave worrying about just how long it will be before you can come back again. You'll have experienced one of the most teeming, creative and dynamic cities on the planet – and you may not want to leave at all.

A CITY AGAINST THE GRAIN

Like Venice, the Distrito Federal, or DF, as it's often known, has survived against considerable geographical odds; but it has often had to struggle, too, for its political existence. Since 1824, it has been the nation's only district to be politically dependent on federal powers. Surrounded by the much larger state of Mexico but with a separate administration, it has always been denied the level of autonomy enjoyed by states, in a situation roughly analogous to that of the District of Columbia in the USA. Citizen pressure has eked gradual gains from the central government – a local assembly with limited powers in 1991; an elected mayor in 1997, and so on. Full statehood, the next step in the process, hasn't been achieved yet mainly since the rightist party, PAN (National Action Party), lost its enthusiasm for the project when, in 1997, the city voted overwhelmingly for the leftist PRD (Party of the Democratic Revolution). A liberal island in a conservative sea, in politics as in so much else, DF runs against the grain of the rest of the country.

And it is increasingly determined to highlight that difference. In November 2006, just months after its candidate, Andrés Manuel López Obrador, lost the presidential elections to the PAN by a extremely narrow margin, the Left used its majority in the DF assembly to pass a law permitting civil partnerships, homosexual and otherwise. The Catholic Church hierarchy snapped into action, issuing warnings that the city was on the brink of becoming a Mexican Sodom; but it was nothing compared to the campaign the Church launched weeks later against a legal reform on abortion. In April 2007, the PRD decriminalised the termination of pregnancies of less than 13 weeks, with free on-demand treatment for all women, residents and non-residents, making DF the only place in Latin America aside from Cuba and Puerto Rico to allow women such rights.

In their crusade to prevent this, massed bishops denounced the legislation, calling on the faithful to demonstrate. But the measure was approved, with polls showing that the law commanded majority support, and threatened mass protests never materialised. Around the same time, the archbishop of Mexico City published a report on his webpage stating that only between six and nine per cent of baptised Catholics attended mass on Sundays. And as if

to illustrate the city's secular, progressive credentials, two weeks later, in May 2007, US photographer Spencer Tunick persuaded 18,000 *chilangos* – more than twice as many as were featured in his previous largest group shot, 7,000 in Barcelona – to strip off in the city's main plaza. The image of so many naked bodies covering the Zócalo, one of the world's largest squares, was an eloquent demonstration of DF's irreverent, art-loving spirit.

> **'The city's artificial beaches are eagerly welcomed by those who have never felt sand and water on skin.'**

Indeed, art and Mexico City go together like salt and tequila. In 2007 and 2008, Frida Kahlo's and Diego Rivera's individual retrospectives attracted a total of five million viewers; and in 2008, Gregory Colbert's Ashes and Snow exhibition drew the largest museum attendance figures ever recorded, with some sources putting attendance at eight million over a three-month run. Current mayor Marcelo Ebrard's decision to turn the Zócalo into the world's biggest ice rink each winter, and to set up artificial beaches around the city in an echo of Paris's urban *plages*, all with free admission, might be branded as mere populism by upper-class regulars at swish Cancún resorts and Colorado ski pistes; but they are eagerly welcomed by tens of thousands who have never seen a piece of ice larger than those in their freezers, nor experienced the feeling of sand and water on their skin. As art cafés and galleries spring up in neighbourhoods previously untouched by high culture and gay couples sport wedding rings, young people find it difficult to believe that the sex scenes so common on TV used to be edited out even in cinemas. But that's how it was.

Just a generation ago, under the 71-year PRI regime that ended in 2000, *chilangos* were used, along with all Mexicans, to the moral and religious censorship of films, blatant pro-governmental bias in the press, and having to exercise their sexual and entertainment preferences semi-clandestinely. A trademark of Mexico City in the 1970s and 1980s were its *hoyos funkys* (funky holes), illegal venues to which local rock bands were confined. Only the universities and a few independent newspapers provided a space in which social activism, political humour and critical journalism could thrive. The turning point came in 1985, when the government's failure to respond adequately to two massive earthquakes that caused

Superslums and the megacity

The shoeshiner on the corner; the woman selling home-made sweets outside the subway; the man walking the median strip, hawking anything from tortillas to pirate DVDs as he inhales fresh carbon dioxide: visitors to Mexico City brush shoulders with countless of its slum-dwellers without a second thought for where they live. According to the United Nations' landmark 2003 habitat survey,

Challenge of the Slums, as much as 85 per cent of Mexico City's population lives in what can be broadly defined as a slum – whether that's a shack in one of the *ciudades perdidas* (inner-city shanty towns); a hastily-constructed house in one of the sprawling *colonias populares* that can be glimpsed through the smog as they creep up the mountainsides encircling the city; *vecindades,*

thousands of deaths and injuries forced citizens to act on their own behalf. It was a traumatic wake-up call, and it marked the seismic beginnings of popular democracy in the city.

CITIES WITHIN THE CITY

Nevertheless, the social and economic fragmentation found throughout Latin America still disfigures DF. The cycle is vicious: poor *chilangos* live in certain neighbourhoods; *chilangos* who live in certain neighbourhoods tend to be poor. PAN's strongholds are located in the richer, 'whiter' areas to the west and south of the city, while the north and the east are poorer, 'darker', with worse public services.

Bad traffic, on the other hand, is like death: it comes to everyone. And if a visitor can fall all too easily into a rut, seeing the sights without

straying from the well-worn trail, so too can *chilangos*. Many spend a lifetime in a particular area without getting to know the others, and it's partly because transport is so bad. The Metro network is one of the largest in the world, complemented since 2005 by the Metrobús, a low-emission rapid-transit bus system running from north to south. Yet some commuters still spend up to eight hours a day simply crossing DF in a series of anarchic *micros* (minibuses) and *combis* (vans): a desperately slow way for the city's lifeblood – its people – to circulate.

This has resulted in a kind of urban Balkanisation. Many *chilangos*, for example, would be astonished by the cosmopolitan, gentrified neighbourhood Condesa has become, where hippy artists mix with publicists, soap opera stars and actors, and enriched wannabes where poor families live in crumbling buildings long abandoned by the wealthy; or the many dilapidated housing projects that dot the city.

Seen alongside the first world's sleek metropolises, Mexico City seems a savage and crazy place; but statistically speaking, it represents the norm. In 2005, the human race hit a landmark: for the first time in history, more of us live in the cities than outside them. As author Mike Davis writes in his 2006 book, *Planet of Slums*, 'in 1950 there were 86 cities in the world with a population of more than one million ... by 2015 there will be at least 550'.

According to Davis, the growth of slums like Mexico City's constitutes an approaching urban apocalypse that will see our cities overburdened with waste, crime and social decay. With the state in retreat, either unwilling or unable to act, those who can will escape to gated communities, eventually leaving the city to the poor masses that derive scant economic nourishment from it.

Economists scratch their heads as to why urban population growth and urban economic growth don't line up. Davis blames neoliberal development models under which poor countries borrow funds on the condition that they cut spending, privatise public services and drop the subsidies and trade barriers that protected their farmers. Mass migration towards capital cities when the governments are saddled with debt means infrastructure can't keep up, forcing newcomers to build their shanties and scrape about for work where there is none. In this way, millions have exchanged tough but decent lives in the countryside for unemployment, squalor and social exclusion in ever-growing cities.

Whatever the causes, Davis's grim vision is playing out all over the world, from Lagos, the world's fastest-growing megacity, whose 10 million citizens welcome 6000 new neighbours each day, to Buenos Aires, where middle-class residents regard with horror the ever-expanding, *favela*-style *villas miserias* growing around the city's outer ring.

So what does the future hold for Mexico City? While successive city and national governments have displayed a fairly laissez-faire approach to the spread of *colonias populares*, both the state and NGO sectors are offering limited but innovative programmes to support some of the poorest neighbourhoods, from organic vegetable farming to community-run schools and childcare centres.

For now, Mexico City's population has stabilised, with many choosing a risky border crossing to the USA over DF's slums. Strengthening political institutions in Mexico make it easier to imagine a sound long-term policy that might transform the *colonias populares* – perhaps offering residents official title over their homes and land, allowing them to borrow against their property and create micro-enterprises. But in the meantime, the millions living each day without basic services like running water, sewers and electricity – let alone decent schools and hospitals – demand an urgent solution that seems beyond any government's capacity to deliver.

and impoverished magnates, plus a generous sprinkling of expats, dine out in style.

Condesa couldn't be more different from Tepito, a pre-Columbian neighbourhood of criminals, boxing champions, poets, traders, smugglers and painters, with a distinct culture that includes *tepiteño*, a playful slang with a unique accent, rich with word play, and a sense of identity that has led its inhabitants to repeatedly challenge the authority of the city government. Executing an arrest warrant here requires hundreds of policemen to confront the uprising they will likely face.

CRIME AND PUNISHMENT

Mexico City's reputation as a crime capital was forged in the 1970s, when Arturo 'El Negro' Durazo was the all-powerful police chief. Enemies of Durazo were liable to turn up dead in the sewers; and a *chilango* in a dark street with a police car at one end of the road and a mean-looking gang on the other would instinctively run to the latter for protection. By the mid- to late 1990s, the situation was at its worst, and in 1998, annual reported crimes for DF hit a figure of almost 238,000.

No sooner had crime peaked, however, than it began to fall. Many believe the turning point was the election of Cuauhtémoc Cárdenas, the city's first democratically elected mayor, in December 1997; but whatever the reason, since 1998, the crime rate has fallen year on year to a figure of around 149,000 in 2006. Supporters of democratic institutions in the city claim that this is one of the dividends of accountability.

But the crooks have not been the only ones to suffer: the war on crime has also led to tragic 'collateral damage'. In June 2008, a botched police raid on the News Divine, a bar selling alcohol to under-age customers, started a stampede in which 12 people – nine teenagers and three police officers – died. The immediate result was the sacking of the city police chief, the city prosecutor and the borough chief.

And despite improvements in DF's crime statistics, the country as a whole is, at time of writing, being battered by a wave of highly publicised drug-related violence that threatens to taint Mexico's image abroad. A BBC report dated September 2008 stated at least 2,700 Mexicans have been killed and 300 kidnapped in 2008 alone, mostly in drug-related violence.

It's a national tragedy for Mexicans; and even though it's exceptionally rare for foreigners to find themselves caught up in such violence, it's also bad news for the country's tourism industry. But the Mexican people themselves, caught between the rock of vicious drug gangs locked in turf wars and power struggles and the hard place of corrupt police and government officials who acquiesce in the violence, are fighting back. Mass anti-crime rallies were held across the country in 2008, and one candlelit procession, held in the Zócalo on 30 August, drew 150,000 protestors, most of them dressed in white.

Mayor Marcelo Ebrard.
See p23.

CLEANER AIR ACT

DF has had better luck tackling its other perennial bugbear, pollution. Surrounded by volcanoes and mountains, the giant metropolis sits at the bottom of a sealed-in natural basin, a geographical oddity that translates into thin air and heavy smog, worst in winter, when cold weather makes gases heavier. Rapid industrialisation and growing car ownership mean many millions of cubic kilometres of gases each year, and there are days when flying into the city through a brown-grey cloud feels like diving into an unattractive pool. Better, then, to arrive at night, when an immense blanket of light spreads across the valley like a swarm of fireflies hovering over an inky lake.

At the peak of the problem in the 1980s, 'imecas' – the Spanish acronym stands for 'metropolitan environmental quality index' – became as familiar to *chilangos* as tacos, as did *contingencias ambientales* (environmental emergencies) – crisis days on which all activities must cease. Children would stay at home, cars would be banned from running, and workers would be given the day off. The 1990s were a decade of drastic anti-pollution measures, including the banning of a fifth of all vehicles from driving one day a week; the setting of limits on factory emissions; and control of car emissions. The efforts have had a certain degree of success, though there are still occasional *pre-contingencia* alerts that shut down some factories. But the ozone levels that trigger a *contingencia* or *pre-contingencia* were reached on four out of every five days from 1990 to 1994, while there were, in total, only four *pre-contingencia* alerts in 2007.

FUTURE OF THE MEGAMETROPOLIS

Much has improved in DF; but there's still a long way to go, and a sense that the city's potential hasn't yet been fully realised. That translates into a certain sense of frustration. Many *chilangos* can't understand why Mexico City is still considered a backwater metropolis. Still, the sense that the city's golden years are yet to come works like a roaring engine, pushing hard up a steep mountain.

In 2010, the country is set to mark two important anniversaries – 200 years since the start of the Independence movement, and a century since the country's Revolution. Mexico City will, of course, be the focal point for the celebrations, and as the city gears up to host them, there's probably never been a better time to go. For a place with such a long history, DF has a remarkably youthful attitude: brash and daring, brave and open-minded; joyfully getting naked in front of its cathedrals, and inviting the rest of the world to come and watch.

Aztec revivalist, Basílica de Guadalupe.

Aztec Traces

What did the Mexica ever do for us?

You cannot fully appreciate Mexico City or its history without understanding its Aztec legacy, ever-present in a visible, physical sense but also psychologically, sociologically and metaphysically speaking.

Nearly 500 years have passed since the Spanish conquistadores ostensibly destroyed the Aztec nation. Those temples, palaces and pleasure gardens that had survived the city's desperate final siege, radiating out from the site of today's Zócalo (also the principal plaza in the pre-conquest capital), were razed, partly as a power gesture on the part of the Spanish as they set about constructing their colonial capital. Though many of the city's marketplaces and shopping areas can still be found in the very same places they always have been, there's nothing left today to indicate that Avenida Hidalgo, which heads west from the Centro, was once a causeway spanning the lakes that surrounded the Aztec capital, Tenochtitlán; and the last of the city's canals, once its main thoroughfares, which had led the European invaders to describe the city as a New World Venice, were filled and paved over in the early decades of the 20th century. Almost every

Aztec trace you'll see in Mexico City today is the result of historical accident to one degree or another — lost, buried or dismissed as insignificant at the time of the conquest, and fortunately so, since 'official' interest in Aztec civilisation really only began following Mexican independence from Spain.

But once you start exploring, physical traces of the ancient civilisation begin to reveal themselves – and Mexicans themselves may be the most direct connection. In contrast with cities built by the Spaniards in parts of Latin America that were never home to large indigenous populations, the faces of many *chilangos* show a near total reflection of the Mesoamerican physical type. Moctezuma is a surname you can still find in the Mexico City telephone directory; and Náhuatl, the living Aztec language, is spoken by 1.5 million in and around the modern capital.

THE ETERNAL CAPITAL

On the eve of the Conquest, Tenochtitlán was the most populous city in the Americas, larger than any European city except Naples and Constantinople and the capital of a far-flung empire stretching from the Gulf of Mexico to the Pacific, and from the deserts of northern Mexico to as far south as present-day Guatemala and Nicaragua. At the time, the Valley of Mexico, now Greater Mexico City, was a region divided into dozens of municipalities and supported a population of 1.2 million – a density it would not achieve again until the early 20th century. But even at the end of three centuries of political dominance, Spaniards remained a minority among the Native American and *mestizo* (Spanish-indigenous mixed) populations. And although the Spanish language took firm root, without ever extinguishing the native Náhuatl, even today, strictly Spanish culture and religion are at times little more than nuancing elements, or a thin veneer laid over longstanding indigenous habits. It's often commented, for example, that Mexican Catholicism verges on the polytheistic, with the Saviour sidelined and far more attention paid to the Virgin and to innumerable saints, official and otherwise. Relations are often drawn between those legions of saints and the equally vast number of deities – from big ones like Quetzalcoatl, the plumed serpent sky god, down to household gods protecting every trade and profession – that made up the Aztec pantheon. Even the Virgin of Guadalupe, it is suggested, bears more than a passing resemblance to Tonantzin, an Aztec lunar goddess (*see p85* **One lady: two faiths?**).

Serpent stone, Museo de la Ciudad.

THE PHYSICAL CITY

In physical terms, some of the most tangible Aztec traces are to be found right at the heart of the city. Much as the colonial overlords hoped to erase the previous civilisation and impose their own, in some of the earliest buildings they constructed, they used stones from the rubble of Aztec ruins. South of the Zócalo, at the corner of Pino Suárez and República de El Salvador, a colonial palace houses the Museo de la Ciudad de México. The house's cornerstone – a fearsome serpentine idol, unmarked and barely noticed in the urban fray – is a direct connection to city life six centuries ago. And as you change subway lines in Pino Súarez Metro station, check out the small temple that's visible there – it was unearthed during the station's construction and left in place.

> **'In Xochimilco, crops are still raised on chinampas – fertile fields created on the lake bed by Aztec farmers.'**

Aztec archaeological treasures have been discovered time and again under the city's skin, stumbled across during municipal maintenance works such as the digging of Metro tunnels and water mains, and in the laying of cables. The most dramatic example of this is the Templo Mayor, the most complete and impressive ruin of ancient Tenochtitlán, whose central location beside the cathedral, right on the Zócalo, seems incredible – until you remember that this has always been the city's core, right from the start. What *is* incredible is that it lay for so many centuries, forgotten, under a row of colonial buildings beside the cathedral. Once the ceremonial centre of the entire Aztec Empire and the setting for human sacrifices, it is in fact not one pyramid but seven, built one on top of the another between 1375 and 1502.

Further afield within the city, the ruins of Tenochtitlán's sister city, Tlatelolco, form part of the Plaza de las Tres Culturas (Plaza of the Three Cultures), and are another place in which visitors can make physical contact with Aztec civilisation – and indeed, with the 'layer cake' of Mexican history, as it was memorably described by the writer Carlos Fuentes. And in Xochimilco, in the south of the city, crops are still raised on the *chinampas* – fertile fields made by driving piers and packing earth onto the lake bed – created by Aztec farmers along miles of peaceful waterways.

Accidental archaeological finds invariably unleash an emotional, and for some, religious, reaction. As recently as October 2006,

Traditional *charro* costumes embroidered with Aztec imagery at Holy Week, Iztapalapa.

excavations between the Templo Mayor and the Metropolitan Cathedral turned up an idol believed to portray Tlaltecuhtli, an earth deity popularly celebrated as 'La Diosa' ('The Goddess'). Many Mexicans saw an ominous portent in the discovery – a resurgence of ancient Aztec power that dovetailed conveniently with unrest in Mexico at the time in response to the controversial, some say fraudulent, presidential elections.

On the other hand, in April 2006 the ruins of a pyramid supposedly destroyed by Cortés's soldiers were discovered in Mexico City's gritty Iztapalapa neighbourhood (you can visit the temple in Parque Cerro de la Estrella). While most local people were delighted by the importance it afforded the area, its excavation was halted so as not to interfere with Iztapalapa's famous and, it was felt, equally important Holy Week Passion play: the crucifixion (*see p163* **Thank God it's Friday**) is re-enacted on the very same hill on which the ruin was discovered.

SOUVENIRS AND SYMBOLISM

Beyond the religious, Aztec imagery is very much to the fore in the Mexican capital. The appeal of a romanticised Aztec stereotype is powerful, evident in the many kitsch modern representations of a buff Aztec warrior who appears on posters, calendars, T-shirts, blankets and assorted knick-knacks across the city. Handsome, strong and with impressive muscle tone, he bears his virginal, bare-breasted and swooning princess towards Mexico City's

twin volcanoes, Popocatépetl and Ixtaccíhuatl. Tellingly lighter-skinned than most Mexicans, he embodies a host of ideals as rudely macho as they are whimsically romantic.

The last Aztec emperor Cuauhtémoc lives on as a fierce warrior emblazoned on the blood-red 100-peso note, and cast in bronze at one of the city's pivotal intersections, Reforma and Insurgentes, where he raises his spear permanently at those approaching from Spain. Emblazoned on the national flag, the eagle-and-serpent insignia depicts an omen the Aztecs were told they would see in the place they should found their civilisation, and there's a monument on the southern side of the Zócalo indicating where the eagle supposedly landed in 1325. Schoolchildren learn the story as a historical event, and it's as much a part of the Mexican national mythology as it was for the Aztecs, who, once they began to flourish and conquer, undertook a systematic programme of rebranding, sanitising and aggrandising their origins while fashioning a legendary history, from which comes the eagle and serpent story, among others. Thus, in layers of memory and myth as multiple as the city's archaeological vestiges, the Aztec culture admired in the 21st century is the idealised version of a past created, in turn, by Aztec intellectuals and politicians in the mid 14th century.

Perhaps the most striking embodiment of Mexico's Aztec fascination are the *concheros* – Aztec revivalists dressed in robes, loincloths, noisemaking shells and extravagant feathers, who gather in groups comprising dozens of dancers, drummers, and conch-blowers to pay homage to their heritage through dance and song in the Zócalo, at Plaza Morelos, or in front of the Basílica of Guadalupe. The groups attract a diverse set of adherents, from working-class types to latter-day hippies, environmentalists and intellectuals. Most are motivated by a straightforward desire to preserve vanishing cultures, though a small minority has more a pointedly political and even right-wing agenda. And while some of the dancers are pagan believers, many of the other participants believe it's not incompatible with their Catholic faith.

The supposed greatness and splendour of Cuauhtémoc's era feeds a characteristically Mexican nostalgia for a time when society was orderly, fierce and technologically superior to its neighbours, and was governed by noble warriors instead of dubious bureaucrats. Ever alive to an opportunity, though, politicians have often sought to tap this well of Aztec aspiration. In 2008, government-sponsored ads in the Metro encouraged passengers to come and 'celebrate the 488th anniversary of the Spaniards' defeat' at a festival. The 'defeat' referred to the 1520 Spanish retreat from Tenochtitlán, known as La Noche Triste (the Sad Night) – in fact a mere blip on the sure road to the Spanish conquest. And if Carlos Fuentes wrote of the usefulness to Mexico's ruling class of encouraging this nostalgia for an Aztec past, author Octavio Paz went further in his fierce

critiques (particularly in the essay 'The Other Mexico') of the Mexican fascination with the Aztecs, pointing out that in fact the Mexica, as the Aztecs called themselves, were a cruelly oppressive society that struck fear into the hearts of people across Mesoamerica. 'Although the Conquest destroyed the indigenous world and built another, different one on its remains', Paz writes, 'there is an invisible thread of continuity between the ancient society and the Spanish order: that of domination.'

'Tortillas, tamales, beans, chilli peppers, squash and huitlacoche were the core elements of Aztec cuisine.'

Less controversially, when it comes to food and drink and Aztec traces, the proof is on the plate. Iguanas and gophers may have fallen from favour in the Mexican culinary universe; but tortillas, tamales, beans, chilli peppers, squash and *huitlacoche* – corn smut or fungus – were the core elements of a workingman's lunch in 15th-century Tenochtitlán, and they are still staples half a millennium on. At Don Chon (*see p102*), one of the Centro's finest restaurants, Aztec-style sautéed ant larvae (*escamoles*), crocodile in green *mole* sauce, swamp-fly eggs (*ahuatli*) and fat, crispy, deep-fried moth larvae (*gusanos de maguey*) are eaten with relish by the restaurant's Mexican patrons – and with the kind of insouciance that is the mark of the true gourmet in the non-Mexican. Far from being mere novelties, these are genuine delicacies, still widely enjoyed in Mexico. Aztec completists will want to wash them down with *pulque*, the foamy, fermented maguey sap once drunk by priests, warriors and lovers and associated with a whole range of Aztec deities, including the awesome god of alcohol, Two Rabbit or Ometotchtli. For prisoners of the Aztecs, *pulque* was the last thing they ever imbibed. They were force-fed the white liquor and then made to dance and sing as they marched to their gory end atop a sawn-off pyramid. Parts of their bodies, it is thought, were sometimes then eaten – but this, even for the boldest of gourmets, is probably a gastrofad too far.

Perhaps it's because European influence prevailed, eventually, that Aztec heritage is so treasured in Mexico as a valuable cultural counterweight. It's concrete, too, since as many of the city's colonial buildings subside thanks to their imperfect, muddy lake-bed base, Aztec traces multiply, revealing themselves all over the city. The plumed serpent is, it seems, ready to strike every time a pick strikes the pavement.

Aztec awakening – a *conchero* dancer

Death in Mexico by DBC Pierre

My guide, though middle-aged, has the wary eyes of a child who has spied a murder through a keyhole. We meet at midnight beside a monument in the heart of Mexico City. 'I wouldn't call us vampires,' he says, warming his hands on a takeaway coffee. 'Maybe angels of death.'

Five of his associates mill around. One is dressed like a gangster, complete with hat. A moll in lurid eveningwear hangs on his arm. Six nights a week, they gather here like latter-day hunters, cars at the ready: they are journalists and photographers for Mexico's lurid death press. They talk between crackles and chatter from radio scanners.

'Stabbing, San Felipe,' calls a reporter. 'Man in the road – not breathing!'

We scramble into a convoy. I look around the endless churning organism of Mexico City as we go, and wonder about its willingness to contemplate horror. Its pre- and post-Hispanic layers had different tastes for death, and these have mixed into one unique Mexican flavour. The city's people and their arts are steeped in it. Repulsed by Aztec human sacrifice, Spanish conquerors merely replaced it with the church's own brand of the macabre; in later centuries this included disinterring and displaying the corpses of those whose families were in arrears with the rent on their graves – a practice continued until 1984. In Mexico City, the ex-Convento Del Carmen in San Ángel still displays its mummies – corpses preserved by mysterious conditions of air and soil.

Around Hallowe'en, in a coincidence of Aztec and Christian timing, Mexico's Day of the Dead celebration is a smoky cocktail of skulls and crosses, with sugar and chocolate versions for the kiddies. The church at Mixquic, outside the city, best embodies the cocktail, its yard heaped with bones and its baptismal font an altar once used to sacrifice children. The Aztecs were a materialistic people: they believed in offering something in return for a god's favour, and that something was mostly blood. The altar's chill was also meant to shock valuable tears from a child, the better to encourage rain. Such history seems brutal, but today Mexico's romance with death is a cosy one, its painted skeletons as whimsical and charming as puppies and as plentiful. There's hardly a corner on which *calaveras* don't roam in print, pottery or papier maché, going like Disney characters about their everyday business, dressed up, dressed down, pushing prams, playing trumpets, playing tennis. And even the death press has its light side, credited with being a vital watchdog over the city's denizens of the night.

This night, though, the police beat us to our stabbing. Disappointment settles over the returning convoy. In *colonia* Doctores, a shrine to Santa Muerte flashes past us and sets me musing. Saint Death, the skeleton in holy virgin's robes, originally a cult for delinquents, now has worshippers across the ranks of society and I realise: she is a return to the materialism of the Aztecs. A full circle through the hoopla of morality back to those temperamental humours, that lottery of fortune, neither good nor bad, that has always governed this ancient city, Mexico City – Tenochtitlán.

She is an agent through whom death can be bartered with; and as with so many things in Mexico City, she works both ways. The radio crackles. 'Crash on Viaducto!' hisses a reporter. Phones light up as a web of informants sets about confirming the victim's status. But the reporter's face soon falls.

'Damn it. Just a broken leg.'

Booker-prize-winning author DBC Pierre grew up in Mexico City.

¡Viva la Lucha!

Masked-up, leotard-wearing superheroes you can touch.

If you want an insight into the significance of comedy and violence in Mexican culture and the role of masks in popular entertainment, read a book by Octavio Paz or Carlos Fuentes.

If, on the other hand, you want a lively, possibly fun and certainly weird night out in Mexico City with plenty of beer, banter and brawling, a night at a *lucha libre* arena is not to be missed. You'll see grown men in skin-tight masks being carried along on waves of animal passion, both inside and outside the ring. You'll see pneumatic women prancing around in glittery swimming costumes, or fighting each other in leotards, long hair flying. You'll watch gangs of diehard fans cheering on their idols and yelling insults at their idols' opponents – or, as is more likely, bellowing startling revelations vis-à-vis the sexual appetites and poor characters of those fighters' mothers.

Above all, you'll see wave on wave of elaborately choreographed martial arts routines, blurring the line spectacularly between sport and art. In *lucha*, nothing is as it seems; and that, coupled with the fact that nobody appears to mind much, is its strength.

SAINTS AND SUPERHEROES

In the first decades of the 20th century, Mexican wrestling was mostly an amateur, regional affair. But in 1933, the Empresa Mexicana de Lucha Libre (Mexican Wrestling Company) was created to encourage the sport both in the capital and in the far-flung provinces. When bouts began to be televised in the 1950s, just as TV itself was crackling into life, *lucha libre* took off as a national passion.

El Santo (The Saint, pictured above in silver mask), the unsurpassed *luchador* par excellence, appeared on the scene in 1942, and on his debut in Mexico City won an eight-man 'battle royal', a triumph often cited by his fans despite the fact that – whisper it, and take care who to

Fight facts

Where?

There are two principal Mexico City arenas for top-drawer *lucha libre*: the run-down but enormously atmospheric Arena Naucalpan, far out in the suburbs, where fighters walk a battered red carpet into the ring through clouds of dry ice; and at the other end of the spectrum, the massive Arena México, which holds 17,000. Naucalpan's capacity is a mere 1,500. The crowd here is noticeably more affluent, with front-row seats going for MX$500 (the minimum daily wage is MX$51).

The rules

Contests usually consist of three bouts per match. Most matches are nominally 'tag' bouts: when a player is tied or injured, he can touch his co-fighter and swap places. All fights descend rapidly into chaos, however, with wrestlers piling in to help their compadres, fighting in and out of the ring, and competitors falling into the audience.

Good vs evil

Luchadores (wrestlers) are divided into *técnicos* (good guys) and *rudos* (bad guys), making each bout a battle between good and evil. *Rudos* favour black costumes and make their attempts to cheat obvious, going for groin grabs and indulging in much swaggering and posing. *Técnicos* play fair, and like to wave at children in the audience.

Referees

The referees are also split between *técnicos* and *rudos*. A pro-*rudo* ref will turn a blind eye

to ganging up during tag-team fights, for instance, or to a chair being brought into the ring. But their main function is to make panicking gestures and express faux bewilderment or outrage as the fights spiral, predictably, out of control.

Audience participation

In the arenas, it's more fiesta than fight club: spectators don the masks of their favourite *luchadores* and children dash around wearing sequinned capes. Teams of supporters scream and chant the names of their adopted teams between mouthfuls of popcorn, and and plastic horns sound continuously. Hawkers work their way down the rows selling beer, street food and merchandise.

Grudge matches

Many deep-seated feuds are resolved in well-publicised fights in which the winner tears off the mask of the defeated wrestler – causing him to lose face, literally – and, sometimes, shaves off his hair. The loser's popularity plummets; earnings can too. Many *luchadores* have scars on their foreheads from having their masks violently ripped off.

The front row

Anyone in the front row risks being spattered with blood (some fake, some not), and *luchadores* frequently fly out of the ring, intentionally or otherwise, landing in the first few rows of seats. If you're not prepared to have a 250-pound masked man crash-land in your lap, consider sitting a few rows back.

– bouts are rigged by the promoters and their outcomes are, by and large, preordained.

El Santo became an icon, starring in a series of B-movies of the likes of *El Santo vs the Vampire Women* and featuring in his own *Marvel*-style comic. In public, he never once stepped out of character – that of a working-class hero fighting for justice for the common man. Behind the scenes, however, El Santo was also fighting for higher pay for wrestlers and to turn *lucha libre* – or at least, his own fights – into a lucrative professional franchise.

In 1985, El Santo died. ¡Viva El Hijo del Santo! Yes, not long after the last funeral taco had been scoffed, the Saint's son emerged as a worthy successor. Of his father, he recalls, 'El Santo started as a *rudo* [heel or baddie], but he became like Spider Man or Batman, not through magical powers but through faith.' He can be

forgiven, perhaps, a moment's confusion between the superhuman and mortal powers, respectively, of those venerated superheroes, because he gets it spot on where it most counts: 'We Mexicans,' he continues, 'are first and foremost adorers of the Virgin of Guadalupe, and it is through faith that El Santo became a *técnico* [goodie]. Faith made him good, and it made the people love him. His silver mask became a symbol of justice.'

El Santo turned *lucha libre* into the third most popular sport in Mexico, after football and baseball, and El Hijo del Santo says he wants to see it grow even bigger. With a degree in media and communications, he takes pride in the fact that 'Lucha nights now attract high society, media people and artists', and sells his own merchandise from a themed coffee bar in swanky Condesa. Like his father before him,

he has taken on arena managers to get higher wages for fighters, but says there is still a long way to go in the fight for wrestlers' rights. 'I am a superstar like Hugo Sánchez in football and Julio César Chávez in boxing, but I don't earn what they earn. Sadly, the *lucha libre* promoters and venues have got used to taking all the money and treating fighters as second-class citizens. There are even cases of wrestlers getting as little as US$10 a fight.'

El Hijo del Santo is happy to share his theories about Mexican wrestling: '*Lucha libre* is an art, a sport, a spectacle. You need to be in good shape, of course, but it is not merely a sport. It is also theatre in the sense that a mask is used and a character is adopted. The wrestler adopts the persona just like an actor in a theatre. He loses himself in the *lucha*.'

Spectators also lose themselves, he says, and forget their daily troubles: 'I think it is a sort of therapy for the general public, because it's a way in which they can get things off their chests. Unlike other spectacles, in *lucha libre* we invite spectators to express their aggression verbally at the wrestlers.

'When they see a *rudo*, they probably think of their boss, their enemy, perhaps their mother-in-law. But take a look at these same people when they are leaving the stadium and you'll see the great majority of them smiling, contented, free of stress. They return to the old laws of mutual respect and tolerance, having experienced a sort of catharsis.'

Rayo de Jalisco Jr.

Which brings us back to those clever writers. Octavio Paz has written that Mexicans are naturally drawn to dissimulation and hiding: 'Our whole way of life is a mask designed to hide our intimate feelings… [The Mexican man] is condemned to play his role throughout life.' Television and radio commentator Carlos Hernández Valdés keeps it simpler regarding Mexicans' view of the *luchadores*: 'They're considered superheroes you can touch.' Their names – Místico, Fray Tormenta (Brother Storm), Black Warrior, Mephisto – and their lurid, figure-hugging costumes seem to bear this out.

GOING GLOBAL?

These days, *lucha libre* events are more like rock concerts than sporting matches. With big-brand advertising, tickets touted for as much as US$200 and live TV broadcasts, it's a millions-of-pesos money-spinner. Big-name *luchadores* turn up in music videos; El Hijo del Santo is about to feature on a postage stamp; and Silver King nabbed a role as Ramses in Jack Black's 2006 *lucha* comedy, *Nacho Libre*.

The next step is to take *lucha* to the world. For decades, wrestlers have moved between the USA's WWE and the Mexican codes. In 2008, twenty big-name *luchadores* took their show to London's Roundhouse theatre, and advertising billboards have been spotted broadcasting their imminent arrival as far south as Argentina. With a little luck (and a lot of promotion), *lucha libre* could prove to be as highly exportable a slice of mexicana as mariachi music, tequila and tacos.

Where to Stay

Where to Stay   **36**

Features

Where to Stay

Sleep easy in DF's chic hotels, colonial inns and cheap and cheerful hostels.

With the hundreds of hotels you'd expect in a city its size, DF nevertheless has a relatively compact range of really great hotels. Choosing accommodation is a straightforward affair: work out where in the city you'd like to be and take it from there; though if it's huge, luxury hotels that make your heart sing, the choice is made for you. You'll very likely be resting your head somewhere along Paseo de le Reforma or in posh Polanco, in trad-classic **JW Marriott** (*see p46*), or the edgy **W Mexico City** (*see p46*). Other picks of the Polanco pack are cosy **Casa Vieja** (*see p45*) and slick **Habita** (*see p46*) – the original in DF's crop of design hotels.

Visitors with business affairs in corporate, high-rise Santa Fe are well advised to choose lodgings there, since its geographical isolation makes transport a drag. Better to base yourself close to your associates and make excursions into the Centro and beyond. Zona Rosa is a traditional hotel hotspot – the **Calinda Geneve** (*see p43*) remains a popular choice – but has lost ground in recent years to wider and better selections in other neighbourhoods, including Polanco and indeed, the Centro.

Because no matter how chic and cheerful other parts of the city might be, short stays in DF are perhaps best appreciated from one of the Centro's excellent spread of hotels in the heart of the city. Centro gems include, at the top end, the **Sheraton Centro Histórico** (*see p37*) and the **Hotel Isabel** at the other (*see p41*).

Hotels are scarce in Coyoacán, a village-like neighbourhood in the south of the city; but the **Chalet del Carmen** (*see p50*) is a good pick there. And with the boutique hotel wave yet to break fully over DF, if it's due any time soon there's little doubt it will roll in on Condesa and Roma, increasingly popular and surely on the brink of a boutique upsurge. For now, the range is small but includes hip **Condesa DF** (*see p49*) and homely **Red Tree House** (*see p49*).

Our hotel listings are organised by area and price including tax (IVA), then in alphabetical order. Taking the cost of the lowest-priced double room as a rough guide, we've sorted hotels into one of the following categories: **Deluxe** (more than MX$2,500); **Expensive** (MX$1,500-$2,500); **Moderate** (MX$750-$1,500); and **Budget** (under MX$750).

W Mexico City. *See p46.*

The best Hotels

For colonial charm
Best Western Hotel Majestic (*see below*); **Calinda Geneve** (*see p43*); **Casa Vieja** (*see p45*).

For haute decor
Condesa DF (*see p49*); **Habita** (*see p46*); **W Mexico City** (*see p46*).

For killer views
Fiesta Americana Grand Chapultepec (*see p46*); **Hotel Maria Isabel Sheraton** (*see p43*); **NH Hotel** (*see p43*).

For business pleasure
JW Marriott Hotel (*see p46*); **Hotel Marquis Reforma** (*see p43*); **Sheraton Centro Histórico** (*see below*).

For a home from home
Casa Comtesse (*see p49*); **The Red Tree House** (*see p49*).

For peso pinchers
Hostal Frida (*see p50*); **Hostal Virreyes** (*see p41*); **Hotel Isabel** (*see p41*).

Centro

Expensive

Best Western Hotel Majestic
Madero 73 (5521 8600/01800 509 2350/www. majestichotel.com.mx). Metro Zócalo L2. **Rates** MX$1,440-$2,760 double. **Rooms** 84. **Credit** AmEx, MC, V. **Map** p267 M4 ❶
Too beautiful to be part of a bland chain of hotels, the Majestic is irresistibly Mexican, resplendent in blue and white tiles and set around a lovely flower scented, shady courtyard that comes as a pleasant surprise, given the hotel's downtown location. Its colonial-style standard single and double rooms are cosy without being cramped, and come complete with views of the Zócalo, busy *calle* Madero or the indoor courtyard, with the latter the best bet for light sleepers. Oversize bathtubs in the vintage bathrooms make a relaxing soak after a long day's sightseeing something to look forward to, while the terrace restaurant, with its open-air section, offers magnificent views of Mexico City's main square, the Zócalo (*see p103*). The hotel's in-house travel agency arranges trips in and around DF as well as to other parts of the country.
Bar. Business centre. Concierge. Disabled-adapted rooms. Internet (free wireless, shared terminal). No-smoking rooms. Restaurant. TV: cable.

Gran Hotel Ciudad de México
16 de Septiembre 82 (1083 7700/01800 088 7700/ www.granhotelciudaddemexico.com.mx). Metro Zócalo L2. **Rates** MX$1,670-$2,800 double. **Rooms** 60. **Credit** AmEx, MC, V. **Map** pp267 M4 ❷
An immense chandelier reputedly donated by 19th-century dictator Porfirio Díaz lights your way into the breathtaking atrium of this gloriously old-fashioned hotel in the heart of the Centro Histórico. There, art nouveau lines sweep your gaze up to the tremendous Tiffany stained-glass vaulted ceiling, forged in Paris and shipped to Mexico piece by piece in the early 20th century. Original elevators fashioned in the same workshop are reserved for arriving guests, but the inhabitants of the matching birdcages chirp their greetings to all and sundry. All the rooms have spacious bathrooms and air conditioning, and are decorated in the hotel's signature French-colonial style – a tad chintzy, but not oppressively so. Some rooms (mainly suites) come with striking views of the Zócalo – the trade-off being, as always, that interior rooms are quieter. The public areas look a little tired despite a 2005 refit, but the hotel's sparkling original features make such minor failings exceptionally easy to forgive. *Photo p45.*
Bar (2). Business centre. Concierge. Disabled-adapted rooms. Gym. Internet (free wireless, shared terminal). No-smoking rooms. Parking (MX$90). Restaurants (3). Room service. TV: cable.

Sheraton Centro Histórico
Juárez 70 (5130 5300/www.sheraton.com.mx). Metro Bellas Artes L2, L8 or Juárez L3. **Rates** MX$1,440-$5,400 double. **Rooms** 457. **Credit** AmEx, MC, V. **Map** pp266 K4 ❸
This is one of Mexico's foremost business hotels, with an unusually relaxing, almost Zen-like atmosphere. The air-conditioned rooms are both opulent and contemporary, and each comes with a work area and a spacious bathroom. Most staff members speak English and they tend to be very helpful, giving sightseeing and transport advice cheerfully at the busy front desk. Spoil yourself with an upgrade to a corner room – a mini-suite with panoramic views of the Alameda park and Bellas Artes; and wake up on sunny days with a swim in the roof garden pool, with brunch afterwards at La Terraza restaurant. Or head straight for on-site eaterie El Cardenal (*see p102*), famous for its gourmet Mexican breakfasts and lunches. It is rumoured that this Sheraton will become DF's only downtown Hilton in 2009.
Bars (2). Business centre. Concierge. Disabled-adapted rooms. Gym. Internet (MX$102 p/24hrs high-speed/wireless). No-smoking rooms/floors. Parking (MX$102). Pools (1 indoor, 1 outdoor). Restaurants (3). Room service. Spa. TV: pay movies.

---

❶ Green numbers given in this chapter correspond to the location of each hotel as marked on the street maps. See pp259-267.

THE ELEGANCE OF ART NOUVEAU

GRAN HOTEL
CIUDAD DE MÉXICO

Moderate

Holiday Inn Zócalo

5 de Mayo 61 (5130 5130/www.ichotelsgroup.com).
Metro Zócalo L2. **Rates** MX$1,140-$1,400 double.
Rooms 105. **Credit** AmEx, MC, V. **Map** pp267 M4 **4**
Despite the typically bland lobby, this Holiday Inn,
scheduled for a refit in 2009, is atypical. The air-
conditioned rooms have a rustic feel, with wooden
floors and colonial details; and though standard
rooms are a little on the small side, the suites – complete with immense jacuzzis – look out on to the
Zócalo through double-glazed windows that reduce
noise from the busy plaza below. The terrace
restaurant offers impressive views of the square
and free wireless internet.
Bar. Business centre. Concierge. Disabled-adapted
rooms. Gym. Internet (free wireless, shared terminals
1st 30mins free). No-smoking rooms. Parking.
Restaurant. Room service. TV: cable, pay movies.

Hotel Catedral

Donceles 95 (5518 5232/01800 701 8340/www.
hotelcatedral.com). Metro Zócalo L2. **Rates** MX$685-
$1,040 double. **Rooms** 116. **Credit** AmEx, MC, V.
Map pp267 M4 **5**
There's retro chic – and then there's 1970s furniture
twinned with cheap 1980s textiles, including bizarre
pastel fabric wall hangings. But despite its design
eccentricities, Hotel Catedral offers good value for
money. Twin terraces with bar service are its finest

features, offering suntrap spots plus shaded seating
areas and wireless access. The rooms are clean and
often spacious, some with bathtubs, others with balconies. Junior suites include lounges and jacuzzis,
and while there is no air conditioning, fans are provided. The in-house travel agent can change flights
or book trips across the country.
Bar. Concierge. Internet (free wireless throughout,
MX$30/hr shared terminal). No-smoking hotel.
Parking. Restaurant. Room service. TV: cable.

Hotel de Cortés

Hidalgo 85 (5518 2181/www.hoteldecortes.com.mx).
Metro Bellas Artes L2, L8 or Hidalgo L2, L3. **Rates**
MX$980-$1,610 double. **Rooms** 28. **Credit** AmEx,
MC, V. **Map** pp266 K3 **6**
This colonial beauty, once part of the Best Western
chain, is set to become an independent boutique hotel.
Its pleasant, leafy courtyard offers shelter from the
city's hustle and bustle, with a relaxed feel that goes
way, way back. From 1660 up until the late 19th century, the establishment served as a hostelry for
Augustinian friars visiting Mexico on evangelising
missions, and the ornate, baroque building's 28 rooms
began their lives as monastic cells. Rescued from dere-
liction in 1943, it has served, on and off, as an upmarket guesthouse ever since. The hotel is undergoing a
full refit at time of writing.
Bar. Concierge. Restaurant. Room service.

Hotel Tulip Inn Ritz

Madero 30 (5130 0169/01800 201 5256/www.
tulipinnritzmexico.com). Metro Bellas Artes L2, L8
or Zócalo L2. **Rates** MX$1,140-$1,290. **Rooms** 120.
Credit AmEx, DC, MC, V. **Map** pp267 L4 **7**
This mid-range option is well located on a busy, safe
street. Upstairs, the bright yellow open-plan lobby
merges with a bar and television area, giving this
small hotel something of a hostel feel. The clean,
comfortable rooms have original 1930s features, and
it's well worth stretching to a junior suite where, for
a minimal outlay, you'll get a much larger room with
a separate seating area. There's no air conditioning,
but fans do the trick unless an unusual heat-wave
strikes. Friendly English-speaking staff are a plus,
but the buffet breakfast can be a bit hit and miss.
Bar. Internet (free wireless, shared terminal).
No- smoking rooms. Parking (MX$50). Restaurant.
Room service. TV: cable.

Budget

Hostel Catedral Mundo Joven

República de Guatemala 4 (5518 1726/01800 823
2410/www.hostelcatedral.com). Metro Zócalo L2.
Rates MX$480-$670 double; MX$145-$155 dorm
bed. **Rooms/dorm beds** 6 rooms, 40 dorm beds.
Credit MC, V. **Map** pp267 M4 **8**
This well-equipped, sociable hostel right on the
Zócalo has single-sex or mixed dorms for four to six
people, with individual lockers (bring your own pad-
lock). Aimed at young travellers unlikely to be
bothered by noise from the bar, Hostel Catedral

**Hostal
Virreyes.**
See p41.

Where to Stay

Habita forming

Want to sleep in style? Meet the Habita group, consisting of seven design hotels that add a dab of idiosyncratic fun and high style to Mexico's hotel world, as well as containing some of the country's hottest bars and restaurants. The presence of a Habita hotel has become a litmus test of an area's transition from up-and-coming to international sensation ever since the group, owned by the Micha brothers Rafael, Moisés and Jaime, plus partner Carlos Couturier, opened its first hotel, **Habita** (*see p46*) in Polanco in 2000. It quickly became associated with the now thriving Mexico City art and design renaissance, and the hotel and its sister, **Condesa DF** (*pictured, see p49*), are packed most nights with designers, artists, hipsters, media types, celebs, and a host of quite convincing wannabes.

At their best, the spaces are impeccable, with a real sense of drama and intrigue surrounding the journey from street to guest room – one of the industry's holy grails, if only more hoteliers knew it. At Condesa DF, an elegantly understated entrance and lobby suddenly segue into an open-air atrium that's part noughties minimalism, part tight white pants in Acapulco, on a yacht, circa 1972.

Flagship Habita has the work-hard, play-harder crowd's number, with an compellingly spartan design scheme that practically dares you not to stay calm and efficient. The rooftop bar, however, is hedonism central.

At the other end of the scale are the group's Playa del Carmen properties, **Deseo** (www.hoteldeseo.com) and **Básico** (*see p233*), which have a more casual and indeed, verging on the louche seaside feel, Mexican style. Deseo plays the design straight guy, albeit still wildly camp, to Básico's exuberant, melodramatic industrial look; and it's that audacious design edge that's a signature quality of the group. With that in mind, tranquil **Azúcar** (www.hotelazucar.com), two hours north of Veracruz on the Gulf of Mexico, may be the group's most singular property, so blessedly far from civilisation and so simple that you have little choice there but to detach and unwind. In Puebla, close to DF, **La Purificadora** (www.lapurificadora.com), has injected some kicky energy into the sleepy colonial town, with architect Ricardo Legorreta's re-imagining of the 19th-century water purification plant blending tradition and modernity to stunning effect. And with its eye on still further expansion, the group opened **Habita MTY** in Monterrey in late 2008.

Even if you only drop in for a cocktail, don't miss taking a look at some of these, Mexico's hottest hotels. They represent the real Mexico just as vividly as do ancient ruins, endless metropolis, traffic jams and taco stands.

Where to Stay

offers discounts to Hostelling International and ISIC cardholders. Services include a kitchen, a launderette, 24-hour security and a book exchange. Bilingual staff are available around the clock and an in-house travel agency offers good value tours. The Terraza bar has cut-price drinks, a view over the plaza and an area in which you can soak up the sun. *Bars (2). Internet (free wireless, MX$15/hr shared terminals). No-smoking rooms.*

Hostal Virreyes

José María Izazaga 8 (5521 4180/www hostal virreyes.com.mx). Metro Salta del Agua L1, L8. **Rates** MX$345 double; MX$130 dorm bed; monthly from MX$2,550. **Rooms/dorm beds** 140 dorm beds. **Credit** MC, V. **Map** p267 L5 ❾

A flawed yet funky, affordable place to stay in the Centro Histórico, Hostal Virreyes has a stylish foyer, lounge and bar area equipped with 1960s furniture, and a quirky lift decorated with vintage wallpaper. Street-facing rooms, particularly on upper levels, offer impressive views of the city; but it comes at a price: the hotel's location on Eje Central makes sleeping like trying to snooze through an incessant movie car-chase. Ask for an interior room, or bring earplugs. Reasonable monthly rates make the Virreyes a good option if you're sticking around. Your fellow long-term guests will be mostly artists, writers and filmmakers, adding to the bohemian, Chelsea Hotel feel as do the regular events that take place here, from book launches and film showings to live music and lobby parties, held periodically at weekends, that bring Mexico City nightlife to your door. Continental breakfast included. *Photo p39. Bar. Concierge. Gym. Internet (free wireless, shared terminals).*

Hotel Gillow

Isabel La Católica 17 (5510 0791/www.hotel gillow.com). Metro Allende L2 or Bellas Artes L2, L8. **Rates** MX$635-$865 double. **Rooms** 103. **Credit** AmEx, MC, V. **Map** p267 M4 ❿

Hotel Gillow is having something of an aesthetic identity crisis, the 19th-century elegance of this, one of the city's oldest hotels, increasingly giving way to a bizarre, 1970s Swiss-chalet-style decor. Even so, it's a decent all-rounder, with secure and comfortable rooms – request one with a terrace for spectacular views of the city. Restaurant La Capilla serves Mexican food and hearty breakfasts for an additional cost. There's a same-day dry-cleaning service and a 24-hour taxi service, and for travel assistance, try the in-house Sablons travel agency. *Bar. Business centre. Concierge. Internet (free wireless, shared terminals). Restaurant. Room service. TV: cable.*

Hotel Isabel

Isabel La Católica 63 (5518 1213/www.hotel-isabel.com.mx). Metro Isabel la Católica L1 or San Juan de Letrán L8. **Rates** MX$280-$405 double. **Rooms** 71. **No credit cards. Map** p267 M5 ⓫

Hotel Isabel is a great budget option, with bags of character and legions of devoted fans. The vintage

1980s furniture distracts attention from the rooms' faded decor, and as in Hostal Virreyes, artists and writers are among the hotel's permanent residents. Noise carries from the hostel next door, so avoid rooms at the back at the adjoining wall. Multiple occupancy rooms on the top floor are furnished with old-fashioned brass beds; and the cheapest rooms, with shared bathrooms, can only be requested on arrival. *Bar. Disabled-adapted rooms. Internet (shared terminals MX$10/20mins). No-smoking rooms. Restaurant. Room service. TV: cable.*

Paseo de la Reforma

Deluxe

Four Seasons

Avenida Paseo de la Reforma 500 (5230 1818/ www.fourseasons.com/mexico). Metro Chapultepec L1 or Sevilla L1. **Rates** MX$2,600-$9,030 double. **Rooms** 240. **Credit** AmEx, MC, V. **Map** p264 F6 ⓬

It's central, it's slick, it's expensive: it's a Four Seasons hotel. The lobby has been polished until it gleams, the service is impeccable, and each room is an acme of quiet luxury in that uptight and ultra-conservative style Four Seasons does so well. The manicured central courtyard, alive with geraniums, azaleas and myrtle and a tinkling fountain, is an outstanding feature, as is the pool which, though small, is a lovely spot for a pre-breakfast dip. *Bar. Business centre. Gym. Internet. (free wireless, shared terminals). No-smoking floors. Pool (outdoor). Restaurant. Spa. TV: cable, pay movies.*

Expensive

Embassy Suites

Avenida Paseo de la Reforma 69 (5061 3000/www. embassysuitesmexicocity.com). Metro Hidalgo L2, L3. **Rates** MX$1,670-$2,915 double. **Rooms** 160. **Credit** AmEx, DC, MC, V. **Map** p266 I4 ⓭

This newly minted Hilton franchise offers three types of suite: superior, premier and corner, with heavy double glazing to keep traffic noise down. The decor is simple and pretty, with white bedspreads and throws in pinks and rusts, plus plasma TVs and iPod-ready clock radios. There's a 'manager's cocktail' plus snacks every day from 6pm-8pm in the lobby bar which is delightfully free of charge; or for those who prefer a shot of java, there's a Starbucks in the lobby. *Bars (2). Business centre. Concierge. Disabled-adapted rooms. Gym. Internet (wireless MX$11/day). No-smoking floors. Parking (MX$8). Pool (1 indoor). Restaurant. Room service.*

Gran Meliá Mexico Reforma

Avenida Paseo de la Reforma 1 (5063 1000/ www.meliamexicoreforma.com). Metro Hidalgo L2, L3. **Rates** MX$1,640-$2,990 double. **Rooms** 489. **Credit** AmEx, DC, MC, V. **Map** p266 J4 ⓮

With an address not even DF's worst taxi driver could botch, the Meliá Mexico Reforma is a swanky symphony in pink. If its spacious spa, equipped with

yoga room, beauty salon and separate male and female relaxation areas fails to soothe sufficiently, guests can indulge in a neck massage in the lobby, while executive floors with their own lounges, check-in, internet stations and meeting rooms are designed to make life easier for the business traveller.
Bar. Business centre. Concierge. Disabled facilities. Gym. Internet (wireless MX$17/day). Parking (MX$12). Pool (1 indoor). Restaurants (2). Room service. Spa. TV: pay movies.

Hotel María Isabel Sheraton

Avenida Paseo de la Reforma 325 (5242 5555/ www.sheraton.com). Metro Chapultepec L1 or Sevilla L1. **Rates** MX$1,440-$4,205 double. **Rooms** 755. **Credit** AmEx, V. **Map** p264 G5 ⓯
This generic hotel is made more interesting by its magnificent location overlooking el Ángel, Mexico City's beautiful golden homage to the Independence movement. The rooms are comfortable in a contemporary and understated style, with plasma-screen TVs as standard plus a predictably good business centre. There are two rooftop tennis courts for guests' use – a better bet for working up an appetite for the sushi bar than is the tiny pool. Hearty Italian dishes are served up in Ristorante Amici.
Bars (2). Business centre. Concierge. Disabled-adapted rooms. Gym. Internet (wireless/shared terminal, 1st 30 mins free/day, MX$152 after). No-smoking floors. Parking. Pool (1 outdoor). Restaurants (3). Room service. Spa. TV: cable, pay movies.

Moderate

Hotel María Cristina

Río Lerma 31 (5703 1212/5566 9688/www.hotel mariacristina.com.mx). Metro Insurgentes L1. **Rates** MX$895-$1,140 double. **Rooms** 150. **Credit** AmEx, MC, V. **Map** p264 H5 ⓰
Its lush gardens brimming with bougainvillea, this terracotta-hued former colonial mansion is an attractive and reasonably priced alternative to the breeze-block style hotels that tend to dominate in this neighbourhood. The wood-panelled lobby overlooks an internal courtyard with a fountain centrepiece and the rooms are comfortable and quiet, but their decor doesn't quite live up to the promise of the lobby, and the reception service could be friendlier.
Bar. Business centre. Internet (wireless MX$40 p/hr). No-smoking rooms. Parking. Restaurant. Room service.

Hotel Marquis Reforma

Avenida Paseo de la Reforma 465 (5229 1200/ 01800 901 7600/www.marquisreforma.com). Metro Chapultepec L1. **Rates** MX$2,220-$5,705 double. **Rooms** 209. **Credit** AmEx, MC, V. **Map** p264 F6 ⓱
The Marquis Reforma's unsightly pink high rise exterior conceals the very good business hotel within. More luxurious than trendy, the hotel is decked out in polished marble of various hues, from the lobby to guest bathrooms. All the rooms are fully air-conditioned, with single rooms small yet spacious enough to fit in a king-size bed dressed in crisp white

linen. The sizeable pool, decent gym and sauna and the full-service spa and beauty salon round things out nicely.
Bar. Business centre. Concierge. Disabled-adapted rooms. Gym. Internet (wireless MX$200/day, shared terminal MX$150/hr). No-smoking floors. Parking (MX$130/day). Pool (1 indoor). Restaurants (2). Room service. Spa. TV: cable, pay movies.

Zona Rosa

Expensive

Calinda Geneve

Londres 130 (5080 0800/www.hotelgeneve.com.mx). Metro Insurgentes L1/ Metrobús Insurgentes. **Rates** MX$1,415-$1,955. **Rooms** 270. **Credit** AmEx, MC, V. **Map** p264 H6 ⓲
Owned by telecoms tycoon Carlos Slim, this belle époque hotel is furnished with a collection of antiques that helps recreate the ambience of the era. Guest rooms are unfussy and elegant and the courtyard, lined with ornate pillars, makes a refined setting for breakfast, lunch or dinner. A fully equipped business centre includes secretarial services.
Bar. Business centre. Concierge. Gym. Internet (free wireless, shared terminals MX$60/hr). No-smoking hotel. Parking. Restaurants (2). Room service. Spa. TV: cable, pay movies.

Moderate

Hotel Marco Polo

Amberes 27 (5080 0063/1800 900 6000/www. marcopolo.com.mx). Metro Insurgentes L1 or Sevilla L1/Metrobús Insurgentes. **Rates** MX$1130-$1,820 double. **Rooms** 76 (including 13 long-stay suites). **Credit** AmEx, MC, V. **Map** p264 G6 ⓳
Hotel Marco Polo is a small, attractive hotel with well equipped, spacious rooms and a European feel about it. Discount rates can be often found through online agents, but whatever you pay, a big Mexican or continental breakfast is included in the price. In-room spa treatments start from MX$850.
Bar. Business centre. Concierge. Gym. Internet (free wireless, shared terminals). No-smoking floors. Parking (MX$70/day). Restaurants (2). Room service. TV: cable.

NH Hotel

Liverpool 155 (5228 99285229 1551/ www.nh-hotels.com). Metro Insurgentes L1. **Rates** MX$945-$1,670 double. **Rooms** 302. **Credit** AmEx, DC, MC, V. **Map** p264 G6 ⓴
The NH Hotel is a bit of a 1970s throwback, which sometimes gives the impression that its glory days might be behind it. That said, the rooms are comfortable, the service is generally friendly, and it's located right in the heart of the Zona Rosa, with sweeping, stunning views of the city from floor-to-ceiling windows in the gym and 14th-floor lounge. Be warned: the Wi-Fi doesn't reach rooms on the third, fourth and fifth floors.

THE HIPPODROME HOTEL

AV México 188 . COL Hipódromo Condesa . 5212 2110

www.thehippodromehotel.com

Don't stop

Gone are the days when the thought of hotel bars conjured up gloomy lobbies in which hollow-faced salesmen might numb the pain of the road with a lukewarm gin and tonic. Likewise, hotel restaurants have progressed in leaps and bounds; and if DF hotels have been slow to jump on the lodging-as-lifestyle bandwagon, they seem to be making up for lost time now. The rooftop bar at **Condesa DF** (*see p137*) has charming views over the leafy colonia, with blankets and heat lamps provided on chilly nights, and sake and passion fruit martinis for that inner glow.

Or at the Whiskey bar at the **W Mexico City** (*see p46*), red-and-white minimalism draws an after-work crowd of media and business types who watch the world go by through the floor-to-ceiling windows. Order ceviche or quesadillas to go with your raspberry mojito.

For the best view of the Zócalo, hit the terrace at the **Gran Hotel Ciudad de México** (*see p37*). This art deco gem was recently refurbished, and its giant birdcages, gilt cage elevators and stained-glass ceilings give the lobby a roaring 1920s feel (*pictured*). It's not always easy for non-guests to get in, so be prepared to blag, or book ahead.

Hungry? The **Presidente Intercontinental**'s Au Pied de Cochon (*see p112*) is a glamorous French bistro that's open around

the clock, and it's ideal for post-witching-hour *haute cuisine* and Mexican celeb spotting. Or at the other end of the showy-subtle spectrum, the Hip Kitchen (*see p120*) inside the design-focused **Hotel Hippodrome** is a small, intimate restaurant with moody lighting and an Asian-inspired menu. A variety of unusual martini flavours are also available, including mandarin, cucumber and coffee.

Bar. Business centre. Concierge. Disabled-adapted rooms. Gym. Internet (wireless MX$383/hr or MX$1,382/day). No-smoking floors. Parking (MX$100/24hrs). Pool (1, outdoor). Restaurants (2). Room service. TV: pay movies.

Budget

Zona Rosa Hostelling International & Suites

Cerrada de Hamburgo 5, Hamburgo 153 (5525 6318/zonarosa@hostellingmexico.com). Metro Insurgentes L1. **Rates** MX$525 double; MX$140 dorm bed. **Rooms/dorm beds** 5 rooms, 35 dorm beds. **Credit** AmEx, DC, MC, V. **Map** p264 G6 ㉑
Affiliated to Hostelling International, this small hostel is a haven in hectic Zona Rosa, tucked down a picturesque cul-de-sac with a fountain at the end. Staff members are welcoming and happy to share their local knowledge. The restaurant-bar next door, decked out with a medley of Mexican souvenirs, spills out into the street at night and hosts live music at weekends. Breakfast and hot water are included in the room rate, and the hostel is open 24 hours. *Bar. Internet (free wireless). Restaurant.*

Polanco

Deluxe

Casa Vieja

Eugenio Sue 45 (5282 0067/www.casavieja.com). Metro Auditorio L7 or Polanco L7. **Rates** MX$2,825-$5,175 double. **Rooms** 10. **Credit** AmEx, MC, V. **Map** p262 B5 ㉒
Close to the nicest bits of Polanco and Bosque de Chapultepec, Casa Vieja is one of the city's most charming boutique hotels, with a deeply comfortable ambience that sets it apart from the Mexico City pack, and an almost flawless attention to detail. The lobby is a gorgeous visual jumble of brightly coloured tiles, while a stunning, shady roof terrace on the top floor is where breakfast, lunch, dinner and cocktails are served. Deep, jewel colours are used in the individually decorated rooms, which come with a kitchenette stocked with coffee and a percolator; pot plants and picture books make you feel like an honoured guest in someone's lovely home. *Photo p50.*
Internet (free wireless). Restaurant. TV.

Habita

Avenida Presidente Masaryk 201 (5282 3100/
www.hotelhabita.com). Metro Polanco L7. **Rates**
MX$2,350-$3,910 double. **Rooms** 36. **Credit** AmEx,
DC, MC, V. **Map** p262 C4 ㉒

Habita has been doing designer chic, Mexico City-
style, since the turn of the millennium, and doing it
supremely well. The glass façade that sheathes the
building and its box-like shape prepare you for a
degree of modern-design hi-jinks inside, and it does
not disappoint. Stripped-down cool in the lobby carries through into the rooms, where it ramps up (or
down) a notch into full-blown, white-on-white minimalism with a delightfully agreeable feel. Equipped
with silent electric blinds and piped-in, fashionable
music – ask the porter to show you how to turn it
off – the rooms are as simple, functional and comfortable as minimalism was always meant to be.
See p40 **Habita forming**.
Bar. Gym. Pool. Restaurant. Spa.

Hotel Camino Real

Mariano Escobedo 700 (5263 8888/www.camino
real.com/mexico). Metro Chapultepec L1. **Rates**
MX$4,080-$7,935 double. **Rooms** 712. **Credit** AmEx,
MC, V. **Map** p263 E5 ㉔

Though it's showing its age slightly, and renovations over the years have marred some aspects of
architect Ricardo Legorreta's original 1968 show-
stopper, built for that year's Olympic Games, the
Camino Real is still a top-notch hotel, particularly
for design fans. On the down side the rooms are
generic, though spacious and clean, and the service
doesn't always live up to the five-star billing. But it's
in an impeccably ritzy Polanco location, with a glam
lobby and bar scene and excellent power-lounging
opportunities around the pool.
Bars (2). Business centre. Concierge. Disabled-
adapted rooms. Gym. Internet (MX$173/day).
No-smoking rooms. Parking (MX$112). Pool
(1 outdoor). Restaurants (5). Room service.
TV: pay movies.

JW Marriott Hotel

Andrés Bello 29 (5999 0000/www.marriott.com/
hotels/travel/mexjw). Metro Auditorio L7. **Rates**
MX$2,740-$6,605 double. **Rooms** 312. **Credit**
AmEx, MC, V. **Map** p262 B5 ㉕

Once inside the JW Marriott, you could be anywhere from Houston to Hong Kong. The JW, nevertheless, may be the best-run hotel in Mexico City,
with an impeccable level of service that mitigates
the hefty price tag. High-end business travellers are
particular fans of this grand hotel's slick, deluxe
style and the tranquillity and lack of hassles that
come as part of the package. There are no major
surprises here, and that's the point. The rooms are
as plushly appointed as you'd expect, with spectacular city views.
Bar. Business centre. Concierge. Disabled-adapted
rooms. Internet (MX$22/day). Gym. No-smoking
rooms. Parking (MX$50/hr, $100/day). Pool (1
outdoor). Restaurant. Room service. Spa. TV:
pay movies.

W Mexico City

Campos Elíseos 252 (9138 1800/www.starwood
hotels.com/whotels). Metro Auditorio L7. **Rates**
MX$2,620-$6,095 double. **Rooms** 237. **Credit**
AmEx, MC, V. **Map** p262 B5 ㉖

The Mexico City outpost of Starwoods' 'boutique
chain' (their oxymoron, not ours), the W is slick,
colourful and sexy, with a restaurant, bar and
lounge that have become magnets for DF's fast
crowd. The haute decor style carries into fashionably uncluttered guest rooms featuring cloud-soft
beds and dramatic – if somewhat confusing – show-
ers. *Photo p36.*
Bars (2). Business centre. Concierge. Disabled-
adapted room. Internet (MX$19/day). Gym. No-
smoking rooms. Parking (MX$9). Restaurant. Room
service. Spa. TV: pay movies.

Expensive

Fiesta Americana Grand Chapultepec

Mariano Escobedo 756 (2581 1500/www.fiesta
americana.com). Metro Chapultepec L1. **Rates**
MX$1,495-$4,075 double. **Rooms** 203. **Credit**
AmEx, MC, V. **Map** p263 E6 ㉗

The Fiesta is well placed on the very edge of Bosque
de Chapultepec, with unrivalled views of stunning
Chapultepec Castle. Housed in an attractive art deco
building, the hotel is smaller than its skyscraping
Polanco neighbours, with a cosy two-tier reception
area and small restaurant and bar on the upper level.
The rooms are spacious, with large windows, and
the club rooms and suites come with in-room exercise bikes and Nespresso coffee machines.
Bar. Business centre. Concierge. Disabled-adapted
rooms. Gym. Internet (wireless MX$100/hr,
$150/12 hrs, $250/day). No-smoking rooms.
Parking (MX$110/day). Pool (outdoor).
Restaurant. Room service. TV: pay movies.

Hotel Polanco

Edgar Allan Poe 8 (5280 8082/www.hotelpolanco.com).
Metro Auditorio L7. **Rates** MX$1,675-$1,940 double.
Rooms 71. **Credit** AmEx, MC, V. **Map** p262 A5 ㉘

This small, pleasant hotel puts you within easy
walking distance of Polanco's principal attractions
at a fraction, relatively speaking, of the price of the
big boys on the nearby blocks. Remarkably bland
decor does a good job of ensuring there's no wow
factor to speak of here, and the rooms can be a little
tight on the space front; but it's very clean, and the
staff are friendly and helpful.
Business centre. Gym. Internet. No-smoking rooms.
Parking (MX$8.50/free for guests). Restaurant.
TV: cable.

Intercontinental Presidente Mexico City

Campos Elíseos 218 (5327 7700/www.ichotelsgroup.
com). Metro Auditorio L7. **Rates** MX$1,545-$5,665
double. **Rooms** 661. **Credit** AmEx, MC, V.
Map p262 B5 ㉙

This 661-room behemoth towers above the northern edge of Bosque de Chapultepec in Polanco's hotel hub, making it a good option for those looking for an affordable super-hotel experience. The lobby is a city within a city, featuring a newsagents, fashion and jewellery stores, a travel centre, Mexicana and American Airlines offices, and seven international restaurants including the highly regarded Zhen Shanghai and Au Pied de Cochon. *See p112.*
Bar. Business centre. Concierge. Disabled-adapted rooms. Gym. Internet (wireless MX$200/day). No-smoking rooms. Parking (MX$100/day). Restaurants (6). Room service. TV: pay movies.

Residencia Polanco
Newton 272 (5203 9144/www.residencia polanco.com). Metro Polanco L7. **Rates** MX$1,610-$1,900 double. **Rooms** 23. **Credit** AmEx, MC, V. **Map** p262 D4 ③⓪
Size does matter at the Residencia: the suites are huge, with living areas and one or two bedrooms providing an apartment-like feel. It's by no means a luxury property, but the public spaces are nicely appointed and everything is satisfyingly clean and orderly. Polanco's main attractions are a little walk away, as the hotel is on the neighbourhood's fringe.
Bar. Business centre. Internet. No-smoking rooms. Parking. Restaurant. Room service. TV: cable.

Santa Fe

Expensive

Camino Real Santa Fe
Guillermo González Camarena 300 (5004 1616/ www.caminoreal.com/santafe). Metro Tacubaya L1, L7, L9, then minibus, taxi colectivo or RTP bus marked Santa Fe. **Rates** MX$1,590-$3,680 double. **Rooms** 300. **Credit** AmEx. MC, V.
This very modern glass and steel structure is in sharp contrast to the city's original Camino Real in Polanco, yet it has a very simple and practical character. For those for whom business commitments make Santa Fe the place to be, this is a very good option. The rooms are bright, with floor-to-ceiling windows and hip decor touches that include animal-skin patterned armchairs and abstract artworks. Request a front-facing room for a ringside view of the helicopter pad on the adjacent Mercedes Benz building , and be sure to check out the Sky Bar on the top floor in the evening for cocktails, live music and sushi.
No-smoking rooms. Parking (MX$70/day). Restaurant. Room service. Spa. TV: pay movies.

Sheraton Suites Santa Fe
Guillermo González Camarena 200 (5258 8500/ www.starwoodhotels.com/Sheraton). Metro Tacubaya L1, L7, L9, then minibus, taxi colectivo or RTP bus marked Santa Fe. **Rates** MX$1,725-$5,020. **Rooms** 194. **Credit** AmEx, MC, V.
Opened in 1995, the Sheraton Suites was one of the first hotels to go up in a burgeoning Santa Fe and its age is beginning to show, with the carpets, walls, furniture and even the white courtyard in the centre of the building showing signs of wear and tear. Still, if it's suites in Santa Fe you're after then this the place: it has 194 in total, including 16 master suites and a presidential suite, each spacious and featuring a small kitchenette, no hobs. There's a club floor with a lounge, and the hotel has all the necessary business facilities plus a modern, well-maintained gym.
Bar. Business centre. Concierge. Disabled-adapted room. Internet (MX$150/day). Gym. No-smoking rooms. Parking (MX$40/day). Restaurant. Room service. TV: pay movies.

Bed, breakfast and balconies at **Condesa Haus**. *See p49.*

DF eye

Avenida Amsterdam, the oval avenue that defines the Condesa neighbourhood, is one of my favourite places in Mexico City. I love its art deco houses and the pedestrian path that runs down the middle of its green boulevard. It's also close to all the best parts of La Condesa, including my favourite park, Parque México.

Jessica Abel, graphic novelist, author of *La Perdida*.

Condesa

Deluxe

Condesa DF
Avenida Veracruz 102 (5241 2600/www.condesadf. com). Metro Chapultepec L1 or Sevilla L1 or Chilpancingo L9. **Rates** MX$2,140-$6,060 double. **Rooms** 40. **Credit** AmEx, MC, V. **Map** p264 F7 ⑪
Representing, in many ways, the crème de la crème of the DF hotel scene, Condesa DF scores instant points for its location, on the cusp between Condesa and Roma. A neoclassical façade gives way inside to a patio enclosed by soaring white panels that rise to the roof terrace. The panels are shuttered at night to set the hotel apart from the hubbub of its popular terraces: El Patio restaurant (*see p120*) and La Terraza roof-top bar (*see p137*), both hotspots for cool *chilangos*. The clamour of happy hipsters can infiltrate rooms despite the shutters, so you might want to request a pair of earplugs. The rooms are as neat, slick and cleverly designed as you'd expect, iPods and all, though in some cases, their compact dimensions verge on the cramped. *Photo p40.*
Bar. Internet (free wireless). Restaurant. Room service. TV.

Expensive

Hippodrome Hotel
188 Avenida México (1454 4599/www.stashhotels. com). Metro Sevilla L1 or Chilpancingo L9/Metrobús Sonora. **Rates** MX$1,930-$3,440 double. **Rooms** 15. **Credit** AmEx, MC, V. **Map** p264 G8 ⑫
Just around the corner from lush Parque México, this new hotel has one of the nicest locations in DF, at the heart of Condesa with the park to one side and charming *calle* Amsterdam to the other. An imperfect gem of a boutique hotel thus far (it opened in 2007), the Hippodrome gets most things right, such as complimentary hors d'oeuvres delivered to your room; but it slips up in places where a little more passion and attention to detail might have saved it. But blessed with charming and helpful staff

and the buzzing Hip Kitchen restaurant downstairs (*see p120*), the place has plenty going for it.
Internet (free wireless). Restaurant.

Moderate

Condesa Haus
Cuernavaca 142 (5256 2494/www.condesahaus.com). Metro Patriotismo L9. **Rates** MX$1,165-$1,395. **Rooms** 5. **Credit** MC, V. **Map** p264 E9 ⑬
This boutique bed and breakfast in a restored 1930s house in the heart of Condesa has kept its original granite and tile floors, moulded fittings, arched doorways and wrought-iron balconies. Themed rooms include Playa del Carmen, with a balcony overlooking the street, dark wicker furniture and a billowy mosquito net, while Porfirio, with its large, free-standing bath, is particularly lovely. Close to many restaurants and bars, this is a good option for medium-stay business travellers tired of big hotels. There are no phones in the rooms, but guests are provided with a local mobile phone. *Photo p47.*
Internet (free wireless). No-smoking rooms. Parking. TV: cable.

Budget

Casa Comtesse
Tamaulipas 103-8. (4084 3670/www.casacomtesse. com). Metro Patriotismo L9. **Rates** MX$580-$755 double. **Rooms** 3. **No credit cards.** **Map** p264 F8 ⑭
A dearth of mid- and mid-priced accommodation in Condesa has led to a new wave of B&Bs, many of which, like this one, are private homes with one or two rooms fitted out for guests. In an eighth-floor apartment with a cactus-lined balcony overlooking the treetops, this light-filled lodging isn't quite as spruce as it looks on its website, but it comes close. The king-size front bedroom with a private bathroom is a bargain, and the downstairs communal area is as comfy as being in someone's living room. The owners are planning to move the B&B to a nearby house with more rooms.
Internet (free wireless).

The Red Tree House
Culiacan 6 (5584 3829/www.theredtreehouse.com). Metro Chilpancingo L9/Metrobús Chilpancingo. **Rates** MX$600-$1,745 double. **Rooms** 7. **Credit** AmEx, MC, V. **Map** p264 F9 ⑮
Staying at this lovely seven-room B&B, one block from Parque México, feels like dossing down in a stylish friend's house. Guests are encouraged to make themselves at home in the lounge, and in the terracotta-tiled courtyard, a disco ball shares the space with a huge jacaranda tree. The comfortable rooms are decorated with paintings by local artists and boast beautiful lighting, quality linens, fresh flowers and flat-screen TVs. The penthouse suite, with outdoor terrace and a kitchenette, is stunning.
Internet (wireless). TV: Cable.

Roma

Expensive

La Casona

*Durango 280 (5286 3001/www.hotellacasona.
com.mx). Metro Sevilla L1.* **Rates** MX$1,440-
$2,900 double. **Rooms** 29. **Credit** AmEx, MC, V.
Map p264 F7 ㊱
The smart quarters of this restored, pink-painted
1920s mansion are filled with antique furniture;
and if the rooms aren't quite as luxurious as the
rates might suggest, they are comfortable, and the
staff are friendly. Close to Bosque de Chapultepec
and Condesa, La Casona makes a nicely central
base from which to head downtown and beyond.
*Bar. Business centre. Concierge. Internet (free
wireless). Gym. Parking. Restaurant. Room service.
Spa. TV: cable.*

Budget

Hostel Home

*Tabasco 303 (5511 1683/www.hostelhome.com.mx).
Metro Sevilla L1/Metrobús Álvaro Obregón.* **Rates**
MX$140 dorm bed. **Rooms** 3. **No credit cards**.
Map p264 G7 ㊲
The best thing about this place, besides its cheap
rate, is its location on a lovely tree-lined street in
café-filled Roma, within walking distance of
Condesa and Zona Rosa. On the other hand, the
bunk-filled (six or eight) dorm rooms in this converted family home are small and stuffy, as are the
shared bathrooms. But there's a nice common area
with wooden floorboards, high ceilings and white
leather couches, plus a covered terrace set with
tables and chairs.
Internet (free wireless).

Coyoacán

Moderate

Chalet del Carmen Coyoacán

*Guerrero 94 (5659 1611/5554 9572/www.
chaletdelcarmen.com/info@chaletdelcarmen.com).
Metro Coyoacán L3.* **Rates** MX$745-$945 double.
Rooms 7. **Credit** MC, V. **Map** p259 E2 ㊳
There are only a handful of good places to stay in
this neighbourhood, and the Chalet del Carmen is
definitely the most attractive. The owners, Manuel
of Mexico and Margrit of Switzerland, have converted part of their home into five tastefully decorated
rooms and two sprawling suites. Spacious rooms
with hardwood floors overlook a small leafy courtyard, and umbrellas, magazines and books are available on loan. Book well in advance.
Internet (free wireless). TV: cable.

Budget

Hostal Frida

*Francisco Javier Mina 54. (5659 7005/www.hostal
fridabyb.com.mx/mghme@aol.com) Metro Coyoacán
L3.* **Rates** MX$575 suite. **Rooms** 5. **No credit
cards**. **Map** p259 E2 ㊴
Popular with visiting university professors and writers drawn to the neighbourhood's literary scene,
Hostal Frida is an unmarked house on a leafy residential street and consists of a former B&B now converted into suites. If you're looking for luxury, look
elsewhere; but you'll find simple comforts here that
cover all the basics. The three suites and two clean
and cosy rooms are all equipped with toaster, oven
and coffee maker, and the suites have kitchenettes.
Children and pets not allowed.
Internet (free wireless). TV: cable.

The sumptuously cosy Suite Agustin Lara at **Casa Vieja**. *See p45.*

Where to Stay

Sightseeing

Introduction

Your key to the city.

If you land at Mexico City's Benito Juárez airport on a clear day, you'll be treated to a view of the capital's infamous urban sprawl stretching right across the Valley of Mexico and beginning to climb up the sides of the mountains that surround it. Once you step outside of the airport, or as you approach, if arriving overland, you'll soon see just how much of the city is an unforgiving maze of concrete jungle.

With its 1,500 square-kilometre (580 square-mile) area and an estimated population of 19.2 million, getting to grips with the Distrito Federal, or DF as it is frequently called, can be a daunting prospect for anyone used to smaller conurbations – London, say, or Paris. Perhaps

this accounts for the fact that the majority of visitors to Mexico bypass Mexico City altogether or pass through in a hurry, headed straight for the coast. But these provincial types are missing something very special, because DF is home to some of the most fascinating pockets of history and culture in Latin America. Its extraordinary archaeological riches, churches and museums, plazas and parks, wide, palm-lined avenues and winding, cobbled streets all add up to a potentially very rewarding sightseeing experience. And it's also, contrary to expectations, relatively easy to navigate.

MEXICO CITY FOR BEGINNERS

Right at the heart of things is the **Centro Histórico**. Formerly the site of the Aztec capital, Tenochtitlán, it was subsequently the colonial capital of New Spain. The enormous central plaza, the **Zócalo**, and the **Alameda** park are the two focal points of a busy, gripping city centre that's in the process of being restored from the foundations up. Many of the best museums can be found in the blocks between these two open spaces.

The area to the east of the Zócalo is generally a bit shabbier and more run down than that to the west. Street markets and vendors and decaying buildings are more common around here, and the place oozes character, from quiet, unassuming Plaza de Loreto to the colourful bustle of Calle Moneda that leads into the stately **Palacio Nacional**.

To the west of the Zócalo, the grid of commercial streets is lined mostly with scruffy local shops, with a few western fashion chains mixed in as well as the odd café and dusty bookshop. Take an elevator to the top of the **Torre Latinoamericana** (*see p62* **Arriba, arriba**) or catch a show across the road at the magnificent **Palacio de Bellas Artes** (*see p69*). Within spitting distance from here are also the stunning **Casa de los Azulejos** (*see p61*) and the **Palacio Postal** (*see p64*), a magnificent central post office that's still open for business.

Further west, **Avenida Paseo de la Reforma** is the grand avenue whose central section runs westwards from the Alameda in the Centro Histórico all the way to the massive **Bosque de Chapultepec** (*see p74*), often known as Chapultepec Park in English. Much loved by *chilangos*, as the inhabitants of Mexico City are known, stately Paseo de

Towering **Torre Latinoamericana**.

la Reforma is one of the city's main arteries. Important national monuments line the avenue, including the golden **Ángel de la Independencia** (*photo p55*), focal point of celebrations and protests alike. North of the avenue is the Plaza de la República, home to the **Monumento a la Revolución**, one of the city's most imposing memorials. To the south, after Paseo de la Reforma has crossed another major street, Avenida Insurgentes, is the lively neighbourhood of **Zona Rosa**, packed with hotels, cafés, bars and clubs.

WITH A LITTLE MORE TIME ...

If you've more than a couple of days to spend in the city, you might be grateful for a break from the traffic-heavy streets of the Centro. The most attractive and accessible alternative is the quiet, verdant haven of the massive **Bosque de Chapultepec** that lies to the west of the centre, just below the posh neighbourhood of **Polanco** and east of the city's glass-and-steel business district, **Santa Fe**.

Aside from its expanses of greenery and vegetation, the park is also home to a set of world class museums including the **Museo de Antropología** (*see p79*) for ancient relics; the **Museo Rufino Tamayo** (*see p80*) and the **Museo de Arte Moderno** (*see p80*) for contemporary art shows; and the stunning hilltop **Castillo de Chapultepec** (*see p78*) with its long views and its history museum.

Heading south from the centre of Mexico City, the beautiful adjacent neighbourhoods of **Condesa** and **Roma** are studded with private galleries, boutiques, cafés and restaurants. Once the centre of the horse-racing track that gives the area its oval street layout, lush and tropical **Parque México** is an excellent starting point for anyone of a mind to spend the day hopping from one café to another, taking in the rich mix of art deco buildings and chic modern glass and concrete structures along the way

... AND WITH LONGER STILL

With a little more time on your hands, you might consider venturing further afield. To the south of the city, a few kilometres down Avenida Insurgentes, lie the neighbouring districts of **San Ángel** and **Coyoacán**. A bit out of the way but well worth the journey, these two former villages have retained a large part of their colonial character and give you some idea of how Mexico City must have looked a century ago.

Once home to Mexico's most celebrated artists, Diego Rivera and Frida Kahlo, both neighbourhoods are packed with references to the couple, from museums to memorabilia. Frida's family home, **Museo Frida Kahlo** (*see p91*) is open to the public, as are the artists'

The best Sights

Ancient relics

No trip to Mexico City would be complete without an excursion to the pyramids of **Teotihuacán** (*see p95*). In the heart of the city, the ruins of the **Templo Mayor** (*see p60*) are less impressive but still of interest, while archaeology buffs and novices alike will adore the **Museo de Antropología** (*see p79*).

Art and soul

The **Museo Nacional de Arte** (*see p64*) houses a fantastic collection of Mexican art from the 16th century onward, while Chapultepec's **Museo Tamayo** (*see p80*) is the place to go for contemporary shows.

Park life

Mexico City's green giant is sprawling **Bosque de Chapultepec** (*see p74*), filled with museums plus a funfair, a zoo and a boating lake. For something more compact, there's Condesa's lush **Parque México** (*see p81*) or the Centro's **Alameda** – an urban park since Aztec times (*see p64*).

Muralism

See Diego Rivera's epic historical works at the **Palacio Nacional**, or his *Dream of a Sunday Afternoon in Alameda Park* at the **Museo Diego Rivera** (*see p69*). The **Palacio de Bellas Artes** (*see p69*) has murals by Rivera, and José Clemente Orozco, Rufino Tamayo, David Alfaro Siqueiros and Jorge González Camarena.

Colonial streets

Head to the old-time neighbourhoods of **San Ángel** and **Coyoacán** (*see p86*), whose cobbled streets are punctuated by plazas, haciendas and monasteries from the days of New Spain.

studios in San Ángel. Just north of the Centro, the **Basílica de Guadalupe** (*see p84*), one of Latin America's most sacred sites, is worth a visit any time of the year, but especially on 12 December and the days leading up to it, when hundreds of thousands of pilgrims congregate for the festival of the Virgin of Guadalupe.

As far as venturing a little further still is concerned, some exceptionally rewarding day trips are possible from Mexico City. A visit to the astonishing truncated pyramids and ancient city complex at **Teotihuacán** (*see p95*) is, if time permits, more or less compulsory. You can

Sightseeing

also head south towards the smoking cap of **Popocatépetl** volcano (*see p98*), once visible from the city centre but now obscured by haze.

GETTING AROUND

Walking in Mexico City – sprawling, polluted, car-loving Mexico City – might sound insane, but in fact the distances are not as vast as they might appear on the map, especially along main thoroughfares like Paseo de la Reforma. The streets of the Centro are often so crowded with people that the only way to get from A to B is with an iron will and a firm pair of shoulders; and in Condesa and Roma, it would be a crime not to do a bit of strolling since these lovely *colonias* (neighbourhoods) lend themselves perfectly to it. (*See p83* **Walk on**). The cobbled back alleys of San Ángel and Coyoacán can, in turn, only really be traversed on foot.

Although traffic can be a problem and indeed, an obstacle in Mexico City, taxis are cheap relative to other major international cities, and a very easy way to get around. You'll be warned repeatedly, not least by taxi drivers themselves, of the dangers of hailing taxis off the street. In practice, convenience leads many visitors to do so anyway and problems are the exception, not the norm; but you should take a moment to read the notes on this in our Directory section (*see p237*), and remember that taxis taken from *sitios* (ranks) are generally more reliable, though there's a small surcharge for that peace of mind.

The Metro is extremely cheap and, with a large though not comprehensive trajectory, a reliable transport option, though it can sometimes get very hot and crowded. The city's new, low-emission Metrobús line runs in a special lane up and down Avenida Insurgentes, and is a great way to get to San Ángel from Condesa and Roma, then back up to Paseo de la Reforma. There is also a minibus that stops frequently along the Paseo de la Reforma, and local buses that circumvent all other parts of the city, though they can be difficult to work out, especially if you don't speak Spanish.

Tours

An excellent way to see the major sights in one go and get your bearings is to take the **Turibús**, an open-top double-decker bus whose route passes many of the city's tourism highlights, with a jump-on, jump-off system that makes it perfect for getting an overview before you zoom in on points of interest. Tickets cost MX$100 on weekdays and MX$115 at weekends – see www.turibus.com.mx for the route map. There's also a tram that rumbles through the Centro Histórico, starting at Avenida Juárez 66, at a stop between the

Alameda Park and the Palacio de Bellas Artes. It takes in the area's key sights in about 45 minutes, running between 10am and 5pm daily.

Free walking tours of the Centro Histórico are given by the **Mexico City Historic Centre** (5345 8000), starting at 10.45am every Sunday from the Casa de los Condes de Heras y Soto, on the corner of República de Chile and Donceles. Tour routes vary from week to week and last for approximately two hours. The history of the city's Jewish community is the focus of **Mónica Unikel's Jewish Tours** (5507 6908/www.jewishtours.com.mx). **Ticket 2 Fútbol** (5754 3145, www.ticket2futbol.com) offers excursions to football matches, *lucha libre* and bullfighting events, as well as running atmospheric trips to Teotihuacán for a traditional, ritual *temazcal* (sauna) in sight of the pyramids. Personalised city tours are available from MX$250, depending on the size of the group. If your Spanish is up to it, tours of the city's archaeological sites and museums are run by the government's **Instituto Nacional de Antropología e Historia** (5553 3822/www.inah.gob.mx/tci). Prices range from MX$166 for one-day tours to MX$3,509 for multi-day excursions.

Most museums charge a nominal fee for entry, and card-holding students can generally enter for free. The majority of museums are closed on Mondays, and many of the state-owned institutions are free to enter on Sundays.

Sightseeing

Ángel de la Independencia. *See p53.*

Centro

Wide open spaces, historic streets and the archaeological heart of the Aztec city.

Brace yourself: this is the clamorous, chaotic centre of Mexico City, and it's not for the faint-hearted. Neither is it to be missed. A trip to the Centro can be hot and tiring – and surprising, and awe-inspiring; and it's the only way to place yourself at what has been the centre of the region's political and cultural activity for centuries: for Aztecs, for colonists and clerics, and for later generations in an independent Mexico. It's a concentrated cornucopia of museums, churches, plazas and cantinas, with the government and commercial activity that has always gone on here providing the lively hum you'd expect at the heart of a city this size.

History is piled on layer upon layer in the Centro, thanks to successive waves of civic planning and architects who have raised their new structures on the ruins of the old. Churches and former monasteries are often constructed from the rubble of volcanic rock

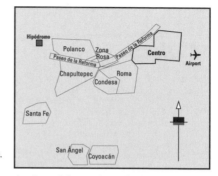

Calle Moneda. *See p60.*

that formed the temples and palaces of the Aztec empire, while modern renovations are coming to the rescue of old colonial structures bending, stooping, and sinking into the mud upon which the city has been built.

The historic district has been a mainly daytime attraction for many years; but it's getting livelier at night, and indeed, some of the city's best restaurants, cantinas and bars are to be found here. One day is enough to see the highlights around the Zócalo and the Alameda, but it would take several days, and be well worth doing, to see the area in depth. So walking shoes on, keep your wallet close by, grease up those crowd-budging elbows and dive in.

Zócalo

Map p267

Metro Zócalo L2.

The Plaza de la Constitución or simply '**Zócalo**', as it is almost always called, has been at the heart of Mexico City life since before the Spanish conquest, when it was the religious and ceremonial centre for the Aztecs of Tenochtitlán. When Cortés and his men took control of the city, they razed most of the buildings in the centre to the ground, building their own cathedrals and palaces in the same spot, often with stone from the demolished buildings.

The Zócalo is an indispensable national space: it's where people come to protest, gather and hang out, like Beijing's Tiananmen Square or the Plaza de Mayo in Buenos Aires. Its name comes from the Spanish word *zócalo*, meaning pedestal, after the empty plinth that stood in the

Sightseeing

square awaiting a monument to Independence in the 19th century that was never realised. The plinth was removed, but the name stuck and many still consider the space to be a symbolic plinth for the Mexican soul. Today, a massive Mexican flag billows overhead, though its solitary poignancy is often dampened by the erection of various temporary structures in the centre of the plaza, from concert stages to art galleries. In December 2007, much of the square was iced over to make a wildly popular ice-skating rink: a sight to see and a joy to use, which is some consolation, perhaps, for the one-time visitor who misses the chance to see the square in all its empty, expansive glory.

It's a great place to begin or end a bout of downtown sightseeing, and is particularly magical at sunrise and sunset, when the high-altitude light augments its beauty to perfection. The square is flanked on all sides by giants of colonial and Aztec architecture: the **Catedral Metropolitana** to the north, the **Templo Mayor** to the north east, and the **Palacio Nacional** to the east, with commercial and municipal buildings to the south and west.

The plaza is always abuzz with a mix of tourists and locals; touts and hawkers are decreasing in number as new laws are enforced to keep them out of the Centro Histórico. You may also spot bands of befeathered Aztec revivalists performing traditional dances and incense ceremonies outside the Cathedral and the Templo Mayor.

Like so many areas of the city, the Zócalo is built upon the soft mud of Lake Texcoco, into which it is slowly sinking. The Catedral Metropolitana was once raised above street level; visitors now descend a flight of steps to enter the building, which is also leaning to one side, and much work has been done underneath it to prevent it from collapsing altogether.

The cathedral took no less than 277 years to complete, hampered over time by perennial flooding and shifts in command. Today, it's one of the largest cathedrals in the western hemisphere, with five naves, a sacristy and a bell tower, as well as a sizeable side chapel, the Sagrario Metropolitano, constructed in the mid-18th century in elaborate Churrigueresque (Spanish Baroque) style. Perpendicular to the cathedral, taking up the entire length of the enormous block that runs the length of the Zócalo, is the Palacio Nacional. Today, its extensive grounds house government departments as well as the president's office. It's worth bearing in mind, as you wander freely through its courtyards and hallways, that you're walking above the ruins of the former palace of Aztec supremo Moctezuma, demolished by Hernán Cortés and replaced

The **Zócalo**, in the heart of the Centro Histórico.

with a rather flash castle-residence – a vanity project that prompted accusations that the conquistador was squandering the country's newfound resources for his own benefit.

By far the highlight of a trip to the Palacio Nacional is Diego Rivera's mural over the main staircase, showing the epic evolution of Mexican history. Highly detailed, it features scenes from ancient Aztec times and the Spanish conquest through to the battle for independence and the French occupation. Rivera's mural continues around the walls of the first-floor cloisters, depicting idealised tableaux of rural Indian life before colonisation.

Just to the north of the Palacio Nacional are the sad ruins of the Templo Mayor, destroyed by Cortés's soldiers in the 16th century. The remains of the pyramid were rediscovered in 1979 by electricians laying cable behind the cathedral. You can see some of the ruins from the square, but for a tour around the remains and to see some of the artefacts that were dug up when the pyramid was unearthed, including a superb sculpture of Coatlicue, goddess of Life and Death, you'll need to enter the site itself. A more extensive collection of artefacts from the site is kept in the **Museo de Antropología** (*see p79*). The location is impressive; but for anyone who's visited the superbly restored pyramid complex at Teotihuacán just outside the city, this rather unidentifiable pile of remains may be a bit of an anti-climax.

Across from the Templo Mayor, along calle República de Guatemala, is the **Centro Cultural de España**, a chance to take in some contemporary art inside a renovated colonial mansion that comes as light relief after the weighty antiquities of the Zócalo. The terrace café-restaurant is a great place for a coffee or a snack with views of the cathedral. The serene courtyards of the **Antiguo Colegio de San Ildefonso** on Justo Sierra, one street behind the Centro Cultural de España, are a lovely place in which to unwind and take in the architectural charm of a building that's one of the best examples of civic colonial architecture. Today, it's a lively cultural centre with exhibitions and performances, a great café on the second floor, and a series of dazzling murals by Diego Rivera, Jean Charlot, Ramón Alva de la Canal, Fermín Revueltas and José Clemente Orozco.

Three blocks south of the Zócalo is the Plaza de Jesús and the **Museo de la Ciudad de México**. Suitably situated across the road from a plaque that marks the first meeting place of Cortés and Moctezuma on 8 November 1519,

Catedral Metropolitana.

DF eye

The Centro is the most diverse wasps' nest I know, besides Calcutta. It's full of surprises and always open to rediscovery. Go to the Zócalo at sunset when the light changes; go to a protest; and go to see Fermín Revueltas's Virgin of Guadalupe mural at the Antiguo Colegio de San Ildefonso. An atheist artist painting a symbolic virgin linked to the fight for independence is totally Mexico City.

Paco Taibo, detective novelist, *An Easy Thing*.

the museum serves as a beginner's crib of the city's history and also shows cutting-edge contemporary art, mainly by Mexican artists.

Antiguo Colegio de San Ildefonso

Justo Sierra 16 (5702 6378/www.sanildefonso. org.mx). Metro Zócalo L2. **Open** 10am-6pm Tue-Sun. **Admission** MX$45; MX$22.50 reductions. *Building only* MX$15; MX$7.50 reductions. Free Tue. **Map** p267 N4.

Founded by Jesuits in 1588 as housing for youngsters studying in surrounding colleges, this complex became a school in its own right in 1611, and was expanded a century later to become the impressive, three-storey edifice standing today. The manicured courtyards are a peaceful refuge from the hubbub beyond, with the walls around the enclosure adorned with murals by Diego Rivera, José Clemente Orozco, David Alfaro Siqueiros and other 20th-century masters of the genre, all of whom were relatively unknown at the time the college commissioned them. Today, the college also serves as an art museum and cultural centre, and occasionally stages dance and music performances in its quads.

Catedral Metropolitana

Plaza de la Constitución (Zócalo) (5510 0440). Metro Zócalo L2. **Open** *Cathedral* 8am-7pm daily. *Bell tower* 10.30am-6pm daily. **Admission** *Cathedral* free. *Sacristy* MX$10 suggested donation. *Bell tower* MX$12. **Map** p267 M4.

Construction on this cathedral began in 1573, to replace a smaller building commissioned by Cortés directly following the Spanish conquest of Tenochtitlán. It was almost three centuries in the making and, as a result, it was subject to a whole range of styles, with most of the work shared between architects Claudio de Arciniega in the late 16th century, and Mexican-born José Damián Ortiz de Castro, assigned to complete the bell tower and the upper part of the façade in the 1780s. The Sagrario Metropolitano, a little crooked chapel next to the cathedral, is also worth a visit, open daily from 7.30am to 7.30pm.

Centro Cultural de España

Guatemala 18 (5521 1925/www.ccemx.org). Metro Allende L2 or Zócalo L2. **Open** 10am-8pm Tue, Wed; 10am-11pm Thur-Sat; 10am-4pm Sun. **Admission** free. **Map** p267 M4.

Inaugurated in 2002 to mark the 25th anniversary of renewed (that is, post-Franco) diplomatic relations between Spain and Mexico, this cultural centre is located behind the Zócalo. The building has had a number of uses over the years, including as a convent, a guesthouse and a warehouse. In 1997, it was handed over to the Spanish government, who refurbished it. The centre is primarily a showcase for young photographers and contemporary artists, and also offers various creative computer workshops and a lovely top-floor terrace restaurant (*see p131*), with regular live DJs and jazz events in the evenings in a glorious setting.

Museo de la Ciudad de México

Pino Suárez 30 (5522 9936). Metro Pino Suárez L1, L2. **Open** 10am-5.30pm Tue-Sun. **Admission** MX$20; MX$10 reductions; free Wed. **Map** p267 M5, N5.

This museum leads visitors through the city's story by using images and documentation from various historical eras. It starts with an informative video about the Spanish conquest, though frustratingly, it's only shown in Spanish. The building, originally the home of Cortés's cousin, is made from volcanic rock that once formed the walls of an Aztec temple. Don't miss the original Aztec serpent's head on the southwest outside corner of the building.

Palacio Nacional

Plaza de la Constitución (9158 1259). Metro Zócalo L2. **Open** 10am-5pm daily. **Admission** free. **Map** p267 N4.

The official seat of the president of Mexico, who in fact spends most of his time at Los Pinos, his Chapultepec residence, this massive edifice is far more pleasant on the inside than its rather stern exterior would suggest, with some pleasant courtyards among its labyrinthine layout. In addition to the offices of Benito Juárez and the first Chamber of Deputies' hall of debates, the palace's biggest attraction is the huge panoramic mural painted by Diego Rivera between 1929 and 1935, depicting the history of Mexico. In true Rivera style, the mural is an account of class struggle over the centuries, with time periods blending seamlessly into each other as it takes you through the world of the ancient Mesoamericans to the foundation of Tenochtitlán, the conquest and colonial era, and the wars and revolutions that followed. Officials will ask to see ID at the door, so remember to take a passport or driver's licence.

Templo Mayor

Seminario 8 (5542 4943/www.templomayor.inah. gob.mx). Metro Zócalo L2. **Open** 9am-5pm Tue-Sun. **Admission** MX$37; free reductions. **Map** p267 N4.

The recently renovated modern museum building that stands behind the ruins of the Templo Mayor to the north of the Zócalo houses a huge collection of

Sightseeing

artefacts, which were found when the pyramid was rediscovered in 1979. With a glazed façade that looks out on to the remains of the pyramid, the museum consists of eight exhibition halls spread over four floors, with an auditorium showing a good film, playing on a loop, about the history of the temple.

East of the Zócalo

Map p267

Metro Zócalo L2.

Calle Moneda (*photo p56*), the street that runs between the north face of the Palacio Nacional and below the Templo Mayor, is at the core of one of the less developed quarters of the Centro Histórico. With its teetering buildings, brightly coloured façades and tucked-away churches and plazas, it's also among the neighbourhood's more picturesque areas.

A small cul-de-sac to the left called Licenciado Verdad will lead you to **Ex-Teresa Arte Actual**, a large and somewhat off-kilter baroque former church that doubles as as a contemporary art space. It's worth a visit just to see the towering, skewed interior of the church, even if there is no exhibition scheduled when you go.

Attached to the back of the Palacio Nacional is the **Museo Nacional de las Culturas**, a former mint turned museum of bits and pieces of mainstream world history, from arts and handicrafts to unspectacular copies of Greek statues, and mediocre 'multimedia' exhibits such as a Mesopotamian timeline consisting of a few ageing maps. Further up Calle Moneda and off to the left on Academia is the **Museo José Luis Cuevas**, a 16th-century convent building now dedicated to the works of modernist painter Cuevas, as well as art by his contemporaries. His massive sculpture, La Giganta, a nine-metre-high androgynous bronze statue, towers over you in the courtyard as you enter. The museum's permanent collection, which includes works by Cuevas as well as items from the artist's private and wide-ranging stock of purchased artworks, is housed in rooms around the courtyard on the first and second floors. Keep an eye out for a collection of pieces by Picasso also exhibited in the museum.

Ex-Teresa Arte Actual

Licenciado Verdad 8 (5522 2721/www.exteresa. org.mx). Metro Zócalo L2. **Open** 10am-6pm Mon-Fri. **Admission** free. **Map** p267 N4.

Leaning at angle due to some heavy subsidence, this atmospheric baroque-style church is now used as a contemporary art space for multimedia exhibitions, events and workshops. The programme can be a little erratic, so it's worth checking the website for upcoming shows. Guided tours can be arranged, but it's best to call as far in advance as possible to maximise your chances.

Museo José Luis Cuevas

Academia 13 (5522 0156/www.museojoseluiscuevas. com.mx). Metro Zócalo L2. **Open** 10am-6pm Tue-Sun. **Admission** MX$20; $10 reductions; free Sun. **Map** p267 N4.

Housed in the 16th-century Convento de Santa Inés (look up to the fabulously colourful dome), this museum is filled with the work of Mexican artist José Luis Cuevas, as well as pieces by other artists from his private collection. A member of the revolutionary 'Rupture' generation of the 1950s, Cuevas is also known for his more racy images, and there's an entire room at the museum devoted to erotic artworks that shouldn't be missed.

Museo Nacional de las Culturas

Moneda 13 (5542 0165). Metro Zócalo L2. **Open** 9.30am-6pm Tue-Sun. **Admission** free. **Map** p267 N4.

A rather stale collection of (mostly) copies of historical artefacts from around the world, the museum is housed in a nonetheless beautiful old building from 1567 that used to be the colonial mint.

West of the Zócalo

Map p267

Metro Allende L2, Bellas Artes L2, L8, Isabel la Católica L1, San Juan de Letrán L8 or Zócalo L2.

The area to the west of the Zócalo, in contrast to the streets to the east, is in considerably better shape, with established shops, restaurants and chain stores lining the narrow thoroughfares between Monte de Piedad at the edge of the Plaza Mayor and the Alameda.

A short walk of three blocks from Monte de Piedad down Calle Brasil will take you to the Plaza de Santo Domingo, the second largest open square in the Centro Histórico, presided over by the Iglesia Santo Domingo. The centre of the city's intellectual life during colonial times, the plaza was originally the site of Emperor Cuauhtémoc's palace before Dominican monks built a monastery here. All that remains of the Dominican's complex is the terracotta-coloured Capilla de la Expiación on the upper east side of the square. On the north-eastern corner, the Palacio de la Inquisición was the macabre HQ and site of the Spanish Inquisition, and later a medical school. The Portal de los Evangelistas is an arcade on the east side of the square that houses an assembly of lowly scribes, the latest in a long line of writers who have combined their services with those of the printers on Leandro Valle. Here, a dozen or so men and women stand by their portable typewriters and printing presses offering to make anything from wedding invitations to business cards.

Just opposite the printers is the **Centro Cultural del México Contemporáneo**,

I was so in love, though; I was delirious with Mexico. I was avoiding thinking about the inevitable, the ticket in my backpack that meant the end of the affair, until finally I bit the bullet and looked. I had missed my plane by a week.

(The Zócalo)

That's when I knew I was staying.

Panel from *La Perdida*, a graphic novel by Jessica Abel, showing the Zócalo.

a great modernised space with towering palm trees, redolent of a Polynesian retreat. It's built around a Dominican convent that uses some of its space for contemporary art exhibitions. Be prepared for a curious overabundance of distrustful security guards, who appear to take a perverse pleasure in repeatedly telling you that just about everything, from snapshots to entering the library to any independent navigation of the space whatsoever, is *estrictamente prohibido*.

Avenida Madero, which runs from the Zócalo to the Alameda, is home to a major landmark: at a height of 45 storeys, the lofty **Torre Latinoamericana** stands head and shoulders above other buildings in the area. Weather permitting, it's one of the best attractions in the Centro Histórico thanks to the spectacular views from the 'Mirador' at its top.

By contrast, at the foot of the tower, just opposite its entrance, is the **Iglesia y Ex-Convento de San Francisco**. It's one of the oldest convents in the centre of the city, and was one of the largest in its day, covering an area of over 32,000 square metres (350,000 square feet). Built on the site of Moctezuma's *'casa de las fieras'*, or 'house of wild beasts', most of the complex was destroyed in the mid-19th century when the Franciscans were banished from Mexico. The church – with its elaborate Churrigueresque façade – remains, however, and is open to visitors.

Stately Palacio de Iturbide, a block from the ex-convent and built from the same red volcanic rock, tezontle, is a former colonial palace that was bought by Banamex bank in the 1960s, and now contains an art space among its offices. Entry is free and the exhibitions usually revolve

around classical Mexican painting or history. Dry as it may sound, they are usually very interesting, with multimedia aspects and an abundance of helpful and informative staff.

One building on Avenida Madero that you mustn't miss is the 16th-century **Casa de los Azulejos**, whose Spanish/Moorish influenced exterior is completely covered with blue tiles imported from China during the 18th century. You can wander through sections of the Casa, which today houses a branch of Sanborn's department store and restaurant (*see p105*). It's the perfect spot for a bit of cake and a sit down in exquisite surroundings; and there's also a very nice bar upstairs. Look out for Orozco's mural 'Omniscience' on the landing between the first and second floors. The Casa, located at Madero 4, is open from 7am to 1am daily.

Back towards the Zócalo, Avenida Madero crosses Isabel la Católica, a street named after Spain's Isabella I, mother of British queen for-a-stretch Catherine of Aragon, who was a renowned sympathiser with the Amerindian cause. On the corner here is the **Museo del Estanquillo**, a quirky little exhibition space devoted to Mexican cartoons and comic books that was recently set up by well known writer Carlos Monsiváis. Entry is free; and if the cultural references are lost on you, just head up to the roof for a fantastic view of the Templo de la Profesa across the street.

A few blocks down Isabel la Católica and onto Calle Regina – the faint buzzing in your ears means you're passing through the sewing-machine-selling district – is the **Casa Vecina**, a cultural centre owned by Carlos Slim, which has exhibition spaces and a full programme of workshops and courses for children and adults.

Arriba, arriba

Every tourist knows, or soon discovers, that this is one of the biggest cities in the world. But spending time on the ground can never give you a full appreciation of its size. For that, you need to go up.

Seeing Mexico City from the top of a tall building is a sight guaranteed to render you speechless. While other cities such as São Paulo and Los Angeles disappear into an impenetrable haze at the not too distant horizons, it's the way you can see the vastness of DF encroaching on the hills to the south, dense suburbs creeping up the green mountains in all directions, that really makes you catch your breath. See it from the city's tallest building, the **Torre Mayor** (Paseo de la Reforma 505, admission MX$40); or combine it with a well-made cocktail or budget-busting fine dining experience at Miralto restaurant (Marder 1, www.miralto.com.mx), on the 40th and 41st floors of the **Torre Latinoamericana**.

Assuming that a new city government initiative to improve pollution by greening the rooftops of big buildings really takes off – first up, the city's transit authority will have its massive roof covered with bushes

and grass – the view should become increasingly pleasant.

But for a bird's-eye view of the city, if you're good for the fare – more than US$1,000 per hour – you can't beat a ride in a helicopter. Contact pilot Oscar Ruiz Cardeña (04455 3302 5865/ oruiz@mac.com); or settle for viewing his spectacular aerial photographs online, at www.imagenes aereasdemexico.com. *See photo left and p57.*

Close by, quaint **Casasola Bazar de Fotografía** is the perfect place to follow up a lunch at Casino Español (*see p105*), three doors down. Its exhibition of antique photos includes many from the same period as Casino Español, the Porfiriato – the 35-year rule of dictator Porfirio Díaz, which lasted until 1911.

Need to post the postcards you've just picked up? Then look no further than the corner of traffic-infested Eje Central and calle Tacuba, to the magnificent **Palacio Postal**, also known as the Correo Mayor – possibly the most exuberantly baroque post office in the world. It's crammed with rococo and art deco extravagance, and guarded on exterior walls by iron dragons perched on top of the light fixtures. With its regal staircase and glimmering, gilded interior, the place is more akin to a stately home than your average post office, but contrary to appearances, it's fully functional for stamp buying and package sending.

A little further along Tacuba, diagonally across from the Palacio Postal and behind an intermittent cluster of covered art and crafts stalls, is the Plaza Manuel Tolsá. The square is named after the neoclassical sculptor who came to Mexico from Spain in 1791 and embarked upon a series of urban design projects, including the relocation of the Alameda Park. His statue of Spanish King Carlos IV, 'El Caballito', stands in the square in front of the Museo Nacional de Arte.

Despite its rather uninviting grey exterior, the **Museo Nacional de Arte** (MUNAL), with its extensive collection of Mexican art dating back to the 16th century, is one of the best sights in the Centro Histórico. Spanning two seemingly limitless floors, and grouped thematically according to period, the museum boasts a spread that only mad dogs and art lovers would dare to attempt in one go. The building's severe look is due to its original function as the Palacio de Comunicaciones, once considered one of the best examples of 20th-century Mexican architecture for its art nouveau interior. You can also visit the Telegraph Museum, situated on the ground floor.

Casa Vecina Espacio Cultural

*Esquina Calle Regina y 1R Callejón de Mesones
(5709 1117/www.casavecina.com). Metro Isabel la
Católica L1.* **Open** 11am-7pm Tue-Fri; 11am-4pm
Sat. **Admission** free. **Map** p267 M5.
This no-frills cultural centre was founded to build
bridges between the various communities in Mexico
City. The small exhibition rooms span two floors of
an unassuming building located amid the renovations
on Calle Regina, and it's a far cry from the other high-
flying galleries and museums in the area. While you're
in the neighbourhood, pop next door to check out the
Hostería La Bota (*see p130*), a very cool, kitsch open-
air café draped in bullfighting posters and other
tongue-in-cheek memorabilia from times gone by.

Casasola Bazar de Fotografía

*2nd floor, Isabel la Católica 45 (5521 5192/
www.casasolafoto.com). Metro San Juan de Letrán
L8.* **Open** 10.30am-7.30pm Mon-Fri; 10.30am-3.30pm
Sat. **Admission** free. **Map** p267 M4.
This quaint, compact museum-cum-shop is run by
the fourth generation of a family that has been in the
photography business since Agustín V Casasola, a
photographer and journalist, began capturing
Mexico City's street scenes and events on film at the
turn of the 20th century. Occupying one room on the
second floor of an office building, it's filled with fascinating photographs and ephemera from a long
century of city history. Reproduction images on sale
include impressively moustachioed revolutionaries
and fine ladies – in separate photos, natch.

Centro Cultural del México Contemporáneo

*Leandro Valle 20 (5526 3997/www.ccmc.org.mx).
Metro Allende L2 or Lagunilla LB.* **Open** 10am 6pm
Tue-Sun. **Admission** free. **Map** p267 M3.
Tucked behind the back of the Iglesia de Santo
Domingo, and built into and reconstructed around
a crumbling Dominican convent, the CCMC is a
great example of how the glass and steel of modern
architecture can come to the rescue of crumbly
degeneration. The exhibition spaces themselves are
confined to a few rooms around the upper mezzanine, while there is a library on the ground floor
displaying a set of old murals.

Museo del Estanquillo

*Isabel la Católica 26 (5521 3052/www.museodel
estanquillo.com). Metro Zócalo L2.* **Open** 10am-6pm
Wed-Mon. **Admission** free. **Map** p267 M4.
Devoted to Mexican comic books and cartoons, this
museum is particularly strong on the works of the
artists Leopoldo Méndez and Gabriel Vargas, author
of the much-loved strip 'La Familia Burrón'. There's
a cine club on the fourth floor, and a terrace with a
shop, refreshments and a wonderful view.

Museo Nacional de Arte

*Tacuba 8 (5130 3400/www.munal.com.mx). Metro
Bellas Artes L2, L8.* **Open** 10.30am-5.30pm Tue-Sun.
Admission MX$30; MX$15 students with ID; free
Sun. **Map** p267 L4.
Mexico's National Gallery is home to the country's
most comprehensive collection of national art since
colonial times. The hundreds of paintings housed in
this former communications office building are
grouped chronologically, and the rooms of the museum follow the development of Mexican art and the
evolution of a true Mexican style through the ages.
The three main sections of the museum cover the
paintings of New Spain from 1550 to 1821; the birth
of a nation during the 19th century; and the development of modernism up until 1955. Highlights
include the 17th-century *Martyrdom of San Lorenzo*,
derived from a very Sevillian style and attributed to
José Juárez, as well as some fantastic landscapes capturing Mexico City before the onslaught of modern
development, such as José María Velasco's rendition
of the Mexico Valley as seen from the Santa Isabel
hill in 1875. Yes, that is Popocatépetl in the back-

Palacio de Bellas Artes. *See p69.*

ground, visible through a palpable lack of smog. The museum also has a space for temporary exhibitions, often by foreign artists, on the first floor.

Palacio Postal

Tacuba 1 (5510 2999/www.palaciopostal.gob.mx).
Metro Bellas Artes L2, L8. **Open** 10am-6pm Tue-Fri;
10am-4pm Sat, Sun. **Admission** free. Map p267 L4.
This turn-of-the-20th-century gothic/baroque edifice was designed by Italian architect Adamo Boari, who was also responsible for the Palacio de Bellas Artes. The details of the marble and gilded bronze interior were sculpted by dozens of local artisans in stone, wood and metal, while the building itself is made from white rock quarried from Pachuca. *Photo p66.*

Torre Latinoamericana

Eje Central Lázaro Cárdenas 2 (5518 7423). Metro
Bellas Artes L2, L8. **Open** 9am-11pm daily.
Admission MX$50; MX$40 children. **Map** p267 L4.
At 182 metres (597 feet), the Torre Latinoamericana was the tallest building in Latin America from its opening in 1956 until the construction of the 211-metre Torre Ejecutiva Pemex in 1984. There's a museum inside the skyscraper, as well as a café and viewing deck on the 44th floor. Upon admission you'll be given a wristband which you can use for re-entry for the whole day – handy if you fancy seeing the city by night. Note that the cost of a cocktail at the restaurant/bar one floor below is about the same as admission to the viewing deck – with no queues. (*See p62* **Arriba, arriba.**)

Around the Alameda

Map p266

Metro Balderas L1, Bellas Artes L2, L8, Hidalgo L2,
L3 or Juárez L3.
With its colourfully tiled art deco domed roofs and grandiose façade, dripping with winged seraphs and chunky marble cherubs integrated with the odd Aztec motif (*see photo p63*), the **Palacio de Bellas Artes** is one of the most unmistakeably lavish buildings in the city. An opera house by design, the Palacio also houses a chic restaurant, an art museum, a museum of architecture, an extensive bookshop and various gift shops (think upmarket Louvre or Met-style silk scarves, money clips and handbags). Climb up to the upper mezzanine floors for a look at murals by all the big names including Diego Rivera, José Clemente Orozco, Rufino Tamayo, David Alfaro Siqueiros and Jorge González Camarena. The most famous is Rivera's *Man, Controller of the Universe*, a reworking of the famous piece commissioned by Nelson Rockefeller that was eventually withdrawn and destroyed due to Rivera's refusal to remove the figure of Vladimir Lenin. This second version includes not only Lenin but also Trotsky, whom Rivera was yet to meet, plus a figure with a striking resemblance to

Rockefeller himself, surrounded by cocktail-sipping, card-playing capitalists against a backdrop of a collage of sexual disease.

Directly outside the Palacio is the edge of the Alameda, the area's one mercifully green space. Spanning over 77,000 square metres, the area was originally set aside as a park by the Spanish on the site of a former Aztec market, and later became a promenade for the city's socialites, who would parade themselves in high fashion in the afternoon under the shade of the hundreds of trees that filled the park back then.

Today, the Alameda, so called for the abundance of *álamos* (poplar trees) that originally filled its grounds, is a respite from the bustle of the Centro Histórico, with police on horseback languidly patrolling the walkways, sculptures and fountains of the park. It's also worth passing by the Hemiciclo a Juárez, a giant semicircle of fluted Ionic columns on the south side of the park, which forms a rather triumphal monument to Mexico's first full-blooded indigenous, much-loved president.

North of the Alameda is a frequently bypassed little square, the Plaza de Santa Veracruz, which faces the Avenida Hidalgo and is flanked on both sides by two rickety old churches that are literally sinking into the ground, to almost comic effect. When crossing from the Alameda, the church on the left-hand side, the Iglesia de San Juan de Dios, is connected to another building, a former hospice and refuge for prostitutes, which has been transformed into the **Museo Franz Mayer**. With a remarkably extensive collection of Mexican artefacts gathered together over seven decades by German immigrant Franz Mayer, the museum also hosts a programme of more contemporary design shows on the first floor. Be sure to look at the courtyard, and have a coffee or even lunch at its peaceful outdoor café.

Right next door is the much smaller and more manageable **Museo Nacional de la Estampa**, which chronicles the development of printing as an artistic technique while showcasing some big names in classical Mexican and contemporary global art.

Another couple of museums also worth popping into, east of the Alameda, are the **Museo Mural Diego Rivera** and the **Laboratorio Arte Alameda**. The former is home to Rivera's masterpiece, *Dream of a Sunday Afternoon in Alameda Park*, as well as a rotating exhibition of the work of Rivera and his contemporaries on the second floor, while the latter is a showcase for art more firmly entrenched in the 21st century, especially of the electronic and digital variety. And if your art lust still isn't sated, then head down to **Museo de Arte Popular** on the corner of

Walk on History central

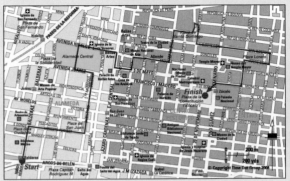

If you're ready for a break and a coffee, then this is the spot. Or for something a little stronger, carry on to **Bar La Nueva Ópera** (*see p128*), glancing up from your drink at the hole in the ceiling, said to be from a bullet fired by Pancho Villa.

From there, turn left up Filomeno Mata and walk for two blocks until you reach the Plaza Tolsá, site of the **Museo Nacional de**

Start: Plaza de la Ciudadela
Finish: El Zócalo
Length: 5.2km (3.2 miles)

Set out heading north from Metro Balderas, past the food stalls along the eastern edge of the citadel building at **Plaza de la Ciudadela**. The yellow-walled artisan's market to the north of the square is a good and inexpensive place to pick up a few souvenirs. At the corner of the market, turn right on to Calle Pugbet for three blocks to reach another market, **Mercado San Juan.** This one is a favourite among local cooks and gourmands, who come here to buy all manner of food, from quails to mussels to sushi rice.

Carry on half a block from the market and turn left into the Plaza de San Juan, passing another artisan's market to your right and heading up Dolores, all the way to the Alameda. Once you reach the edge of the park, and you can see the **Palacio de Bellas Artes** to your right, turn left and walk along the park's southern edge until you reach the semi-circular monument to Benito Juárez.

Here, you can cut across the centre of the Alameda north to the picturesque **Plaza de la Santa Veracruz,** home to the Museo Franz Mayer and the Museo de la Estampa, each building flanked on one side by a church.

Now head east on Avenida Hidalgo, around the back of the Plaza de Bellas Artes, and turn right onto Lázaro Cárdenas, ducking in for a glimpse of the glittering interior of the Palacio Postal, and out and left down to Avenida 5 de Mayo. Another left turn will take you past the beautifully tiled edifice of **La Casa de los Azulejos,** which also houses one of the finest Sanborns restaurants in the city (*see p105*).

Arte. Turn right and head east along Tacuba, passing Café Tacuba on the left (another nice place for coffee or a meal, and so famous its name was adopted by one of Mexico's most famous bands, Café Tacuba) until you arrive at República de Chile. Turn left and walk three blocks along these streets, once teeming with street vendors but remarkably clear now, thanks to a city government crack down in 2007–2008, until you reach Belisario Domínguez. On the southeast corner is a wonderfully authentic cantina, La Dominica. It's not elegant, but it is a nice place for a pitstop. Exit the cantina, turning left on to Belisario Domínguez and you'll land bang in the centre of the Plaza Santo Domingo.

Noticing the scribes under the Portal de los Evangelistas – and, as at all times, being aware of your wallet and possessions as you go, it's round the square and off again along Luis González Obregón, the continuation of República de Cuba (Centro streets change their names willy nilly, sometimes thrice in as many blocks.) Head three blocks east to **Plaza de Loreto.** A quiet square with two churches and a fountain, it's a bit off the beaten track, but a charming colonial plaza.

To the south of the plaza runs Justo Sierra. Follow that street west for two blocks, then left on to Correo Mayor, the main street that runs through the heart of the run-down but lively commercial zone east of the Zócalo, packed with jewellery and camera shops. Turn right on to Calle Moneda, passing the north entrance of the **Palacio Nacional,** and keep straight on until you find yourself in the vast expanse of the Zócalo.

Independencia and Revillagigedo, a showcase for 'popular' Mexican arts and crafts including maquettes, carvings and the signature national papier-mâché sculptures.

Four blocks down from here along Avenida Balderas is the Plaza de la Ciudadela, a large, verdant square flanked by stalls selling T-shirts, *lucha libre* masks, and plenty of food, from fresh fruit to hot tacos. The 'citadel' after which the square is named is a huge, stately looking compound to the south that has had various incarnations as a tobacco factory, a military barracks and a prison. Today, it houses the **Biblioteca de México**, the country's national library, as well as the photography museum, the **Centro de la Imagen**. On the opposite side of the square is the bright yellow outer wall of the **Centro de Artesanías La Ciudadela**, an extensive arts and crafts market that's definitely worth seeing (*see p151*).

Centro de la Imagen
Plaza de la Ciudadela 2 (9172 4724/http://centrodela imagen.conaculta.gob.mx/ http://centrodelaimagen. blogspot.com). Metro Balderas L1, L3. **Open** 11am-6pm Tue-Sun. **Admission** free. **Map** p266 J5.
The Centro de la Imagen is Mexico City's leading contemporary photography museum. It hosts a photography biennale, and, in alternate years, it is one of the venues for 'Fotoseptiembre', a series of exhibitions and happenings that take place across the city. The space is fairly large and usually allows for two or three separate exhibitions.

Laboratorio Arte Alameda
Dr Mora 7 (5510 2793/www.artealameda.inba. gob.mx). Metro Hidalgo L2, L3. **Open** 9am-5pm Tue-Sun. **Admission** MX$15; MX$7.50 reductions; free Sun. **Map** p266 K4.
Established in 2000 by the national advisory for art and culture for the express purpose of furthering electronic arts such as video and interactive installations, the LAA, like so many museums in the area, is housed inside a former convent, that of Saint Diego, originally built in 1591. Its cutting-edge programme changes frequently, but stays within the bounds of contemporary digital art. Screened, projected or installed, these works contrast well with their classical surroundings.

Museo de Arte Popular
Revillagigedo 11, entrance on Independencia (5510 2201/www.map.df.gob.mx). Metro Juárez L3. **Open** 10am-6pm Tue, Wed, Fri-Sun; 10am-9pm Thur. **Admission** MX$40; free reductions. **Map** p266 K4.
This museum of contemporary Mexican arts and crafts is a colourful showcase of giant papier-mâché devils and dragons, along with elaborately painted wooden animals, pottery, toys, masks, textiles and other handiworks. The shop on the ground floor is great for souvenirs, and the hip café right opposite is a good place to rest your pins.

Museo Franz Mayer
Avenida Hidalgo 45 (5518 2266/www.franzmayer. org.mx). Metro Bellas Artes L2, L8 or Hidalgo L2, L3. **Open** 10am-5pm Tue, Thur-Sun; 10am-7pm Wed. **Admission** MX$45; MX$25 reductions. **Map** p266 K4.

Gilt complex: gloriously baroque **Palacio Postal**. *See p64.*

Slim city

Even the most cursory dash through the Centro Histórico reveals that the neighbourhood has some serious issues. Lack of residents is one: a third of the area's inhabitants fled for the suburbs after the damage done by the 1985 earthquake. This came in the wake of another exodus, decades earlier, which saw the relocation of a large part of the community when the University vacated most of its numerous sites in the centre to move to the south of the city.

And then, of course, it's sinking. Built, as it is, on the swampy turf of a drained lake in a region of high seismic activity, the Centro isn't exactly a prime candidate for real estate speculation. The streets surrounding the Zócalo are full of exquisite colonial buildings gradually subsiding into the ground, often at angles that seem to defy gravity.

In the past couple of decades, crime has also been a problem. Although somewhere around a million people, mostly government workers, come to work in the centre every day, the lack of permanent residents has meant that the streets were all but deserted at night, and thus fertile ground for all manner of illicit and violent activity.

But help is at hand thanks to the shared efforts of the government and one of Mexico's most controversial characters. With a net worth of MX$60 billion, Mexico's wealthiest man, Carlos Slim, recently overtook Bill Gates in the Forbes rich list to become the second richest person in the world, behind investor Warren Buffett.

The son of a Lebanese immigrant, Slim started his soaring empire by buying stock at the age of 12, having already sharpened his skills in the playground by trading baseball cards. He is now the most powerful businessman in the country, with stakes in more than 220 companies including the telephone giant Telmex; electricity supplier Condumex; the CILSA construction firm; Swecomex oil; and everybody's favourite newsagent-cum-restaurant, Sanborns.

With about eight per cent of the national GDP under his belt in a country in which 40 per cent of the population lives below the poverty line, Slim has come up against a lot of criticism: it's a running joke that the average Mexican can't drive a car, watch the news, make a phone call, or even turn on the lights without contributing in some way to one of Slim's ever-swelling enterprises.

Unlike Gates and Buffett, Slim is portrayed as a reluctant philanthropist by the media, despite a number of charitable institutions being set up in his name. One of those is the Fundación Centro Histórico, a project committed to the rejuvenation of properties in Mexico City's ailing downtown area. The Fundación has bought up dozens of historic buildings, now in various stages of renovation, while the city, first under Andrés Manuel López Obrador and now under Mayor Marcelo Ebrard, has committed itself to improving and maintaining the area's infrastructure and cleanliness. In all, more than MX$600 million of both government and private money has been poured into the Centro Histórico since the launch of the project in 2002, and the results are already evident in the repaving of many of the streets in the area, general improvements in services such as electricity supplies and sewage, and the ousting of the more than 15,000 street vendors and hawkers who used to dominate the Centro's streets.

The government is also granting a series of tax breaks to developers renovating buildings in the area; and since there is always the risk, with regeneration, of creating fossilised façades that please only snap-happy tourists, the authorities are also treading carefully so as not to allow too much gentrification. Thus developers bear the expense of relocating existing residents while working on their homes so as to ensure they come back when the work is finished: in the words of Carlos Slim, 'The project is not to restore buildings but to revitalise the centre. To revitalise means to have life again, with more people working, living and studying there.'

Slim's father, who came to Mexico from the Ottoman Empire in 1902, and who kick-started the family fortune with the bold and canny purchase of downtown real estate at the height of the Mexican Revolution, would presumably heartily approve.

Chilango bingo

With characters like Death, the Devil, the Drunkard and the Scorpion nestling in the pack alongside the Rose, the Pear, the Sun and the Boot, Mexican children's bingo (*lotería*) cards pack an existential punch to match their rich colours and vivid images. As you roam the city, try your luck at spotting each item in our special set, and be sure to sing out '¡lotería!' for a full house.

GREEN VW TAXI

1 - Green VW taxi

Thronging the streets since 1964, when production began in Puebla, near DF, the classic *vocho*'s days are numbered. The last one rolled off the line in 2003, and they are being phased out of use as taxis. Climb aboard while you can (*see p238* **Taxi tips**).

BLUE CORN

4 - Blue corn

Given the choice between a pale yellow tortilla and one with a deep indigo hue, many Mexicans will pick the latter, safe in the knowledge that blue corn is home-grown, and not the cheap subsidised maize imported from its neighbours under the NAFTA agreement.

SAINT DEATH

2 - Saint Death

Spy a shrine to la Santa Muerte, an unofficial but deeply revered patron saint. Once exclusive to gangsters and drug lords, criminals and prisoners, the cult of Saint Death is growing in popularity in Mexico and beyond. Extra points for spotting a neck tattoo.

AZTEC REVIVALIST

5 - Aztec revivalist

Dancing and drumming, whirling and spinning outside the Basílica de Guadalupe or at the Zócalo square, Mexico's proud, plumed Aztec revivalists cut a fine, old-fashioned figure, reinventing tradition with a nod to their roots.

ELECTRIC SHOCKER

3 - Electric shocker

A way for macho men and fierce women test their mettle, in practice it's mainly drunken revellers who keep the *toque* men in business. At Plaza Garibaldi (*see p192* **Cry me a Río**) or in a cantina, they'll crank up the voltage for a few pesos. Extra points for over 50v.

DEAD SPARROW

6 - Dead sparrow

A far less common sight these days, at the peak of Mexico City's pollution problems during the early 1990s, sparrows and pigeons could often be found dropped dead on the street, like a metropolitan, *chilango* versions of the coalmine canary.

This museum showcases an eclectic range of objects of art and design, sculpture, pottery, fabric and furniture from the 17th century onwards, all part of the personal collection of the German-born Franz Mayer, including hundreds of editions of *Don Quixote*. Design, antique and collecting enthusiasts will be thrilled; others will be more tempted by the bookstore and the pleasant café in the courtyard.

Museo Mural Diego Rivera

Colón (no number), esquina Balderas (5518 0183/ www.museomuraldiegorivera.bellasartes.gob.mx). Metro Hidalgo L2, L3. **Open** 10am-6pm Tue-Sun. **Admission** MX$15. **Map** p266 K4.

This museum's raison d'être is the exhibition of one mural by Diego Rivera, and probably his most famous. *Dream of a Sunday Afternoon in Alameda Park* was originally painted at the Hotel Prado in 1947, but it was dismantled and brought to this location after the 1985 earthquake, when the hotel was demolished. This 14-metre-long, four-metre-high painting depicts well-known Mexican personalities from the time of Cortés on, promenading in the park that lies directly across the road. Rivera has painted himself as a child holding the hand of the fashionably dressed skeleton in the centre of the image, while the adult Frida Kahlo stands maternally behind him, clutching a circular ying-yang symbol.

Museo Nacional de la Estampa

Avenida Hidalgo 39 (5521 2244). Metro Bellas Artes L2, L8 or Hidalgo L2, L3. **Open** 10am-6pm Tue-Sun. **Admission** MX$10; free Sun. **Map** p266 K3

This relatively small showcase of the history and development of the engraved and printed image is situated right next to the Museo Franz Mayer, and with just a MX$10 entry fee, it's worth a spin around. Among the works on show are prints, etchings and lithographs by the likes of José Clemente Orozco, José Guadalupe Posada and David Alfaro Siqueiros, as well as some foreign artists including Ilya Kabakov, Richard Serra and Barbara Kruger.

Palacio de Bellas Artes

Avenida Juárez y Eje Central Lázaro Cárdenas (5130 0900/www.bellasartes.gob.mx). Metro Bellas Artes L2, L8. **Open** 10am-6pm Tue-Sun (guided tours 10am-5pm). *Box office* 11am-7pm Mon-Sat; 10am-7pm Sun. By phone (Ticketmaster) 5325 9000. **Admission** MX$35; free reductions; free Sun. **Map** p267 L4.

Hindered by structural hurdles and the disruption caused by the 1910 revolution, the Palacio de Bellas Artes, Mexico City's principal opera house, was almost three decades in the making. The interior is a polished marble art deco extravaganza, and even the ticket counters have been preserved to perfection. The main stage has hosted world-class acts from Placido Domingo to the Bolshoi Ballet, and has a regular programme of local music and dance shows too. (*See p204.*) On the second and third levels are the Museo de Bellas Artes and the Museo Nacional de la Arquitectura, the former usually reserved for big budget monograph shows. *Photo p63.*

JACARANDA

7 - Jacaranda

If it's autumn, you're out of luck with this card. Come again in springtime, when Mexico City parks explode in a joyful, magnificent purple riot of jacaranda blossom. Parque México and the Alameda are our tips for guaranteed violet views, overhead and scattered underfoot.

8 - Wonky church

Settling silently, inexorably and unevenly into the lakebed of what was once Lake Texcoco, the city's heavy churches and monuments are particularly prone to sinking at odd angles. Keep your eyes peeled in the Centro Histórico.

WONKY CHURCH

9 - Fresa

Preppies by any other name, Mexico's bourgeois kids, *fresas*, can be seen in their natural habitat in city malls and Condesa bars, peppering their speech with English and rocking loafers, labels and an unquestioning, profound sense of entitlement.

FRESA

Sightseeing

Paseo de la Reforma & Zona Rosa

A walk along DF's grandest avenue is a trip through Mexican history.

Paseo de la Reforma, the monumental avenue that runs from Bosque de Chapultepec to the Centro Histórico, began its life as a twinkle in the eye of the Emperor Maximilian, who dreamed of a fast track from his residence at the Castillo de Chapultepec through open fields to the Palacio Nacional in the centre of town. It was laid out in its present grand form by the dictator Porfirio Díaz decades later and, named to commemorate liberal reforms carried out in the 19th century under much-loved President Benito Juárez, it soon began to take shape as a grand avenue in the European style, studded with statues, *glorietas* (roundabouts) and mansions. Today, most of the mansions have been replaced by modern high-rise offices in this, the heart of Mexico's traditional financial district; but the Parisian-style grandeur of the two-mile-long Paseo remains, refreshed and invigorated in recent years by a growing collection of new sculptures and statues, permanent and temporary.

Walking the avenue from end to end is a trek, so try to work out where you plan to go in advance. Metro stations Chapultepec and Hidalgo are located at each end of the Reforma's main central stretch, while Insurgentes, Cuauhtémoc and Revolución are also relatively close.

Zona Rosa is the neighbourhood directly to the south of Paseo de la Reforma and to the west of Avenida Insurgentes. A fashionable bohemian neighbourhood in the 1960s, it has become a little rougher around the edges over the years, and is easily outshone as a sightseeing destination by many other of the city's more historic *colonias* (neighbourhoods). Nevertheless, with its central location it makes a pleasant enough base, and there's plenty of diversion to be had in its countless cafés, bars, clubs, shops and markets.

Paseo de la Reforma

Maps p262 & p267
Metro Chapultepec L1 or Hidalgo L2/Metrobús Revolución or Reforma.

Starting at the eastern end of Paseo de la Reforma (the side closest to the Alameda park

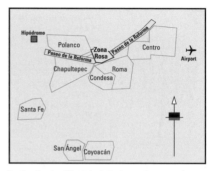

in the Centro Histórico), look out for two of the area's most unmistakeable landmarks: the bright yellow swishes and curves of *El Caballito*, a huge sculpture set outside the Torre de Caballito, and the stunning 1920s art deco building that houses the Lotería Nacional just opposite. The piece is a modern reworking of an original sculpture of Spanish king Charles IV by Manuel Tolsá – itself a work whose presence became so contentious during the struggle for Independence that it was relocated from Paseo de la Reforma to Plaza Tolsá.

Nearby, a couple of blocks north of Paseo de la Reforma, is the Plaza de la República and the Monumento a la Revolución, an enormous dome perched on a quadrangle of arches made from a combination of marble and basalt. The space was originally intended to house a new parliament building for Porfirio Díaz, but the project was abandoned in the wake of the dictator's ousting in the 1910 revolution. It wasn't until 1933 that it was decided that parts of the iron structure and the cupola should be incorporated into a monument to the uprising. It was completed in 1938, and the remains of revolutionaries like Venustiano Carranza and Pancho Villa were later transported to the monument and interred in its columns. It's possible to go up into the dome on weekends from 10am to 5.30pm.

Built into the ground underneath the monument is the **Museo de la Revolución**, a showcase of objects and documents that illustrate the six decades of Mexican history from 1857 up to 1920. Most interesting are the articles evoking the social history of the period – antique outfits and costumes; a late 19th-century printing press; and copies of a series of undelivered letters from Pancho Villa to Emiliano Zapata explaining his reasons for wanting to attack the United States.

The nearby **Museo Nacional de San Carlos** holds one of the best collections of European art in Mexico. Housed in a 19th-century mansion designed by Manuel Tolsá and formerly the (art) Academy of San Carlos, the collection is relatively small, with a notable emphasis on Spanish art from 1500 to 1900. Among the highlights are Cranarch's *Adam and Eve*, and Pelegrin Clavé y Roque's *La Primera Juventud de Isabel la Católica,* which is hung alongside the artist's sketches and preliminary studies for the piece.

The Monumento a la Madre is located on the edge of the Jardin del Arte, a verdant plaza to the north of Paseo de la Reforma. The area around the large social-realist statue dedicated to the mothers of Mexico is currently a mini-shanty town of tents and temporary homes set up by a small population of protestors who have established a campaign HQ in the city.

Adjacent to the Jardin del Arte is contemporary art space El Eco Experimental Museum, revived from hibernation by UNAM's architecture faculty to host exhibitions, performances, film screenings and conferences. You can soak up some avant-garde culture before crossing the park to Río Lerma for a visit the **Museo Casa de Carranza**, the former residence of Venustiano Carranza, one of the most prominent figures of the 1910 revolution and the president under whose term the country's current constitution was drawn up.

Back along Paseo de la Reforma, dozens of statues, busts and other artworks line the avenue, among which perhaps the most impressive are the Monumento a Cuauhtémoc, a homage to the last Aztec ruler; the Monumento a la Independencia; and the fountain **Diana Cazadora** – Diana the Huntress (*photo p73*). The first is a late 19th-century sculpture by Francisco Jiménez of the Aztec emperor, nephew of Moctezuma, who fought the Spanish invaders while still in his teens and who was captured and

A safe pair of hands: public art on **Paseo de la Reforma**

Paseo de la Reforma.

tortured by Cortés' army in a bid to discover the location of the mythical Aztec gold. The last two are on successive roundabouts approaching the gateway to Bosque de Chapultepec. The Ángel de la Independencia, as it is often called, is a popular symbol of Mexican autonomy and was one of the last sculptures to be inaugurated by Porfirio Díaz. You can enter the monument – just take care traversing the Avenida. If you do make it across, you can view the grisly remains of 12 revolutionaries, including Miguel Hidalgo's skull.

Museo Casa de Carranza

Río Lerma 35, (5535 2920). Metro Insurgentes L1. **Open** 9am-6pm Tue-Sat; 9am-5pm Sun. **Admission** MX$35; free reductions; free Sun. **Map** p266 H4.
Housed inside a French-style mansion that was once home to former president Venustiano Carranza, this museum celebrates the life and career of the revolutionary leader. A museum space to the side hosts exhibitions themed around Carranza and his era.

Museo de la Revolución

Monumento a la Revolución, Plaza de la República, Paseo de la Reforma (5566 1902/www.cultura.df. gob.mx). Metro Revolución L2. **Open** 9am-5pm Tue-Fri; 9am-6pm Sat, Sun. **Admission** MX$14; MX$7 reductions; free Sun. **Map** p266 I4.
Beneath the Monumento a la Revolución, this museum charts Mexican history from 1857 to 1920.

Museo Nacional de San Carlos

Puente de Alvarado 50, Paseo de la Reforma (5566 8085/www.bellasartes.gob.mx). Metro Hidalgo L2, L3 or Revolución L2. **Open** 10am-6pm Wed-Mon. **Admission** MX$25; MX$12.50 reductions; free Sun. **Map** p266 J3.
This is Mexico's largest collection of European art, spanning four centuries from the Renaissance onwards. The collection includes works by Rodin, Goya and Cranarch, among others.

Zona Rosa

Maps p262 & p265
Metro Insurgentes L1/Metrobús Hamburgo or Insurgentes

The Zona Rosa lies directly south of the Paseo de la Reforma. Most of the streets here are named after major European cities, for example the two arteries that run the length of Zona Rosa, Hamburgo and Londres. A popular haunt of the cultural elite during the 1960s, the Zona Rosa has suffered a decline in popularity in recent years, and is now mostly favoured by students, who come for the cheap beer in its relatively low-priced bars. Think London's Camden, but without the punk posturing – for that, head for El Chopo market on a Saturday; *see p156*. Legend has it that Zona Rosa was named after the pink glow given off by its profusion of neon signs. The fact that the 'pink zone' is now Mexico City's best-known area for gay bars and nightlife is pure coincidence.

There's not much to see in the area, which is more suited to hanging out in shops, cafés and restaurants, or hunting for local arts and crafts at the artisans' market on the corner of Liverpool and Florencia streets. However, you might want to take a look at the **Museo Ripley** and its neighbouring waxwork museum, the **Museo de Cera**. The former is one of a worldwide chain of 'Odditoriums' started by cartoonist, amateur

---

DF eye

Paseo de la Reforma is so beautiful with its fountains, trees, museums, cafés, roundabouts, palaces and mansions. You can smell the coffee of the corporate world there, linger in museums, dance in the Gay Pride carnival, or catch a glimpse into the lives of those who march for better conditions, passing along the avenue under the gaze of its statues.

Liliana Flores, actress and TV presenter, VH1.

anthropologist and entrepreneur Robert Ripley who founded the 'Ripley's Believe It or Not!' franchise with the sole purpose of collecting and displaying the weird, the wonderful and the utterly freakish. The museum on *calle* Londres is hard to miss thanks to its medieval castle-style exterior and the busloads of school children queuing to get in on any given weekday. Its collection includes shrunken African heads and the genuine skeleton of a two-headed human and might not be for the delicate of stomach. The **Museo de Cera** (Waxworks Museum) next door is almost an extension of the Ripley museum, and is Mexico City's answer to Madame Tussaud's (minus the enormous queues and endless hype). You're unlikely to be bowled over with admiration here, but the motionless figures, which include Harry Potter and a rather sweaty-looking Tom Cruise, might at least put a smile, even if only a bemused one, on your face.

El Eco Experimental Museum

Sullivan 43, Avenida Paseo de la Reforma (5622 0305/www.muca.unam.mx). Metro Revolución L2. **Open** 10am-7pm Tue-Fri; 10am-6pm Sat, Sun. **Admission** free. **Map** p266 H4.

El Eco showcases experimental contemporary art in its many forms. Originally founded in the 1950s by visionary German artist Matías Goeritz, it was later turned a nightclub before being reclaimed and reinvented as an art space by the Universidad Nacional Autónoma de México (UNAM).

Museo de Cera

Londres 6, Zona Rosa (5546 7670/www.museode cera.com.mx). Metro Cuauhtémoc L1 or Insurgentes L1. **Open** 11am-7pm daily. **Admission** MX$60; MX$45 reductions. **Map** p266 I5.

In an annexe of the Museo Ripley (*see below*), this waxwork museum might not be the most technically impressive in the world, but it's your one chance to come face to face with the great figures of Mexican history, including Miguel Hidalgo, Pancho Villa, Benito Juárez, Emiliano Zapato and Frida Kahlo.

Museo de lo Increíble ¡Ripley Aunque Usted no lo Crea!

Londres 4, Zona Rosa (5546 7670/www.ripleys.com). Metro Cuauhtémoc L1 or Insurgentes L1. **Open** 11am-7pm daily. **Admission** MX$60; MX$45 reductions. **Map** p266 I5.

One of a global chain of museums dedicated to the weird, wonderful and wacky. You can buy a joint ticket for this museum and the adjacent Museo de Cera (MX$100 for adults and MX$80 for reductions and children).

The dramatic **Diana Cazadora** (Diana the Huntress) fountain. *See p71.*

Polanco & Chapultepec

Natural beauty meets high-class streets in posh Polanco and lush Chapultepec.

Polanco

Map p 262
Metro Auditorio L7 or Polanco L7.

One of Mexico City's classiest, most expensive neighbourhoods, Polanco is known for its fine collection of designer boutiques and luxurious bars and restaurants, spread throughout an area that stretches from the top of the first section of **Bosque de Chapultepec** to the Avenida Ejército Nacional to the north.

The land here was relatively undeveloped as recently as the 1930s, when it was home to the Hacienda de los Morales, a farm that harvested silk from the worms nesting in the mulberry trees that grew here before the bulldozers moved in. Reincarnated as a very upmarket restaurant, the farm is still standing today.

Development proceeded apace through the 1940s, with many buildings going up in a decorative, baroque-influenced 'mission revival' style first popularised at the turn of the 20th century, which echoes early Spanish missionary constructions in California. Many of those houses, which with their turrets and elaborate façades often look like mock fortresses and castles, are standing in perfect condition next to the über-modern concrete-and-glass structures that also characterise the area.

Walking around Polanco, you'll notice that most of the street names are dedicated to philosophers, poets and writers, with one or two exceptions, the most prominent being the thoroughfare named after the first president of Czechoslovakia, Tomás Masaryk. Polanco's main artery, Avenida Presidente Masaryk is littered with top-notch boutiques of the likes of Chanel, Burberry and Escada, plus high-street standards like Diesel, Zara and Massimo Dutti. Sleek cars and sleek shoppers give it an air of New York's Fifth Avenue, London's Sloane Street or any number of high-class shopping meccas the world over; but if you're planning a wallet-busting day here, best to wear something other than the Manolos, as Masaryk stretches over three kilometres.

For a more condensed shopping experience, you might want to try out the impressive Antara mall (*see p141*). An architectural diversion in itself, this well-laid-out outdoor mall houses all the main international high-street names as well as a few local brands, several restaurants and a multi-screen cinema.

Between Avenida Masaryk and the top of Bosque de Chapultepec is the compact and serene Parque Lincoln, bordered by Avenida Emilio Castelar and semi-circular Virgilio, both to the north and both of which house a number of superb restaurants, food markets and small shops. One block south of Parque Lincoln is Campos Eliseos, a road named after the legendary French boulevard that houses the district's grand hotels, including the W, the Intercontinental and the JW Marriot (*see p46*).

Polanco is also known for its sizeable Jewish community, and there are 12 synagogues in the area. If you're feeling starved of church visits, head up to Horacio 921, to the spectacular Catedral San Agustin, built in an arrestingly modern style.

Bosque de Chapultepec

Map p262
Metro Auditorio L7, Chapultepec L1 or Constituyentes L7.

Often referred to as Chapultepec Park in English, Bosque de Chapultepec, a vast expanse of greenery that covers some 1,655 acres, serves as the city's overworked lungs. To most *chilangos*, it's a place to escape from the noise and pollution of the city, although the chaos on the streets is transferred to the park at weekends, when thousands of day-trippers come to spend time strolling, picnicking, rowing on the lake, or visiting one of the park's many museums, most of which are free on Sundays.

Chapultepec, meaning 'grasshopper hill' in Náhuatl, has had quite a history, having served as a temporary home to Aztec and colonial rulers alike, all of whom cherished the notion of a verdant haven away from urban influence.

The park is split into three sections, named accordingly the first, second and third sections (*primera*, *segunda* and *tercera secciones*). The first and easternmost section is the most popular, containing a number of world-class museums including the **Museo Nacional de Antropología** and the **Castillo de Chapultepec** (Chapultepec Castle), as well as a large lake and a zoo with an adjoining butterfly sanctuary. A little further to reach on foot, the second section is more child-oriented, with the rollercoaster of the Feria Chapultepec Mágico peeking out over the trees beside the technology museum and the excellent children's museum, **Museo del Papalote** (*see p165*). *Papalote* means butterfly in Náhuatl, the local indigenous language, and is also a synonym for 'kite' in Mexican Spanish. The third section of the park – the westernmost section – is remote and less well frequented than the other sections, though by the same token, it's also considered to be the quietest and most attractive part.

Avenida Paseo de la Reforma runs along the northern edge of the park, and you'll find a tourist information booth just where it passes by the anthropology museum. If you fancy touring on two wheels, bikes can be rented near the entrance to Chapultepec Metro. Consult the park's offical website (www.chapultepec.com) for more information. To get to Bosque de Chapultepec by Metro, you can go to one of three stops: Auditorio, Constituyentes or Chapultepec; given the size of the park, you might want to think ahead to find out which one best fits your plans. The most striking entrance to the park is the one near Chapultepec Metro. A wide walkway extends from the city's main boulevard, Avenida Paseo de la Reforma, through the main gate of the park and up to the dramatic Monumento a los Niños Héroes. Six pillars shoot up from the base of this lofty white marble memorial, each adorned with a large black eagle and topped with a sculpted burning flame. The pillars represent the six *niños héroes* or 'heroic boys' young cadets who lost their lives fighting the US army at the Battle of Chapultepec in 1847. Castillo de Chapultepec (Chapultepec Castle) was a military academy at the time of the battle, and with the Mexican side losing ground to the Americans, the Mexican cadets were ordered to retreat from the castle. Six of them stayed on to fight to the death, and the story goes that the last of the boys, Juan Escutia, wrapped himself in the Mexican flag and threw himself from the top of the castle –

Sightseeing

A welcome dose of leafy green: the city seen from **Bosque de Chapultepec**.

a final act of patriotism that prevented the enemy from claiming the standard.

Just behind the monument, on top of a hill partially concealed by the park's trees, is the Castillo de Chapultepec. Directly aligned with Avenida Paseo de la Reforma, it's a bit of a climb up the hill to the park's entrance (there's also a mini-train that makes regular trips there and back for MX$10); but the castle and the museums within it are first class, as is the stunning view over the park and the city.

Initiated in the late 18th century by the Viceroy Bernardo de Gálvez, the castle's construction was drawn out over several years as project leaders came and went and funds became low. Its future was uncertain until 1833, when it was decided that it should be used as a military academy.

It wasn't until the arrival of Emperor Maximilian, brother of the Archduke of Austria, and his Belgian wife Carlotta in 1864 that the castle really came into its own as a regal residence. Maximilian chose Chapultepec as his home over the rundown Palacio Nacional in the town centre, and got to work building upon the existing structure to bring it in line with the neoclassical style then predominant in Europe. The colossal boulevard that stretches from the foot of the castle into the city centre was

Carlotta's idea, intended to echo Avenue Louise in her native Brussels. Today, it is the traffic-clogged but nevertheless impressive Avenida Paseo de la Reforma.

Maximillian was executed by firing squad in 1867 and the castle went on to become the residence of a string of Mexican presidents including Porfirio Díaz, Venustiano Carranza and Álvaro Obregón. This continued until the 1940s, when President Lázaro Cárdenas decreed that the castle should become a museum. The presidential residence was transferred to Los Pinos.

Today, the castle houses Mexico's **Museo Nacional de Historia** as well as a temporary exhibition space and an exhibition of some of the presidential living quarters. Don't miss Carlotta's bedroom and bathroom, among the most lavishly decorated rooms in the castle, or the breathtaking stained-glass representations of the five classical goddesses of womanhood, made in Paris for Porfirio Díaz and installed in a corridor on the top floor of the building.

On the way up or down from the castle, it's worth stopping at the **Museo del Caracol** or 'snail' museum, so called for its innovative spiral shape, cut into the hill and winding downwards into the museum. Enter from the top via a path that spirals around the roof and descends into the entrance lobby. It's a museum of Mexican

A touch of tranquility at **Lago de Chapultepec**.

history, primarily intended for children, with extensive use of dolls and scale models to illustrate some of the key moments in the country's past, including Hidalgo's 'shout of independence' from the church steps in Dolores, Maximilian's execution and the 1847 assault on the Castillo de Chapultepec.

A short walk from the castle's main entrance is the **Museo de Arte Moderno**, a circular building on two floors housing the country's most extensive collection of Mexican modern art. Appropriately for a 'modern' rather than a 'contemporary' art museum, the collection is firmly rooted in the 20th century, with two huge permanent collection rooms, one devoted principally to art from the first half of the century, the other to the second. If you're not familiar with 20th-century Mexican art, this is an essential stop. Temporary visiting exhibitions help to keep things fresh, and there are occasional monograph shows from the works of artists in the collection.

For contemporary art, cross the road to the **Museo Rufino Tamayo**. Ostracised by the art world in Mexico for his affiliation to European movements such as Cubism and Fauvism, and in political circles for his refusal to join the Rivera/Orozco socialist bandwagon, Tamayo made a fortune selling his work in the USA. He said that the purpose of the museum, in response to David Siqueiros's famous declaration, 'Ours is the only path', was to open up what he considered to be the very closed and introspective art community in Mexico.

Aside from the museum's permanent collection, which contains only a handful of works by Tamayo himself, the lion's share of the space and the spotlight are given to its programme of contemporary shows and installations, which have recently included Wolfgang Tillmans, Jeff Wall and Thomas Hirschhorn. There's a very basic café by the entrance that serves coffee good enough to boost you on to your next destination, and the tables and chair under the concrete awning over the front door provide an all-weather vantage point for views over the park.

From the Museo Tamayo, it's possible to cross back over Avenida Paseo de la Reforma and re-enter the first section of the park via the Jardín Botánico (botanical gardens), which contain a mixture of evergreens, cacti, domesticated, medicinal and ornamental plants, as well as some carnivorous specimens and an arboretum. The garden as it is today was conceived in 2004 as part of a plan to revive Mexico's ancient botanical traditions. It's a pleasant enough stroll around the manicured grounds, though hardly a world-class botanical showcase. The ordered, freshly dug beds look

Castillo de Chapultepec.
See p75.

a little sparse in comparison with the rest of lush Bosque de Chapultepec, while the deserted greenhouse adds a further air of dilapidation.

Right next to the Jardín Botánico is the park's huge lake, **Lago de Chapultepec**, created under the watch of President Porfirio Díaz in 1908 as part of a project to convert what was rough forest land into a public park. It's immensely popular, especially at weekends when you can barely see the water for the boats that can be rented from the lake's shore. It's MX$40 per hour for a kayak, MX$50 for a pedal boat and MX$60 for a dinghy with oars. On quieter days, being out on the water here can be a pleasantly serene experience, especially with the view of the Castillo de Chapultepec up on the hill reflected on the surface of the lake.

On the western shore of the lake, the Casa del Lago is a stately dwelling that dates back to the beginning of the 20th century. Originally an automobile club and later the park's administrative headquarters, it was the residence of former President Adolfo Huerta for a brief period in the early 1920s and later became a cultural centre. Today, the house sits alone, looking rather romantic beside

Sightseeing

the lake, and is used by UNAM university for art exhibitions and music, film and theatre events.

Another nearby art space, not so lively as the Casa del Lago, is the **Sala de Arte Siqueiros**. Located on the quiet residential street of Tres Picos, just outside the park as you leave via the exit closest to the Gandhi monument, this museum was the home and studio of one of Mexico's most renowned social realist painters, who was part of the muralist movement along with Diego Rivera and José Clemente Orozco. Siqueiros bequeathed the site to the public just before his death in 1974.

The museum contains a series of murals covering the walls and floor, executed in the Chihuahua-born artist's signature modernist style, with and angular forms seeming to punch out from the painting's surface and a set of revolutionary themes reflecting Siqueiros's Marxist convictions. It also contains a temporary exhibition space for contemporary art by Mexican and international artists.

One building that's hard to miss is the gigantic concrete-and-glass **Auditorio Nacional** (www.auditorio.com.mx). Built in the 1950s by the same architects who went on to design the nearby Museo Tamayo, this 20,000-person capacity arena is the city's prime concert venue. Winner of the 2007 Billboard Touring best concert venue in the world, the auditorium is also home to the largest pipe organ in Latin America. Even if you're not going there to see a concert, it's worth having a wander around the enormous concrete entrance hall, if it's open, to get a feel for the impressive scale of the place. There's another, smaller venue called the Lunario whose entrance is tucked away to the side of the auditorium. It's a good place for smaller gigs, and there are weekly double-bill film showings for just MX$50. (*See p191*.)

Further afield, closer to the Constituyentes entrance to the park, is the **Museo de Historia Natural**, Mexico City's Museum of Natural History, set under a complex of Jetsons-style brightly coloured domes. Unfortunately, the exhibits inside are not quite so arresting – the result of a less futuristic, more antiquated approach to museum curating that's rather pedestrian and dry. The faded display cabinets are crying out for a revamp, while a soundtrack of seagulls cawing incessantly in the background may lift the hairs on your neck in a manner to make Hitchcock proud.

A startled looking polar bear and a wolverine frozen in action in the museum's lobby will give you a taste of the cornucopia of taxidermy that lies ahead in the second dome, with dozens of stuffed creatures placed in mini savannahs and tiny forests behind the glass of the display cabinets. Add these unsettling qualities together and you have quite an eerie museum experience, though undoubtedly something children might enjoy.

If you are accompanied by children, consider making the short walk to the **Museo Tecnológico**, or MUTEC, situated right next to the screaming rollercoasters of the park's fairground (*see p165*). Funded by the electricity board, the technology museum might sound like dullsville nerd heaven, but in fact it's one of the most diverting museums in the city. Designed with children in mind, the museum is split into various sections that cover everything from the development of technology to electricity and the science behind natural disasters.

In the park's second section nearby is the Tláloc fountain, easy to find by dint of its sheer size and elaborate design. The Fuente de Tláloc is Diego Rivera's homage to the Aztec rain god, who was also revered for his incarnations as hail, thunder and lightning. Built in 1952, the circular pool features Tláloc emerging spreadeagled from the water, covered in small mosaic tiles and volcanic rock pebbles. Behind the fountain is a small domed pavilion housing the mural *El Agua, Origen de la Vida* – a fresco in polystyrene and rubber that Rivera completed one year before the fountain.

Casa del Lago

Bosque de Chapultepec, 1st section (5211 6093/ www.casadellago.unam.mx). Metro Auditorio L7 or Chapultepec L1. **Open** 11am-5pm Wed-Sun. **Admission** free. **Map** p262 D6.
This lonely looking lakeside house, with spectacular views of the water and the surrounding park, is a cultural centre used for art exhibitions, courses, workshops, seminars, screenings and performances. It has a lively, ever-changing schedule of events, so it's worth checking the website in advance.

Castillo de Chapultepec

Bosque de Chapultepec, 1st section (5241 3100/ www.mnh.inah.gob.mx). Metro Auditorio L7 or Chapultepec L1. **Open** 9am-5pm Tue-Sun. **Admission** MX$48; free reductions; free Sun. **Map** p262 D7.
Stunning Chapultepec Castle, set on top of a hill in Mexico City's largest park, is split into three main sections: the Museo Nacional de Historia, a segment of the castles residential wing; the Alcázar; and a space devoted to temporary exhibitions. Entrance to the museum covers the first two, but there's usually a separate fee for temporary exhibitions. The museum covers events from the time of the conquest and into the 20th century, and consists of a well-curated display of illustrations, paintings and artefacts from across the centuries, including the fabled standard of the Virgin of Guadalupe carried by Miguel Hidalgo during the march for independence. Also keep an eye out for David Siqueiros's remarkable

The shock of the old

The **Museo Nacional de Antropología** makes for a gripping introduction to the variety of civilisations that inhabited Mexico prior to the Spanish invasion. Inside an extraordinary 1960s structure created by Pedro Ramírez Vázquez, architect of other landmarks such as the Museum of Modern Art and the Templo Mayor museum in the Centro Histórico, the museum boasts a unique collection of historic and pre-historic artefacts, plus reconstructions of pre-Columbian tombs and pyramid segments, some set outside in the museum's gardens.

Go in through the main entrance hall and out into the huge courtyard, set around a giant concrete umbrella (*el paraguas*) on a pillar carved with bas-reliefs from Mexican and European history. You might catch one of the museum's series of temporary themed exhibitions, for which you'll pay a separate entrance fee; but there's more than enough to be getting on with in the museum's permanent collection, from diverting little models of the first Mesoamerican settlers and their fanged feline friends, to cabinets full of Aztec, Maya and Toltec relics alongside enormous stone sculptures.

The exhibition rooms encircle the main courtyard and are divided over two levels, the lower of which is the archaeological section, and the upper, the ethnographic.

Starting from the right-hand side as you go in, the exhibits are laid out in more or less chronological and geographical order.

One of the most impressive spaces is the Aztec hall, which contains a model of old Tenochtitlán, the Aztec island city on which Mexico City was built after the Spanish conquest, as well as scores of other sculptures, vessels and engraved stones. Perhaps the most impressive item on show is the hall's central piece, the 25-ton Sun Stone (*left*). Unearthed in the Zócalo in 1790, it contains carvings representing the beginning and end of the Aztec world, and is often mistaken for an Aztec calendar.

Other must-see exhibits are the giant Olmec heads in the Gulf Coast room. Weighing in at around 20 tons each, these sculptures are the remnants of one of Mexico's oldest cultures, often dubbed the 'mother culture', which came to dominate the Veracruz and western Tabasco regions around 1,200 years ago.

If you're planning to visit Teotihuacán (*see p95*), a trip to the museum beforehand or, failing that, afterwards, will multiply your pleasure and understanding considerably, helping you put into context an excursion that will likely leave you bristling with questions. Similarly, if you're heading further afield in Mexico – to Palenque, say, or to the Riviera Maya – be sure to tour the Maya hall first, for maximum benefit later.

Museo Nacional de Antropología

Paseo de la Reforma y Gandhi (5533 6381/ www.mna.inah.gob.mx). Metro Auditorio L7 or Chapultepec L1. **Open** 9am-7pm Tue-Sun. **Admission** MX$48; free reductions; free Sun. **Map** p262 D6.

Sightseeing

series of murals entitled 'From the Dictatorship of Porfirio Diaz to the Revolution' in the Hall of the Revolution, just to the left of the main entrance to the museum. The superbly restored Alcázar is the two-storey east wing of the castle that was home to Mexican rulers from Maximilian onward, until Cárdenas moved the official residence to Los Pinos. Visitors meander through the various presidential rooms and out on to the black-and-white tiled terraces, with superb views over the park and the arrow-straight Avenida Paseo de la Reforma. The south-facing verandas have been reinforced with steel and glass, adding a more progressive edge, while behind them, in the centre of the east-wing courtyard, is what used to be an observatory, used for a short period at the end of the 19th century.

Museo de Arte Moderno

Avenida Paseo de la Reforma y Gandhi (5553 6233/ www.bellasartes.gob.mx). Metro Chapultepec L1. **Open** 10am-5.30pm Tue-Sun. **Admission** MX$20; free reductions; free Sun. **Map** p263 E6.

With 2,800 works in its permanent collection, the Museum of Modern Art affords a comprehensive survey of Mexican art in the 20th century. Owing to space limitations, however, only a small proportion of the total collection is on display at any given time. The museum has works by Frida Kahlo, Diego Rivera, David Siqueiros, Rufino Tamayo and Remedios Varo. The sculpture gardens around the museum, home to a host of scampering squirrels, are good for a stroll, and there's also a second building, previously a café and educational centre, under renovation at time of writing.

Museo del Caracol

Bosque de Chapultepec, 1st section (5241 3144/ www.chapultepec.com.mx). Metro Chapultepec L1. **Open** 9am-4.15pm Tue-Sun. **Admission** MX$37; free reductions; free Sun. **Map** p262 D6.

A snail-shaped museum featuring scale models and miniature *mises-en-scène* behind glass that depict key moments in the country's history, this is a fun, informative museum for kids and anyone not acquainted with the events of the last 500 years in Mexico. Note that all text is in Spanish.

Museo de Historia Natural y Cultura Ambiental

Bosque de Chapultepec, 2nd section (5515 2222/ www.sma.df.gob.mx/mhn). Metro Constituyentes L7. **Open** 10am-5pm Tue-Sun. **Admission** MX$20; MX$10 students; free Tue.

The city's Natural History Museum offers – to borrow the phrase – a brief history of time, from the origins of the universe to the emergence and evolution of life on earth. Despite its quirky external appearance of several brightly coloured domes, the museum itself is a little outmoded. However, any child or adult with an interest in the boned, pickled, stuffed, preserved or set in acrylic will no doubt be captivated by the museum's jam-jar approach to biology. The highlight of the museum, which you can hardly miss, is

the 25-metre (82-foot) diplodocus in the 'Origins of Life' section. It's a cast made from the remains of three dinosaurs unearthed in Wyoming in 1899 by archaeologists working for American millionaire Andrew Carnegie. The models were donated to several countries around the world as tokens of peace during World War I, and this one is an exact replica of the Natural History Museum's original in London.

Museo Rufino Tamayo

Avenida Paseo de la Reforma y Gandhi (5286 6519/ www.museotamayo.org). **Metro** Auditorio L7 or Chapultepec L1. **Open** 10am-6pm Tue-Sun. **Admission** MX$15; free Sun. **Map** p262 D6.

Oaxacan artist Rufino Tamayo founded this namesake gallery in 1981, when he was in his early eighties, to house his collection of international modern art, which includes works by Warhol, Picasso, Mark Rothko and Francis Bacon. An affiliate of the New Museum in New York, the gallery is one of the most exciting in the city thanks to its strong permanent collection plus regular exhibitions of the works of the world's leading contemporary artists. The concrete, marble and glass building was designed in the 1970s by Teodoro González de León and Abraham Zabludovsky, and has echoes of Aztec architecture in the sloping walls of its squared, geometric shapes.

Museo Tecnológico

Bosque de Chapultepec, 2nd section (5516 0964/ www.cfe.gob.mx/Mutec). Metro Constituyentes L7. **Open** 10am-5pm Tue-Sun. **Admission** free. **Map** p262 B8.

This educational interactive museum is geared towards a younger audience, with exhibits designed to be basic so that little ones can fully appreciate them, but good fun for adults too. 'Electrópolis' is a survey and demonstration of the different types of electrical manifestation, while another temporary exhibition about natural disasters features an earthquake shed in which you can experience for yourself the terror of a tremor, as well as a glass tornado box (not recommended for women wearing skirts), a wind tunnel, and a miniature tsunami maker, where you can cause your own (mini) giant wave to crash over an unsuspecting tropical landmass.

Sala de Arte Público Siqueiros

Tres Picos 29, Polanco (5203 5888/www. siqueiros.inba.gob.mx). Metro Auditorio L7. **Open** 10am-6pm Tue-Sun. **Admission** MX$10; free reductions; free Sun. **Map** p262 C5.

This former home and studio of one of Mexico's most famed muralists was bequeathed to the public by Siqueiros, and is now a small museum. Containing murals by the artist that stretch over two floors, as well as works made during his time in the USA and South America, there's also a space on the ground and first floors reserved for contemporary multimedia shows. There's room to relax in a seating area in the centre of the gallery, on the ground floor, while Siqueiros's archive of books, drawings, film and photographs can be found at the very top of the building.

Condesa & Roma

Low buildings, high culture and parklife galore in these fashionable barrios.

Condesa and Roma are Mexico City's most bohemian neighbourhoods, home to many of the capital's artists, writers and musicians as well as a multitude of restaurants, cafés, bars, coffee shops and boutiques. Located either side of noisy Avenida Insurgentes, both areas are reassuringly calm and well ordered; and with a number of parks and verdant plazas, they offer unexpected oases of silence in the centre of the city.

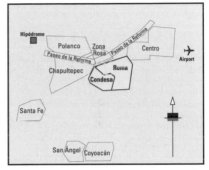

Condesa

Map p264

Metro Chilpancingo L9, Patriotismo L9 or Sevilla L1/Metrobús Campeche, Chilpancingo or Sonora.

By the 1950s, small, leafy, low-slung Condesa had established itself as the *colonia* of choice for glamorous film stars and artists. Popular wisdom has it that Condesa was badly damaged in the 1985 earthquake; but in fact it was neighbour Roma that suffered most due to its exceptionally soft and muddy foundations. Nevertheless, many of Condesa's wealthier inhabitants were spooked, and fled to Polanco and Lomas. Prices fell and a new generation of artists and writers took

Parque México.

advantage, moving in and providing the sort of neighbourhood regeneration that's part of the life cycle of cities the world over. Today, Condesa is an expensive place to live again, with old hacienda-style dwellings sitting side by side with art deco mansions, California colonial-style buildings, and modern glass-and-steel edifices.

Leisure and pleasure in Condesa revolve around its two parks: **Parque España** and **Parque México**, the latter almost never known by its official name of Parque San Martín. Both parks are luscious green jungles of palm trees and exotic shrubs, though the former serves more as a thoroughfare while the latter is painstakingly manicured and best known for its breathtaking springtime display of purple jacaranda blossom. Parque México is very popular with families, who flock here at weekends with their dogs, rent bicycles, and peruse the mini-market that sporadically sets up shop at weekends. Dog school, held in the park most mornings, presents the fascinating tableau of a classful of assorted dogs handed over by their owners to learn to lie down, heel and, impressively, to sit quite still as all park life whirls around them.

The former racetrack, the Hipódromo de la Condesa, which is now Avenida Amsterdam, runs in an oval around Parque México. It's worth a stroll around its tree-lined perimeter to get a look-in at the various cafés and other small shops that dot its circumference.

The hub of restaurants and nightlife in Condesa lies mostly along Avenidas Michoacán and Tamaulipas, the latter a long and colourful road that stretches from the Parque España to Avenida Benjamín Franklin, several blocks

Sightseeing

down. At the far end, at the crossroads with Benjamin Hill, is the **Centro Cultural Bella Época**, a massive bookstore, art gallery, café and screening room all rolled into one. The shop has a broad selection of mostly Spanish books, as well as a children's play area.

Across the road at number 219 is a café and gift shop belonging to the famous *lucha libre* wrestler El Hijo de Santo. It's nice spot for a cup of tea, and for buying shiny silver masks, tacky mugs and comic books. A couple of block down, on the corner of Tamaulipas and Alfonso Reyes, is the church **Parroquia Santa Rosa de Lima**. Built in 1943, it's cool and welcoming, with a fantastic, colourful altarpiece featuring the Virgin encircled by plump, kitsch cherubs.

Another highlight, also on Tamaulipas, is the bright yellow market on the junction between Michoacán and Tamaulipas. Emblazoned with lettering and graffiti art, it's hard to miss, and it's a good place to pick up some old-school *tortas* (sandwiches). Just down from the market is the Village Plaza, a tiny square housing, among other things, the boutique-cum-café Boutique Secretos (*see p147*).

Roma

Map p265

Metro Chapultepec L1, Insurgentes L1 or Sevilla L1/Metrobús Álvaro Obregón or Durango.

This one-time bourgeois neighbourhood, once home to wealthy immigrants from Europe, isn't quite as gentrified as adjacent Condesa, but it's well on its way and is notable for an abundance of art galleries (*see p181*) scattered among a good selection of cafés and bookshops.

The largest square in Roma Norte is the mainly residential Plaza Río de Janeiro, with lush green spaces and a playing fountain from which an oversized replica of Michelangelo's *David* rises. The buildings around the plaza serve as a quick resumé of the area's history, from colonial-style mansions, some of which never recovered after the earthquake, to both art deco and modern blocks of flats. Hit Roma at the weekend and you'll be treated to a stroll through the antique, crafts and bric-a-brac market along Álvaro Obregón, 10am to 4pm.

Casa Lamm, on the corner of Álvaro Obregón and Orizaba, is a cultural centre housed inside one of the area's fine old mansions. It hosts frequent exhibitions and has a general interest and arts bookshop on the lower floor, a library and a space for events, plus a beautiful restaurant (*see p123*).

Casa Lamm

Álvaro Obregón 99, Roma (5511 0899/www. galeriacasalamm.com.mx). Metro Insurgentes L1/ Metrobus Álvaro Obregón. **Open** 10am-6pm Tue-Sun. **Admission** free. **Map** p265 I7.

A cultural centre inside a turn-of-the-century mansion, Casa Lamm's two galleries show contemporary painting in a grand setting – so grand that it can tend to overshadow the exhibitions at times. A glassed-in restaurant annexe is a well-executed object lesson in mixing old and new architecture.

Roma.

Walk on Roma free

Start: Durango and Mazatlán
Finish: Plaza Río de Janeiro
Length: 4.6 kilometres

A good place to start any walk through Condesa and Roma is at trendy **Kurimanzutto** gallery (*see p180*) on Avenida Veracruz, at the crossing with Durango and Mazatlán. It's only three blocks from Chapultepec Metro and will give you an idea of the statelier side of Condesa's architecture, another excellent example of which is the chic **Condesa DF** hotel (*see p49*), on the intersection of Veracruz and Parque España. Pop in for a look at the inner courtyard, or head to the top floor for a cocktail or some sushi on the roof terrace.

From here, take a path through Parque España to Avenida Tamaulipas, Condesa's main hub of restaurants and bars. Check out the yellow-walled *mercado* (market) or stop for lunch at one of the many cafés with tables and chairs lining the streets. Try **La Sabia Virtud** (*see p121*).

Turn left from Tamaulipas on to Campeche and follow for three blocks before turning left again on to Saltillo. Bookworms should make a beeline for **El Péndulo** bookstore and café (*see p143*), which keeps a small selection of books in English. Cross the main road from here and continue down Ozuluama, which will spit you out at the bottom corner of Parque México. This is a great place to hang back, take a break, and weirdly, listen out for bagpipes – a local band of which practises here regularly. Make your way on to where Calle Laredo hits the park to witness the weekday morning spectacle of several dozen pedigree dogs at dog school.

After you've reoxygenated in the park, make your way east along Michoacán out of bonny Condesa and on to the concrete-and-traffic jungle of Avenida Insurgentes. Cross over and keep following Michoacán, which after a couple of blocks returns you to the relaxed atmosphere of Roma. The **Mercado Medellín** is a large, bustling food market that's well worth a stop for some fresh juice or whatever catches your eye, and then keep straight on Michoacán until you hit Calle Orizaba, where you can hang a left and take a break at **Plaza Luis Cabrera**; or halt for a drink at **Belga**, a great little beer shop on the corner of Querétaro and Orizaba that stocks all manner of unusual brews from around the world.

Walking up Orizaba, you'll see a profusion of old mansion houses, most dating from Roma's upper-middle-class heyday. Some of these have been renovated and are now either residential buildings or public buildings such as colleges and arts centres; one of the best examples is the **Casa Lamm** arts centre on the corner of Álvaro Obregón and Orizaba. Duck in for a look at the lovely courtyard or for a browse in the bookshop, **Librería Pegaso** (*see p143*). Turn right on to Álvaro Obregón here, where, at weekends, the road's central median is choc-a-block with stalls selling bric-a-brac and other quirky goods.

Continue for four blocks until you reach the **Jardín Pushkin**, also a popular market venue (weekends only), and then turn left again on to Tabasco, one of the most attractive residential streets in Roma. Follow it all the way back to Orizaba and turn right to walk another two blocks to the Plaza Río de Janeiro, where you can visit the **Galería OMR** (*see p181*) or stop in for a bite to eat at lively restaurant **El Malayo** (*see p123*), housed in a red-brick art deco building at No.5 in the square.

Sightseeing

Beyond the Centre

Religious fervour, colonial cobbles and the largest university in Latin America.

Basílica de Guadalupe

Map p258

Metro La Villa-Basílica L6/Metrobús Deportivo
18 de Marzo.

The **Basílica de Guadalupe**, in the north of the city a simple Metro or Metrobús ride from the centre, is the most important Roman Catholic site in Mexico and indeed, in the Americas. Every year on 12 December, the day of the festival of the Virgin of Guadalupe, hundreds of thousands of people make the pilgrimage to the Basílica, many travelling for hundreds of miles, some on their knees in the last part of the journey, to pay homage to the Virgin Mary, who, it is said, appeared to the farmer Juan Diego in 1531. As well as being a Catholic icon of exceptional importance, the Dark-Skinned Virgin ('La Virgen Morena') is also a symbol of Mexican Independence, since her image was on the standards carried by the rebel armies in the struggle for independence from Spain.

The site of the Basílica consists of the original 18th-century building with its baroque façade, as well as a modern, circular basilica created by Pedro Ramírez Vázquez, architect of the Estadio Azteca and the Museo Nacional de Antropología, when it was discovered, in the mid 1970s, that the older edifice was sinking.

The two basilicas stand perpendicular to each other in starkly contrasting styles, deliberately constructed close to the site of Juan Diego's vision. The house in which Juan Diego is said to have lived is still standing next to the Capilla de Indios, another, smaller chapel on the site. Close by is the dazzling **Capilla del Pocito**, another baroque structure with blue- and white-tiled domed roofs, considered to be one of the most impressive chapels in the country. It is built on the spot of the Virgin's fourth and last appearance to Juan Diego, at which time, it is said, she emblazoned the famous image of the Virgin of Guadalupe on to his cloak so that he could prove to the local bishop that he had indeed encountered the Holy Mother. The cloak is still on show inside the new basilica, where worshippers and visitors are shepherded by means of a slowly moving walkway past the ancient icon that has become Mexico's most sacred symbol.

Signs of devotion: a photo opportunity at the **Basílica de Guadalupe**.

Sightseeing

Bridging the faith gap

For those with the faith, devotion or curiosity to join the many thousands of believers (some say millions) who make the pilgrimage to the Basílica de Guadalupe every year on 12 December, there might be an unexpected addition to the proceedings.

Each year, hundreds of native Mexicans clad in brightly coloured and beaded traditional garments, with plumes of feathers exploding from headdresses crowned by human and animal skulls, congregate in the plaza in front of the Basílica. There, in their tribal groups, they perform traditional dances around images of the Virgin of Guadalupe before proceeding into the Basílica itself.

In Mexico, the indigenous people's acceptance of the conquistadores' religion was a key factor in the success of colonisation, as well in as the spread of Catholicism. Juan Diego, an indigenous farmer who was named Cuauhtlatoatzin before his conversion to Catholicism – and who was canonised in 2002 – encountered the Virgin just a decade after the arrival of the Spanish, and it is thought that Diego's vision of the Virgin as a dark-skinned *mestiza*, 'La Virgen Morena' as she is commonly called in Mexico, was a key factor in reaching out to and converting many people to Christianity during this early 'hearts and minds' period.

The plot thickens. The Basílica stands on a hill called Cerro de Tepeyac, close to the location of the Virgin's apparition to Juan Diego, which was also once the site of a popular shrine to the Aztec goddess Tonantzin. It's thought that for a long time following the introduction of Catholicism to Mexico, the two deities were somehow fused by, or for the benefit of, native religious practices.

Indeed, many historians believe the Virgin's image to be a thinly veiled portrait of Tonantzin, who is believed to have been a lunar deity as well as the mother goddess. The icon at Guadalupe, it is suggested, was intended as a syncretic symbol, bridging the gap between indigenous religious practices and those of Catholicism.

Santa Fe

Map p258

Metro Tacubaya L1, L7, L9, then minibus, taxi colectivo or RTP bus marked Santa Fe.

Barely 20 years ago, the hotbed of high-rise buildings that is Mexico City's ultra-modern business district Santa Fe, to the west of the city, was a landfill that doubled as a sand mining pit. Today, it's a strange, somewhat incongruous suburb – a business hub in a set of skyscrapers in which some 70,000 people work. The incentive to develop the area came after the devastation of the 1985 earthquake that forced a lot of businesses out of the city centre. Development was fast, with so much money initially poured in that a great deal of the space has remained unused.

No visitor to Mexico City would have reason to go to Santa Fe unless it was for work purposes, while for some business travellers to the city, shiny, glass-and-steely Santa Fe is the only glimpse they get of the city.

Somewhere between a futuristic utopia and an apocalyptic social experiment, the streets of Santa Fe are a far cry from the gritty city you see elsewhere. And despite the fact that the area is furnished with several excellent restaurants and hotels, they are still only really used by businessmen and residents, since the journey from the centre is arduous in traffic, and reaching the area by public transport is difficult.

These transport problems highlight Santa Fe's sense of isolation and its status as something of a bubble on the outskirts of the city. A visitor coming into the district will notice the shabbiness of the surrounding neighbourhoods, including the low-income *pueblo* Santa Fe right next door, which predates the urban makeover.

One of the biggest draws of the area, however, is its shopping mall, **Centro Santa Fe** (*see p141*), which is the largest in the country. It contains some 300 stores, including Mexico's Saks Fifth Avenue, and it gets thoroughly packed out at weekends.

Apart from inside the mall, there's not much need or call for strolling in Santa Fe, a district whose wide, busy roads were clearly designed for cars. If you're desperate to stretch your legs, get off the main road and head over to

Festival of the Virgin of Guadalupe: an explosion of culture and colour. *See p84.*

calle Guillermo González Camarena, which is
effectively at the heart of the neighbourhood.
This road, which runs in a one-way loop,
contains many of Santa Fe's restaurants and
hotels, and even has a green space resembling
a park on one side.

San Ángel and Coyoacán

Map p259

*Metro Coyoacán L3, Miguel Ángel de Quevedo L3 or
Viveros L3/Metrobús Altavista, Dr Gálvez, Olivo or
La Bombilla.*

Rewind 500 years to the heyday of Teotihuacán
and the arrival of the conquistadores, and
both San Ángel and Coyoacán were small
settlements on the shores of Lake Texcoco,
connected to the metropolis by man-made
causeways. As recently as 50 years ago, they
were still considered, collectively, to be a
quiet suburb outside Mexico City; but they
have since been absorbed by the relentlessly
expanding megametropolis.

But despite their hectic surroundings, the
colonial hearts of San Ángel and Coyoacán
have been well preserved, and both are
worth a visit to see their intact colonial cores,
made up of Spanish-style houses, churches,
museums and markets laid out in a labyrinth
of delightful cobbled streets and plazas.

Hernán Cortés was among the first of the
conquistadores to install himself in Coyoacán,
reputedly establishing a headquarters there
while a new capital city was being built on the
rubble of the defeated Tenochtitlán. The area is
also famed for its more recent residents, Frida
Kahlo and Diego Rivera, whose former houses
and studios have been converted into museums,
as has the home and place of assassination of
their exiled friend and colleague, Leon Trotsky.

San Ángel

At the heart of San Ángel is the Plaza San
Jacinto, which might be a quaint and peaceful
square if it didn't double as the area's most
sought-after parking lot, flanked by a couple of
restaurants and a few boutiques, that renders
itself almost unrecognisable on Saturdays when
the crowds arrive to peruse the immensely
popular **Bazar del Sábado** (*see p151*). The
17th-century building that houses the indoor
crafts market is set around a small courtyard
and café which serves a lunch buffet on market
days, and is closed during the rest of the week.

A couple of doors west of the *bazar* at No.15
in the square is the **Museo Casa del Risco**,
a small museum of European antiquities
contained within a 17th-century house. Head
west, too, from the plaza by way of *calle* Juárez
for a look at the Iglesia de San Jacinto and its

beautifully manicured courtyard, garnished with swathes of bright pink *trinitaria* – a type of pansy – cascading over the walls.

The famous twin buildings, joined by a walkway, of the the **Estudio y Casa de Diego Rivera**, lie a little way out of the centre of San Ángel, where Avenida Altavista, a smart shopping street to rival Polanco's Avenida Presidente Masaryk, crosses the *calle* Diego Rivera. The straightforward functionality of the studio befits Rivera's leftist lifestyle: his small bedroom is like an ascetic's cell, although it's difficult to imagine a man his size sleeping in such a rudimentary hospital bed as the one on display here.

Across the road from the studio is the **San Ángel Inn**, the neighbourhood's most renowned restaurant. A converted hacienda, it boasts a gorgeous colonial courtyard and is also known for its excellent margaritas (*see p125*).

Across the busy Avenida Revolución from the quieter centre of San Ángel is the **Ex-Convento y Museo del Carmen**, originally dedicated to San Ángelo Mártir, from whom the neighbourhood took its name. Be sure to see the macabre collection of mummified corpses in the crypt, which were unearthed, some say, by Zapatistas looking for treasure. A small portion of what was once a huge orchard containing around 13,000 trees, from apple and pear to Lebanese cedars, can be seen behind the monastery, as can the remains of an aqueduct that was part of an ingenious hydraulic irrigation system that drew water from the river to the trees in the orchard.

A short walk from the Convent, the Jardín de la Bombilla is a verdant neighbourhood park in which canoodling couples sit on benches circling the striking monolith of the Monumento a Álvaro Obregón. The memorial was unveiled in 1934 to commemorate the death of the former revolutionary general turned president, who had been assassinated on that very spot six years previously, while dining at the erstwhile La Bombilla restaurant. Up until the late 1980s, it was still possible to see the rather gruesome spectacle of Obregón's arm, lost in battle against Pancho Villa in 1915, suspended and preserved in a jar of formaldehyde. However, by 1989, the arm had reached such an advanced state of decay that the decision was taken to cremate the limb and inter it with the rest of his body in his home state of Sonora.

If you've still got the yen for galleries, there are a couple in San Ángel that are worth at least a brief visit. The **Museo de Arte Carrillo Gil**, located a couple of minutes' walk down the busy Avenida Revolución from the Museo del Carmen, houses a good showcase of contemporary Mexican art as well as temporary

exhibitions by groups of international artists. In the other direction along Avenida Revolución is the **Museo Soumaya**. This small modern art gallery, owned by Carlos Slim and named after his wife, is located in the Plaza de Loreto, an old paper mill that has been converted into an outdoor shopping plaza.

Ex-Convento y Museo del Carmen

Avenida Revolución 4-6, San Ángel (5616 2816/ www.museodeelcarmen.org). Metro Miguel Ángel de Quevedo L3/Metrobús Dr Gálvez. **Open** 10am 5pm Tue-Sun. **Admission** MX$25; free students; free Sundays. **Map** p259 B3.

This 17th-century former Carmelite convent is now a museum displaying a wide variety of curios, from oil paintings by colonial masters such as Cristóbal de Villalpando and Juan Correa to religious artefacts and antique furniture. The highlight of the museum is a tiled underground crypt that holds the mummified bodies of 18th-century monks, nuns and gentry.

Museo de Arte Carrillo Gil

Avenida Revolución 1608, San Ángel (5550 6260/ www.macg.gob.mx). Metrobús Altavista. **Open** 10am-6pm Tue-Sun. **Admission** MX$15; MX$9 students; free Sun. **Map** p259 B3.

Considered one of the leading collections of 20th-century Mexican art, this gallery houses a sizeable collection of works collected by Doctor Alvar Gil and his wife between the 1930s and the 1960s. Within the museum's permanent collection are 164 works by José Clemente Orozco, 47 paintings and drawings by David Alfaro Siqueiros, and a selection of cubist works by Diego Rivera. The building itself, of 1950s design, wasn't constructed until the mid 1970s, and it's notable for its functionalist simplicity in the midst of hectic Avenida Revolución.

Museo Casa del Risco

15 Plaza de San Jacinto, San Ángel (5616 2711/ www.isidrofabela.com). Metrobús Dr Gálvez. **Open** 10am-5pm Tue-Sun. **Admission** free; guided tours MX$35. **Map** p259 B3.

This private museum, founded by 20th-century politician and writer Isidro Fabela, is set around a 17th century courtyard housing an incredible fountain adorned with pieces of broken crockery. Decked

Got the Frida fever?

The first stages are unmistakeable and usually mild: you might start with a trip to the Frida Museum in Coyoacán, or to Diego Rivera's famous murals at the Palacio Nacional and the Museo Mural Diego Rivera in the Centro Histórico. But as the virus sets in and the affliction grows more intense, you may soon find yourself in the frenzied clutches of full-blown Frida-Diego fever – an obsession with the artistic couple that compels the sufferer to visit every outpost in Mexico City that bears one of their names or that has any connection at all with their convoluted biographies.

They're everywhere: in bookstores, souvenir shops, at markets, emblazoned on jewellery boxes and pendants, matchboxes and toilet roll holders. The frequency of Frida's appearance on decorative wooden crucifixes in the country just about rivals that of the Virgin of Guadalupe, and you'd be forgiven for thinking she was some kind of saint.

Although Diego Rivera was considered one of the greatest Mexican artists during his lifetime, it was not until the 1980s that Kahlo's work began to enjoy the acclaim that it does today and indeed, in some ways, to surpass that of Rivera. In the three decades of her career, Kahlo produced 200 artworks, most of which are now owned by international museums and private collections and so are hard to see here in Mexico City. However, the story of Frida and Diego's relationship is beginning to crystallise into a national myth:

the exceptionally talented star-crossed lovers whose mutual obsession transcended infidelity, sickness, divorce and remarriage.

About 240,000 visitors make the pilgrimage each year to Frida's Casa Azul in Coyoacán, and many continue on to the Estudio Diego Rivera (*pictured*), the studio in San Ángel that the artists shared for many years. Any true Frida-maniac will have watched the 1984 Mexican movie, *Frida, Naturaleza Viva*, by Felipe Cazals, and the 2002 biopic starring Selma Hayek and Alfred Molina, and will waste no time in revisiting other sites immortalised on celluloid: Trotsky's house in Coyoacán (yes, there are even pictures of them in there) and the historic site of Teotihuacán that Frida and Trotsky famously visited together.

Had enough? No? Then head further afield to the Museo Dolores Olmedo Patiño in Xochimilco (*see p94*), a quasi-shrine to the artists bequeathed by collector Dolores Olmedo Patiño, who posed for Diego on many occasions, was his patron and, it is rumoured, one of his mistresses. Her former estate is a well-enclosed diamond in the rough in the shabby outskirts of this southern suburb, and it's well worth a visit both for the extensive collection of Rivera's works – although with a profusion of flattering works of Olmedo and her grandchildren, it's perhaps not the finest collection of Rivera's works – and for the beautifully manicured gardens, wandered by peacocks and by *escuincles*, Mexico's famous hairless dogs.

out in stodgy European aristocratic style, the upstairs rooms are filled with dark religious oil paintings and portraits of European nobility.

Museo Estudio Diego Rivera

Diego Rivera 2 at Altavista, San Ángel Inn (5550 1518). Metrobús La Bombilla. **Open** 10am-6pm Tue-Sun. **Admission** MX$10; free students; free Sun. **Map** p259 A3.

Constructed by architect Juan O'Gorman in the early 1930s to provide a living and working space for Diego Rivera and Frida Kahlo, these two buildings were used as a set in the 2003 movie, *Frida*, and they are immediately recognisable from the street thanks to the innovative cactus fence that runs round the periphery. This was the place in which Diego and Frida lived from 1934 to 1940, and where Diego eventually died in 1957. It was also the place where Kahlo painted the iconic image of *The Two Fridas*, and where Diego executed many preparatory drawings for his murals. There's not much art to see as the studio is mostly filled with memorabilia and a collection of little Aztec sculptures. But look in the corner behind the door of Rivera's studio, and you'll find the small, iconic 1934 drawing of *Juanita Rosas*.

Museo Soumaya

Plaza Loreto, Avenida Revolución y Río Magdalena, San Ángel (5616 3731/www.soumaya.com.mx). Metrobús Dr Gálvez. **Open** 10.30am-6.30pm Mon, Wed Thur, Sun; 10.30am 8.30pm Fri, Sat. **Admission** MX$10 suggested donation; MX$5 students; free Mon, Sun. **Map** p259 B4.

This small gallery was opened in 1994 as a non-profit institution with the aim of collecting and preserving key artworks of Mexican and European history. The permanent collection includes works by masters such as Rodin, Brueghel, Van Dyck, Van Gogh and Picasso, as well as a selection of pieces by colonial artists such as Juan Correa and Juan Sánchez Salmerón.

Coyoacán

A good place to start any excursion into Coyoacán is from the Metro stop at Viveros, which leads directly into the **Viveros de Coyoacán** (open from 6am to 5.30pm), a park at the edge of the centre of historic Coyoacán that was set up as one of the city's first tree nurseries in 1908, thanks to the foresight of pioneering environmentalist Miguel Ángel de Quevedo. Still a functioning arboretum with a plant shop located inside, the Viveros (literally, 'breeding grounds') is also a very pleasant spot for an afternoon stroll along dusty paths shaded by the trees. Keep an eye out for skulking black squirrels and the matador training-rink at the centre of the park. Animal rights activists can rest easy: there are no live bulls here to practise on, just wheelbarrows with horns.

A short walk from the Viveros, where Avenida Universidad meets Avenida Francisco Sosa, is the stunning terracotta-coloured façade of the Iglesia de San Antonio Panzacola, a small 17th-century church perched above a littered stream that is all that is left of the Río Magdalena, provider of nourishment to the orchards during the colonial era. Legend has it that the cobblestoned bridge was the scene of a fight between the revolutionary armies of Venustiano Carranza and Pancho Villa.

If watercolours are your thing, you might want to pop into the **Museo Nacional de la Acuarela** on Calle Salvador Novo to check out its display of various aspects of watercolour painting through the ages, before continuing further along the superbly scenic Avenida Francisco Sosa towards the Jardín del Centenario. Look out for Plaza Santa Catarina along the way, a much quieter and more picturesque square than its counterparts at the centre of Coyoacán. Here, you're likely to encounter guitar players, storytellers and students sitting in front of the bright yellow Iglesia de Santa Catarina, built in stages between the 16th and 18th centuries. On the south side of the square is the Casa de la Cultura Jesús Reyes Heroles, a university arts centre set in the premises of what was originally a mill and paper factory in 1780. The gardens are dotted with sculptures that include an Aztec calendar and a bronze cast of Frida and Diego, and there's also a café in which to take a break from your wanderings.

Coyoacán is one of the city's best neighbourhoods for walking; but if you fancy taking it a bit easier, then look out for an antiquated tram, painted bright yellow and red, which does a circuit of the area between 10am and 5pm Monday to Friday, and between 11am and 6pm at weekends. It costs MX$45 for adults and MX$30 for children, and you can get more info from the tourist office at No.1 Plaza Hidalgo (5050 4027/www.transviade coyoacan.com.mx).

The bustling double-plaza of Plaza Hidalgo and Jardín Centenario, at the centre of old Coyoacán, is more often than not teeming with people, especially at weekends, when families come in their droves to buy snacks and knick-knacks from the stalls in the square, although recently the council has made moves to try to curb stallholders' activity in the area. Still, it's a prime spot for people-watching, and there are some good cafés with outdoor seating around the leafy Jardín Centenario. Look out for the famous 'chewing-gum tree' to one side of the gardens – a tree whose trunk is studded with colourful bits of chewed gum. To the south-east of the Plaza Hidalgo is the Parroquia y

Ex-Convento de San Juan Bautista, one of the first churches to be built in Mexico after the Spanish conquest. Constructed by Dominican monks at the end of the 16th century, the sculpted stonework of the baroque exterior is still in its original form.

Down Calle de la Higuera, which leads west from the Plaza Hidalgo, is the gorgeous, leafy Plaza de la Conchita, fronted by the charmingly archaic **Capilla de la Purísima Concepción**. Constructed in 1521, it's thought to be the first church building erected in the city – a designation that makes itself evident in every worn groove of the Moorish-style carvings that adorn the centre strip of the building's exterior. Cross the road at Calle Fernández Leal and you'll come to the Jardín de Frida Kahlo, a small park dedicated to the artist that houses a statue of her wearing a dress typical of the Oaxacan town of Tehuantepec.

You'll find the Mercado de Coyoacán on the way from Plaza Hidalgo to the Museo Frida Kahlo. It's open Monday to Saturday from 8am to 6pm, and is an excellent place to swing by, whether you're drawn by its enormous selection of colourful fruit and veg, the art and crafts section towards the back, or the profusion of *tostada* stalls scattered around the centre that serve up tasty tortillas with a variety of ingredients that you can custom build. There are also a number of vendors offering fresh fruit juices made with everything from oranges to watermelons, bringing the number of stalls up to a massive 464.

Given the contagiousness of the Frida-mania that pervades Mexico City (*see p88* **Got the Frida fever**), especially here on the painter's home turf of Coyoacán, a trip to the Museo Frida Kahlo at the **Casa Azul**, Frida's family home and studio on the corner of Londres and Allende, is definitely in order. Within its famous cobalt blue walls, the museum contains some of Kahlo's works and much in the way of memorabilia from her life. Her decorated plaster back support and the paintings of dead babies on the headboard of her bed, symbols of her miscarriages, are visceral reminders of the physical difficulties with which she struggled.

Five blocks away is a homage to another of Coyoacán's notorious residents, the **Museo León Trotsky**. When Trotsky and his wife, Natalia Sedova, arrived in Mexico in 1937 on the umpteenth leg of their exile, they were greeted and taken in by Diego Rivera and Frida Kahlo, and indeed, stayed in Frida's Casa Azul until an affair between Kahlo and Trotsky made things a little awkward, and the Trotskys again moved out and down the road to Avenida Río Churubusco.

A bit further afield in Coyoacán is the neighbourhood of Churubusco, the site of a famous battle in August 1847 between an 8,000-strong American invading force and the 800 defending Mexican fighters under the command of Generals Manuel Rincón and Pedro María Anaya, who used the convent at Churubusco as their fortress during the campaign. The story goes that the defenders resisted until they ran out of ammunition. Among them were the remaining Irish combatants who had deserted the US Army to join the Mexican side to form the Saint Patrick's Battallion, who were captured and hanged. A commemorative statue of General Anaya stands in the centre of the fragrant park crammed with western red cedar trees next to the convent. The Ex-Convento de Churubusco is in excellent condition and has, ironically, been converted into the **Museo de las Intervenciones**, dedicated to showcasing the numerous invasions of Mexico by foreign powers since the first Spanish incursions.

There are a number of sites around Coyoacán related to the conquistador Hernán Cortés, though many people dispute the historical accuracy of reports and the extent to which the original 16th-century buildings are still intact. In 1521, after the fall of Tenochtitlán, Cortés chose to build his temporary headquarters in Coyoacán, which at the time was connected to the city via a causeway that spanned Lake Texcoco. He established a residence in a

Leon Trotsky's grave, Coyoacán.

The city's first church, the **Capilla de la Purísima Concepción**, Plaza Conchita.

building on the north side of Plaza Hidalgo, the Casa Cortés, which is now the Casa Municipal, a complex of government offices. Legend has it that it was around this site in Coyoacán that the Aztec prince and emperor Cuauhtémoc was tortured at the hands of gold-hungry Spanish troops, and there's a chapel inside the Casa Municipal with murals by Diego Rosales that depict Cuauhtémoc's torture.

One of the most infamous sites in the neighbourhood is the Casa Colorada, otherwise known as the Casa de la Malinche, at Higuera 57. The house was inhabited 500 years ago by the infamous Doña Marina, or La Malinche, who was Cortés's indigenous interpreter, mistress and mother of one of his children. La Malinche inspires mixed feelings among historians and Mexicans in general, who are split between seeing her as a traitor to her people or as a saviour of the Aztec culture and language. The plot is as thick as blood, however, since Cortés's wife was found strangled in the same house, a crime for which Cortés himself was accused and tried, though the results of the trial were kept secret and the question of the conquistador's guilt never settled. You can only see this scandalous hotbed of a house from the outside, as it is currently inhabited by an artist couple.

Cortés's principal officer during the first occupation of Tenochtitlán, Pedro de Alvarado, is also reputed to have built a house in Coyoacán, an updated version of which can be seen at Casa de Alvarado at Avenida Francisco Sosa 383 (**Map** *p259 E3*). Alvarado cuts a dark figure in Mexican history thanks to his commanding role in the notorious massacre at the main temple in Tenochtitlán. The

two-storey house attributed to him is itself an impressive example of Andalucian country estates and houses of the era.

Casa y Museo León Trotsky
Avenida Río Churubusco 410, El Carmen (5554 0687/http://museocasadeleontrotsky.blogspot.com) Metro Coyoacán L3. **Open** 10am-5pm Tue-Sat. **Admission** MX$35; MX$20 students. **Map** p259 F1.
The house that was Trotsky's Mexican refuge, which became a mini-fortress after several attempts on his life, is still standing more or less as he left it following his abrupt assassination by ice pick in his study in August 1940. Windows were bricked up and the doors reinforced following a raid by armed gunmen months earlier that left gaping bullet holes in the masonry in Leon and Natasha's bedroom. The house is a fascinating insight into the final years of one of the 20th century's most important revolutionaries, whose ashes, along with those of his wife, are buried under a stone memorial in the garden under the Communist flag.

Museo Frida Kahlo
Londres 247, Del Carmen (5554 5999/www. museofridakahlo.org). Metro Coyoacán L3. **Open** 10am-5.45pm Tue-Sun. **Admission** MX$45; MX$20 students; free under-6s. **Map** p259 F2.
This is the house in which Frida Kahlo was born in 1907, grew up with her family, and lived with husband Diego Rivera in the later years of their marriage. The outer walls of the building are an unmistakeable cobalt blue, while the interior courtyard and rooms are equally bright, their sunniness offset by the artefacts that are dark reminders of Frida's incessant pain. There are historical tidbits and personal relics aplenty in the form of Frida and Diego's photographs, books, sketches and Marxist memorabilia. Artworks are otherwise thin on the ground in this mainly nostalgic monument to Mexico's most famous artist, although there is a

The Biblioteca Central at **UNAM**.

wonderful set of *ex-voto* paintings from Kahlo's personal collection. (*See p183* **Painted prayers**.)

Museo de las Intervenciones

Esquina Calle 20 de Agosto y General Anaya, San Diego Churubusco (5604 0981/www.inah.gob.mx). Metro General Anaya L2. **Open** 9am-6pm Tue-Sun. **Admission** MX$37; free students and under-13s; free Sun.

This museum chronicles the invasions by various foreign forces into Mexico during the post-Columbian era, set alongside old monastic artefacts from the days when the building at Churubusco was a monastery. The crooked walls and undulating floors of the convent form the backdrop to souvenirs from numerous military campaigns and events, including the plaster-cast death mask of the ill-fated Hapsburg emperor Maximilian.

Museo Nacional de la Acuarela

Salvador Novo 88, Coyoacán (5554 1801). Metro Miquel Ángel de Quevedo L3 or Viveros L3. **Open** 11am-6pm Tue-Sun. **Admission** free. **Map** p259 D3.

Set in a two-storey house with beautifully kept gardens, the gallery is dedicated to the history and development of watercolour painting and technique going as far back as the Aztecs. There's an additional space in an adjacent building that showcases exhibitions of contemporary watercolour artists.

UNAM

Map p258

Metro Universidad L3/Metrobús Ciudad Universitaria. A bit of a schlep from the city centre, although not far from Coyoacán and San Ángel, is the campus of UNAM, the Universidad Nacional Autónoma de México. The largest university in Latin America, it's home to some striking art and architecture and to more than 280,000 students

and 33,000 members of staff. It moved here, to the area around Avenida Insurgentes, in the 1950s after a long stint in the Centro Histórico, where it still retains some premises.

The campus is huge – about 1,800 acres – so it's a good idea to either come with your own transport or make judicious use of the university-run minibuses that bolt between the various faculties, also passing the Universidad Metro stop.

If you're approaching from Insurgentes, you can't miss the massive stadium built for the 1968 Olympics, which features a relief mural by Diego Rivera emblazoned over the front entrance. Across Insurgentes from the stadium is the Ciudad Universitaria, the heart of the campus, which includes a rectory tower adorned with paintings by fellow muralist David Alfaro Siqueiros, and the singular Biblioteca Central, whose exterior is completely covered by a stunning mosaic by Juan O'Gorman depicting Mexico's scientific and cultural history.

Just a short drive from the Ciudad Universitaria is the Jardín Botánico, a pleasant reserve arranged into a variety of themed areas, from a cactus garden to a section for medicinal plants, an arboretum and a little café and shop.

Well worth a look and possibly the most impressive part of the campus is the extraordinary Espacio Escultórico – a massive landscape sculpture installation consisting of 64 giant concrete triangles circling a rocky bed of solidified lava. It's a wonderfully atmospheric and tranquil place to visit – that is, if you don't mind tripping over the scores of students who escape to its peaceful surrounds for a sly smoke or a long, sustained snog.

MUCA Museo Universitario de Ciencas y Arte

Costado Sur Torre de Rectoria, Ciudad Universitaria (5622 0305/guided tours 5622 0273/www.muca. unam.mx). Metro Copilco L3/Metrobús Ciudad Universitaria. **Open** 10am-6pm Tue-Sun. **Admission** free.

The university's on-campus museum, reserved for shows in art and science, has a well-earned reputation for it excellent contemporary art exhibitions. Attention, nevertheless, is bound to be taken away from this tiny exhibition space in early 2009 with the opening of the giant MUAC, the Museo Universitario de Arte Contemporáneo, which will also be housed on the university campus and is set to become the city's largest contemporary art space.

Xochimilco

Map p258

Metro Tasqueña L2, then tren ligero to Xochimilco.

Named Xochimilco (pronounced so-chee-MIL-ko), meaning 'garden of flowers', by the Aztecs, this neighbourhood 20 kilometres south of the centre of the city was once the agricultural heartland of Tenochtitlán. Right on the edge of Lake Texcoco, its shallow waters and naturally nutrient-rich mud were fertile ground for raising crops. Farming advances transformed the shores of the lake into a series of canals around thousands of acres of specially raised fields called *chinampas*, also sometimes (misleadingly) called 'floating gardens', which were capable of providing for most of the population of Tenochtitlán.

Go to Xochimilco during the weekend and you'll think you've gatecrashed a fiesta, since the area has become a leisure hotspot for *chilangos,* who come here in droves to hire one of the many *trajineras* – long, wooden, brightly coloured canal boats – and be punted, by gondolier-like punters, around a network of canals that stretches for some 180 kilometres.

The boats can seat anything from a pair of honeymooners to an extended family of 20. Official price lists are posted on the dock at the *embarcaderos*, the embarkation landings – expect to pay somewhere in the region of MX$15 per hour, per person

In addition to the passenger boats, there's also a fleet of vessels selling food, cold drinks, and transporting mariachi bands from boat to boat, ready to come aboard and play at your behest. If you were thinking of a quieter, more romantic spin around the canals, then your best bet is definitely to aim for a weekday.

To get there from the city centre, take the number 2 Metro line to Tasqueña and change for the *tren ligero* (light train) to Xochimilco, the last stop. From there, several *embarcaderos* are within walking distance, the most popular being San Cristóbal and Saltire. Declared a UNESCO World Heritage Site in 1984, Xochimilco, a bit shabby and run down, may not quite be the 'Venice of Mexico', as the official promotional material claims; but it's a nice day out with a difference for those with more than a couple of days to spend in the city.

Finally, if your hunger for the art of Diego Rivera and Frida Kahlo hasn't yet abated, then the Museo Dolores Olmedo Patiño two stops from Xochimilco is another chance to drink in the works of the maestros. But be warned: if this is your first viewing of Rivera's works, you may feel justifiably underwhelmed. To do his *oeuvre* justice, be sure to also visit some of his magnificent murals.

Gondoliers ply the waterways of **Xochimilco** in colourful *trajinera* boats.

Museo Dolores Olmedo Patiño

*Avenida México 5843, La Noria (5555 1221/
www.museodoloresolmedo.org.mx). Metro Tasqueña
L2, then tren ligero to La Noria.* **Open** 10am-6pm
Tue-Sun. **Admission** MX$45; MX$20 students; free
under-6s. Free Tue.

This storybook hacienda, the Finca Noria, sheltered
by high walls from the shabby surroundings of its
neighbourhood in Xochimilco, houses a large collection of works by Diego Rivera that are part of a private collection bequeathed by his friend and
one-time model, Dolores Olmedo Patiño. Among the
137 works on display by Rivera, which span his
entire career, are portraits of Olmedo as well as a
small nude drawing of Frida Kahlo, several of whose
works are also featured in the museum. The Kahlo
pieces are often loaned out, so it's down to the luck
of the draw as to which you'll see.

Tlalpan

Map p258

*Metro Tasqueña L2, then tren ligero to Estadio Azteca
and pesero minibus to Centro de Tlalpan.*

A suburb of Mexico City just south of the
UNAM complex, Tlalpan is a quiet, quaint
neighbourhood with all the colonial charm of its
more central cousins San Ángel and Coyoacán,
but with less of the crowds, touts and taco
stands. Situated along the road to Cuernavaca
and Tepoztlán, it's some way from the city
centre, and a trip there and back warrants
setting aside the best part of a day. However,
if you're not short of time and feel like an
undemanding excursion, the journey is worth
it to experience an old neighbourhood that's
less frequented by tourists than San Ángel and
Coyoacán, though by the same token, there's
less to do there. But the cobbled streets of
Tlalpan, which served as the district capital
from 1827 to 1830, are perfect strolling grounds,
lined as they are with large houses, trees and
bougainvillea. All footpaths ultimately lead to
the central plaza, which is for the most part
occupied by the offices of the municipal district,
the façade of which forms the background for
some lively, historically themed murals.

Surrounded by cafés to the north side, with a
busting indoor market (El Mercado de la Paz)
on the south side of the square, the centre of
Tlalpan is in fact a lively place to be. During
weekday lunchtimes, the plaza is overrun by
mobs of schoolchildren and students grabbing
a bite to eat, businessmen having their shoes
shined, and nuns in wimples going about their
morally edifying errands. On weekends, finding
a parking space or an empty table in the cafés
resembles an Olympic challenge, but it's fun all
the same, thanks to comedy and music shows in
the plaza and a generally festive atmosphere.

To the east of the plaza is the wrought-iron
gateway of the church of San Agustín de las
Cuevas. Pass through an attractive garden to
reach its terracotta façade, built by Franciscan
monks in 1647, and see if you can also enter
the small cloisters to the right of the church.

Other points of interest in Tlalpan are the
Museo de Historia de Tlalpan (Plaza de
la Constitución 10, 5485 9048, closed Mon), a
showcase of the area's history housed inside
an old house known as La Casona, as well as
the small art gallery at **Casa de Cultura de
la UAEM** (Trionfu de la Libertad 9, 5513 5802,
closed Sat & Sun) run by the Universidad
Autónoma del Estado de México and featuring
group and student shows.

Los Portales de Tlalpan.

Day Trips

Volcanoes, art galleries, and an archaeological site that everyone digs.

Teotihuacán. The Pyramid of the Sun, seen from the Pyramid of the Moon.

Teotihuacán

Looking up at the astonishing bulk of the 65-metre- (213-foot) high Pirámide del Sol (Pyramid of the Sun) today, you might wonder how Hernán Cortés and his men rode so nonchalantly past this stunning archaeological megalith in 1520, believing it to be a mere grassy mound. But amazingly enough, excavation didn't begin on Teotihuacán, a spectacular site that dates back more than 2,000 years, until the mid 1900s.

Some 50 kilometres (31 miles) north-east of Mexico City, Teotihuacán, a must-see for visitors, features two superbly restored pyramids as well as a palace housing a number of murals and sculptures that are in surprisingly good condition. The area covered by the current site is barely a fraction of the 20 square kilometres the city spanned in its heyday between 150 and 450AD, when it is thought to have been home to 125,000 people and possibly considerably more, making it larger than any city in Europe at the time, bar Rome.

Not a great deal is known about the city or the culture that built it: the name Teotihuacán, meaning 'the place where men become gods', was given to the city by the Aztecs many years after its collapse. The abundance of temple structures suggests that it might have been a religious centre, and indeed, the bodies of sacrifice victims have been found during recent digs. Teotihuacán's influence extended to almost every culture in the rest of Mesoamerica as far south as Honduras and, to the north, beyond the region: its gods, ceramics and sculptures were highly regarded in the Colorado plateau, in today's USA, by the Anasazi (Pueblo) and the Mogollon peoples.

Teotihuacán is thought to have been deserted by around 650AD, though the exact cause of its demise remains a mystery. There is evidence of fire around the temple and palace buildings, which points, perhaps, towards either a siege by invading forces or an internal uprising. A major drought in the area around the time of its decline provides another possible clue, in combination with a number of malnourished bodies that have been exhumed from the site, as to why people might have abandoned the city so suddenly.

The giant **Pyramid of the Sun**, the third largest pyramidal structure in the world, is undoubtedly Teotihuacán's highlight, and if you've managed to adapt to the thin air at this

Pulp art

In the gritty industrial town of Ecatepec, half an hour north of Mexico City and halfway to the sun and moon pyramids of Teotihuacán, amid pulping and pasteurising vats and fruit-filled trucks delivering crates of mango, pear and guayaba, lies another only-in-Mexico experience: Latin America's biggest private art collection, housed in the heart of a fruit-juice factory.

Set amid the giant Jumex factory grounds, in a white cube warehouse with a rainbow-coloured sign on the roof reading, 'Love Invents Us', La Colección Jumex is the pet project of juice heir and thirtysomething international playboy Eugenio López, who has invested millions of the

family fortune in assembling more than 18,000 pieces of contemporary art. Open to the public since 2001, the gallery features works by big-name international art stars such as Marcel Duchamp, Jasper Johns, Damien Hirst, Jeff Koons and Tracy Emin alongside Latin American and Mexican artists, including Gabriel Orozco and Minerva Cuevas. In doing so, the collection shifts the traditional focus of Mexican art from last century's muralists to a more contemporary scene. The gallery also recently purchased a set of prints from nightlife photoblogger Domestic Fine Arts.

Works like Mexican artist Abraham Cruzvillegas' tennis-racquet-and-wooden-box construction are shown alongside Jeff Koons's basketballs floating in a fish aquarium – a juxtaposition whose effect is to bring diverse artists into the same arena, putting Mexicans on a par with their foreign counterparts and creating a dynamic that's as playful as it is internationalist. Adding to the mix, guest curators are brought in from around the world, including a recent exhibition of works from the collection curated by Jessica Morgan of London's Tate Modern.

It's a bit of a schlep to get to Jumex, which might recommend it to die-hard art lovers only. But even for those only casually interested in contemporary art, it's well worth the effort, if only to savour the experience of viewing world-class works inside one of Mexico's most iconic factories.

A taxi from the city centre will set you back around MX$200, plus anywhere upwards of half an hour's travel time. Go in the middle of the day to avoid Mexico City's crushing rush hour, which can add several painful hours to the journey. The independent, adventurous or simply strapped for cash can take the Metro to Indios Verdes and then a Route 30 bus heading for San Cristóbal por abajo. Ask to be let off at La Costeña, the canned food factory right next door to the Jumex complex.

The extensive art library is open all year round to researchers and students, with gallery visits limited to exhibitions – two per year on average – that draw on works from the permanent collection. Entry is free, but only by appointment (phone or email).

Fundación/Colección Jumex
Vía Morelos 272, Santa María Tulpetlac. (5775 8188/www.lacoleccionjumex.org). **Open** 10am-5pm Mon-Fri.

altitude, the climb to join the matchstick-men tourists at the top, as seen from across the site, is not nearly as daunting as it first appears. The pyramid has never been fully excavated, and with the exception of a handful of chambers and a couple of tunnels discovered underneath it, no one knows for sure what, if anything, might be lurking on the inside.

The **Calzada de los Muertos** (Avenue of the Dead), an immense causeway that runs the two-kilometre length of the site, was given its macabre name by the Aztecs, long after the city's decline, although the 'tombs' they thought lined the avenue are in fact merely ceremonial platforms. At one end of it, the **Pirámide de la Luna** (Pyramid of the Moon) is slightly smaller than that of the sun and thus it's a shorter climb to the top, albeit a little more demanding thanks to the steepness of its steps. The view of the complex from the top is unmissable. Descending the steep, narrow steps of the pyramids can feel a little alarming, so it's best to take a more zigzagging route down, pausing occasionally to admire the view as you catch your breath.

Also worth seeing are the **Complejo del Palacio de Quetzalpapálotl** (Quetzalpapálotl Palace Complex) and the stunning **Templo de Quetzalcóatl**. The former is situated near the Pyramid of the Moon and contains some well-preserved murals and sculptures, while the Temple of Quetzalcóatl, aka the Templo de la Serpiente Emplumada (Temple of the Feathered Serpent), is at the opposite side of the Avenue of the Dead. This area is known as the Ciudadela (Citadel), and was thought to have been the spiritual and political centre of the city, and home to members of its elite classes. A handy café-bar back at the entrance makes a nice spot to quench your thirst with something cold and take one last look, through the café's large windows, at the ancient city.

Getting there

Buses run to 'Las Pirámides' (don't ask for Teotihuacán, as you will end up at the nearby town of San Juan Teotihuacán) from Mexico City's Central de Autobuses del Norte terminal every 15 minutes. Alternatively, you could make a deal with a cab driver for the journey. The usual fare for a return journey and a two- to three-hour wait is around MX$750. Try to get there early, since midday sun, a lack of shade and large crowds can combine to make the staggering experience almost dizzying, and don't forget water, sun cream and a hat, though there are plenty of vendors at the entrance to the site who will gladly supply you with a MX$10 *sombrero*.

Tepoztlán

A 90-minute, white-knuckle drive ride through the Alpine-like landscape and plunging ravines to the south of Mexico City is the small town of Tepoztlán, birthplace of the Mesoamerican feathered serpent deity Quetzalcóatl, according to legend. It's set at the bottom of a sheer and dramatic cliff face at the top of which sits the ten-metre-high **Pirámide del Tepozteco**, dedicated to the Aztec god of plenty Ometochtli, a bacchanalian character with an interesting sideline as chief of the 400 rabbit gods of drunkenness. His tipple of preference was *pulque*, and if you should make it to Tepoztlán for the night of 7 September, be prepared to put down some serious amounts of this agave-extract drink during the course of the annual celebrations. If you're hoping to summon all 400 rabbits, though, you'll need to drink quite a lot of it – it's not high in alcohol content.

The pyramid can only be accessed by foot, and it's a 2.5-kilometre hike from the city centre, so wear good shoes and take an anorak if it's the rainy season. It's a trek, there's no doubt about it; but the stunning views from the summit will be ample reward for your exertions. The pyramid itself is accessible each day between 9am and 5.30pm.

Like nearby Cuernavaca – another lovely sidetrip from DF, though one perhaps best enjoyed by those lucky enough to have been invited to a weekend house party – Tepoztlán is popular with weekenders from Mexico City and also attracts a regular influx of hippie travellers, hence the cluster of new age shops and reiki centres on the main street. The town was also made famous by UFO enthusiast and 'alien abductee' Carlos Diaz, who famously reported and filmed many 'alien encounters' in the area during the 1980s and 1990s – so keep your eyes peeled for glowing plasma discs, and try to avoid beckoning invitations from glaze-eyed, glowing humanoids.

The centre of Tepoztlán is small and easily traversable on foot. Avenida 5 de Mayo is the road that cuts into the centre of town and turns into Avenida Tepozteco once it crosses the Zócalo. Right next to the main square is a colourful market that houses everything from taco stands to handicrafts vendors, and directly behind that lies the arched entrance to the imposing walled compound of the **Ex-Convento Dominico de la Natividad** (closed Mondays). Dominican priests built this 16th-century church and monastery, and its interior features a set of well-preserved murals as well as some wonderful views over the surrounding verdant landscape.

Around the back of the church, off *calle* Arq Pablo González, is the **Museo Arqueológico Carlos Pellicer** (closed Mondays). This small but varied compendium of pre-Columbian artefacts formed the private collection of Tabascan poet Carlos Pellicer, and provides a very compact run through Mexican pre-history.

If you haven't already done so elsewhere, be sure to sample some home-made ice-cream from the branch of Tepoznieves here, one of a famous group of parlours that boast hundreds of quirky flavours including shrimp; or treat yourself to a meal at the upmarket El Ciruelo restaurant on *calle* Zaragoza, where the garden affords magnificent views of the cliffs facing the town.

Getting there

Buses run to Tepoztlán from the Central de Autobuses del Sur (Metro Taxqueña), in the south of Mexico City every 40 minutes or so. Otherwise, it's a winding 80-kilometre (50-mile) drive along the autopista México-Cuernavaca. Follow the Cuautla-Tepoztlán detour.

Popocatépetl & Ixtaccíhuatl

Popocatépetl, named the 'smoking mountain' by the Aztecs, is an active volcano 5,420 metres (17,782 feet) above sea level, about 50 kilometres (31 miles) east of Mexico City. If the weather's right, it's a truly remarkable sight: a snow-capped triangular mass rising from the ground with billowing white clouds pumping out from its crater. On flights south to Chiapas or Oaxaca, you may well see the white peak popping above the clouds like an iceberg – a beautiful and rather intimidating sight.

Right beside Popocatépetl is its twin peak, Iztaccíhuatl, at 5,230 metres (17,158 feet) – a popular destination for climbers. If you look at it from the west, you'll notice its four peaks which, together, resemble the form of a sleeping woman, hence its nickname '*La Mujer Dormida*'.

The legend behind the two mountains is a tragic love story of Shakespearean proportions: Iztaccíhuatl (from the Náhuatl *iztac*, meaning 'white', and *cíhuatl*, 'woman') was a princess who fell in love with one of her father's soldiers, Popocatépetl (from the Náhuatl *popoca*, meaning smoking, and *tépetl*, mountain). Popocatépetl was sent to war in Oaxaca and while he was away, the princess was told that he had been killed. Naturally, she died of grief, and when Popocatépetl returned from fighting to find her dead, he also died of a broken heart. Another version of the story goes that they belonged to warring enemy tribes, and that he unwittingly shot her through the heart with an arrow. In both stories, she lies on the ground while the warrior kneels before her in eternal grief, and so the dust of the centuries fell on them. Look from the east and you will possibly see what the ancients saw: Iztaccíhuatl as the figure of a sleeping lady, and Popocatépetl as a bent warrior.

Getting there

Given an early start, a trip to Popocatépetl and Iztaccíhuatl is a viable day trip from Mexico City. Take a bus to the nearby town of Amecameca, stopping for a look round the local market if the fancy takes you, and then catch a minibus from the main plaza; the fare is around MX$4. It's about half an hour's drive through the fir-tree forests along the Paso de Cortés that cuts between the two mountains, which continues as a dirt track down the other side to Cholula and Puebla.

There's a saddle between the peaks that serves as a base camp for hikers, with a modest snack shop and toilets. From here, there's a fantastic close-up view of the volcano (that is, on a cloudless day), as well as a seven-kilometre road that leads further up Ixtaccíhuatl.

It's not currently possible to scale Popocatépetl, and when you see the fumes belching from its innards, you'll know why.

Popocatépetl.

Eat, Drink, Shop

Restaurants

From pre-Hispanic delicacies to molecular gastronomy, DF has the works.

Sanborns. *See p105*.

Complex, colourful and with an extraordinary variety of dishes and ingredients, Mexican cuisine's standard and range puts most other national culinary traditions in the shade. Tacos are a national obsession and you shouldn't leave Mexico City without sampling some, whether you stick to the classic *taco al pastor* made with marinated, spit-roasted pork; delectable lunchtime shrimp and fish tacos; or stride boldly into the realms of cow's head tacos (*tacos de cabeza*) – worth a try, crowned with chopped onion, cilantro and a dash of spicy sauce. Busy taco stands in well-frequented spots are a good bet for street food; but for guaranteed taco heaven, try **El Huequito** (*see p103*), **El Farolito** (*see p115*), **El Califa** (*see p121*) or **Supertacos Chupacabras** (*see p127*).

Or push the boat out and head for the other shore of gastronomic DF. Treating yourself to

a multi-course tasting menu at **Jaso**, **Biko** (for both *see p114*) or **Pujol** (*see p115*) is worth serious consideration, with or without wine-pairing to match. It isn't cheap, but neither will it set you back much beyond the price of a good curry in London or a great sushi dinner in New York; and make no mistake: this is highly accomplished, inventive cuisine, cooked by world-class chefs with the CVs to prove it.

If you should you find yourself dining in a surprisingly solitary style of an evening, wondering where everyone else is, note that lunch is king in DF, and it tends to be long and leisurely. For best results from the city's restaurants it makes sense to follow suit, dining royally at lunchtime and settling for a snack in the evening. Like any cosmopolitan city of its size, DF has a full complement of restaurants serving food from all over the world, and you'll find our pick of these in the pages that follow. In general, though, DF does Mexican food best of all, and that includes food from across the country. Try **Coox Hanal** (*see p102*) or **Xel-Ha** (*see p121*) for a taste of the Yucatan, and **La Bella Lula** (*see p106*) for Oaxacan specialities.

It's always worth calling ahead if you plan to go out of your way to reach a restaurant. They open and close frequently and even the finest of places can find itself *clausurado* – shut down – from one moment to the next. Aguila y Sol, one of the city's most cherished gourmet restaurants, was *clausurado* at the time of writing, with little apparent prospect of its reopening.

Centro

Chinese

Hong King
Donceles 25A (5521 5631/5512 6703). Metro Bellas Artes L2, L8 or Juárez L3. **Open** 10am-10.30pm daily. **Main courses** MX$60-$280. **Credit** MC, V. **Map** p267 L4 ❶
Pick an upstairs seat at this decent restaurant in Mexico City's compact Chinatown, and as you sip the hot jasmine tea that greets each new arrival you can enjoy a bird's nest view of the bustling market below. Or at night, watch Chinese lanterns tremble in the breeze as they light up the street. A good range of set menus is outshone by the ever popular Peking duck à la carte – possibly because Mexicans love to make tacos out of anything.

Italian

Cozzaglia
Rosales 6, Local 11 (5512 0211/www.cozzaglia mexico.spaces.live.com). Metro Hidalgo L2, L3. **Open** 11am-7pm Mon-Sat. **Main courses** MX$65-$140. **Credit** MC, V. **Map** p266 J3 ❷
Hidden behind Reforma's enormous yellow Caballito statue, Cozzaglia is run by three Mexican brothers who learned their trade working for Italians in San Francisco. Murals of the Tower of Pisa and the Golden Gate Bridge overlook diners feasting on food 100 per cent *hecho en casa* (home-made), from the bread to the pasta, proving you don't have to be Italian to cook Italian. Try the chocolate pasta served with a hunk of seared beef, or the seafood risotto, black with squid ink. Finish with Gelato Bereccino – a dollop of vanilla ice-cream topped with a crunchy cone, surrounded by sweet stewed apples.

Trevi Café & Restaurant
Colón 1 (5512 3020). Metro Hidalgo L2, L3. **Open** 8am-11pm daily. **Main courses** MX$40-$70. **No credit cards. Map** p266 K4 ❸
A stone's throw from the Diego Rivera Museum (*see p89*) in the Alameda gardens, jolly, neon-bright

For food with a view
Casa de las Sirenas (*see p102*); **Majestic** (*see p103*); **Plaza Mayor** (*see p103*); **Los Danzantes** (*see p124*).

For oceanic fare
Contramar (*see p124*); **El Jardín del Pulpo** (*see p127*); **La Ostra** (*see p123*); **Segundo Muelle** (*see p119*); **L'Olivier** (*see p112*).

For a veggie oasis
King Falafel (*see p109*); **El Vegetariano del Centro** (*see p105*); **Yug** (*see p109*).

For beautiful surroundings
Ivoire (*see p112*); **Sanbornes** (*see p105*); **El Lago** (*see p119*).

For ancient flavours
El Cardenal (*see p102*); **Don Chon** (*see p102*); **Coox Hanal** (*see p102*).

For a taco hiatus
Al Andaluz (*see p105*); **Ham Ji Bak** (*see p109*); **Hong King** (*see p101*); **Adonis** (*see p115*).

Trevi is an excellent place to stop for lunch while touring the city. Served by aged waiters providing the kind of service that comes with a lifetime in the trade, the menu's Mexican staples and pasta dishes are excellent – but the star of the show is the juicy *pechuga de pollo a la parmesana*, served with tiny ravioli in a meat sauce. *Photo p103.*

Mexican

Café La Blanca
5 de Mayo 40 (5510 0399/5510 9260). Metro Allende L2. **Open** 6.30am-11pm daily. **Main courses** MX$30-$100. **Credit** MC, V. **Map** p267 M4 ❹
Marble floors and old-fashioned laminated tables give away this classic Mexican diner's age – it's been in the business for more than 80 years. Impatient diners can cut to the chase in an overwhelmingly comprehensive menu by choosing the *menu turístico*: a classic combo of soup, rice and a hearty main. The hungry go for *el plato cubano*, a dish in which black beans and rice complement a spicy *picadillo* – minced beef with tomato sauce,

❶ Purple numbers given in this chapter correspond to the location of each restaurant as marked on the street maps. *See pp259-267.*

Eat, Drink, Shop

raisins and olives – served with a fried egg and fried bananas. It's a steal at just over MX$30.

El Cardenal

Calle Palma 23 (5521 8815/5521 8816/www. restauranteelcardenal.com). Metro Zócalo L2. **Open** 8am-6.30pm daily. **Main courses** MX$120-$350. **Credit** AmEx, MC, V. **Map** p267 M4 **⑤**

One of a handful of outstanding DF restaurants that focus on refining and reviving Mexico's ancient culinary repertoire, the emphasis at El Cardenal is on fresh ingredients, with menus that vary according to the season. In September, for example, try the emblematic dish of Mexican independence, *chiles en nogada* (pork-stuffed chillies in a creamy walnut sauce); or indulge at breakfast with hot chocolate made on the premises, and exceptional home-made *pan dulce* (fruit cake). Set inside a perfectly preserved, French-inspired 19th-century townhouse, this is one of two branches, both power-lunch favourites with the city's movers and shakers. (The other branch is at the Sheraton Centro Histórico, *see p37*.)

La Casa de las Sirenas

Guatemala 32 (5704 3345/5704 3273/www. lacasadelassirenas.com.mx). Metro Zócalo L2. **Open** 11am-11pm Mon-Sat; 11am-6pm Sun. **Main courses** MX$250-$350. **Credit** AmEx, MC, V. **Map** p267 N4 **⑥**

There are several downtown roof terrace restaurants with better views, sure; but though Casa de las Sirenas looks on to the back of the cathedral rather than on to the Zócalo, it's still a spectacular sight and the best of the bunch in terms of food, if a little pricey. The shady terrace makes it just right for a long and leisurely lunch, as does the service, smart but unhurried. Equally importantly, the well-rounded selection of appetisers, soups, salads and entrées is delicately prepared and flavourful, using traditional recipes and high-quality ingredients. Unusual desserts are well worth the calories, and afternoons feature not-too-loud live music and on-terrace tortilla-making. There will be gringos among your fellow diners (menus and staff members are bilingual), but well-heeled local patrons prove this is no tourist trap.

Coox Hanal

2nd floor, Isabel la Católica 83 (5709 3613). Metro Isabel la Católica L1. **Open** 10.30am-6.30pm daily. **Main courses** MX$25-$140. **Credit** MC, V. **Map** p267 M5 **⑦**

Mexican families go crazy for the delicious offerings at Coox Hanal (pronounced 'cosh hanal'). Specialising in the cuisine of the Yucatán peninsula, it's well worth the walk five blocks south of the Zócalo, where you'll find it above a pool hall. Zingy *sopa de lima* (chicken and lemon soup) is recommended, as are a selection of taco dishes including *tacos de cochinita pibil* (slow roasted, citrus marinated pork tinted red with annatto seed). The food is a little on the oily side, but pickled slices of red onion help balance it out, while table salsas charged with the

hottest habanero chillis turn up the heat. A carnival atmosphere pervades at weekends, with performances of traditional song and dance – an unlikely cross between flamenco and Morris dancing – all day Friday to Sunday.

Don Chon

Regina 160 (5542 0873/www.restaurantechon.com). Metro Pino Suárez L1. **Open** 1-6.30pm Mon-Sat. **Main courses** MX$200-$500. **Credit** MC, V. **Map** p267 N5 **⑧**

Though it's not much to look at, Don Chon's remarkable menu of pre-Hispanic-style dishes has made it a fixture on the city's restaurant circuit. Esoteric delicacies that merge Mexico's gastronomic past and present include *tacos de escamoles a la mantequilla* (sautéed ant egg tacos), *cocodrilo en mole verde* (crocodile in green mole sauce), and the extravagantly exotic *crisantemos* (chrysanthemum flower and tuna rostis with a sweet mango salsa). Crocodile, falling somewhere between pork and turkey on the chicken-comparison index, is embellished with a delicately spiced sauce, and the protein-rich, salty ant eggs are surprisingly moreish when stuffed into a tortilla together with a generous serving of guacamole. Crispy, deep-fried *gusanos de maguey* (whole worms that live within the plant from which tequila is made), are not for the faint-hearted; and washing them down with the gelatinous 'drink of the gods', *pulque*, a gloopy pre-Colombian beverage, may or may not help. If you've had your fill of acquired tastes, Don Chon keeps a good selection of Mexican and imported wines.

Los Girasoles

Plaza Manuel Tolsá y Tacuba 8-9 (5510 0630/ 5510 3281/www.restaurantelosgirasoles.com). Metro Allende L2 or Bellas Artes L2, L8. **Open** 1pm-midnight Tue-Sat; 1-9pm Sun, Mon. **Main courses** MX$300-$400. **Credit** AmEx, MC, V. **Map** p267 L4 **⑨**

Another classic Centro restaurant serving traditional food with a touch of modern flair – and excellent fresh fruit margaritas – Los Girasoles is frequented by intellectuals and politicians alike thanks to its

DF eye

Real *chilango* food is the kind you find in the street, in the stalls on every corner where they serve tacos, tortas, quesadillas, tamales and *sopes* of every sort. Everyone who comes to Mexico City should try a tamale sandwich: it's tasty and cheap, and accompanied by a hot atole, it's a fundamental part of the diet of the city's workers.

Christian Cañibe, graphic designer, Eramos Tantos.

Trevi Café & Restaurant: great for a light lunch. *See p101.*

location opposite the Museo Nacional de Arte and next to the Senate, and a seat outside puts you in an excellent position to admire the grand surrounding architecture. For complex, intense flavours try the *mole de tamarindo con pavo* (turkey with tamarind sauce) and let its sweetness and spice play upon your palate. Or the *ensalada de arándano y mandarina* (cranberry and mandarin salad), topped off with a zesty dressing, nuts, seeds and crispy beetroot chips – a deliciously light option. The Polanco branch, inside an upmarket shopping mall at Avenida Presidente Masaryk 275, lacks the ambience of the original restaurant.

El Huequito

Bolívar 58 (5510 4199). Metro Isabel la Católica L1 or San Juan de Letrán L8. **Open** 7.30am-11pm daily. **Main courses** MX$80-$130. **Credit** AmEx, MC, V. **Map** p267 L5 ⑩
Tacos rule in Mexico City, and the corner taco stand in a sleepy tin hut is the bedrock of popular Mexican cuisine. You could spend a lifetime in search of your 'perfect' taco; but if you want an excellent taco, a gourmet taco, a taco everyone will tell you to try, just get yourself down to El Huequito. You'll want the *taco de pastor especial*, a mountain of the best pork heaped on to five or six tortillas with chopped onion and coriander, and then you'll want to lash some of the spicy special

sauces on top. El Huequito started nearly 50 years ago as a hole-in-the-wall taco stand, but has expanded into two restaurants, with the second at Pennsylvania 73 in *colonia* Nápoles.

Majestic Terrace Restaurant

7th floor, Best Western Hotel Majestic, Madero 73 (5521 8600/www.majestichotel.com.mx). Metro Zócalo L2. **Open** 7am-11pm daily. **Main courses** MX$70-$200. **Credit** AmEx, MC, V. **Map** p267 M4 ⑪
Sadly, the view from this terrace restaurant is way more majestic than the food and service, both of which disappoint in this grandiose setting. The splendid Zócalo main square spreads its expanse before diners munching on average but acceptable Mexican fare. Perhaps the management takes the unique view for granted? If you do eat there, go for the *molecajete*, a hot stone bowl filled with meats and sauce, or snack on coffee and *crêpes de cajete* (crêpes with toffee sauce). The weekend buffets are a better option than ordering from the menu – and you won't have to rely on the waiters.

Plaza Mayor

16 de Septiembre 82 (1083 7700/www.granhotel ciudaddemexico.com.mx). Metro Zócalo L2. **Open** 1-11pm Mon-Fri; 9am-6pm Sat, Sun. **Main courses** MX$180-$280. **Credit** AmEx, MC, V. **Map** p267 M4 ⑫

A good long gaze at the breathtaking stained-glass canopy over the atrium of this 19th-century building is an excellent distraction from Plaza Mayor's overall need of a makeover. Once inside the restaurant, though, the place's longevity takes on a different hue, with delicate *tostadas de jaiba* (fresh crab salad served over crispy tortillas) a delightfully old-school example of Plaza Mayor's *haute cuisine a la mexicana*. If seafood sounds good (Mexico City is renowned for it) consider ordering the generous tuna steak in rich *crema de chile poblano* with wild rice, or choose from a selection of steaks. A rich *pastel de chocolate* balanced by a strawberry coulis makes a delicious way to finish, then head out the terrace for after-dinner coffees or liqueurs while drinking in spectacular views of Mexico's historic Zócalo. Come for lunch or on Thursday or Friday nights, unless you enjoy eating in eerie quiet to the sound of the clinking of your own cutlery.

Sanborns

Casa de los Azulejos, Francisco I Madero 4 (5510 1331/www.sanborns.com.mx). Metro Bellas Artes L2. **Open** 7am-1am daily. **Main courses** MX$106-$124. **Credit** AmEx, MC, V. **Map** p267 L4 ⓮

In the heart of the historic Casa de los Azulejos, this branch of Sanborns restaurant is the original and best, in a grand setting that's slightly at odds with the menu's workaday Mexican fare. It's all for the best, since it makes lunch here a treat you can afford. Choose from classic dishes like stuffed chillies, enchiladas or *molletes* – or come for breakfast before you hit the sightseeing trail – and then settle down to take in the scenery. There are soaring ceilings and exquisite architectural details wherever you look, from elegant columns and an intricately beautiful upstairs gallery to the huge mural on one wall – and another, by the famous artist José Clemente Orozco, on the staircase to the first floor. In case you should find yourself feeling delicate in the stomach department – it can happen – note that the chicken-and-rice consommé, here or at any branch of Sanborns, makes a spot-on meal once the storm has abated. *Photo p100.*

Middle Eastern

Al Andaluz

Mesones 171 (5522 2528). Metro Pino Suárez L1, L2. **Open** 9am-6pm daily. **Main courses** MX$150-$250. **Credit** AmEx, MC, V. **Map** p267 N5 ⓮

Al Andaluz is an oasis of calm on the busy commercial street of Mesones. Housed within a grand 17th-century former residence, this smart Middle Eastern restaurant is a superb find in Mexico City. The capital boasts a large community of Lebanese descent, but most eateries from the region have 'mexicanised' their menu to some extent (*see p117* **Mexification and Vitamin T**). Al Andaluz is not one of them. The *plato libanés*, ideal for sharing, comes with a vast selection of regional dishes including a refreshing tabouleh salad that is authentically heavy on parsley and lime juice. Vegetarians can sample a range

of aubergine dishes and a perfectly balanced *garbanza molida* (houmous). Finish off with baklava and a pot of smooth but potent Lebanese coffee, either *amargo* – literally 'bitter', but in this context meaning simply unsweetened – or *dulce*, with sugar. Ask for a table on the balcony overlooking the verdant courtyard and linger over a hookah pipe filled with vanilla, cherry or apple-flavoured tobacco.

Seafood

Danubio

Uruguay 3 (5512 0912/5512 0976/www.danubio.com). Metro San Juan de Letrán L8. **Open** 1-10pm daily. **Main courses** MX$100-$400. **Credit** AmEx, MC, V. **Map** p267 L5 ⓯

The walls of elegant Danubio are festooned with hand-written tributes from its famous clientele, including former presidents and celebrated writers like Carlos Fuentes and Gabriel Garcia Márquez. Excellent service and a wide selection of Spanish and Mexican wines encourage diners to linger, so much so that long boozy lunches often merge into dinnertime discussions. An Iberian aspect about the home-cooked food recalls the restaurant's Basque founders, who established the place over 70 years ago. Daily set lunch menus offer good value dining; and *langosti nos al mojo de ajo* (crawfish sautéed with garlic and dried chillies) is a signature dish. Cheese lovers should try the *róbalo a la champagne* (sea bass fillet in a creamy champagne sauce au gratin).

Spanish

Casino Español

Isabel la Católica 29 (5518 4685/5521 8894/www.casinoespanol.com.mx). Metro Allende L2 or San Juan de Letrán L8. **Open** 1-6pm Mon-Sun. **Main courses** MX$120-$300. **Credit** AmEx, MC, V. **Map** p267 M4 ⓰

On the first floor of a beautiful Spanish building, Casino Español is a magnificent, lunch-only restaurant serving impeccable traditional Spanish food. Stone columns line a huge dining hall dressed in warm, light wood and manned by white-coated, efficient waiters; and lest it sounds a little pricey, rest easy in the knowledge that everything is a cheaper than you'd expect. Start with the tortilla española and then go onto the paella valenciana; or if you're ready for a large meal, order *lechón al horno* (spit-roasted suckling pig), the house speciality.

Vegetarian

El Vegetariano del Centro

Filomeno Mata 13 (5510 0113). Metro Allende L2 or Bellas Artes L2, L8. **Open** 8am-8pm daily. **Main courses** MX$50-$80. **Credit** MC, V. **Map** p267 L4 ⓱

Don't be put off by the setting, somewhere between a canteen and a diner; just seize this rare opportunity

to sample veggie versions of traditional Mexican meals. Friendly staff offer extensive breakfast options, good-value set lunches and early dinners, with fresh juices and smoothies including hardcore healthy vegetable blends like celery and beetroot and – ahem – carrot with milk. *Tres mundos* (papaya, orange and apricot) is much more palatable and still vitamin enriched. Traditional bean-soup *frijoles charros* comes without the usual lumps of chorizo and pig-fat, and unexpectedly tasty soy-based meat substitutes mean you can try *puntas al albañil*, at other times made with thinly sliced beef, in a chipotle, *chile cuaresmo* and mushroom sauce.
Other locations upstairs at Madero 56, Centro (5521 6880); Tuxpan 24, Roma Sur (5564 7930).

Paseo de la Reforma

French

Bistrot Arlequin
Rio Nilo 42-C (5207 5616). Metro Sevilla L1. **Open** 1.30-11.30pm Mon-Sat. **Main courses** MX$100-$150. **Credit** MC, V. **Map** p264 F5 ⑱
This tiny bistro, with just eight tables, is a firm favourite with local French and British expats. The owners and most of the waiting staff are French, and they serve unpretentious, provincial French bistro cooking at its best – think lamb casserole, *tarte aux oignons* and steak-frites. Far from the madding crowd, this is an ideal place to sit and sip wine with friends – but choose carefully,

as the wine list is a bit patchy. Reservations are recommended, especially on weekend nights.

Italian

Attenti
Rio Lerma 175 (5525 9341/www.attentiresto.com). Metro Insurgentes L1. **Open** noon-11pm daily. **Main courses** MX$100-$150. **Credit** AmEx, DC, MC, V. **Map** p264 G5 ⑲
This bistro-style Italian restaurant attracts a later dinner crowd from around 10pm. An extensive menu includes a huge range of pasta, pizza, salad and antipasti dishes which vary in quality, from average to decent. The baked provolone comes recommended, though, and the salads are better than most in DF. Attenti's wine list is fairly comprehensive, but ask about their rotating wine specials, as these are often good value. Service is fast although not always as charming as it could be.

Oaxacan

La Bella Lula
Rio Lerma 86, Cuauhtemoc (5207 6356). Metro Insurgentes L1. **Open** 8am-7pm Mon-Fri; 10am-7pm Sat, Sun. **Main courses** MX$50-$100. **Credit** AmEx, MC, V. **Map** p264 G5 ⑳
This restaurant has been serving Oaxacan specialities to a Mexico City crowd since 1982, and judging by the way it packs them in at lunchtime, they're doing something right. The informal eaterie

Los Danzantes. *See p124.*

Sugar and spice

It's no surprise to find that the nation that invented chocolate has a pronounced sweet tooth. What is surprising is the huge variety of confectionery on offer. Most markets have stalls specialising in sweets, or the **Mercado de Dulces de la Ciudad de**

México, next to the Merced market in the Centro Histórico, on Avenida Circunvalación, is a great place to get an overall sampling. But more typically, home-made *dulces* are sold on the street, often at stands set up outside Metro stations or from baskets carried by roaming vendors.

A small sample of what you'll find might include: **alegría** (*right*) a pre-Columbian sweet whose name means 'joy', made from toasted amaranth seeds and honey; **pepitorias** (*top right*), pretty, fan-shaped wafers in bright colours, sandwiched together with **cajeta** (goat milk caramel) or honey, with pumpkin seeds around the edge; **palanquetas** (*below*), peanut-brittle-like candy made with brown sugar syrup and toasted nuts, sold in disks or squares; **candied fruit**, which comes in coloured, sugary lumps of mango, fig, pineapple, tuna (cactus fruit) and just about any other type of fruit you can imagine. **Cicadas** are clusters of coconut stuck together with egg and sugar; and there's **camote,** candied sweet potato, cut into bars and wrapped; **calaveritas** (*below*), sugary skulls made for the Day of the Dead celebrations; **charamusca**, caramelised sugar with peanuts or coconut; and **jamoncillo**, made from milk flavoured with fruits and cooked to a caramel-like consistency.

The Mexican appetite for strong flavours is reflected in its sweets no sooner is the young palate weaned off milk than it's on to chilli. **Miguelitos** (*far left*), sugar mixed with chilli powder, are a popular treat, as are chilli-coated lollipops, tamarind and *chamoy*-flavoured sweets (*chamoy* is a salty, spicy sauce or paste), and chilli-coated *nieve* ('snow'), which is water-based ice-cream.

For those who prefer eye candy to street candy, window shopping in the city's many *panaderías, pastelerías and bizcocherías* (bread, cake and biscuit shops), with their stacked shelves of sugar coated buns and enormous, elaborately decorated cream cakes, may be enough to send your insulin levels soaring. Visit **Pastelería Ideal** (*see p149*), if only so you can check out the fabulously overgrown wedding and *quinceañera* – 15th birthday cakes – on the mezzanine level.

is on two levels, tiled in yellow and orange with an open kitchen area, and the ambience is chatty, festive and full of employees from the surrounding business district. The menu boasts five different moles (a thick, labour-intensive sauce that Oaxaca is famous for): *verde, negro, coloradito, amarillo* and *almendrado* – all of which are well worth a try. Other regional specialities include *tasajos* (thin strips of meat rubbed with chilli paste) with a variety of garnishes, *tlayudas* (large, crisp corn tortillas topped with beans, cheese, chorizo, and so on) and *chapulines* (dried grasshoppers). For those planning post-lunch productivity, the 'light menu' might not bring on a food-induced siesta quite so strongly. Takeaway also available.

Zona Rosa

Basque

Tezka
Amberes 78, Royal Zona Rosa Hotel (9149 3000). Metro Insurgentes L1. **Open** 1pm-5pm Mon-Sat; 8pm-11pm Mon-Fri. **Main courses** MX$200-$300. **Credit** AmEx, DC, MC, V. **Map** p264 H6 ㉑
Tezka's unusual dishes, based loosely on Basque cuisine, are best sampled via the chef's *menú de degustación* (tasting menu). Sample an intriguing array of flavour combinations and sweet/savoury mixes, of which some work better than others. Sea

bass pâté with mamey (a tropical fruit) and suckling lamb with a confit of potato, avocado and a raspberry sauce are examples of the play on sweet versus savoury, and the presentation is exquisite. The dessert menu might have been written by Lewis Carroll, from the intriguingly named 'chocolate hamburgers' to cinnamon ice-cream with parsley sauce, and cones of quince filled with cream cheese mousse and passion fruit. If you're in the mood for a digestif, try *paxaran*, a liqueur from Navarra in Spain, made from wild sloe berries and aniseed.

Korean

Ham Ji Bak

Hamburgo 244, Juárez (5208 8292). Metro Sevilla L1. **Open** 11am-10.30pm daily; closed 2nd and 4th Mon of each month. **Main courses** MX$100-$150. **Credit** MC, V. **Map** p264 F6 ㉒

The Zona Rosa is Mexico City's 'Little Korea', and from the Korean clientele to the Korean TV programmes, Ham Ji Bak does not disappoint. This canteen-style restaurant might not be big on style, but the food is good value and includes a courtesy buffet of around nine different dishes such as pickled cabbage, tofu strips and grilled broccoli. Each table has a built-in domed grill for cooking strips of meat, to which you add vegetables and chilli sauce before wrapping it all up in a lettuce leaf for easy munching. For a filling lunch, try rice with raw egg – rice, sauce and vegetables with a raw egg on top, mixed at the table to cook through in the rice's residual heat.

Mexican

Casa Bell

Praga 14, Juárez (5208 3967). Metro Sevilla L1. **Open** 1-6pm Mon-Sun. **Main courses** MX$100-$250. **Credit** AmEx, MC, V. **Map** p264 G6 ㉓

During the week, this power lunch venue fills to bursting with Mexico City's suited and booted political and business players, while weekend lunches are more family orientated, with free-range children providing the background noise. Sip margaritas and munch on *quesadillas de cazón* (shark) to the trilling of birds both in cages and flying free around the terrace. (You'll be surprised how loud trilling can get.) Shrimp tacos, snapper and sea bass presented in many shapes and forms anchor a menu heavily weighted towards seafood, and whether you sit in the indoor dining room or garden terrace, the atmosphere is formal and the service attentive.

Fonda El Refugio

Liverpool 166, Juárez (5207 2732/5525 8128/ www.fondaelrefugio.com.mx). Metro Insurgentes L1. **Open** 1-11pm Mon-Sun. **Main courses** MX$150-$200. **Credit** AmEx, MC, V. **Map** p264 G6 ㉔

Whitewashed walls hung with copper pots, a lurid pink fireplace and bright blue wainscoting provide the backdrop for a cosy, family atmosphere at this traditional restaurant, where classic Mexican dishes such as *chiles rellenos* (stuffed chillies), *chicharrón* (fried pork rind), *mole poblano de gallina* (chicken with mole sauce) and *carne asada* (grilled beef tenderloin) fill the menu. The portions are satisfyingly generous for appetites whetted with great guacamole, which is not too spicy and not too bland, but Goldilocks-style just right. Help it all down with margaritas served in thick, handmade Mexican glasses so small you may, be warned, need more than one. The service is attentive and friendly, and a cheesy Mexican soundtrack completes the experience.

Middle Eastern

King Falafel

Londres 178, Juárez (5514 9030). Metro Insurgentes L1. **Open** 10am-8pm Mon-Fri; 11am-6pm Sat. **Main courses** MX$20-$50. **No credit cards.** **Map** p264 G6 ㉕

A hole-in-the-wall furnished with plastic chairs and tables, King Falafel is the ideal spot for a cheap, filling lunch to eat in or take away. Basic Middle Eastern fare, from the eponymous falafel to tabouleh, houmous and stuffed vine leaves, is available in various formats, depending on how hungry you are. The falafel sandwich (four falafel in a pita bread with houmous and tahini) is a bargain at around MX$40.

Vegetarian

Yug

Varsovia 3, Juárez (5525 5330/5533 3296/ www.lovegetariano.com). Metro Insurgentes L1. **Open** 7am-9pm Mon-Fri; 8.30am-8pm Sat-Sun. **Main courses** MX$50-$100. **Credit** AmEx, MC, V. **Map** p264 G6 ㉖

This vegetarian restaurant is one of a handful in Mexico City serving up veggie staples such as soy burgers, vegetarian lasagne, salads and brown rice and lentil dishes. The menu also features soy-based versions of Mexican favourites such as tacos and *carnitas* (usually seasoned pork simmered in lard), and drinks include juices, smoothies, non-alcoholic beers and wines. It's not exactly a party atmosphere, but the lunch buffet is very reasonable and it's a good place to top up on the veggies that are often lacking in Mexican food. That said, meat-free does not necessarily mean healthy: the soy burger comes loaded with cheese and a good side of fries.

Polanco

Argentinian

Como

Horacio 253 (5250 1596/www.restaurantcomo.com). Metro Polanco L7. **Open** 1pm-2am daily. **Main courses** MX$250-$350. **Credit** AmEx, MC, V. **Map** p262 D4 ㉗

"MEXICAN WOMAN FROM CHIAPAS WITH CEL PHONE, AT PAXIA RESTAURANT"

OUR MEXICO   OUR CUISINE   PAXIA
OUR MEXICAN CUISINE

Menu decoder

BASICS

Agua water; **almuerzo** traditionally a midmorning meal often translated as 'lunch'; **antojito** snack; **azúcar** sugar; **bocadillo** finger food; **botana** snack or appetiser, often taken with drinks in a bar or before a meal; **caldo** soup or broth; **carne** meat; **carta** menu; **comida** lunch, **comida corrida** set menu; **cena** dinner; **cuenta** bill; **desayuno** breakfast; **ensalada** salad; **huevo** egg; **leche** milk; **mantequilla** butter; **manteca** lard; **pan** bread; **picante** hot, as in spicy; **plato fuerte** main dish; **propina** tip; **queso** cheese; **sopa** soup.

LOCAL SPECIALITIES

Breakfast: Atole, a hot, thick drink made from corn meal; **pan dulce** sweet rolls, eaten for breakfast; **huevos rancheros** corn tortilla with fried eggs and spicy tomato and onion salsa; **chilaquiles** tortilla chips with red or green chilli sauce, cheese and cream, with chicken or egg on top; **molletes** toasted bread with beans and melted cheese.
Any time: Burritos a filling, usually shredded or dried meat, often mixed with chilli sauce, wrapped in a large, thin flour tortilla; **cazuelitas** a thin layer of tortilla dough molded into a cup, deep fried and filled with shredded meat and other taco fillings; **chapulines** dried grasshoppers; **chillis en nogada** stuffed mild chilli filled with ground meat, fruits, nuts and spices, covered in a white nut sauce and pomegranate seeds; **cochinita pibil** Yucatán-style marinated pork wrapped in banana leaves and slow roasted in a pit; **enchiladas** corn tortilla wrapped around a filling of chicken, meat or cheese, garnished with more sauce and cheese; **guacamole** avocado dip with onion, chillis, tomato, lime juice and cilantro; **gorditas** tortilla pockets filled with beans, meat or pork skin, and cheese; **huarache** a large, flat, thick, oval-shaped tortilla topped with meat and chillis; **jocoque** a type of cheesy yoghurt; **mole** a dark brown stew, traditionally chocolate-and-chilli flavoured, but also in green, yellow, white and red; **panuchos** Yucatán-style tortilla filled with fried black beans, then fried and topped with more shredded meat; **papadzules** enchiladas or soft tacos filled with hardboiled egg and topped with tomato and pumpkin-seed sauces; **pipián** similar to mole, usually containing ground squash

seeds and nuts; **pozole** pre-Columbian soup made with hominy, pork or chicken, beans, cabbage, avocado, oregano, radish, cilantro and lime; **quesadillas** tortillas folded over a cheese filling, sometimes with an epazote leaf, squash blossom or other ingredient; **sincronizada** deep fried tortilla filled with beans, ham and cheese, with guacamole on top; **tacos** tortillas wrapped around a filling; **tacos al pastor** tortillas filled with thin slices of marinated pork, cooked on a spit; **tamales** pre-Hispanic dish made with masa (tortilla dough) filled with meat, seafood, insects, vegetables or fruit, wrapped in a corn husk and steamed; **torta** sandwich roll stuffed with meat, beans and avocado; **torta cubana** torta with ham, cheese, egg, sausage, milanesa, chipotle; **tortilla** flat, thin bread made from corn or wheat; **totopos** fried tortilla chips.

MEAT

Aguayón sirloin; **aguja** cut of chuck steak; **albóndiga** meatball; **arrachera** skirt steak; **barbacoa** meat smoked in earthen pits; **bistec** beefsteak; **carne de res** beef; **carnitas** chunks of pork simmered in lard; **picadillo** filling made of ground meat.

SEAFOOD AND SHELLFISH

Almeja clam; **calamar** squid; **camarón** shrimp; **cazón** shark; **ceviche** seafood marinated in lime juice; **huachinango** red snapper; **jaiba** crab; **langosta** lobster; **mariscos** seafood; **moro** grouper; **ostión** oyster; **pescado** fish; **pulpo** octopus.

VEGETABLES/PULSES/CEREALS

Achiote annato seed, used to make a seasoning paste; **elote** fresh corn (as opposed to maíz or dried corn); **flor de calabaza** squash blossom; **frijoles** beans; **huitlacoche** fungus that grows on corn, like a cross between a mushroom and a truffle; **jitomate** tomato; **maíz** dried corn; **nopal** prickly pear cactus leaf

DESSERTS

Budín pudding; **cajeta** caramel made with cooked goat's milk and sugar, like dulce de leche; **camote** cigar-shaped sweets made from sweet potato and fruit; **cocada** sticky sweet made with coconut; **flan** custard tart made with milk or cream and eggs; **helado** ice cream; **natillas** custard; **pastel** cake; **rompope** Mexican style eggnog.

Less formal than most Polanco eateries, this popular Argentinian restaurant offers reasonable wines, well-cut steaks and rich pastas at moderate (for the neighbourhood) prices, in a buzzy, fun atmosphere. Decent salads and tasty empanadas are good options for a lighter meal, and locals rave about the 'imported' South American waiters, who know how to run a proper restaurant and look good at the same time.

Rincón Argentino

Masaryk 177 (5254 8775/5254 8744/ www. rinconargentino.com.mx). Metro Polanco L7. **Open** 12.30pm-12.30am Mon-Sat; 12.30-11.30pm Sun. **Main courses** MX$165-$675. **Credit** AmEx, MC, V. **Map** p262 C4 ❷⓮

This classic steakhouse in the centre of Polanco has been around for more than 20 years, and although the atmosphere inside is a little Disneyesque – a log-cabin interior, farmhouse memorabilia and a trompe l'oeil 'sunny day' ceiling – the food, namely the steak, is among the best in DF. And that's saying something in this city in which Argentinian meat is so highly regarded, and in which *chimichurri*, a spicy sauce for steak that was always a delicious aberration in condiment-shy Argentina, has found its true natural habitat, close to the Mexican heart. The butterflied rib-eye and the top sirloin are especially mouth watering, as is the chorizo argentino. The portions are enormous and eminently shareable.

Asian

MP Café Bistro

Andrés Bello 10 (5281 0592). Metro Auditorio L7. **Open** 1.30-11.30pm Mon-Wed; 1.30pm-12.30am Thur-Sat. **Main courses** MX$120-$220. **Credit** AmEx, MC, V. **Map** p262 B5 ❷⓲

This Asian fusion restaurant tucked between the hotel megaliths of Polanco and Bosque de Chapultepec is the brainchild of local culinary-guru-turned-Buddhist, Mónica Patiño. The menu combines Japanese and Mexican flavours to mostly successful effect; try the tuna carpaccio with a garlic, soy and lemon dressing, or the *tataki* (lightly seared thick cut chunks of tuna). Steer clear of the rolls, however, if you're not a big fan of cream cheese. The dress code is Polanco chic to go with the low-lit bistro-with-an-Asian-twist interior, and 1980s aficionados are in for a treat at weekends, when the DJ sticks on a medley of low-volume Smiths and Depeche Mode classics.

Delicatessen

Klein's

Avenida Presidente Masaryk 360 B2 (5281 0862). Metro Polanco L7. **Open** 7am-12.30am. **Main courses** MX$60-$200. **Credit** AmEx, MC, V. **Map** p262 B4 ❸⓪

Mexico City's facsimile of a New York deli is far from kosher, but has plenty of merits of its own. Among them are the Polanco price break – it's not dirt cheap, but it's an improvement on the robust prices of some of its neighbouring eateries – the solid sandwiches and soups, and the choice people- and pooch-watching opportunities here on Polanco's main drag. The decor is down-at-heel formica and the service no-nonsense.

French

Au Pied de Cochon

Campos Elíseos 218, Hotel Presidente (5327 7700/ www.aupieddecochon.com.mx). Metro Auditorio L7. **Open** 24 hrs. **Main courses** MX$160-$280. **Credit** AmEx, MC, V. **Map** p262 B5 ❸⓵

This far-from-home outpost of the famed Parisian brasserie takes the theme to its logical conclusion, with prices that must creep somewhere close to the original's. Wildly popular nevertheless with power-brokers and major-league señoras who lunch, it offers an enormous menu of solidly prepared French bistro classics from a vantage point inside the Hotel Presidente. Late nights lower the median age, if not income: Au Pied de Cochon is one of very few upscale restaurants operating 24-7, and is a last resort for the beautiful people when local nightclubs let out. If you're up on this season's *telenovelas* (soap operas), you're sure to see stars.

Ivoire

Emilio Castelar 95 (5280 0477/5280 7912/ www.ivoire.com.mx). Metro Polanco L7. **Open** 1.30-3pm, 7-9pm Mon-Sat; 1.30-3pm Sun. **Main courses** MX$200-$350. **Credit** AmEx, MC, V. **Map** p262 B5 ❸⓶

This must be one of the loveliest rooms in Mexico City – several different rooms, in fact, including the popular garden terrace and rooftop bar – with delicious food and charming service to match. The restaurant specialises in familiar French favourites which it calls 'colonial cuisine', presented with creative international twists from the former Gallic empire such as couscous, curries and far-Eastern flavours. There's an extensive wine list and the desserts are also excellent. And as is the case in so many Polanco hotspots, great crowd-watching means you'll never be bored. Sink into a banquette and pretend that every day of your life is as comfortable and civilised as this one.

L'Olivier

Avenida Presidente Masaryk 49C (5545 3133). Metro Polanco L7. **Open** 1.30-11pm Mon-Sat; 1.30-5pm Sun. **Main courses** MX$150-$250. **Credit** AmEx, MC, V. **Map** p262 D4 ❸⓷

A spacious, sunny Mediterranean outpost on Polanco's west side, L'Olivier offers well-prepared Provençal standards like soufflés, salade niçoise and onion soup, as well as steaks. Fresh seafood is a particular specialty, and a welcome emphasis on healthy ingredients and light preparations make it a good option when you've grown tired of too many *enchiladas suizas* and *tacos al pastor*. Note: dinner can be extremely quiet. If that's not what you're looking for, stick to lunch.

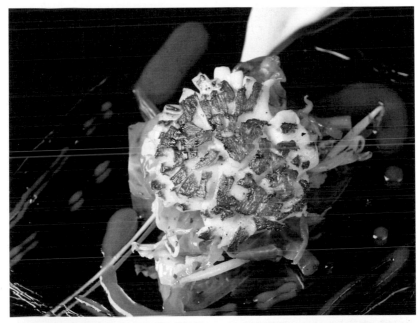

Modern cooking with a French slant at **Jaso**. *See p114.*

International

Biko

Avenida Presidente Masaryk 407 (5282 2064/
www.biko.com.mx). Metro Polanco L7. **Open** 1.30-
5pm, 8-11pm Mon-Sat. **Main courses** MX$100-$370.
Credit AmEx, MC, V. **Map** p262 B4 ③④
Comprising traditional dishes deconstructed with a
touch of genius and a dash of whimsy, Biko's menu
is a thrill to read, even if it does make you giggle.
Reductions, airs, smears, brushstrokes and spheri-
fications alert you to the fact that you are in the field
of molecular gastronomy. If the thought of foie gras
and yoghurt mousse wrapped in lettuce spun in a
cloud of candy floss has you snorting into your
beard, Biko may not be for you; but you'll have
missed something a bit special, because crazy as it
sounds, it's a silky moment of delight when popped
in the mouth. Beef in bean sauce with pigs' ear and
pine nuts is another little star, the tasty, toothsome
ear chopped mercifully small. As Basque chef and
part owner Mikel Alonso insists, this might be food
evolved a fair way from its traditional roots, but the
bottom line is, your mother should be able to like it.
As long as you've concealed the bill from her successfully, she probably will.

Jaso

Newton 88 (5545 7476/www.jaso.com.mx).
Metro Polanco L7. **Main courses** MX$195-$350. *Set menus* from
MX$600. **Credit** AmEx, MC, V. **Map** p262 C4 ③⑤
Open since early 2006, Jaso has quickly rocketed into
position as one of the best restaurants in Mexico City.
Owned by husband-and-wife chef team Jared
Reardon and Sonia Arias, Jaso excels in serving modern haute cuisine with a New York touch and just a
soupcon of frenchification. *Garra de léon* is a signature dish of scallops on a cauliflower puree with mandarin sauce, and the seafood in general is particularly
good, though you might want to save space for the
dessert menu, Arias's speciality, and for arguably the
best magdalenas in the city. Tasting menus of five or
nine courses are highly recommended, and if you can
stretch to the tasting menu plus wine matching, you'll
be treated to a parade of dizzyingly good food paired
with exceptional wines, including some of Mexico's
finest. If you prefer to choose your own wine, 15
Lineas is a solid choice, while Casa Grande Reserva
– a chardonnay from Ensenada – is a buttery, creamy,
pineapple and lychee delight. *Photo p113.*

OW9

Oscar Wilde 9 (5280 2723). Metro Polanco L7.
Open 1-6pm Mon-Sat. **Main courses** MX$100-$200.
Credit AmEx, MC, V. **Map** p262 B5 ③⑥
OW9 is a tiny bistro offering a selective menu of contemporary recipes that's part New York, part DF. The
salads and appetiser soups are standouts, with a delicacy and variety not always seen on Mexican menus.
Entrées include traditional fish such as red snapper
and trout. Vegetarians will find plenty to like too. The
dining room is intimate, but not cramped, with quirky
touches in hidden corners. It's only open for lunch and
has no liquor licence.

Italian

Primo Bacio

Emilio Castelar 121K (5280 9945). Metro
Auditorio L7 or Polanco L7. **Open** 1-11pm Mon,
Tue; 1pm-midnight Wed-Sat; 1-8pm Sun. **Main**
courses MX$59-$138 **Credit** AmEx, MC, V.
Map p262 A5 ③⑦

Pujol.

A moderately priced restaurant serving down-to-earth Italian fare in the heart of swanky Polanco, Primo Bacio is an unpretentious little joint with something of a Condesa air about it, thanks to its relaxed, friendly service. Bruschetta topped with rich mozzarella and roasted red pepper is a good choice as a starter, and the crisp, thin-crust pizza is also recommended. Free Wi-Fi makes it a good option for a solo lunch, though if you're dining alone thanks to a broken heart, the 'first kiss' photo collection on the walls – a reference to the restaurant's name – might make the terrace the best choice, with its leafy views of nearby Parque Lincoln. Pick your moment carefully, though, since traffic noise can spoil the effect a bit at rush hour.

Mexican

Estoril

Alejandro Dumas 24 (5280 9828/www.estoril.com. mx). Metro Polanco L7. **Open** 1-11.30pm Mon-Fri, 1-11pm Sat; 1-6pm Sun. **Main courses** MX$200-$300. **Credit** AmEx, MC, V. **Map** p262 B5 ❸❽

A Mexico City tradition since 1971, Estoril offers a very haute brand of Mexican cuisine – forget about greasy enchiladas here – nuanced with plenty of old-school Parisian touches. The extensive menu features updates on appetisers like *pata negra* ham with fried parsley; tortilla, chilled avocado and other traditional soups; and entrées like whole roast suckling pig and Veracruz-style snapper. The desserts are delicious and the service is both impeccable and, thankfully, unstuffy, though the same can't always be said for your fellow diners. Dress up and bring *dinero*.

El Farolito

Newton 130 (5531 9779/www.taqueriaselfarolito. com). Metro Polanco L7. **Open** 11am-2am Mon-Thur; 11am-3am Fri-Sat; 11am-1pm Sun. **Main courses** MX$20-$100. **Credit** AmEx, MC, V. **Map** p262 C4 ❸❾

An informal, budget Polanco option located in the centre of the neighbourhood's attractive shopping district, El Farolito is a traditional and popular *taquería* serving many different kinds of this wonderful staple, including *tacos al pastor*, the spit-grilled marinaded pork version that locals adore. Yes, there's a mark-up due to location, but neither your belly nor your wallet will be empty when you leave. Things might seem fast-paced, but don't be afraid to linger as long as you like.

Izote

Avenida Presidente Masaryk 513 (5280 1671/5280 1265). Metro Polanco L7. **Open** 1pm-midnight Mon-Sat; 1pm-6pm Sun. **Main courses** MX$250-$350. **Credit** AmEx, MC, V.

Famed chef Patricia Quintana practically invented the *nueva cocina mexicana* (traditional Mexican ingredients married to the latest international culinary trends), and her flagship restaurant routinely appears on the ten-best lists at home and abroad. Many consider this the city's finest Mexican restaurant, though the service can be somewhat haughty. For visitors it's a great place to try exceptionally high-quality local specialities like *huitlacoche* (yes it translates as 'corn fungus', but believe us, it's delicious), *flor de calabaza* (squash blossom) and *nopales* (cactus leaves). Design freaks will appreciate the modernist recipes, presentation and decor.

Pujol

Francisco Petrarca 254 (5545 3507/www.pujol. com.mx). Metro Polanco L7. **Open** 1.30-5pm, 7-11.30pm Mon-Fri; 1.30-11.30pm Sat. **Main courses** MX$195-$395. *Set menu* from MX$700. **Credit** AmEx, DC, MC, V. **Map** p262 D4 ❹❶

Quality traditional Mexican food can be found in many places in Mexico – from cantinas, *taquerías* and fondas to street stalls. But with a brilliant line in high-quality Mexican standards, elegantly served in a sophisticated atmosphere, Pujol is one of the big, posh boys on the block. Everything dazzles here, from the wine glasses, tableware and prices to the chef, Enrique Olvera, who has become well known in Mexico for his high-class spin – a dash of foam here, a drizzle of reduction there – on local favourites. Yet another contender for the hotly contested Mexico City foodie crown, the pursuit of which keeps fine restaurants like Pujol eternally on their toes.

Middle Eastern

Adonis

Homero 424 (5250 2064/5531 6940). Metro Polanco L7. **Open** 1-11.30pm Mon-Wed; 1pm-2am Thur-Sat; 1-7pm Sun. **Main courses** MX$100-$150. **Credit** AmEx, MC, V. **Map** p262 C4 ❹❶

An institution among members of Mexico City's Lebanese community, Adonis makes for an exotic change of pace with its traditional Levantine specialities. Prices are moderate to high but the service attentive and friendly. The 'casbah bordello' look makes a great backdrop for group outings, which lend themselves to the easy-to-share menu as well, with the house 'buffet selection' tasting menu perfect for noshing en masse. Happy-hour piano serenades and weekend belly-dancing provide a fun, campy touch.

Chapultepec

Japanese

Suntory

Montes Urales 535 (5202 4711). Metro Auditorio L7, then 15min walk or taxi. **Open** 1-11.30pm Mon-Thur; 1pm-midnight Fri, Sat; 1-9pm Sun. **Main courses** MX$95-$380. **Credit** AmEx, MC, V.

A short taxi ride or brisk stride from the centre of Polanco, this old-school, upmarket tepanyaki joint has been a local fixture for several decades now, and may not have had a makeover in as long. A rather kitsch bamboo garden dotted with fountains

Eat, Drink, Shop

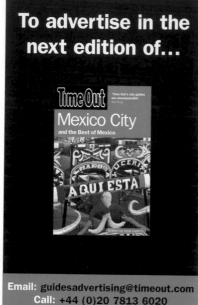

Mexification and Vitamin T

Mexicans take their fast food seriously. Perhaps that's why the *Guinness Book of Records*' fattest man is Mexican – he has since lost half his 560kg body weight, putting him in the running for the book's man who lost the most weight – and Mexico now rivals the USA at the top of the world's obesity ranking. Tasty, greasy *antojitos* (literally, 'little whims') are this country's speciality and delight. For that reason, just about every street corner with a reasonable level of passing trade is occupied by somebody tending a sizzling vat or hotplate, with a tarpaulin and plastic chairs on the footpath where everyone from besuited business types to mums and kids halt to feast on lard-dipped delicacies. Any time of day, in any part of town, you'll find Mexicans stocking up on the day's all-important Vitamin T: tacos, tortillas, tortas, tamales and *tlacoyos* (corn dough, sometimes green or blue, dating back to pre-Hispanic times, filled and cooked on a griddle).

Yet when Taco Bell ventured south of the border in 1992, Mexicans boycotted the US chain in droves. Tex-Mex on home turf (whoever heard of hard-shelled tacos?) proved one insult too many for a nation in which the humble *taquito* ('little taco') holds pride of place in the national cuisine. (Taco Bell has since made a second attempt, this time taking out half-page newspaper ads announcing 'a fast-food alternative that does not pretend to be Mexican food'.)

But while Mexicans might baulk at gringo-fied versions of their maize-based staples, the same is not true in reverse. It seems that, to the Mexican palate, there's nothing that can't be improved with a little chilli and lime, and that includes ice-cream, fresh fruit, vegetables and chocolate. Many Western foods have been cheerfully 'Mexified' to suit local tastes. You'll find sushi deep fried in chipotle batter; 'pastes' – variations on the Cornish pastie, filled with frijoles or mole; a Dominos pizza called 'Hawaiian Diablo' – pineapple with spicy chilli topping; and Argentine *parrillas* (grills) serving Mexican cuts like *arrachera* over the traditional *vacio* and *bife de chorizo*. Even the classic *taco al pastor* is believed to be an adaptation of the spit-grilled shawarma brought to Mexico by Lebanese immigrants. Maybe it's an example of Mexico's mestizo culture, absorbing and modifying everything it touches; or it could be payback for the Tex-Mex phenomenon. Or perhaps it's just a case of Moctezuma, still having his revenge.

Wanted. Jumpers, coats and people with their knickers in a twist.

From the people who feel moved to bring us their old books and CDs, to the people fed up to the back teeth with our politicians' track record on climate change, Oxfam supporters have one thing in common. They're passionate. If you've got a little fire in your belly, we'd love to hear from you. Visit us at **oxfam.org.uk**

Be Humankind (Ⓧ) **Oxfam**

Registered charity No. 202918

and waterfalls encompasses a large dining space of tepanyaki tables of various sizes, to which chefs in tall white hats come and sizzle your food before your eyes. Fresh lobster fished from a tank is also available, as is good sushi, but the sake on the limited menu is extortionate. Book ahead, even during the week.

Mexican

El Lago
Lago Mayor, Bosque de Chapultepec, 2nd section (5515 9585/www.lago.com.mx). Metro Auditorio L7. **Open** 7.30am-11pm Mon-Sat; 10am-4.30pm Sun. **Main courses** MX$200-$300. **Credit** AmEx, MC, V. **Map** p262 A7 **42**
This is one of Mexico City's most dramatic gastronomic settings: Elago's enormous gilded dining room is set beneath a soaring arched roof with spectacular lake and skyline views. Classic Mexican dishes, some with a contemporary twist, join steaks, chops and seafood on an excellent menu, and an extensive wine list offers enough reasonably priced bottles to keep most people happy. Live covers of 1970s pop hits add a *Love Boat* vibe to the room that, given that there's no accounting for tastes in this world, is either a pro or a con.

El Lago de los Cisnes
Prado Norte 391 (5282 4501/5282 4347). Metro Auditorio L7. **Open** 8am-2am Sun-Wed; 8am-6am Thur-Sat. **Main courses** MX$50-150. **Credit** AmEx, MC, V.
Some believe the *tacos al pastor* at El Lago de los Cisnes (formerly the Lomas branch of the legendary Charco de las Ranas) to be among the best in the city. They are good; but their high score on the tacometer may also have something to do with the lively, vociferous scene that makes this joint a late-night favourite and a top spot to soak up the alcohol with a heartstopping (but delicious) *sincronizada al pastor* (spit-grilled pork swimming in melted cheese in a flour tortilla). Walk off the calories tomorrow but consider getting to El Lago in a taxi tonight, since public transport is woefully lacking in this part of town.

Santa Fe

Mexican

Los Canarios
Guillermo González Camarena 1600 (5081 1481/ www.loscanarios.com.mx). Metro Tacubaya L1, L7, L9, then minibus, taxi colectivo or RTP bus marked Santa Fe. **Open** 1-11.30pm Mon-Sat; 1-6pm Sun. **Main courses** MX$80-$320. **Credit** AmEx, MC, V.
A long-time staple choice with business lunchers, Los Canarios, with its spacious, airy ambience, is a surprisingly classic and cordial venue in the centre of the financial neighbourhood. Serving up a hybrid of Mexican and international fare, with outstanding *quesadillas de flor de calabaza* (quesadillas with squash blossom), the restaurant is one part lofty burgundy-

tinted brasserie, complete with giant French-style mirrors behind the bar, and one part pleasant conservatory, decked out with white cages full of the twittering canaries that give the place its name.

Peruvian

Segundo Muelle
Juan Salvador Agraz 40 (5292 5550/www.segundo muelle.com). Metro Tacubaya L1, L7, L9, then minibus, taxi colectivo or RTP bus marked Santa Fe. **Open** 1-6pm Mon, Tue; 1pm-1am Wed-Sat; 1-8pm Sun. **Main courses** MX$95-$220. **Credit** AmEx, MC, V.
This chic Peruvian joint, on the second floor of a Santa Fe high-rise, is a favourite with a slightly trendier business crowd and offers a fantastic skyline view of the suburb. Ceviche here is a must, particularly the restaurant's speciality Ceviche Segundo Muelle. Also good are the spicy *picante de mariscos* and the *róbalo* (snook) with butter and capers. Efficient waiting staff are happy to take orders for half portions, allowing you to range widely over the menu; and don't leave without trying the house tipple: a pisco sour, made with the Peruvian spirit plus lemon and egg white – dangerously gluggable.

Condesa

Argentinian

Fondo La Garufa
Michoacán 93 (5286 8295/www.garufa.com). Metro Patriotismo L9. **Open** 8am-1am Mon-Sat; 8am-11pm Sun. **Main courses** MX$85-$150. **Credit** MC, V. **Map** p264 F8 **43**
Started 16 years ago with three friends and a set of plastic tables on the pavement of their leafy *colonia*, Fondo La Garufa prepared the way for Condesa's alfresco dining boom, and as the oldest kid on the block, it retains a credibility that many of its neighbours lack. The crowd here is definitely more *Sex and the City* than *comida corrida*, and while the menu's Argentinian roots show through clearly – you can still get a sirloin steak or an *empanada* – try some of the more exotic creations, such as the tasty *fettucini hindú* (chicken breast cooked in ginger, yoghurt and chilli *piquín* on a bed of home-made, coriander pasta). If you score an outdoor table, expect to be serenaded by buskers.

La Parrilla Pizzería Quilmes
Alfonso Reyes 193 (5516 1438). Metro Patriotismo L9. **Open** 1pm-10pm Mon-Thu; 1pm-11.30pm Fri-Sat; 1pm-8pm Sun. **Main courses** MX$160-$250. **Credit** AmEx, MC, V. **Map** p264 F9 **44**
Framed, signed football jerseys from Mexico and Argentina adorn the walls of this unpretentious, family-friendly *parrilla* (steakhouse). Servings are substantial and definitely enough to share between two. Traditional Argentinian cuts such as *ojo de bife* (rib-eye), *vacío* (flank) and *lomo* (tenderloin) are outshone by the Mexican *arrachera*, a tender, thin slice

Eat, Drink, Shop

of beef, ideally washed down with a jug of *clericot* – a punch-like drink of fruit juice, fruit and wine.

International

Hip Kitchen

Hippodrome Hotel (5212 2120/ www.thehippodrome hotel.com). Metro Chilpancingo L9 or Sevilla L1. **Open** 7-11am, 2-11pm Mon-Wed; 7-11am, 2pm-12.30am Thur-Sat. **Main courses** MX$210-$260. **Credit** AmEx, MC, V. **Map** p264 G8 **⑮**
Just through the diminutive lobby of the excellently located Hippodrome Hotel, the Hip Kitchen looks cramped at first sight; but once you're settled at a table at one of the two long rows, you start to feel right at home, and indeed, there's something very romantic about the low-lit, contemporary space. A signature edamame bean starter tossed with prosciutto, dried shrimp and chilli sets the tone for a menu that matches international flavours with Mexican staples – try, for example, the duck tacos with ginger and garlic and a raspberry sauce. The risotto of *huitlacoche con callo* – corn fungus with scallops and asparagus – is another good choice from an ambitious, tempting menu.

Orquídeas Café Bistrot

Mexico 117 (5574 7464). Metro Chilpancingo L9. **Open** 9am-1am daily. **Main courses** MX$70-160. **Credit** AmEx, MC, V. **Map** p264 G9 **⑯**
Overlooking one of the city's most splendid parks, Parque México, this low-key, cosy eatery offers up a grab bag of European flavours with the Latin American twist typical of restaurants in this chic neighbourhood. Start out with the excellent trio of tender ceviches, a fresh Greek salad or a bowl of French onion soup, and continue on to one of the many pastas, *chapata* (ciabatta) sandwiches or more substantial meat dishes, all the while sipping a glass of red wine. Or if you'd like to try a locally brewed draught beer, go for the chocolaty, dark Cosaco Negra. Pieces by local artists adorn the walls, jazz bands perform live on Wednesday nights, and surfers will be pleased to find that the Wi-Fi is free.

El Patio

Condesa DF Hotel, Avenida Veracruz 102 (5241 2600/ www.condesadf.com). Metro Chapultepec L1, Sevilla L1 or Chilpancingo L9. **Main courses** MX$180-$240. **Credit** AmEx, MC, V. **Map** p264 F7 **⑰**
A buzzing, lovely and happening spot in the Mexico City restaurant firmament, El Patio – the little-used name for the restaurant at the chic Condesa DF hotel – is the kind of place in which you win extra cred if you're able to greet people at other tables as you arrive. Watch hipster antennae twitch as the place fills up and new arrivals are led in, and be grateful you're a nobody, free to soak up the atmosphere and enjoy the very good service. Black cod in tequila miso and chicken satay signal the Asian pretensions that appear to function as shorthand for 'contemporary' in DF. The food is of a very high standard, but it's not what most people come for.

Rexo

Saltillo 1 (5553 1300). Metro Chilpancingo L9 or Patriotismo L9/Metrobús Chilpancingo. **Open** 1.30pm-1am Mon-Wed; 1.30pm-2am Thur-Sat; 1.30pm-midnight Sun. **Main courses** MX$90-$170. **Credit** AmEx, MC, V. **Map** p264 F9 **⑱**
The location of this three-level restaurant and bar, on a corner facing one of Condesa's main thoroughfares, appeals to its thirtysomething clientele, with the other main attraction being its copious cocktail list, where martinis take centre stage. Some 75 different spirits and liqueurs are available by the bottle, and a limited wine menu also includes a handful by the glass. Though the street-level bar is tiny, full-length windows on two sides, an open floor plan and two elevated dining areas give the space an airy feel. It's uncrowded and casual at lunchtime, but weekend evenings draw the fashionable set and getting a table without a reservation may involve a lengthy wait. While not outstanding, the food is tasty and attractively presented, and the service is friendly and efficient. You can order off the regular menu or check out the slate wall listing daily food and drink specials; and on Sundays, three-course set meals feature dishes from a different country each week.

Casa Lamm. *See p123.*

La Vinería

*Fernando Montes de Oca 52A (5211 9020/
www.lavineria.com.mx). Metro Patriotismo L9.*
Open 2-11pm Mon-Sat. **Main courses** MX$70-
$150. **Credit** AmEx, MC, V. **Map** p264 F8 ⓵
Finding good Italian food is no small task in this city,
so for those wanting their pasta *al dente* and at a reasonable price, this is a good option. The pasta Ramos
(named after the chef) with garlic, chile serrano and
parmesan, is tasty and simple, as is the grilled egg-
plant stuffed with goat cheese in red pepper sauce.
White tablecloths, a warm wooden bar and tables
spilling onto the footpath make this cosy, elegant
eaterie a pleasant, relaxing place to dine.

Mexican

El Califa

*Altata 22 (5271 7666/5271 6285). Metro
Chilpancingo L9.* **Open** 1pm-7am daily; closed
on Yom Kippur. **Main courses** MX$40-$100.
Credit AmEx, MC, V. **Map** p264 F9 ⓵
Legions of fans claim that El Califa's tacos are the
best in Mexico City; so unless you're an extremely
fussy taco gourmand, it's a fair bet you'll like the
tacos here. They're certainly more expensive than
those at your average *taquería* but well worth it if
fresh, clean, delicious tacos and quality ingredients
are what you're after (read: for those too wary to try
street food). In the heart of Condesa's bar and club
district, this an obligatory on-the-way-home stop for
many revellers, and there are sometimes queues
until 7am. Everyone from Tom Cruise to Spencer
Tunick has tried these tacos; for us the *tacos al pastor* and the *gaonas* (sliced lean fillet, topped with
cheese) are stand-outs.

Orígenes Orgánicos

*Plaza Popocatépetl 41A (5208 6678/5525 9359/
www.origenesorganicos.com.mx). Metro Chilpancingo
L9.* **Open** 8am-10pm Mon-Fri; 9am-7pm Sat; 10am-
6pm Sun. **Main courses** MX$40-$95. **Credit** AmEx,
MC, V. **Map** p264 G8 ⓵
Located on a quiet corner, this cosy café and organic food store is part of a slowly growing trend for
organic goods in Mexico City. Vegetarians in particular will be delighted with a menu featuring 12 varieties of salad you can mix and match with other
dishes, plus a variety of options that includes tofu
burgers, veggie fajitas and quiches. Meat and fish
eaters need not fear, since beef burgers, chicken
enchiladas and grilled salmon are also on offer. In a
deliciously shady corner of Condesa, it's a pleasant
spot, particularly for breakfast (until 1pm) or a light
lunch, but quantities sometimes run short. Home
delivery service available.

La Sabia Virtud

*Tamaulipas 134B (5211 8416/5286 6480).
Metro Patriotismo L9.* **Open** 1-11.30pm Mon-
Thur; 1pm-midnight Fri, Sat; 1-7pm Sun.
Main courses MX$80-$180. **Credit** AmEx,
MC, V. **Map** p264 F9 ⓵

It's rare to go to a restaurant and want to order
everything on the menu, but you could find yourself
in such a quandary at La Sabia Virtud. Make it easy
on yourself and choose from the staples; one of the
red, green or almond moles (special sauces) made
from ancient poblano recipes, *pipian* (green sauce
made from ground pumpkin seeds); or *chile en nogada*, a stuffed, green chilli in walnut sauce with pomegranate seeds, representing the green, white and red
of the Mexican flag. This is *alta cocina mexicana* at
reasonable prices, in a white-tableclothed bistro,
with outdoor tables and the odd French touch (the
crepas Sabia Virtud are crêpes suzette). One of the
best moles poblano outside Puebla is served here,
made with 27 ingredients.

El Tío Luis

Cuautla 43 (5553 2923). Metro Chapultepec L1.
Open 2-10pm Mon-Sat; 1-7pm Sun. **Main courses**
MX$75-$150. **Credit** MC, V. **Map** p264 F8 ⓵
Opened in 1939, El Tío Luis claims to be the oldest
restaurant in Condesa. With its original decor of
wood-panelled walls – with framed photos of bullfighters, ex-presidents and the former pope – plus a
pianist tinkling away in a corner, it retains a feel of
lost worlds and past glories. The recently added outdoor tables are a nod to the neighbourhood's newfound cosmopolitanism, but the rest is authentically
unchanged, down to the home-style cooking. The specialty is *pollo* Tío Luis – deep fried chicken, served
with rice, vegetables and sautéed potatoes. Or if that's
a bit rich for your cholesterol count, the nopal salad,
made with a cactus said to possess cholesterol-lower-
ing properties, is as delicious as it is healthy.

VIPs

*Durango 259 (01800 710 6352/www.vips.com.mx).
Metro Sevilla L1.* **Open** 7am-midnight Sun-Thur;
7am-1am Fri, Sat. **Main courses** MX$42-$105.
Credit AmEx, MC, V. **Map** p264 G7 ⓵
If you've ever been to a Little Chef or a Denny's and
liked it, you'll feel right at home at VIPs. With more
than a touch of the US-style big-chain diner about
it, VIPs is all about pleasant, accomplished service
in unostentatious surroundings at a reasonable
price. You know it's good value because there are
always pensioners in VIPs, munching contentedly
on *enchiladas suizas* (chicken enchiladas with spicy
sauce and cheese) or on *flautas de res* (crispy tortillas filled with beef, rolled, and covered with a
spicy green sauce). Take our advice and hit VIPs for
one of its range of large breakfasts, all of which
include juice, toast and tea or coffee.
Other locations across the city.

Xel-Ha

Parral 78 (5553 5968). Metro Chapultepec L1. **Open**
noon-1am Mon-Sat; 11am-7pm Sun. **Main courses**
MX$90-$150. **Credit** MC, V. **Map** p264 F8 ⓵
The bright lights, laminated tables and flat-screen
TVs are at odds with the apricot walls and hotel-
lobby-style fountain, but this cantina/restaurant's
identity crisis is actually the key to its success. Tuck

into the salted nut and *chicharrón* (deep fried pork belly) *botanas*, or order more substantial Yucatecan stomach-fillers such as house specialities *sopa de lima* (a chicken and lime broth), *cochinita pibil* (slow-roasted pork), or *panucho de cazón* (pre-cooked tortilla with shredded shark). The homemade *flan de queso* (cheese quiche) is delightful. Beware the *ixnipec*; this innocent-looking bowl of onion salsa is made with habanera chillis, and the name literally means 'dog's nose', for its ability to make the nose run and the eyes water.

Seafood

La Ostra
Nuevo León 109 (5286 3319/www.laostra.com). Metro Chilpancingo L9. **Open** noon-8.30pm Mon-Thur; noon-10.30pm Fri, Sat. **Main courses** MX$40-$150. **Credit** AmEx, MC, V. **Map** p264 F8 ⑤⑥
If you have neither the budget nor the fancy duds for a splash-out meal at Contramar, this could be your next best bet. Bernardo Massieu opened this hole-in-the wall seafood joint four years ago and has been serving up the freshest, best priced seafood from his native Baja California ever since. The menu is a chalkboard and the offerings kept simple: tacos, tostadas, ceviches and cocktails made with a choice of seafood, though freshwater crab is also a speciality. The sashimi is excellent as are the tuna tostadas – heavenly when washed down with an ice-cold *michelada* (beer with lime juice and ice, served in a salt-rimmed glass). The atmosphere is unpretentious despite a clientele that includes models, TV soap actors and young execs. There's a DJ from 6pm on Fridays and Saturdays.

Roma

Asian

El Malayo
Plaza Río de Janiero 56 (5514 7686). Metro Insurgentes L1/Metrobús Álvaro. Obregón. **Open** 2pm-1.30am Mon-Sat; 2-6pm Sun. **Main courses** MX$110-$230. **Credit** AmEx, MC, V. **Map** p264 H7 ⑤⑦
While the name appears to be a postmodern play on words – the menu makes culinary stops in just about every Asian cuisine *but* Malaysian – the international crowd seem sophisticated enough to take the joke. The decor, which nods towards Lower East Side cool – dark tables, tiled floors, designer wallpaper, date-friendly mood lighting – is better than the food. Despite the efforts of Singaporean chef Eugene Ong to create Asian fusion cuisine, Mexican tastes dominate: the tom yum tastes more like *caldo de camarón* (prawn broth), and the green curry is reminiscent of a spiced-up mole. Two menu items worthy of praise are the saké-braised octopus – giant, tender tentacles that sprawl across the plate and melt in your mouth – and the mojito Malayo, made with tequila and basil instead of rum and mint.

Italian

Non Solo Panino
Plaza Luis Cabrera 10 (3096 5128/www.nonsolo.com.mx). Metro Insurgentes L1. **Open** 1pm-midnight Mon-Sat. **Main courses** MX$50-$70. **Credit** MC, V. **Map** p265 I7 ⑤⑧
Set on beautiful Plaza Luis Cabrera, this simple Italian restaurant is an excellent place for lunch in Roma. The niçoise is good, with tuna, egg and anchovy; or try a caprese, with ham, tomato and mozzarella. But, as the name suggests, it's not all about the sandwiches. There's pasta too, and a delicious *huitlacoche* omelette filled with dark and tasty corn fungus.

International

Travazares Taberna
Orizaba 127 (5264 1421/5264 3039). Metro Insurgentes L1/Metrobús Álvaro Obregón. **Open** 1pm-2am daily. **Main courses** MX$70-$160. **Credit** AmEx, MC, V. **Map** p264 H7 ⑤⑨
Travazares Taberna's owner has created a space that encourages lingering – he also runs the bookshop, gallery and cultural centre, Atrio (www.atrio.com.mx), upstairs – with even the outside seating looking like someone has dragged the lounge furniture on to the footpath. Inside, a maze of rooms filled with mismatched second hand tables and chairs, candles, exposed beams and paintings by local artists creates the mood of a bohemian dinner party. Red wine is served by the generous glassful and diners typically stay late. The salads and pastas are excellent choices for a light lunch.

Mexican

Casa Lamm
Álvaro Obregón 99 (5514 8501-4/www.lamm.com.mx). Metro Insurgentes L1/Metrobus Álvaro Obregón. **Main courses** MX$90-$275. **Open** 8am-3am Mon-Fri; 9am-3am Sat; 9am-5pm Sun. **Credit** AmEx, MC, V. **Map** p265 I7 ⑥⓪
Casa Lamm's restaurant is a real treasure. It provides a contemporary but not overly minimalist centrepiece to this cultural centre (*see also p82*). Floor-to-ceiling glass panes replace two entire walls, giving uninterrupted views of the lush courtyard, and opening up to let the air in from February to May. The food is exquisite, but extremely rich and on the saucy side. Start with a palate-cleansing trio of ceviches of zingy seasoned prawns, octopus and raw Acapulco white fish, pickled in lime juice. If Latin sushi is not your thing then try the posh *tacos de pato* (duck tacos) with a piquant salsa verde, or the *atún fresco* (fresh tuna) which, dressed in a sweet-and-sour tamarind and chipotle chilli sauce is simply mouthwatering. Take your time in one of the city's most delightful settings for a romantic meal; and even if you skip pudding, enjoy a coffee, nightcap or lunchtime digestif, flopping as elegantly as you can into one of the sofas on the upper level. *Photo p120.*

La Tecla

Durango 186-A (5525 4920). Metro Insurgentes L1.
Open 1pm-midnight Mon-Sat; 1-6pm Sun. **Main
courses** MX$70-$130. **Credit** AmEx, MC, V.
Map p264 G7 ⑥①
A little bit posh and yet reasonably priced, this veteran of Mexican *alta cocina* is a great place to try
inventive concoctions strong on local ingredients. The
entrée of squash flower (*flor de calabaza*) stuffed with
goat's cheese in chipotle sauce is delicious, as are the
deep-fried parsley tostadas (not on the menu – ask!).
Situated below Pecanins gallery, the restaurant has
a clientele that leans to the arty side, and with prices
this reasonable, many of the diners are regulars.

Seafood

Contramar

*Avenida Durango 200 (5514 9217/www.contramar.
com.mx). Metro Sevilla L1 or Insurgentes L1/
Metrobús Durango.* **Open** 1.30pm-6.30pm Mon-Thur;
1-6.30pm Fri, Sat. **Main courses** MX$250-$350.
Credit AmEx, MC, V. **Map** p264 G7 ⑥②
Mexico City's casual-dining seafood restaurant par
excellence, Contramar has shoals of devoted fans who
come back again and again for the spankingly fresh
fish, the light and delightful atmosphere, and the
sheer ease with which this Roma star tackles the fine
art of running a packed, buzzing restaurant. The
tostados de atún – tender raw tuna on a crispy taco
shell – are outstanding, emblematic of the beautiful
simplicity that is Contramar's signature style. You
can't go far wrong with anything from the menu, but
the grilled snapper, opened out butterfly style and
rubbed with bright red spice one side and deep green
herbs the other, is as delicious as it is spectacular. Hot
young actors and even the likes of Gabriel García
Márquez can be spotted enjoying long luncheons
here. Lunches go on so long, in fact, that reservations
are a very good idea if you'd like to eat before 4pm.

San Ángel

French

Cluny

*Avenida de la Paz 57 (5550 7350/5550 7359).
Metrobús La Bombilla.* **Open** 12.30pm-midnight
Mon-Sat; 12.30-11pm Sun. **Main courses** MX$110-
$180. **Credit** AmEx, MC, V. **Map** p259 B3 ⑥③
San Ángel residents have been dining on French
fusion fare under the vaulted ceilings of this celebrated crêperie, on the ground floor of a converted
mansion, since 1974. The most popular crêpes are
crammed with fillings like gruyére and gouda or
chicken in béchamel sauce; Mexican veggies including corn, chilli poblano and squash blossoms; or
given unusual twists like the chicken curry crêpe
with cucumber yoghurt raita and fruity chutney.
Bistro-style dishes include the steak frites and
moules marinieres. For dessert, try a Nutella-and-

banana-stuffed crêpe topped with whipped cream
or, if you've grown pancake-weary, sample a scoop
of home-made ice-cream. *Photo p127.*

Mexican/International

San Ángel Inn

*Diego Rivera 50 (5616 1402/5616 2222/www.
sanangelinn.com). Metrobús Bombilla.* **Open** 1pm-
1am Mon-Sat; 1-9.30pm Sun. **Main courses**
MX$130-$340. **Credit** AmEx, DC, MC, V.
Map p259 A3 ⑥④
The elegant 17th-century building and sculpted
grounds of the San Ángel Inn have seen previous
service as a Carmelite monastery, and as a factory
for producing *pulque*, a cactus wine. Choose between
a table off the flowered courtyard or in the cosy dining room, which connects to a handsome cantina
with a mahogany bar. The chefs cook up unusual
blends of local ingredients, such as sea bass
wrapped in fragrant *hoja santa* leaf covered with
pulque, or fettuccini with *huitlacoche* (dark corn fungus) sauce. More traditional dishes include tortilla
soup with all the trimmings; grilled steaks with
beans, rice and strips of chile poblano; and buttery
escamoles (ant larvae) served with guacamole and
warmed tortillas. Dinners are pricey, and with a
drink or dessert, you'll leave feeling you've spent a
small fortune on food that is good but not fantastic.
But it's the surroundings and fine service that make
dining here special. Reservations recommended.

Coyoacán

International

Moheli

*Francisco Sosa 1 (5554 6221). Metro Coyoacán
L3 or Viveros L3.* **Open** 8am-10.30pm Sun-Wed;
8am-11pm Thur-Sat. **Main courses** MX$80-$120.
Credit AmEx, MC, V. **Map** p259 F3 ⑥⑤
Bag a table on the pavement outside Moheli, set on
a cobblestone street near Coyoacán's main plaza. It
looks like a café but has an extensive menu, with
everything from omelettes and bagels to lasagne and
fondue. The pecan and goat's cheese raviolis with
pungent puttanesca sauce are a great choice, and the
enormous salads are ideal for splitting, as are the
many-layered baguette sandwiches with savoury
ingredients including cured ham, artichoke hearts
and smoked salmon. Those not after a full-on feast
can opt for a coffee and home-made dessert, or just
a glass of wine. Moheli also has a deli which sells
wine and cheese.

Mexican

Los Danzantes

*Plaza Jardín Centenario 12 (5658 6054/5658
6451/www.losdanzantes.com). Metro Coyoacán
L3.* **Open** 1.30-11pm Mon-Wed; 1.30pm-midnight

Fresh fish, simple preparation and laid-back style at **Contramar.**

Restaurants & Bar

Polanco • Roma • Centro Histórico

nonsolo.com.mx

NON SOLO PASTA

— Colonia Polanco —
Julio Verne 89
Tel. 5280 9706

— Colonia Roma —
Álvaro Obregón 130
Pasaje El Parian
Tel. 5574 8577

NonSolo BAR

— Colonia Roma —
Álvaro Obregón 130
Pasaje El Parian
Tel. 5574 8577

NON SOLO PANINO

— Colonia Roma —
Plaza Luis Cabrera 10
esquina Guanajuato y Orizaba
Tel. 3096 5128

— Colonia Centro Histórico —
Motolinía 37
Tel. 5512 0619

Thur, Fri; 9-11.30am, 1.30pm-midnight Sat, Sun.
Main courses MX$100-$250. **Credit** AmEx,
MC, V. **Map** p259 F3 ⑥⑥

Huitlacoche, a corn fungus delicacy of the Aztecs
that is typically packed into street-stand quesadillas, finds itself stuffed into ravioli and topped with
a zucchini blossom cream sauce at Los Danzantes.
One of a growing number of restaurants in Mexico
City in which chefs transform humble and some
times peculiar traditional ingredients into so-called
nueva cocina mexicana (new Mexican cuisine),
this unpretentious eaterie has everything those with
an adventurous palate could desire, from appetisers
like grasshopper quesadillas, and shredded venison
tostadas to mains of perfectly seared tuna steak with
habanero chile compote, and *cabrito* (roast baby
goat). Portions are small and the bill is big, but ultimately you're really paying for a table view of
Coyoacán's tree-lined main plaza. *Photo p106.*

El Jardín del Pulpo

*Mercado Coyoacán, Malintzin 89 L24 y 25 (5339
5132). Metro Coyoacán L3.* **Open** 10am-6pm daily.
Main courses MX$70-$180. **No credit cards.**
Map p259 F2 ⑥⑦

At this no-frills eaterie, part of the neighbourhood's
market, patrons sit side by side along picnic tables
devouring plates of *pulpo a la diabla* (spicy octopus)
and *huachinango al mojo de ajo* (whole grilled snapper smothered in garlic). Specialities include *sopa de
mariscos* (spicy seafood broth) and tostadas laden
with combinations of soft shell crab or fish. The
shrimp cocktail is tasty, but you may want to tell
them to go easy on the ketchup.

Merendero Las Lupitas

*Plaza Santa Catarina 4 (5554 3353/5554 1345).
Metro Coyoacán L3.* **Open** 8.30am-1.30pm, 7pm-
midnight Mon-Sat; 8.30am-1.30pm, 8-11pm Sun.
Main courses MX$100 $140. **Credit** MC, V.
Map p259 E3 ⑥⑧

On a lovely little plaza a few blocks from Coyoacán
centre, this restaurant has been serving Northern-
style home cooking since 1959. Colourful cut paper
banners hang from the ceiling, paintings of lilies
adorn the walls, and the food is served in earthen-
ware dishes with a smile, though at a snail's pace.
Try the *machaca* burritos (dried shredded meat in a
flour tortilla) and *panuchos* (thick corn tortillas with
different toppings). Also worth a try are the
chivichangas (crisp flour tortillas stuffed with
creamy beans and melted cheese).

Supertacos Chupacabras

*Universidad, under Churubusco overpass. No
phone. Metro Coyoacán L3.* **Open** 7am-3am daily.
Main courses MX$80 per taco. **No credit cards.**
Map p259 E1 ⑥⑨

Businessmen, construction workers and students
alike dig into the greasy but great tacos at this little
stand, which boasts a marinade 'made from 127
secret spices'. The herbal complexity may be over-
stated, but the signature Chupacabra taco, named
after a mythical goat sucking monster, really is
something special. A mix of tangy chorizo sausage,
salt pork cecina and thin strips of bistec steak,
Chupacabra tacos are made to be drenched in lime
and creamy avocado salsa, making a meal fit to sate
anyone's hunger.

Eat, Drink, Shop

A Paris crêperie comes to Mexico City: **Cluny.** *See p124.*

Cafés, Bars & Cantinas

If the tequila doesn't get you, the mescal might.

There are parts of DF in which you could be in a cosmopolitan corner of just about any Western world city. Sipping coffee in the shady cafés and bars around lovely Parque México, shouting over the late-night hubbub in **Pata Negra** bar, or catching a breeze over martinis at **Área**, the Habita hotel's rooftop bar, it's a delight, but not a purely Mexican one. Yet find yourself a table at any one of the city's down-home cantinas, order a beer and a *botana* (bar snack), and you couldn't be anywhere else. The Centro is particularly well endowed with delightful cantinas, and they make perfect spots for regular stops as you wander the historic streets. Don't miss out on trying mescal, tequila's country cousin, which has nothing to do with mescaline and everything to do, at its best, with fine liquor. But don't knock tequila – and definitely don't knock it

back. Ask three Mexicans how to drink it and you'll get three different, elaborate responses, none of them involving downing it in one go. Mixing up a cocktail in your mouth is one appealing, if potentially inelegant option and it goes something like this: lick salt, suck orange, insert tequila; pause; swallow, smile, repeat.

Centro

Bar La Nueva Ópera
5 de Mayo 10 (5512 8959). Metro Allende L2.
Open 1pm-midnight Mon-Sat; 1-5.30pm Sun.
Credit AmEx, MC, V. **Map** p267 L4 ❶
With its rich dark wood, plush red upholstery and gilded, ornate ceilings, la Ópera is a dream come true for baroque-and-gold fans. And if you just visited the giddily rococo Palacio Postal nearby and liked it, you'll find the more-is-more decor standard flown

Eyes down for dominoes at **Covadonga**. *See p138.*

proudly here too. The only diffident detail in the place is an unassuming puncture in the ceiling, the result, allegedly, of a gunshot fired by the revolutionary Pancho Villa. Dignified waiters serve a typical selection of Mexican lunch and dinner dishes for this is, strictly speaking, a restaurant. But the food, while fine, isn't the point. Pick a dram to match the wallpaper instead: a glass of golden tequila with a sidekick of rich red sangrita – a glass of tomato juice, orange, chilli and lime.

Café La Habana
Morelos 62 (5546 0255/5535 2620/cafehc2@ yahoo.com.mx). Metro Balderas L1, L3 or Juárez L3. **Open** 7am-11.30pm Mon-Thur; 7am-1.30am Fri, Sat; 8am-10pm Sun. **Credit** MC, V. **Map** p266 J4 **2**
Enormous, yellowing photos of Havana adorn the high walls of this historic café in which Che Guevara and Fidel Castro supposedly plotted the Cuban revolution. Located a couple of blocks from the offices of broadsheet newspapers *Excelsior* and *El Universal*, this is still an infamous spot for rendezvous – these days, between politicians and hacks. You'll feel like you are in the know as you sip coffee or linger over breakfast amid the murmur of hushed conversation. For a substantial but speedy lunch, try the *torta cubana*, a large bap (*pan rustico*) filled with roast pork, chorizo, cheese, avocado, refried beans and a smoky chipotle chilli (MX$69). Request *café ligero* (light) for a moderate caffeine fix, or for a full-on, palpitation-inducing direct hit, go for *cargado* – literally meaning 'charged'.

Café Tacuba
Tacuba 28 (5521 2048). Metro Bellas Artes L1. **Open** 8am-11pm daily **Credit** AmEx, MC, V. **Map** p267 L4 **3**
You could be anywhere in Mexico – anywhere that's cool, shady and refined, that is – once tucked inside the hushed, tiled tunnel that is one of the city's most famous cafés. The downtown street outside is just a blur seen past gleaming copper water jugs, stained glass windows and a shop front crammed with cream cakes. Inside, white-uniformed waitresses swish about kindly, plimsolls creaking on polished floors as they deliver ice cream sundaes to frilly dressed little girls whose dads watch fondly over coffee. Mexicans speak highly of the café's homemade *pollo con mole*, whose MX$136 price tag reflects the time, care and many ingredients that go into that most elaborate of Mexican dishes; but it's as a sedate and lovely spot for coffee and cake that Café Tacuba most shines. *Photo p135.*

Churrería El Moro
Eje Central Lázaro Cárdenas 42 (5512 0896/5518 4580). Metro San Juan de Letrán L8. **Open** 24hrs daily. **No credit cards. Map** p267 L5 **4**
Established in 1935, this traditional café serving long Mexican doughnuts or *churros* is a firm favourite with local families seeking a sugar rush. Choose Special (with cinnamon), French, Spanish or Mexican hot chocolate served with four churros

(MX$48) for maximum delight. In fact they all taste similar, with Spanish the sweetest, Mexican the lightest, made with water, and French – also known as *a la reina* or 'fit for a queen' – somewhere in between. Milkshakes or *malteados* are a popular choice, though slightly synthetic for the non-Mexican palate. Savoury options include tacos or *tortas al pastor* (MX$20). Open all hours, El Moro is also a popular option for clubbers lingering after a night on the town. *Photo p131.*

El Gallo de Oro
Venustiano Carranza 35 (5521 1569/5512 1145/ gallooro@prodigy.net.mx). Metro San Juan de Letrán L8 or Zócalo L2. **Open** 10am-midnight daily. **Credit** AmEx, MC, V. **Map** p267 L5 **5**
One of the city's oldest cantinas, El Gallo resembles a shrine to alcohol, with stained-glass windows honouring bottles of Spanish liquor in lieu of religious icons – and so they should, since they've been the cantina's lifeblood since 1874. El Gallo also offers an extensive menu, with mixed grills and diverse cuts of meat. Those with a penchant for black pudding should try the *morcilla de burgos* baked with onion, red pepper and chilli in a terracotta dish (MX$45); and the *empanadas* – spiced meat or

1 Pink numbers given in this chapter correspond to the location of each café, bar and cantina as marked on the street maps. *See pp259-267.*

Great views and modern style at **La Terraza,** Condesa DF hotel. *See p137.*

cheese pies with sweetcorn or spinach – make a perfect beer snack (MX$20). Don't be put off if the green
shutters are down outside: if the saloon-style door
is visible, then this cosy tavern, with its large
leather booths and intimate tables, is almost certainly open for business.

La Gioconda

*Filomeno Mata 18-E (5518 7823/giocondis69@
yahoo.com). Metro Bellas Artes L2, L8.* **Open** 5pm-
midnight Mon-Wed; 5pm-2am Thur-Sat. **No credit
cards. Map** p267 L4 ❻
Rustic decor gives this bar the feel of a poet's
garret despite its location on the ground floor.
Taking its name from the *Mona Lisa*'s alternative
title, La Gioconda doubles as a tiny gallery for local
artists, and between exhibitions the walls are decorated with Da Vinci prints. Unusually good draught
beer – *clara* (light) or *oscura* (dark) – sold in pint or
medium-sized glass mugs, is a favourite. This
European-style drinking establishment also offers
good-value snacks and light meals, chiefly pasta,
salads and baguettes (MX$40-$65).

Hostería La Bota

*Regina 48 (5709 1117/www.casavecina.com).
Metro Isabel la Católica L1.* **Open** 11am-9pm
Mon, Tue; 11am-1.30am Wed-Sat. **No credit
cards. Map** p267 M5 ❼
A gem barely known outside DF's arty crowd, La
Bota is attached to the Casa Vecina Espacio Cultural.
Prepare to feel irresistibly cool as you drink or dine
among Mexico City's up-and-coming film-makers,
writers, painters and musicians. Endless collages of
bull-fighting memorabilia, photographs from the
1940s, eye-catching old product design, cigar boxes,
and empty wine bottles cover the walls, and reasonable Spanish and Italian food includes pasta, small
pizzas (*pizzetas*) and antipasti, though service from
the kitchen is slow. In the interest of safety, it is
worth taking a cab at night, as this is located slightly outside the Centro's habitual bar circuit.

Locazión

*3rd floor, Filomeno Mata 11 (1450 3991/1450
3992). Metro Bellas Artes L2, L8.* **Open** 10am-8pm
Mon-Thur; 10am-1am Fri, Sat. **No credit cards.
Map** p267 L4 ❽
This unusual combination of mid-week eaterie and
weekend salsa bar is found tucked away on the
third floor of a 19th-century townhouse. Affordable
Mexican fare is on offer for breakfast, lunch and
early dinner, but things only really spice up at night.
Frenetic salsa bands attract captivating dancers
who make for a great show to accompany your
drinking. Those brave enough to strut their stuff
among the experts on the sizeable dancefloor can
take a salsa class here (6.30-8pm Thur-Sat).

Salón Cantina La Mascota

*Mesones 20 (5709 7852). Metro Isabel la Católica
L1.* **Open** 9am-11pm Mon-Sat; 9am-8pm Sun.
Credit MC, V. **Map** p267 L5 ❾
Since the early 2008 closure of Mexico's ancient cantina El Nivel, the quest has been on for a sufficiently old-school replacement. La Mascota is a real
contender. A Mexican version of an old man's pub,
the cantina is all dark wood detail and tiled walls. A
deliciously lugubrious atmosphere is fuelled by a
crooner-dominated 1980s jukebox, and fellow customers can be found playing dominos or sinking one
of 20 varieties of tequila (MX$48-$68 per shot). A
place for reflective, potentially hard drinking, the
Salón maintains the tradition of offering free meals
to customers who consume at least three alcoholic
beverages, and plates of salted peanuts – ready to
dress with lime juice and hot sauce – flow freely.

Salón Tenampa

*Plaza Garibaldi 12 (5526 6176/www.salontenampa.
com). Metro Garibaldi L8, LB.* **Open** 1pm-3am daily.
Credit MC, V. **Map** p267 L3 ❿
A safe port in the mariachi storm that is Plaza
Garibaldi, inside Salón Tenampa you're shielded from
the worst excesses of the iconic square beyond –

rubbish scattered underfoot, swaying drunkards and the occasional ineffectual fight. Inside the Salón, the mariachi madness continues as eight-strong bands, trumpets and all, serenade paying punters under the painted gaze of the radio stars of yesteryear. Weep along to your MX$70-a-pop song, which may tell of a no-good woman and a man who shoulda known better, and you'll be smiled upon fondly. Sweet service and good bar snacks mitigate the messiest aspects of the Plaza Garibaldi experience, with the deep dish of melted Chihuahua cheese and spicy chorizo creating a damn good foundation for the tequila and beer that flow as freely here as tears. *See p192* **Cry me a río**.

La Selva Café

Bolívar 31 (5521 4111). Metro San Juan de Letrán L8 or Zócalo L2. **Open** 8am-10pm daily. **Credit** MC, V. **Map** p267 L4 ⑪
This branch of Mexico's upmarket organic coffeeshop chains boasts a particularly pleasant setting. Filling the courtyard of a soaring colonial building, complete with central fountain, it's light and airy by day and romantic by night. The fairtrade company sources its eight varieties of coffee from more than 1,360 indigenous farmers in Chiapas, southern Mexico. Choose between 22 types of coffee, from the humble cappuccino to liqueur blends. La Selva Café also offers breakfast, light lunches, and sweet and savoury snacks.
Other locations throughout the city.

La Terraza del Centro

Centro Cultural de España, República de Guatemala 18 (5510 4077/www.myspace.com/terrazaccemx/ www.ccemx.org). Metro Zócalo L2. **Open** 9.30am-8pm Tue; 9.30am-1am Wed; 9.30am-2am Thur-Sat; 9.30am-4pm Sun. **Credit** MC, V. **Map** p267 M4 ⑫
Meander through the centre's delightful gallery to reach the Terraza del Centro, a spacious bar and restaurant overlooking the rooftops at Mexico's metropolitan cathedral. A contemporary design utilising glass and industrial metal sits surprisingly well with the elegant lines of this grand 18th-century townhouse. Authentic, well-presented Spanish tapas (MX$50 $128) and a good drinks selection, including cocktails (MX$50-000), are another draw. Try the *pimientos del piquillo* stuffed with spiced tuna and finished with fresh garlic and rich olive oil; or the *pantomate*: high-quality Serrano ham served on tomato-topped toasted rye bread. The terrace is a popular nightspot with live musicians and DJs.

Paseo de la Reforma

El Bar

Four Seasons Hotel, Avenida Paseo de la Reforma 500 (5230 1818/www.fourseasons.com/mexico). Metro Chapultepec L1 or Sevilla L1. **Open** 7am-1am Mon-Fri; 8am-1am Sat; 8am-midnight Sun. **Credit** AmEx, MC, V. **Map** p264 F6 ⑬
The library-style bar at Mexico City's grandiose Four Seasons (*see p41*) might not be the first place you consider for a nightcap; and the bar itself, with

its overstuffed chairs and the scent of money heavy in the air, is indeed a touch suffocating. But out on the terrace, it's quite a different matter. Set in a courtyard garden – a phrase that doesn't even start to do justice to the place's impressive dimensions and the soaring hotel that encloses it on four sides, with skyscrapers peeping in beyond that – the terrace is a delight. Fairy-lit shrubs and blazing torches along the walls make the cheap option – a snifter of mescal at MX$35 – well worth the price; and then step politely past the Russian oligarchs and their beautiful friends and out the front door, round the back and behind the hotel to Calle Hamburgo for a tasty, dirt-cheap taco.

Bar Milán

Milán 18-24 (5592 0031). Metro Insurgentes L1. **Open** 9pm-3am Tue-Sat. **Credit** AmEx, MC, V. **Map** p266 I5 ⑭
This popular bar – cool, but not too cool – is a little off the regular party circuit but fills up quickly on Thursday and Friday nights with a fashionable but unpretentious crowd of journalists and creative types. It's not so much a place to be seen but rather a place to drink (strong) margaritas, sing along to 1980s tunes and hang out with friends. The lack of windows and dark decor give it the feel of a basement speakeasy. Milán has its own currency, *milagros* (miracles), which you have to purchase at the cash desk on your way in.

El Moro. *See p129*.

La Cantina de los Remedios
Río Tiber 113 (5208 8922). Metro Insurgentes L1.
Open 1.30pm-2am daily. **Credit** AmEx, DC, MC, V.
Map p264 G5 🄯
If you're looking for spring-break-style partying, Cantina de los Remedios is where it's at. Not a place for sophisticated cocktails or elegant conversation, this vast two-storey cantina is filled to the rafters on weekend nights with gringos and Mexicans enjoying loud music, tequila shots, beer pitchers, mariachi music and the rest. Get there early (or late) if you want to get a table.

Zona Rosa

Konditori
Génova 61 (5511 0722/5511 2300/www.konditori.com.mx). Metro Insurgentes L1. **Open** 7am-11pm Mon-Sat; 8am-11pm Sun. **Credit** AmEx, MC, V.
Map p264 H6 🄯
Despite its location directly opposite a McDonald's, Konditori is a good spot for people-watching, especially given some of the interesting outfits – and the people inside them – that pass on by in this colourful neighbourhood. Classical music and free Wi-Fi accompany the juices, coffee, cakes and pastries on offer, but the waiters aren't always impressed by those just wanting a coffee and a place to while away a few hours. On Saturdays and Sundays there's an all-inclusive brunch buffet – fruit, cereals, pastries, eggs, and so on – served from 9am to 1pm.

Polanco

Área
Habita Hotel, Avenida Presidente Masaryk 201 (5282 3100/www.hotelhabita.com). Metro Polanco L7. **Open** 7-11pm Mon-Wed; 7pm-1am Thur-Sat.
Credit AmEx, MC, V. **Map** p262 C4 🄯
The Habita Hotel's (*see p46*) rooftop bar has been a fixture on the scene since 2000, and it's showing its age – but in a good way. Refusing to blind its clientele with the science of the constant makeover, Área is a slick, classy joint with a pedigree it has no need to shout about. Instead, it sits atop one of the city's best design hotels and serves up cool cocktails to the hip *chilango* set. Gaze up, as you sip on a flavoured martini – all the rage, unless something else has become all the rage since the time of writing – at flickering old films projecting on to a neighbouring building; or peer over the parapet upon the even hipper bar – sorry: VIPs only – downstairs by the pool.

Diagonal
Avenida Presidente Masaryk 169 (2624 3250/www.tapasdiagonal.com). Metro Polanco L7. **Open** 1.30pm-midnight Mon-Wed; 1.30pm-2am Thur-Sat.
Credit AmEx, MC, V. **Map** p262 C4 🄯
Diagonal's stylish but understated space, with tables in the front and a comfy bar out back, fuses sexy Polanco chic with a friendly vibe. The drinks menu boasts over 80 freshly prepared 'artisanal' cocktails,

and the tapas selection is equally exhaustive. Owners Luis Villaseñor and Teresa López Liñán pick the soundtrack: a groovy mix that intensifies as the crowd does, especially on Thursdays and on into the weekend. Dress, if not to kill, then at least to maim. Free Wi-Fi.

Giandolce
Avenida Presidente Masaryk 270 (5282 1234/www.giandolce.com). Metro Polanco L7. **Open** 9am-11pm Sun-Thur; 9am-midnight Fri-Sat. **Credit** AmEx, MC, V. **Map** p262 C5 🄯
This upmarket coffee house makes Starbucks look like a dump. Smack in the middle of the neighbourhood in a spotless old Spanish-revival mansion, Giandolce is the place to go for European-style coffees, free Wi-Fi, freshly prepared sandwiches and snacks and an extensive ice-cream selection. A relaxing place for people-watching on a budget (at least for Polanco), and much classier than Klein's or El Farolito.

King's Pub
Campos Elíseos 269 (5280 1114/www.thekingspub.com). Metro Auditorio L7. **Open** 1pm-2am Mon-Weds; 1pm-3am Thur-Sat. **Credit** AmEx, MC, V.
Map p262 B5 🄯
Homesick limeys won't be fooled by this 'English' pub, but they can still work their fellow customers' anglophilia to advantage. Complete with the mandatory Guinness signs and Fab Four photos, this ample space attracts big crowds most nights. The beer menu is one of the largest west of the Mersey, prices are reasonable, and even the pub grub tastes good after a pint or five. Live music (rock and pop covers) is an added draw – or the reverse – two nights a week. Either way, check the website for the current schedule. Free Wi-Fi.

Pastelería Gino's
Hegel 254 (5545 8847/5531 6141). Metro Polanco L7. **Open** 8am-9pm Mon-Fri; 8am-6pm Sat, Sun.
Credit AmEx, MC, V. **Map** p262 C4 🄯
An obligatory stop if you're travelling with your mother, and a great find even if you're not. Practically frozen in time somewhere around 1909, Gino's is a cheerful tearoom piled high with baroque candelabra, urns and frilly displays laden with mountains of excellent chocolates, pastries and other desserts, all made on the premises. The ice-cream is exquisite, the coffee quite good, and there's also a 'Polanco moderate' menu at lunchtime. Liveried waitresses of a 'certain age' – we're loving those uniforms – won't be in any hurry, so why should you be?

Punta del Cielo
Arquímedes 69-1 (5280 7094/www.puntadelcielo.com.mx). Metro Polanco L7. **Open** 7am-11pm Mon-Fri; 9am-11pm Sat, Sun. **Credit** AmEx, MC, V.
Map p262 C4 🄯
PdC keeps it local by featuring only Mexican coffees in its otherwise international-looking establishments – think the Apple Store in café form. The

Vino, vidi, vici

It's a modest affair compared with that of its Californian cousin to the north, but over 400 years since vines were first planted in Mexico, a resurgence in wine production is giving rise to some exquisite, robust Mexican wines.

Vineyards planted by the Spanish flourished in Mexico until 1595, when King Philip II banned the planting of vines and ordered the removal of existing vineyards to protect the Spanish wine market. Thanks to missionaries who continued to produce wine, viniculture in Mexico survived, and today there are wineries in Coahuila, Querétaro, Aguascalientes and Zacatecas. But it's in Baja California that things are hotting up. Large commercial producers like **LA Cetto**, **Santo Tomás** and **Domecq** are joined by smaller vineyards such as **Monte Xanic** and **Casa de Piedra**, producing wines of a quality that is starting to attract attention. In the Valley of Guadalupe wine hotspot, cold marine currents cause microclimatic changes to the otherwise semi-desert conditions that make all the difference to the grapes and, indeed, shift the climate towards something approximating the Mediterranean.

Currently preparing to create his own wine, **Piluchas**, Adrián García Fernández is a young oenologist from Ensenada, at the heart of the wine boom. García is frank about the challenges facing the region. 'The valley suffers from a shortage of water because most of the zone's water table is assigned to domestic use in Ensenada,' he explains. 'As a result, the grapes acquire less acidity and have a greater concentration of sugar. The soil can suffer from a high concentration of minerals, which is reflected in some wines and gives rise to the special characteristics of Mexican wines: they are powerful, with an acidity that ranges from average to low, and with lots of body and structure.'

Perfect for Mexican food? José Luis Durand of **Sinergi-VT** wines, who alongside the much admired Hugo D'Acosta is one of the stars of Baja Californian wine production, breaks it down: 'I don't think combining spicy Mexican food with red wine is the best option. For both physiological and sensory reasons, it's best to pair Mexican food with white or rosé wines with less tannin. But not all Mexican food is spicy,' he goes on, recommending Ícaro, one of his most popular wines, as a match for local cuisine. Created with a blend of nebbiolo, merlot and petite sirah grapes, Ycaro is typical of the varieties used in Mexican wine. 'There are no regulations for establishing the varieties that must be used in Mexico,' says García. And by the same token, so far no single variety has emerged in Mexico as the wine grape *par excellence*. 'A great deal remains to be tried and tested,' says García, 'to find out if there is a variety that can be expressed better in Mexico than in other parts of the world.'

Mexican wines to look out for: *White* Piedra del Sol from Casa Piedra; chardonnay by Monte Xanix; Silvana from Pau Pijoa. *Red* Jala by Tres Valles; Ícaro by Sinergi-Vt; Emblema by Paralelo.

---

signature coffee is rich and flavourful, available in a dizzying variety of presentations, and the snacks are tasty too. The big tables and comfy lounge areas are great for writing postcards and taking advantage of the free Wi-Fi.

Skyy Bar
Avenida Presidente Masaryk 133 (5545 0848). Metro Polanco L7. **Open** 6pm-1am Mon-Wed; 6pm-3am Thur-Sat. **Credit** AmEx, MC, V. **Map** p262 D4 ㉓
It's not clear where the sky fits in to this ground-level establishment. But down on earth you'll find tons of good-looking, well-dressed and animated young men and women table hopping to an eclectic music mix ranging from 1980s pop to the very latest sounds. *Sex and the City*-style girlie drinks are a speciality, but the basics are well covered as well. It's very happening on weekends – as in packed – so be forewarned. ID required.

Black Horse
Mexicali 85A (5211 8740/www.caballonegro.com). Metro Patriotismo L9. **Open** 6pm-2am daily. **Credit** AmEx, MC, V. **Map** p264 F9 ㉔
Described by co-owner Juan Alberto Vázquez as a '*chilango*-fied' English pub, the Black Horse mixes Anglo traditions (ploughman's lunches; fish and

chips; football on flat screens) with cantina staples – *botanas* (Mexican snacks) and tequila – to popular effect. The rich mix is echoed in the clientele, which runs the gamut of age and nationalities; the bar claims to have been the meeting place for at least ten international couples since its inception in 2004. There's jazz on Tuesdays and local and foreign bands playing Wednesday through Saturday, with a focus on funk, groove, hip-hop and, occasionally, Latin beats such as Cuban *son*. 'We allow everything except reggaeton, Spanish pop and electronic music,' says Vázquez. DJs play after 8pm.

La Botica
Campeche 396 (5211 6045). Metro Patriotismo L9. **Open** 5pm-midnight Sun-Wed; 5pm-2am Thur-Sat. **No credit cards. Map** p264 F9 ㉕
There's no sign on the door at this bar, known by many as 'La Mezcaleria', and inside there are just seven tiny tables, with blue enamel bowls of chilli-coated *habas* (broad beans). Fifteen varieties of mescal are dispensed from nameless bottles as in an old-style pharmacy, and menus scrawled on cardboard add to the understated style. The arty crowd and the subsequent opening of six other locales seem proof that mescal is in the throes of a too-cool-for-school revival *(see p139* **Tequila forever***)*. All mescals are served with orange slices and worm salt; but if that leaves you peckish, as mescal will, La Botica also offers regional specialities such as banana-leaf wrapped tamales, balls of squeaky Oaxaca cheese, and *chapulines* – fried crickets.
Other locations Alfonso Reyes 120, Condesa; Madero 10-C, Francisco I, San Ángel.

Frutos Prohibidos
Amsterdam 244-D (5264 5808). Metro Chilpancingo L9/Metrobús Campeche. **Open** 8am-10pm Mon-Fri; 10am-6pm Sat-Sun. **No credit cards. Map** p264 G8 ㉖

Tired of tacos? Dying for a salad and a sandwich? Pull up a pew on the footpath one block from Parque México and join the dog-walkers and post-yoga crowd downing fresh juice combinations like Cha Cha Cha (orange, strawberry, kiwi, pineapple, banana and spirulina), or tropical inventions like – when in season – mamey (a sweet pumpkin-like fruit) or the vitamin C-packed guayaba. The *pecados* (Spanish for sins) are wraps made with custom-designed, oversized Bimbo-brand bread loaves sliced and flattened, then rolled and toasted with a choice of fillings. Breakfast options include fresh fruit salad, baked eggs, and *molletes* (open-toasted baguettes with refried beans, tomato, avocado and cheese).
Other locations Antara Food Court, Ejercito Nacional 843, Polanco.

Maque
Ozulama 4 (2454 4662). Metro Chilpancingo L9. **Open** 8am-10pm Mon-Sat; 8am-9pm Sun. **Credit** AmEx, M, V. **Map** p264 F9 ㉗
If your class sensibilities aren't too offended by the Porfirio Diaz-era housemaid's frilly skirts and aprons worn by the waitresses, you'll find that this *pasteleria*, right on the corner of Parque México, serves the best breakfasts in Condesa. On weekends, the queue for brunch stretches around the corner as grannies and hipsters alike wait patiently for light and fluffy *huevos rancheros* or *pastel azteca*, a breakfast 'lasagne' with layers of *huitlacoche*, squash flowers and chicken in tomato sauce. Breakfast is served until 1pm when the menu switches to soups, pastas, mains such as tamarind chicken breast, and Mexican standards such as enchiladas.

El Ocho
Ozuluama 14 (5211 9010/www.elocho.com.mx). **Open** 8am-midnight Sun-Wed, 8am-1am Thur-Sun. **Credit** AmEx, MC, V. **Map** p264 F9 ㉘

Café Tacuba. *See p129.*

DF eye

It is said that you can't come to Mexico and not drink tequila. I beg to differ. You can't come to Mexico and not drink mescal – the true libation of the gods, ideally with a worm in the bottle and accompanied by some oranges and a bowl of fried *chapulines* (crickets).

Iván Nieblas, podcaster, Suena on el Estéreo

A charming place to while away the time in leafy Condesa, this corner café has, although it doesn't really need one, a gimmick. It's boardgames, and lots of them. Scan the racks of colourful boxes and note the suduku cards and assorted pen-and-paper games in your tabletop holder, and your cynical bone might quiver. But look around and you'll see the disarming spectacle of friends quietly getting on with the underrated pastime of a spot of simple play. Full meals and snacks are available, but it's the 30 teas and infusions, the cakes, crêpes and tarts, and the equally sweet service that could make you a regular, however long your stay.

Pata Negra

Tamaulipas 30 (5211 4678/www.patanegra.com.mx). Metro Chapultepec L1 or Chilpancingo L9. **Open** 1.30pm-1.30am daily. **Credit** AmEx, M, V. **Map** p264 F8 ㉙
One of the earliest and most popular nightspots in a neighbourhood now packed with them, elbow room is hard to find in this busy tapas bar, which fills up almost every night of the week. Arrive early (around 6pm or 7pm) if you want a table, or pull up a barstool and yell your order over the DJ's thumping backbeat. Live bands play on Sundays, Mondays and Tuesdays. There's an additional bar upstairs that often stays open late, with a live salsa band Wednesday and Saturday nights.

El Péndulo

Nuevo Leon 115 (5280 4276/5286 9493/www.pendulo.com). Metro Chilpancingo L9. **Open** 8am-11pm Mon-Thur; 9am-midnight Fri, Sat. **Credit** AmEx, MC, V. **Map** p264 F8 ㉚
Eating is an excellent reason to come to El Péndulo, but not the only one. Opened in 1992 as a self-styled cultural refuge for Mexico City's intellectuals, this 'cafebrería' – bookshop, DVD/CD-store, café and bar rolled into one – has become a favourite meeting place for writers, politicians, and students who loiter on the upstairs couches discussing, say, the latest developments in film theory. The Condesa flagship has since spawned four more branches and hosts literary workshops, concerts and book launches while serving bottomless cups of *café americano* and hearty soups, salads and sandwiches. By far the best thing on the menu, though, are the breakfasts, served till 1pm. The *huevos Macondo*, fried eggs over quesadillas stuffed with *huitlacoche* or squash flower, are delicious, washed down with Nopal de Luz, a blend of cactus, pineapple and orange juice. On weekends, there's a live duo playing jazz, which, along with book browsing (most of them Spanish-language titles but with a small, quality English section), makes the sometimes lengthy weekend wait for a table far less burdensome.
Other locations Dumas 81, Polanco (5280 4111); Hamburgo 126, Zona Rosa (5208 2327)

La Terraza

Condesa DF Hotel, Avenida Veracruz 102 (5241-2600/www.condesadf.com). Metro Chapultepec L1/Metrobús Sonora. **Open** 2pm-1.30am Tue, Thur-Sat; noon-midnight Mon, Wed, Sun. **Credit** AmEx, MC, V. **Map** p264 F7 ㉛
Another slick roof terrace bar from the same stable as Habita hotel's trendy Área (*see p133*), La Terraza has the same odd triangular shape as the grand Condesa DF hotel (*see p49*) it serves. Pull up a stool at the bar or talk yourself into one of the rattan table-and-chair booths set all around the terrace; and take a casual swing round the place before you're done, just to check out DF's beautiful people taking their pleasure. Sushi is an option, but if it's dinner you're after, best to move downstairs to the hot right-now restaurant. *Photo p130.*

T Gallery

Saltillo 39 (5211 7942/5211 1222/www.tgallerydesign.com). Metro Patriotismo L9. **Open** 5pm-2am Mon-Sat. **Credit** AmEx, MC, V. **Map** p264 F9 ㉜
Named, or rather initialled, after Anglo-Argentinian owner Tina Hacking, this two-storey bar-in-a-house consists of a series of wallpapered rooms filled with plush couches, chaises longues, mosaic mirrors and dripping chandeliers, all of which are for sale. The place was once an antique furniture shop and old habits, it seems, die hard. Live bands play blues on Tuesday, hip-hop on Thursday and Cuban *son* on Friday, while the model-gorgeous crowd orders Argentinian-style pizzas and empanadas to go with its ginger and apple martinis. The music is loud. *Photo p138.*

Tierra de Vinos

Durango 197 (5208 5133/www.tierradevinos.com). Metro Insurgentes L1/Metrobús Álvaro Obregón. **Open** 1pm-12.30am Mon-Sat; 1-5.30pm Sun. **Credit** AmEx, MC, V. **Map** p264 G7 ㉝
In this nation of beer and tequila drinkers, wine bars are scarcer than hen's teeth (though this may not be the case for much longer; *see p134* **Vino, vidi, vici**). This one, an upmarket, cavernous cellar that doubles as a restaurant and tapas bar, is an excellent place to explore Mexico's emerging wine culture and to sample wines from over 14 different countries, including the USA, Australia and New Zealand. The atmosphere is refined but, despite the wine-friendly cooled air, a little stuffy. Bring a jacket.

Roma

Café de Carlo

Orizaba 115 (5574 5647). Metro Insurgentes L1/Metrobús Álvaro Obregón. **Open** 8am-10pm Mon-Sat; 9.30am-5pm Sun. **No credit cards.** **Map** p264 H7 ㉞

Possibly the best coffee you'll find in Mexico City, the roasted-on-the-premises brew here is strong and full of flavour, unlike the ubiquitous, overcooked *americano* or insipidly milky cappuccino served up in many Mexico City cafés. Frequented by old men discussing politics, poets scribbling, and the occasional man in a black beret watching the world go by, this no-frills establishment is a great spot for either a lengthy daydream or a short, sharp shot of caffeine. Free Wi-Fi.

Covadonga

Puebla 121 (5533 2922/www.banquetes covadonga.com). Metro Insurgentes L1/Metrobús Insurgentes. **Open** 1.30pm-3am daily. **Credit** MC, V. **Map** 264 H6 ㉟

A star in the galaxy of the DF night, Covadonga may not be much to look at under its electric light glare, but it has all the *buena onda* – good vibes – to make up for it. It's attended by efficient, seen-it-all waiters, some of whom look like they might have been here since its inception as one of a wave of joints opened by refugees from the Spanish civil war. At tables scattered around the huge room, the dominoes go *clack clack clack* and the players make use of cunning shelves built into the table legs to avoid spillages. At other tables, people rock back in their chairs with laughter, and luminaries from the art, media and literary crowds converse cleverly. A garish triptych of murals on one wall faces a row of incongruous pictures on the other, suggestive of an artistic clientele unable to pay its bills. Serving very

good Spanish-style food, to top it all off, this is a brilliant place to kick off the evening. *Photo p128.*

Maison Francaise de Thé Caravanserai

Orizaba 101-A (5511 2877/caravanseraimexico @yahoo.fr). Metro Insurgentes L1/Metrobús Alvaro Obregón. **Open** 10.30am-9pm Mon-Fri; noon-9pm Sat-Sun. **No credit cards.** **Map** p264 H7 ㊱

With its velvet recliners, eclectic antique furniture and more than 100 teas served in elegant pots and coloured teacups, this 1920s-style, art deco-inspired den is a pleasant spot for calming nerves frayed by the frenetic pace of the city. You could try La Mujer Acechada (a mix of green and black teas with hints of strawberry, vanilla and bergamot), described by the menu as 'a remedy against the cruelty of the world'; or perhaps Revolution of 100 Flowers (jasmin, rose, mango and citrus). As its name suggests, most of the Maison's teas come from France, and the menu follows the francophile theme with a range of tarts and baguettes. Free Wi-Fi.

Coyoacán

La B

Malitzin 155 (5484 8230). Metro Coyoacán L3. **Open** 1pm-midnight Mon, Tue; 1pm-2am Thur-Sat. **Credit** AmEx, MC, V. **Map** p259 F2 ㊲

Cop a seat at a picnic table in heartthrob actor Diego Luna's trendy bar (previously known as La Bipolar) and knock back some cold Pacífico beers or Baja California wine. A less traditional thirst quencher is the house version of *clericó* (sangría), made with white wine, cucumber and bits of pineapple. Mescal seems to be the most popular order and is reasonably priced at MX$30 a shot; or if the smoky agave spirit is too much for you straight, try a refreshing *martínez* – mescal with cucumber and mint. Spirits

T Gallery. *See p137.*

Tequila forever

Tequila and mescal are made from the flesh of a cactus. Tequila is a more refined version of mescal. The best varieties of mescal come complete with a little dead worm. And a particularly clever way to drink tequila is to mix it with equal parts 7-Up, slam it hard on the bar, gulp the resultant suds in one go, and then balance the shot glass on your head while emitting a primeval roar.

Wrong, wrong, wrong. And wrong again. The first misconception is easy to deal with. Both tequila and mescal are distilled from the juice of the agave plant, also known as maguey. Agaves have sharp, spiny leaves, it's true; and they will hurt you if you sit on them. But they are not cacti.

Tequila is not necessarily better, purer or more refined than mescal, but it *is* more strictly defined. All agave-based distilled liquors are mescals except those made from blue agave in the area surrounding Tequila, a town in Jalisco state. The latter, and only the latter, may be called tequilas. Both mescal and tequila may be sold as *joven* (not aged), *reposado* ('rested' for two months to a year) or *añejo* (aged from to three years); and

mescal, unlike tequila, is made from roasted agave, which gives it a subtle smoky flavour.

The other difference between tequila and mescal is a purely decorative one. Mescal is often bottled with objects that can range from tiny sculptures to scorpions to the famous 'worm' – actually the larva of either a snout weevil or a moth, whose presence in the bottle has no effect on the flavour of the liquor. Nor is it a mark of authenticity: the worm was first added in the 1940s as a marketing gimmick. Mescal is, though, served with '*sal de gusano*' on the side, a mix of salt, red chilli powder and roasted larvae.

Both tequila and mescal have a common ancestor, *pulque*, which was being used as a ritual intoxicant by the Mesoamericans at around the time Jesus of Nazareth turned water into wine. *Pulque* is a gloopy beverage made from fermented (not distilled) agave or maguey sap. Though declining in popularity, it is still drunk today, either from a can or in a *pulquería*; and in the latter, it is customary for drinkers to spill a few drops of the green stuff on to the floor as a sacrifice to the god of pulque, Two Rabbits.

are also mixed with Lulu, an old-time Mexican soft drink. The upstairs space features DJs mixing beats into the small hours most nights of the week.

Café El Jarocho

Cuauhtémoc 134 E, F, G (5658 5029/5554 5418/ www.cafeeljarocho.com.mx). Metro Coyoacán L3. **Open** 6am-1am Sun-Thur; 6am-2am Fri, Sat. **No credit cards. Map** p259 F2 ③

At any given time of the day, lines snake out the door of this Coyoacán institution, which puts Starbucks to shame, selling MX$9 *americanos* and cappuccinos as well as full litres of the highly caffeinated elixirs for just MX$36. The coffee, frankly, isn't the best, but it's a fine spot for a pause nevertheless. There are no tables, so join the coffee drinkers parked on benches along the pavement. **Other locations** throughout the city.

Cantina La Coyoacana

Higuera 14 (5658 5337/1325 6019). Metro Coyoacán L3. **Open** 1pm-10pm Sun-Wed; 1pm-midnight Thur-Sat. **Credit** AmEx, MC, V. **Map** p259 F3 ③

This relatively recent addition to Coyoacán's drinking scene has a squeaky-clean interior that leaves

some purists waxing nostalgic for the grime and grit of an authentic old cantina. But the tables on the grass in the back garden are perfect spots for sitting back, sipping tequilas and snacking on reasonably priced cantina fare, especially at weekends, when musicians play jazz or *trova* folk music in a corner of the garden.

El Hijo del Cuervo

Jardín Centenario 17 (5658 7824/www.elhijodel cuervo.com.mx). Metro Coyoacán L3. **Open** 4pm-midnight Mon-Wed; 1pm-1.30am Thur; 1pm-2.30am Fri, Sat; 1-11.30pm Sun. **No credit cards. Map** p259 F2 ④

Philosophy professors, ageing rockers, students and travellers all come together at this convivial tavern. The pavement tables are always packed with patrons knocking back *jarras* (pitchers) of draught beer. Jazz bands play on Tuesdays and rock groups on Wednesdays, with poetry readings on Saturday afternoons. Snacks range from hangover helpers like *caldo de camarón* (shrimp broth) to fried cheese sticks and nachos – the perfect food to nibble while you're giving yourself something to have a hangover about.

Shops & Services

Markets, hawkers, malls – and food, glorious food.

The capital's commercial lifeblood is in its circuit of markets or *tianguis,* and in the roving traders (*ambulantes*) that spill on to the streets, with their makeshift stalls never far from view although they are far fewer than years ago, particularly in the Centro Histórico. Since the 1994 introduction of NAFTA (the North American Free Trade Agreement), the days of the closed economy, when teenagers had to beg American relatives to smuggle in coveted US sneakers in a suitcase, are gone. But those expecting wickedly cheap international goods at mainstream stores will be disappointed: you'll pay a premium for anything foreign, NAFTA or no NAFTA. Electronic goods are an unwise investment unless money is no object.

Shops tend to open from 9am to 7pm in line with general office hours, but malls and department stores usually start and end business later in the day. Carry photo ID with you if you plan to pay with plastic.

General

Department stores

Liverpool
Mariano Escobedo 425, Polanco (5328 6400/ customer service 5262 9999/www.liverpool.com.mx). Metro Polanco L7. **Open** 11am-9pm daily. **Credit** AmEx, MC, V. **Map** p262 D4.
This doughty department store has nothing to do with Mexico's undying Beatlemania: Liverpool's French founder used to ship desirable European clothing to Mexico from the British port. Today, it

A menagerie of fantastical *alejibres* at **La Ciudadela**. *See p151.*

stocks everything from luxury cosmetics to electronics, with gourmet food halls in several of the larger stores.
Other locations throughout the city.

Palacio de Hierro
Avenida 20 de Noviembre 3, Centro (5229 3154/ www.elpalaciodehierro.com.mx). Metro Zócalo L2. **Open** 11am-8pm Mon-Fri; 11am-9pm Sat; 11am-7pm Sun. **Credit** MC, V. **Map** p267 M5.
Welcome to Mexico's intentionally elitist chain of department stores, home to costly yet classy clothes, cosmetics and typical department-store fare. Acquire epicurean offerings in the gourmet department. iPod on the blink? Drop in at the official Apple store.
Other locations throughout the city.

Saks Fifth Avenue
Centro Santa Fe, Avenida Vasco de Quiroga 3800, Santa Fe (5246 4800). Metro Tacubaya L1, L7, L9, then minibus, taxi colectivo or RTP bus marked Santa Fe. **Open** 11am-9pm daily. **Credit** AmEx, MC, V.
New York's most stylish department store opened its *chilango* chain in early 2008, gracing the ground floor of Latin America's largest mall. Worth a trip if you miss the pzazz of US consumer culture.

Sanborns
Centro Comercial Plaza Insurgentes, San Luis Potosí 214, Roma (5584 9192/www.sanborns.com.mx) Metrobús Sonora. **Open** 7.30am-1am daily. **Credit** MC, V. **Map** p264 G8.
Sanborns is one of Mexico's most historic stores. In December 1916, when Pancho Villa and Emiliano Zapata took control of DF, their revolutionary foot soldiers marched on the Sanborns in the Centro Histórico, the most beautiful though not the largest in the chain, to scoff hot chocolate and pastries. Today, this ubiquitous chain of all-purpose stores could do with a revolution. Service is slow and inefficient and the product range is patchy, although in-store pharmacies include good skincare and toiletry sections. Some Sanborns have restaurants attached.
Other locations throughout the city.

Sears
Centro Comercial Plaza Insurgentes, San Luis Potosí 214, Roma (5230 3940/www.sears.com.mx). Metrobús Sonora. **Open** 11am-9pm daily. **Credit** MC, V. **Map** p264 G8.
Cheaper than Liverpool or Palacio, Sears is fine for replacing forgotten basics that didn't make it into your suitcase. The fashion range is improving and they now stock the 'Naco' ironic T-shirt brand (*see p155* **Naco but nice**) – and Nine West shoes.
Other locations throughout the city.

Malls

Mexicans are big fans of malls. The biggest and best are found beyond the centre, but there are some pleasant ones in central *colonias* too.

The best Shops

For ace souvenirs
Arte Mexicano para el Mundo (*see p151*); **Las Artesanías** (*see p151*); **La Ciudadela** (*see p151*); **Bazar del Sábado y Tianguis** (*see p151*).

For gastronomic delight
Mercado San Juan de Especialidades (*see p150*); **La Naval** (*see p149*).

For leisurely browsing
Antara Polanco (*below*); **Jardín del Arte Sullivan** (*see p151*); **Pasaje Polanco** (*below*).

For bargain hunting
Ciao Masaryk (*p142*); **La Merced** (*see p142*); **Mercado La Lagunilla** (*see p153*); **Villa Plaza Boutique Secretos** (*see p147*).

Antara Polanco
Avenida Fjército Nacional 843B, Polanco (5280 1412/www.webantara.com). Metro Polanco L7. **Open** 11am-8pm daily. **Credit** varies. **Map** p262 A3.
This self-styled 'Fashion Hall' features designer boutiques including Tommy Hilfiger, Burberry and Armani alongside omnipresent Spanish stores such as Zara. For electronics there is Sony and the Sharper Image; for elegant homeware, Casa Palacio. Find fast food on the top floor and high-end eateries around the complex.

Centro Comercial Plaza Insurgentes
San Luis Potosí 214, Roma (5230 3971). Metrobús Sonora. **Open** 11am-8pm daily. **Credit** varies. **Map** p264 G8.
This is a clean and compact mall accessible on foot from Roma and Condesa, complete with a sizeable Martí sports store, great coffee at Punta del Cielo, Mix Up for music and DVDs, and a ten-screen Cinemex showing the latest releases.

Centro Santa Fe
Avenida Vasco de Quiroga 3800, Santa Fe (3003 4300/www.centrosantafe.com.mx). Metro Tacubaya L1, L7, L9, then minibus, taxi colectivo or RTP bus marked Santa Fe. **Open** 11am-8pm Sun-Fri; 11am-9pm Sat. **Credit** varies.
This exclusive mall in the midst of Mexico City's financial district brims with designer boutiques and department stores, plus Saks, Diesel, Levi's, Replay, and Spain's Zara, Bershka and Mango.

Pasaje Polanco
Avenida Presidente Masaryk 360, Polanco (5280 7976). Metro Auditorio L7 or Polanco L7. **Open** 11am-8pm Mon-Sat; noon-6pm Sun. **Credit** varies. **Map** p262 B4.

Eat, Drink, Shop

Where to shop

Polanco

International fashion houses line Avenida Presidente Masaryk, where designer stores cluster and DF ladies both shop and lunch.

Roma and Condesa

Young designers flock to the shabby chic Roma and Condesa neighbourhoods to make a name for themselves in funky fashions, unusual accessories and objets d'art. Retro styles dominate round here, but you can equally snap up subtle, minimalist designs in fashion and furnishings.

Centro

As with most cities in Latin America, DF's traditional shopping zones are organised according to speciality. Stretches of specific streets in the Centro are dedicated to sportswear (Venustiano Carranza), stationery (Mesones), car-parts and repairs (Versalles), and – bizarrely – kitchen appliances (Artículo 123). You'll hear Calle Bolívar's principle trade from streets away; its rows of musical instrument shops are a magnet for troupes of teenagers and browsing rockers. Antique hunters should make a beeline for the La Lagunilla flea market.

Santa Fe

Well-heeled shoppers head to the sophisticated suburb of Santa Fe for its mix of fashion boutiques, beauty salons and US-style malls.

This charming cluster of boutiques has a village feel. It's great for design, women's and children's clothes, and also houses the immense arts and crafts store Las Artesanías.

Reforma 222

Paseo de la Reforma 222, Zona Rosa (5525 0602/ www.reforma222.com). Metro Insurgentes L1/ Metrobús Reforma. **Open** 11am-8pm daily. **Credit** varies. **Map** p264 H5.
This striking shopping centre was created by celebrated architect Teodoro González de León. Sneaker pimps and joggers will love the Nike and Adidas boutiques, and trendy women can cruise the shoes at Brazil's Via Uno. Also contains restaurants and an 11-screen cinema. *Photo p156.*

Discount malls

Ciao Masaryk

Avenida Presidente Masaryk 340, Polanco (5282 3033). Metro Polanco L7. **Open** 10.30am-8pm Mon-Sun. **Credit** varies. **Map** p262 B4.
You can pick up top brand goods from Ralph Lauren to Roberto Cavalli at around half normal ticket price at this high-end outlet. End-of-month specials are cunningly timed to coincide with salary cheques. **Other locations** Miguel Ángel de Quevedo 38, Chimalistac (8500 5674).

Markets

Mercado Medellín

Campeche, between Medellín & Monterrey, Roma Sur. Metro Chilpancingo L9/Metrobús Chilpancingo. **Open** 9am-5pm daily. **No credit cards. Map** p264 H9.
A great general market selling everything from *piñatas* to *pescado* (fish) and tasty hot food. The energetic atmosphere and safe, accessible location compensate for higher than usual prices.

La Merced

Rosario, between Santa Escuela & General Anaya, Centro (5522 7250). Metro Merced L1. **Open** 6am-6pm daily. **No credit cards. Map** p267 O5.
This sprawling market includes foodstuffs, handicrafts, clothes and toys. Get the Metro or a cab to avoid the short but risky walk from the Zócalo.

Tepito

Along and to the north of Eje 1 Norte (Héroe de Granaditas), between Jesús Carranza and González Ortega, Morelos (www.barriodetepito.com.mx). Metro Lagunilla LB or Tepito LB. **Open** varies Wed-Mon. **No credit cards. Map** p267 N2, O2.
This immense market seems to stock anything and everything, from everywhere. The market is an experience, but a trip to this area, one of Mexico City's roughest, is not for the faint-hearted. Don't go alone or carry any valuables.

Specialist

Books & magazines

English language

Newsagents inside major international hotels stock foreign newspapers. The Intercontinental Presidente (*see p46*) sells original editions of the *New York Times, Le Monde, USA Today*, the *Wall Street Journal*, and local English-language paper *The News*. Most bookshops plus Sanborns and Mix Up carry a small selection of English titles, but choice is limited.

American Bookstore

Bolívar 23, Centro (5512 0306). Metro Allende L2.
Open 10am-7pm Mon-Fri. **Credit** AmEx, MC, V.
Map p267 L4.
Comprehensive English-language bookstore.
Other locations Avenida Insurgentes Sur 1188, Del
Valle (5575 7901).

Libros, Libros, Libros

*Monte Ararat 220, Lomas Barrilaco (5540 4778/
http://libroslibrosmexico.com). Metro Chapultepec
L1 or Auditorio L7, then microbus along Palmas
to Monte Ararat.* **Open** 10am-7pm Mon-Sat.
Credit AmEx, MC, V.
LLL has been supplying Mexico's English-speaking
population with reading material for four decades,
and its shelves groan with fiction, history, sci-fi,
cookbooks and plenty besides.

La Torre de Papel

*Filomeno Mata 6A, Centro (5512 9703/www.
latorredepapel.com). Metro Bellas Artes L2, L8.*
Open 8.30am-6.30pm Mon-Fri; 8.30am-2.30pm Sat.
No credit cards. Map p267 L4.
Stocks the world's leading foreign titles, as well as
newspapers from Central and South America.
Located underneath Club de Periodistas de México
Prensa Nacional y Internacional (National and
International Press Club).

General

Cafebrería El Péndulo

*Avenida Nuevo León 115, Condesa (5286 9493/
www.pendulo.com). Metro Chilpancingo L9/Metrobús
Campeche.* **Open** *Shop* 8am-11pm Mon-Fri; 9am-11pm
Sat-Sun. **Credit** AmEx, MC, V. **Map** p264 F8.
Part of a small chain of café-bookshops whose art
books and CDs offer plenty of interest for those
who don't speak Spanish. Acoustic concerts are
held in the Zona Rosa branch several nights a week.
See also p137.

Librerías Gandhi

*Avenida Juárez 4, Centro (2625 0606/www.gandhi.
com.mx). Metro Bellas Artes L2, L8.* **Open** 10am-
9pm Mon-Sat; 10am-8pm Sun. **Credit** AmEx, MC, V.
Map p267 L4.
This quality chain stocks some foreign-language
titles, DVDs, videogames and low-cost CDs. Larger
stores contain cafes serving good coffee, herbal teas
and scrumptious cakes. Another draw is the in-store
Ticketmaster sales points.
Other locations throughout the city.

Librería Pegaso, Casa Lamm

*Avenida Álvaro Obregón 99, Roma Norte (5208
0171/www.casalamm.com.mx/libreria.html). Metro
Insurgentes L1/Metrobús Álvaro Obregón.* **Open**
8am-midnight Mon-Sat; 8am-8pm Sun. **Credit**
AmEx, MC, V. **Map** p265 I7.
The recently renovated bookshop in this palatial cultural centre is strong on art, classic literature and
travel, with a limited range of English texts on sale.

Librería Porrúa

*República de Argentina 15, Centro Histórico (5704
7578/www.porrua.com). Metro Zócalo L2.* **Open**
9am-8pm daily. **MC. Map** p267 N4.
Established by three brothers from Asturias in 1900,
Porrúa now also sells CDs, DVDs, videogames and
specialist magazines. This, the flagship store,
includes a reading room, children's area and café.

Used & antiquarian

Pino Suárez metro station doubles as a second-
hand book fair, while Roma is fertile soil for

Mercado Medellín.

Eat, Drink, Shop

bookworms. A section of Avenida Álvaro Obregón, between Tonalá and Orizaba, is stacked with used bookstores, and Centro's Calle Donceles, between Calle Brasil and the Eje Central, has many second-hand bookshops.

La Casona de Aura
Donceles 12, Centro (5518 5707). Metro Bellas Artes L2, L8. **Open** 10am-8pm Mon-Sat. **Credit** AmEx, MC, V. **Map** p267 L4.
This captivating second-hand bookshop a few doors from the Senate building has beautiful antiquarian books at bargain prices. Find English-language books dotted among Spanish texts.

Librería Ático
Avenida Álvaro Obregón 118-B, Roma Norte (5584 7627/teoatic@gmail.com). Metro Insurgentes L1/Metrobús Álvaro Obregón. **Open** 10am-8pm Mon-Fri; 10am-7.30pm Sat; 11am-6.30pm Sun. **Credit** MC, V. **Map** p264 H7.
Literature is Ático's forte, with a section devoted to foreign language novels, including in English. You can also find an appetising selection of English cookbooks. Pop next door to Librería a Través del Espejo for antique and out-of-print texts.

Children

Fashion

Rummage around DF's arts and crafts markets for traditional Mexican children's clothing – it's not all about ponchos, which older children

might find embarrassing. Try **La Ciudadela** (*see p151*) and **San Juan** (*see p151*) for embroidered blouses, dresses, and *manta guayabera* shirts for boys.

Arroz con Leche
Pasaje Polanco, Local 21, Avenida Presidente Masaryk 360, Polanco (5281 4038/www.arrozcon leche.com.mx). Metro Auditorio L7 or Polanco L7. **Open** 11am-2pm, 3-8pm Mon-Sat; 11am-2pm, 3-6pm Sun. **Credit** AmEx, MC, V. **Map** p262 B4.
'Rice pudding' is a designer store that puts a modern spin on typical textiles, creating charming fashion togs for kids. The business invests in Mexico's unique crafts culture by working in partnership with regional women's cooperatives.

Campanita
Londres 127, Local 35-6, Zona Rosa (5533 2557/www.grupocampanita.com.mx). Metro Insurgentes L1. **Open** 11am-8pm Mon-Fri; 11am-9pm Sat; noon-8pm Sun. **Credit** AmEx, MC, V. **Map** p264 H6.
Timeless clothing for babies and infants in soft, natural colours.
Other locations across the city.

Toys

Jugaré
Alfonso Reyes 84, Condesa (5211 7280). Metro Chilpancingo L9 or Patriotismo L9/Metrobús Chilpancingo. **Open** 10.30am-7pm Mon-Fri; 11am-6pm Sat. **Credit** AmEx, MC, V. **Map** p264 E9.
This fun-packed Mexican toyshop is great for drawing, painting and sewing accessories. Your kids will want to adopt one of the delightful cloth teddy bears.

Books

Casa Lamm's bookshop (*see p143*) sells fanciful picture books that overcome the language barrier. The **American Bookstore** (*see p143*) and **Libros, Libros, Libros** (*see p143*) have plenty to offer younger visitors too.

Electronics & photography

General

Department stores stock electronics, but you'll find the lowest prices at the **Plaza de Tecnología** (known colloquially as la Plaza de Computación) in Centro. Cameras and related equipment are sold at Sanborns and Sears. There are Office Maxs, Radioshacks and Apple Stores throughout the city.

Specialist

Low-cost camera stores are clustered in the Centro's Calle Tacuba, on the corner of República de Brasil.

Shops & Services

Camara # 1

Homero 428, Polanco (5255 3668). Metro Polanco L7. **Open** 10am-7pm Mon-Sat. **Credit** AmEx, MC, V. **Map** p262 C4.

Whether you're looking for a generic point-and-shoot box or one of those all-powerful pieces of kit that looks more like a Transformer than a Kodak, Camera #1 probably stocks it.

Plaza de Tecnología

República de Uruguay 17, Centro (5518 2285/ www.apeplazas.com/plazadelatecnologia/repmapa.asp). Metro San Juan de Letrán L8. **Open** 9am-8pm Mon-Sat; 10.30am-6pm Sun. **Credit** varies. **Map** p267 J5.

'Technology square' is a shopping mall that sells computers, games, mobile phones and related accessories. Several shops offer repairs services.

Fashion

DF is not famed as a world fashion capital, and power dressing label-lovers and preppy loafer-wearers still reign supreme. Yet a new generation of uniquely Mexican designers is beginning to break through, bringing a new freshness and vibrancy.

Cutting-edge urban creations are best sought in verdant Roma and Condesa. International designer boutiques are dotted along the manicured streets of Polanco, but don't expect much pzazz for your peso. Spanish high-street stores dominate malls and are often pricier than those in the old country.

00: Warp

Atlixco 118, Condesa (5211 7389/www.00warp.com). Metro Chilpancingo L9 or Patriotismo L9. **Open** noon-9pm Mon-Sat; 1-8pm Sun. **Credit** AmEx, MC, V. **Map** p264 F8.

Condesa cool rides high with this selection of retro trainers, hip tops, T-shirts and Paul Frank accessories. Teen fashions feature Mexican brand Tatei. **Other locations** Supermarket project, Colima 220, Roma (5511 3332).

American Apparel

Avenida Presidente Masaryk 169, Polanco (5250 1348/www.americanapparel.net). Metro Auditorio L7 or Polanco L7. **Open** 10.30am-8.30pm Mon-Sat; 11am-8pm Sun. **Credit** AmEx, MC, V. **Map** p262 C4.

These rainbow-coloured fashions with a 1980s dance feel are splendid for basics or, on the other hand, something spangly. A second store is scheduled to open at Colima 333, Roma in 2009.

King Monster 666

Belisario Domínguez 17, Coyoacán (5658 6973/ www.kingmonster.com.mx). Metro Coyoacán L3/Metrobús Coyoacán. **Open** 1-8.30pm Mon-Fri; noon-8.30pm Sat, Sun. **Credit** MC, V. **Map** p259 E2.

The flagship store of Mexico's rock and skate-inspired male/female fashion label offers original, irreverent T-shirt designs alongside an in-house tattoo and piercing parlour.

DF eye

At Lagunilla market (*see p153*) you can find decades' worth of the city's cast-offs washed up on stalls crammed with bits and pieces from every era, from video games to incense, and from indie T-shirts to antiques (definitely the best part). It's part of a constant process of cultural recycling, and a fascinating way to read the story of the city and its people.

Uriel Waizel, radio DJ, Ibero 90.9

La Primavera

Lázaro Cárdenas 79, Centro (5512 3142). Metro Salto del Agua L1, L8 or San Juan de Letrán L8. **Open** 10am-7.45pm Mon-Sat. **Credit** MC, V. **Map** p267 L3.

Come here for inimitably Mexican clothing and accessories for men and women, including gorgeous, great value men's *guayaberas* in cotton and linen. Check out the *ropa vaquero* (cowboy/girl style clothing) line, including playful shirts and pretty blouses.

Soho Condesa

Atlixco 100B, Condesa (5553 1730). Metro Chilpancingo L9 or Patriotismo L9. **Open** 11.30am-8.30pm Mon,Tue; 11.30am-9pm Wed, Thur; noon-10pm Fri, Sat; noon-8pm Sun. **Credit** AmEx, MC, V. **Map** p264 F8.

Trawl through trendy racks of casual women's clothing and snazzy cocktail and evening dresses. Soho also sells appealing accessories for both sexes, including funky shades, hats and shoes, plus a range of tees and shirts for men.
Other locations Paseo de la Reforma 222, Zona Rosa (5511 8678); Avenida Presidente Masaryk 191, Polanco (5281 1707).

Designer

Paulina and Malinali

El Bazar del Sabado (Mezanine), Plaza San Jacinto, San Ángel (5286 3351/www.paulinaymalinali.com). Metro Miguel Ángel de Quevedo L3/Metrobús Dr Gálvez. **Open** 11am-7pm Sat. **Credit** MC, V. **Map** p259 B3.

Statuesque twins Paulina and Malinali Fosado are professional ballerinas-turned-designers cutting feminine, contemporary fashions inspired by typical Mexican textiles. Call for an appointment if you can't make it to the Saturday market.

Piñeda Covalín

Campos Eliseos 215, Polanco (5282 2720/www. pinedacovalin.com). Metro Auditorio L7. **Open** 9am-8pm Mon-Sat; 10am-2pm Sun. **Credit** AmEx, MC, V. **Map** p262 B5.

Cristina Piñeda and Ricardo Covalín are accessory designers whose upscale creations, sold here, include

Telephone Love

by American Apparel®

Meet Signe. She worked at
our store in Stolkholm before
becoming a photo assistant
in Sweden. She is wearing
the High-Waisted A-Line Skirt,
Nude Micro-Mesh Bodysuit,
Over-the-Knee Opaque Socks
and vintage glasses.

handbags, scarves and ties. Their pieces are inspired by indigenous imagery and iconography.
Other locations throughout the city.

Sicario

Colima 124, Roma (5511 0396/www.sicario.tv/ sicario-roma). Metro Insurgentes L1/Metrobús Álvaro Obregón. **Open** noon-8pm daily. **Credit** AmEx, MC, V. **Map** p265 I7.
Sicario specialises in painfully cool T-shirts by exclusively Mexican designers. This cutting-edge boutique, whose name means 'hitman' in Spanish, offers a killer range of reasonably priced sunglasses and hats, and a small womenswear collection.
Other locations Seneca 41, Polanco.

Discount

If you're in town for seasonal sales, try your luck at department stores and Polanco's 'golden mile' along Avenida Presidente Masaryk. Year-round deals can be snapped up at markets and outlets.

Used & vintage

The bazaar at Portales and the flea market at La Lagunilla (*see p153*) are the city's main hubs for vintage fashion.

Kasi Vintage Boutique

Prado Norte 427, Chapultepec (5540 0177).Metro Auditorio L7, then pesero bus towards Bosques. **Open** noon-7pm Mon-Fri. **No credit cards.**
This intriguing boutique stocks upscale vintage clothes and accessories with a decadent dose of designer labels.

Villa Plaza Boutique Secretos

Tamaulipas 99, Local 2, Condesa (5553 4877). Metro Patriotismo L9. **Open** noon-8pm daily. **Credit** AmEx, MC, V. **Map** p264 F8.
Affordable second-hand items for men and women are the forte at this bohemian café-boutique.

Fashion accessories & services

Clothing hire

Casa Marcelo

Álvaro Obregón 43, Roma (5511 2010/www. casamarcelo.com.mx). Metro Insurgentes L1. **Open** 10am-8pm Mon-Fri; 10am-5pm Sat. **Credit** AmEx, MC, V. **Map** p265 I7.
An enchantingly old-fashioned formal menswear store with an efficient hire service.
Other locations throughout the city.

Fascino

Chihuahua 181, Local D, Roma (5574 7617). Metro Insurgentes L1. **Open** 10.30am-7.30pm Mon-Fri; 10.30am-3.30pm Sat. **Credit** MC, V. **Map** p264 H7.

Those who forgot to pack their glad rags can hire or purchase glamorous evening wear at this Roma boutique. Rent a slinky dress for MX$550 including a matching pashmina and bag.

Cleaning & repairs

DryClean USA International

Mariano Escobedo 506, Polanco (5545 1760/www. drycleanusa.com.mx). Metro Polanco L7. **Open** 8am-7pm Mon-Fri, 9am-6pm Sat. **No credit cards.** **Map** p262 D4.
This efficient drycleaners also offes a one-hour express service, alterations and repairs.
Other locations throughout the city.

Hats

Villagrán

Ayuntamiento 3A, Centro (5521 0462). Metro San Juan de Letrán L8. **Open** 10am-8pm Mon-Sat. **Credit** AmEx, MC, V. **Map** p267 L5.
Villagrán carries a magnificent collection of Stetsons, flat caps, pork-pie and even bowler hats.

Jewellery

Gold and silver jewellery shops flank the Centro's Avenida Madero. Admirers of Mexican silver should browse at San Ángel's Saturday market as well as La Ciudadela (*see p151*).

Daniel Espinosa

Tamaulipas 72, Condesa (5211 3994/www.daniel espinosa.com). Metro Chilpancingo L9/Metrobús Chilpancingo. **Open** 11am-8pm Mon-Fri; 11am-7pm Sat. **Credit** AmEx, MC, V. **Map** p264 F8.
Espinosa's statement-making jewellery has made it big from South Africa to Spain. These minimalist designs can also be acquired at Saks (*see p141*).

Tane

Avenida Presidente Masaryk 430, Polanco (5282 6200/www.tane.com.mx). Metro Polanco L7. **Open** 10am-7pm Mon-Fri; 11am-3pm Sat. **Credit** AmEx, MC, V. **Map** p262 A4.
Classic yet contemporary designs in silver and gold as well as one-off pieces for special celebrations. A selection is also available at Casa Lamm (*see p143*).

Lingerie & underwear

Malls and boutiques are the best places for extending your range of smalls, at chains such as Women's Secret.

Vilebrequin

Lafontaine 110, Local 5, Plaza Zentro, Polanco (5282 0741). Metro Polanco L7. **Open** 11am-8pm Mon-Fri; 11am-7pm Sat. **Credit** AmEx, MC, V. **Map** p262 A4.
Vilebrequin stocks a quirky range of men's swimwear and boxers in original prints.

Intimissimi

Avenida Presidente Masaryk 336, Polanco (5281 8419/www.intimissimi.com). Metro Auditorio L7 or Polanco L7. **Open** 11am-8pm Mon-Sat. **Credit** AmEx, MC, V. **Map** p262 B4.

Intimissimi's compact boutique keeps DF women in sophisticated Italian underwear and seductive Calzedonia bikinis.

Luggage

Sears and Liverpool are good for sturdy suitcases if excess baggage is looking likely.

La Palestina

5 de Mayo 20, Centro (5512 8129). Metro Bellas Artes L2, L8. **Open** 10am-7pm Mon-Sat; 11am-4pm Sun. **Credit** AmEx, MC, V. **Map** p267 L4.

In business on the same site since the 19th century, this is DF's most famous luggage and leather goods shop. Great for bags, wallets and western-style belts.

Samsonite Outlet

Isabel la Católica 30, Local 4, Centro (5521 3559). Metro Allende L2 or Zócalo L2. **Open** 10am-7pm Mon-Sat; 11am-5pm Sun. **Credit** AmEx, MC, V. **Map** p267 M4.

This is the place for Samsonite and other brand cases, hold-alls and handbags at discount prices.

Shoes

Melba

Atlixco 147D, Condesa (5286 4423). Metro Chilpancingo L9 or Patriotismo L9. **Open** noon-8pm daily. **Credit** MC, V. **Map** p264 F8.

Sassy women's shoes demand your attention in this all-round boutique that includes fabulous flats and limited-edition boots fashioned from unusual textiles.

Motivos

Amsterdam 285, Local 1, Condesa (5574 8032). Metro Chilpancingo L9/Metrobús Chilpancingo. **Open** 11.30am-8pm Mon-Sat. **Credit** MC, V. **Map** p264 G8.

Multicoloured flip-flops, flats and funky boots are the star picks in this retro-inspired store in hip Condesa. Look out too for appealing sunglasses and costume jewellery.

Shelter

Colima 134, Roma (5208 6271/www.shelter.com. mx). Metro Insurgentes L1. **Open** noon-8pm Mon-Sat; noon-7pm Sun. **Credit** AmEx, MC, V. **Map** p265 I7.

Head to Shelter for retro-style trainers, funky T-shirts and hoodies for men.

Other locations Campeche 429, Condesa.

Via Uno

Paseo de la Reforma 222, Juárez (5208 5094/ www.viauno.com). Metro Insurgentes L1/Metrobús Reforma. **Open** 11am-8pm Mon-Sun. **Credit** AmEx, MC, V. **Map** p264 H5.

Brazilian sex appeal exudes from Via Uno's ladies' shoes, adding cheeky charm to casual outfits. Prices are reasonable all year round, so when the sales are on, they're a steal.

Food & drink

Bakeries

La Lorena

Avenida Monte Líbano 265, Chapultepec (5202 4594/ http://lalorena.com.mx). Metro Auditorio L7, then bus marked Bosques going north on Paseo de la Reforma. **Open** 8am-11pm Mon-Sat; 8am-6pm Sun. **Credit** MC, V.

Going native

The strapping, stallion-straddling cowboy motif is as familiar in Mexico as it is north of the border, and just as traditional. But though you'll be hard pushed to spot a cowboy making his way around Mexico City, classic cowboy gear is quite another matter. At the Mercado de los Zapatos at **La Lagunilla** (*see p153*), high-quality his-and-hers *botas vaqueras* (cowboy boots) come direct from Mexico's shoe capital, León, Guanajuato. For something uniquely Mexican, go for a pair with winklepicker toes – *estilo Chihuahua*. **El Caballo Mexicano** (Pino Suárez 23, Centro, 5542 6661) offers a colourful range of trad footwear (*pictured*), or for elegant *guayaberas* – stylish linen shirts from the Yucatán – head for **La Primavera** (*see p145*), which also has a great range of *ropa vaquera* (cowboy clothes). Finally, for the *hombre* or *mujer* who can pull off a Stetson, you'll find **Villagrán**'s perfect *sombrero* store (*see p147*) the original and best.

Just ideal: another batch of great pastries at **Pastelería Ideal**.

Mexico City embraces its anglophile sensibilities at this traditional *pastelería*, famous across the city for its lemon glazed carrot cake, English-style scones and teacakes.

Pastelería Ideal
Avenida 16 de Septiembre 18, Centro (5521 2233/ www.pasteleriaideal.com.mx). Metro San Juan de Letrán L8. **Open** 6am-9pm daily. **Credit** MC, V. **Map** p267 L4.
This historic bakery fills three floors. The delicious sweet and savoury pastries, fresh bread and gloriously formal cakes can turn a run-of-the-mill afternoon tea into a special occasion. The early morning opening makes it a good munchies option for the post-club crowd.

Drinks

Cheap and cheerful wines are available at Sumesa. Superama offers a pricier range and a variety of tea and coffee. Oxxo and 7-Eleven are convenient for domestic beers.

Café La Habana
Morelos 62, Juárez (5535 2620). Metro Juárez L3. **Open** 7am-11pm Mon-Sat; 8am-10pm Sun. **Credit** MC, V. **Map** p266 J4.

This famous café, dating from the 1950s, sells a range of specialist coffees by the kilo. *See p129.*

La Europea
Ayuntamiento 21 y 25, Centro (5512 7529/www. laeuropea.com.mx). Metro Salto del Agua L1, L8 or San Juan de Letrán L8. **Open** 9am-8pm Mon-Sat. **Credit** AmEx, MC, V. **Map** p267 L5.
There's a good selection of beers, wines and spirits on offer at this sizeable store. In addition to this central outlet, there are smaller branches across the city
Other locations throughout the city.

Maison Française de Thé Caravanserai
Orizaba 101, Roma (5511 2877). Metro Insurgentes L1/Metrobús Álvaro Obregón. **Open** 10.30am-9pm Mon-Fri; noon-9pm Sat; 3-9pm Sun. **Credit** MC, V. **Map** p264 H7.
This elegant French tearoom sells blends of herbal, black and green teas, providing refreshment to the chattering classes. *See also p138. Photo p150.*

La Naval
Insurgentes Sur 373, Condesa (5584 3500/ http://lanaval.com.mx). Metrobús Sonora. **Open** 9am-9pm Mon-Sat; 11am-7pm Sun. **Credit** AmEx, MC, V. **Map** p264 G8.

Maison Française de Thé Caravanserai. See p149.

La Naval stocks a (perhaps literally) dizzying array of tequilas as well as a surprisingly comprehensive whisky collection. Delivery available.
Other locations throughout the city.

General

Sumesa
Oaxaca y Álvaro Obregón, Roma (5511 0440/ www.lacomer.com.mx). Metro Sevilla L1/ Metrobús Álvaro Obregón. **Open** 7am-11pm daily. **Credit** AmEx, MC, V. **Map** p264 G7.
Sumesa offers slightly cheaper products than its peers, but be careful when buying meat in smaller stores: hygiene standards are not top-notch.
Other locations throughout the city.

Superama
Avenida Homero 310, Chapultepec Morales (5545 4431/www.superama.com.mx). Metro Polanco L7. **Open** 7am-11pm daily. **Credit** AmEx, MC, V. **Map** p262 D4.
This large supermarket chain serves the Polanco area with its bakery, specialist foods and organic produce. Its stores include extensive hair and skincare selections.
Other locations: throughout the city.

Markets

La Fondita Tlacoquemécatl
Parque de Tlacoquemécatl, Del Valle. Metrobús Parque Hundido. **Open** 8-11am daily.
La Fondita is an informal row of stalls famed for their Friday breakfasts and brunches. The makeshift dining area is found behind the plaza's church, where you can sample quesadillas, frijoles and *cecina* (sun-dried pork).

Mercado San Juan Especialidades
Ernesto Pugibet 21, Centro (http://mercadosanjuan. galeon.com). Metro Salto del Agua L1, L8 or San Juan de Letrán L8. **Open** 8am-5pm daily. **No credit cards. Map** p266 K5.
San Juan's most interesting market has produce fit for connoisseurs. Mexican and European specialist cheeses are sold at Baltasar, Local 158-159 (5521 0856); and if you're the kind of person who might like to rustle up an armadillo salad for lunch, you can pick up one of the armoured critters at Los Coyotes butchers (5521 8418).

Tianguis de Parque Sullivan
For listings, see p151.
Enticing food stalls serve artists and Sunday browsers at the Jardín del Arte. Tasty tacos and other traditional foods are prepared alongside fresh fruits, vegetables, meat and fish.

Specialist
Don't overlook the pricey but tantalising food halls at department stores Palacio and Liverpool if you're missing a taste of home.

Celaya
5 de Mayo 39, Centro (5521 1787). Metro Bellas Artes L2, L8. **Open** 10.30am-7.30pm daily. **Credit** AmEx, MC, V. **Map** p267 L4.
Diverse Mexican *dulces típicos* are sold at this traditional sweetshop. Pop in even if you don't have a sweet tooth, for its lavish late 19th-century decor with a rococo feel.
Other locations Orizaba 37, Roma (5514 8438).

Delirio
Monterrey 116, Roma (5584 0068/www.delirio. com.mx). Metro Insurgentes L1/Metrobús Álvaro Obregón. **Open** 11am-8pm Mon-Sat; 11am-5pm Sun. **Credit** AmEx, MC, V. **Map** p264 H7.

Celebrated chef Mónica Patiño presents delectable products in this deli-café, including uncommon artesanal cheeses from Mexico and the world.

Dumas Gourmet
Alejandro Dumas 125, Polanco (5280 8385/www.dumasgourmet.com). Metro Auditorio L7. **Open** 8am-8pm Mon-Wed; 8am-9pm Thur, Fri; 10am-9pm Sat; 11am-6pm Sun. **Credit** MC, V. **Map** p262 B4.
Takeaway lunches from this enticing French deli are perfect for picnics in nearby Parque Lincoln.

Gifts & souvenirs

Markets are unsurpassable for classic Mexican keepsakes, including traditional textiles, painted wooden animal carvings (*alebrijes*) and colourful Oaxacan tin ornaments.

Arte Mexicano para el Mundo
Zócalo y Monte de Piedad 11, Centro (5518 0300). Metro Zócalo L2. **Open** 8am-5pm Mon, Tue; 8am-8pm Wed-Sun. **Credit** AmEx, MC, V. **Map** p267 M4.
Colourful handicrafts with textile, pottery and contemporary jewellery sections split over several floors.

Las Artesanías
Pasaje Polanco, Avenida Presidente Masaryk 360, Polanco (5280 9515). Metro Auditorio L7 or Polanco L7. **Open** 10am-8pm Mon-Sat, noon-6pm Sun. **Credit** AmEx, MC, V. **Map** p262 B4.
Las Artesanías brings together a range of high-quality arts and crafts from all corners of Mexico including pottery from Guanajuato, silver jewellery from Taxco and *rebozos* (shawls) from Jalisco.

Bazar del Sábado y Tianguis
Plaza San Jacinto 11, San Angel (5548 1997/www.fondasanangel.com.mx). Metro Miguel Ángel de Quevedo L3/Metrobús Dr Gálvez. **Open** 9am-4pm Sat. **Credit** varies. **Map** p259 B3.
This is an enchanting arts, crafts, clothing, jewellery and glassware market in a quaint colonial setting. Outside, the *tianguis* offers a mix of textiles, toys, leather goods and more jewellery, and artists exhibit their paintings on Plaza San Jacinto.

La Ciudadela
Balderas 1 & Plaza de la Ciudadela 5, Centro (www.laciudadela.com.mx). Metro Balderas L1, L3 or Juárez L3. **Open** 8am-6pm daily. **Credit** varies. **Map** p266 K5.
This indoor artisan market has good prices, but you should still haggle. This is one of the finest places outside Oaxaca to buy fantastical painted animals known as *alebrijes*. You'll also find silver jewellery, historical photographs and ceramics under one roof, while outside a string of street-stalls stock books, clothes and costume jewellery. *Photo p141.*

Jardín del Arte Sullivan
Serapio Rendón, between Sullivan and Villalonguin, Cuauhtémoc (www.artmajeur.com/jardindelarte mexico). Metrobús Reforma. **Open** 10am-6pm Sun. **No credit cards. Map** p266 H4.

Since the mid 1950s, local artists have congregated here on Sundays to proffer their works. Some 400 members of the Art Garden Association, which exhibits at San Ángel's Plaza San Jacinto on Saturdays, sell sculptures, paintings and photography at reasonable prices. If you get peckish, there's an excellent outdoor food market on the same strip.

Mercado Insurgentes
Londres, between Florencia and Amberes, Zona Rosa. Metro Insurgentes L1/Metrobús Insurgentes. **Open** 9am-5.30pm Mon-Sat; 10am-4pm Sun. **No credit cards. Map** p264 G6.
This is another dedicated artisan market. Prices are higher than at its counterparts in the Centro, so haggle hard for some high quality goods.

San Juan Curiosidades
Ayuntamiento, corner of Aranda, Centro (5512 1263). Metro Salto de Agua L1, L8. **Open** 9am-7pm Mon-Sat; 9am-4pm Sun. **Credit** varies. **Map** p267 L5.
This government-run enterprise sells lovely Mexican handicrafts at good prices. Worth a visit for unusual textiles and trinkets.

Health & beauty

Complementary medicine

Consulta General
Tacuba 40, Despacho 207, Centro (5521 4821). Metro Allende L2. **Open** 4pm-8pm Mon, Tue-Fri; 10am-2pm Sat (by appointment only). **No credit cards. Map** p267 L4.
Established alternative therapy clinic whose services include acupuncture, homeopathy, Chinese herbalism (with Dr Patricia Luján) and dietary advice (Lic. Magali Acevedo).

Mercado de Sonora
Fray Servando Teresa de Mier and San Nicolás, Merced Balbuena, Centro (5768 2701). Metro Merced L1. **Open** 7am-7pm daily. **No credit cards.**
Known as a witch-doctors' market, Sonora is packed with herbal remedies and voodoo-style charms of questionable origin and efficacy. A part devoted to traditional sweets bewitches sweet toothed visitors.

Hairdressers & barbers

Estética Masculín Caesar
Avenida Homero 526, Polanco (5254 3019). Metro Polanco L7. **Open** 9am-8.30pm Mon-Sat. **No credit cards. Map** p262 C4.
At this old-school barbers, basic haircuts cost MX$180. It's a perfect spot for people-watching as the friendly barbers slap-handshake regulars, demonstrating everyone's macho credentials. A manly manicure – very popular in Latin America – is also an option.

Eat, Drink, Shop

Fussion Estilistas

Prado Norte 325, Chapultepec (5540 3326/www.fussionestilistas.com). Metro Auditorio L7. **Open** 9am-6pm Tue-Sat. **Credit** MC, V.
A fancy unisex French-Mexican hair salon (MX$600 for women, MX$450 for men) with a good reputation for colouring and high-lights. Other treatments include facials, waxing, manicure and pedicure.

Opticians

Opticas Lux

Avenida Presidente Masaryk 71, Polanco (5545 1121/www.opticaslux.com.mx). Metro Chapultepec L1 or Polanco L7. **Open** 10am-8pm Mon-Sat. **Credit** AmEx, MC, V. **Map** p262 D5.
A mix of designer and economical frames is available from this, Mexico's largest chain of opticians. Eye tests and contact lens consultations can be arranged by appointment.
Other locations across the city.

Pharmacies

There's no shortage of pharmacies in Mexico, and most medicines can be purchased over the counter. Low-cost generic drugs are available throughout the city at the Farmacias Similares chain (www.farmaciasdesimilares.com.mx).

Music fans love **Tianguis El Chopo**.

Farmacia San Pablo

Cuauhtémoc 114, Roma (5354 9000). Metro Insurgentes L1. Metro Cuauhtémoc L1. **Open** 7am-11pm Mon-Sat. 8am-10pm Sun (24hr delivery service). **Credit** AmEx, MC, V. **Map** p265 I7.
DF's best-stocked pharmacy includes a wide range of international skincare and perfume brands.

Sex shops

Ficus

Anatole France 152, Polanco (5280 4040/www.ficuscompany.com). Metro Polanco L7. **Open** 11am-8pm Mon-Sat. **Credit** AmEx, MC, V. **Map** p262 B4.
Apparent works of art at this swish adult store are, on closer examination, actually sex toys. Their discreet designs should avoid potential embarrassment at customs if you decide to make a purchase.

Spas & salons

Dermal Day Spa & Salon

Ground floor, Paseo de la Reforma 505, Torre Mayor, Chapultepec (5553 2001/www.dermaldayspa.com). Metro Auditorio L7. **Open** 9am-8pm Mon-Fri; 9am-2pm Sat. **Credit** AmEx, MC, V. **Map** p264 F6.
The place for skin treatments and indulgent massages for men and women. Get a free 30-minute facial with substantial purchases of Dermatologica products.

Mani e Piedi

Prado Norte 530, Chapultepec (5520 0751). Metro Auditorio L7, then by taxi. **Open** 9am-7pm Mon-Fri; 9am-6pm Sat-Sun. **Credit** AmEx, MC, V.
This spa and nail salon is a great place to groom. The massage chairs provoke a strange sensation, but relax into it and your body will feel the benefit.

Tattoos & piercings

Tattoo María

Puebla 151-C, Roma Norte (5511 2388/www.myspace.com/tattoo_maria). Metro Insurgentes L1. **Open** noon-7pm Mon-Fri; noon-4pm Sat. **No credit cards. Map** p264 H6.
A complete tattoo and piercing service, offered by the heavily inked María.

House & home

Antiques

Bazar Reto

Fernando Montes de Oca 391, Portales (3330 6441). Metro Portales L2. **Open** 9am-6.30pm. **No credit cards.**
Find antiques, vintage clothes and furniture close to the eclectic Mercado Portales in this southern, working-class neighbourhood. Browse the flea market that spreads out on Saturdays between Libertad and Santa Cruz, halting for beer and a *botana* at the

Instrument shops cluster on *calles* Bolívar and Mesones.

classic Salón Portales cantina (5674 2745) at Victor Hugo 72, open 11am to 10pm daily.

Mercado de Álvaro Obregón

Álvaro Obregón, from Córdoba to Cuauhtémoc, Roma Norte. Metro Insurgentes L1. **Open** 10am-6pm Sat. **No credit cards. Map** p265 I7.

Antiques, artwork and knick knacks are sold at this Saturday flea market on Roma's main avenue. The area's recent gentrification has elevated prices, but it's still worth a stroll along the avenue's tree-lined central reservation.

Mercado de Antigüedades de La Lagunilla

Lateral de Paseo de la Reforma Norte, corner of Francisco González Bocanegra, Centro (5526 6340). Metro Garibaldi L8, LB or Lagunilla LB. **Open** 9am-early evening Sun. **No credit cards. Map** p267 M2.

Arrive early to nab a bargain from this array of antique artifacts, bric-a-brac, second-hand furniture and so much more. A world-class, sprawling street market, Lagunilla blurs into Tepito – a rough area and not recommended – at its northern edge, so stay alert as you meander. Haggling is expected and you'll get a better price if you go with a Spanish speaker.

General

Artefacto

Amatlán 94, Condesa (5286 7729/www.artefacto. com.mx). Metrobús Campeche. **Open** 10am-8pm Mon-Fri; 11am-8pm Sat; 11am-6pm Sun. **Credit** AmEx, MC, V. **No credit cards. Map** p264 F8.

Stylish designs with an ethnic twist include chic cushions and bed linen alongside delightful crockery. **Other locations** Luis G Urbina 74, Polanco.

Casa Palacio

Antara Polanco, Avenida Ejército Nacional 843B, Polanco (9138 3750/www.casapalacio.com.mx). Metro Polanco L7. **Open** 11am-8pm Sun-Thur; 11am-9pm Fri, Sat. **Credit** AmEx, MC, V. **Map** p262 A3.

A mix of contemporary and classic Mexican items for the home can be purchased at this chic spin-off from Palacio de Hierro's homeware department.

Music & entertainment

CDs, records & DVDs

Discoteca

Citlaltépetl 23C, Condesa (5212 0234/www.discoteca online.net). Metro Patriotismo L9 or Chilpancingo L9. **Open** 1-9pm Mon-Wed; 1-10pm Thur-Sat. **Credit** AmEx, MC, V. **Map** p264 F9.

This cool little record shop stocks CDs, DVDs and esoteric music mags, plus fashion by the Fusion design collective.

Mixup

Génova 76, Local 26, Zona Rosa (5525 3011/café 5525 5148/www.mixup.com.mx). Metro Insurgentes L1. **Open** 9am-11pm Mon-Sat; 9am-10pm Sun. **Credit** AmEx, MC, V. **Map** 264 H6.

Mexico's ubiquitous music store stocks CDs, DVDs, books and iPod accessories. The immense Zona Rosa Mixup includes a café, and most branches contain Ticketmaster sales points. **Other locations** throughout the city.

Tianguis del Chopo

Aldama, Buenavista (5525 9380/www.myspace. com/8millas). Metro Buenavista LB/Metrobús Buenavista. **Open** 10am-5pm Sat. **No credit cards. Map** p266 J2.

TANE

Naco but nice

For fans of kitsch, Mexico City is a gleaming motherlode of tacky/cool memorabilia *a la mexicana*. You can find the kind of paraphernalia, religious or otherwise, that Mexicans refer to as *naco* (tacky or ghetto) in its raw, unadulterated state on market stalls across the city, or displayed in a hip, knowing style in the trendy shops of Condesa. *Ser naco es chido*. It's cool to be *naco*.

Plump angels, bold saints, Virgen de Guadalupe glitter domes and Crucifixion bottle openers are vintage *naco* standards, and you'll find all these and more in the streets around the Basílica de Guadalupe (*see* p84). Gaudy shopping bags, T-shirts nightlights, mirrors and bracelets decorated with images of the Virgin abound both in the markets and in hip kitsch boutiques, as do brilliantly coloured *lotería* cards (*see* p68 **Chilango Bingo**) decorating wooden boxes, covering notebooks or reproduced as paintings.

Lucha libre (see pp32-34 **Viva la lucha**) is another deep well in which to dip for kitsch jewels from the Mexican psyche, from wrestling masks and the plastic dolls sold outside arenas to T-shirts and vintage *lucha* comics. Naco is so hip these days that whole businesses have grown out of it. Clothing company **NaCo** (Yautepec 126, Condesa, 5286 1343, www.chidochido.com) produces T-shirts with slogans that play on common Mexican slang and the ways *nacos* supposedly speak, for example '*Estar Guars*' (Star Wars), or a road sign design proclaiming '*One Güey*' (pronounced 'way' but meaning the equivalent of 'mate' or 'dude').

At artisans' markets such as **La Ciudadela** (see p151) and San Ángel's **Bazar Sábado** (see p151) small glazed, 3D tableaux show scenes of skeletons playing pool, getting married, getting drunk or just having their dinner, bearing testament to a strangely jolly Mexican attitude to death (*see* p31 **Death's in Mexico**) – or at least, a calm acceptance of its presence. At **El Milagrito** (Mazatlán 152A, Condesa, 5553 5334), a shop devoted to the art of Mexican kitsch, little shrine ornaments called *el dicho en el nicho* ('the saying in the nook') play on religious imagery and saint worship, offering prayers for protection 'to protect you from hangovers' or 'to shield you from gossip'. A set of tequila glasses, as if they needed it, are emblazoned with a prayer to 'San Honesto' (St Honest). *In tequila, veritas*. Also at El Milagrito, naive-style *ex-voto* religious paintings (*see* p183 **Painted prayers**) run the gamut from the touchingly tragic to the comical, and even to the overtly sexual. Or if you prefer to run your own personal gamut, you can commission a painting depicting your own private miracle.

Rare vinyl mixed with authentic and pirate CDs are on sale at this alternative street market and surrounding shops. To find it, just follow the crowd of punks, *rockeros*, *darkies* (don't worry – it means goths) and emos for whom hanging out at El Chopo has become a rite of passage. Make sure you have a multi-region DVD player before you buy. *Photo p152*.

Cafebrería El Péndulo

For listings, see p143.
A mix of Mexican cinema, arthouse and mainstream films is available at this bookshop.

Musical instruments

Many of Mexico City's musical instrument shops are on Calle Bolívar.

Music City

Bolívar 72 A-B, Centro (5709 6832/www.musiccity. com.mx). Metro San Juan de Letrán L8. **Open** 9.30am-7pm Mon-Sat. **Credit** AmEx, MC, V. **Map** p267 L5.
Electric guitars and amps are the forte, but you can also pick up acoustic and percussion instruments.

Eat, Drink, Shop

Repertorio Wagner

Bolívar 41, Centro (5512 1084). Metro San Juan de Letrán L8. **Open** *10am-7pm Mon-Sat; 11am-4pm Sun.* **Credit** AmEx, MC, V. **Map** p267 L5.

As the name suggests, this music store has a strong classical bias. Includes a great selection of sheet music.

Sports & fitness

A string of sport shops stretches out along Centro's Venustiano Carranza. Kick off at the Eje Central end. Martí, Mexico's ubiquitous sport store, features in most shopping malls.

Martí Outlet

Bolívar 36, Centro (5512 6471/www.marti. com.mx). Metro Isabel la Católica L1 or Salto del Agua L1, L8. **Open** *10am-8pm Mon-Sat; 11am-6pm Sun.* **Credit** AmEx, MC, V. **Map** p267 L4.

Dig around in the racks for sporting bargains galore. **Other locations** throughout the city.

Merrell Boutique

Avenida Presidente Masaryk 360, Local 1R, Polanco (5281 4196/www.merrell.com.mx).

Reforma 222.
See p142.

Metro Auditorio L7 or Polanco L7. **Open** *11am-9pm Mon-Fri; 10am-9pm Sat, Sun.* **Credit** AmEx, MC, V. **Map** p262 B4.

Fashion-conscious outdoor addicts can find some great gear for hiking and camping at DF's Merrell store – but you'll have to pay European prices.

Tickets

Ticketmaster

At most MixUp stores. For listings, see p153.

Online bookings through Ticketmaster, which has a virtual monopoly in Mexico, can only be made using Mexican credit and debit cards, and the agency charges extortionate fees for the privilege. Instead, go directly to box offices or Ticketmaster agents such as MixUp.

Travellers' needs

Shipping

Mailboxes Etc (MBE)

Sucursal Polanco, Galileo 8, Polanco (5280 8705/0). Metro Auditorio L7. **Open** *9am-8pm Mon-Thur; 9am-7pm Fri; 10am-4pm Sat.* **Credit** AmEx, MC, V. **Map** p262 B5.

This international company's professional shipping service includes secure packing of your purchase to ensure it arrives in one piece. Choose DHL, FedEx or UPS to deliver your package from a around a dozen branches distributed around DF.

Travel agent

Hivisa Viajes

Paseo de la Reforma 505, Torre Mayor, The Shops 7, Cuauhtémoc (5212 0812/www.hivisaviajes. com.mx). Metro Chapultepec L1. **Open** *9am-7pm Mon-Fri; 10am-1pm Sat.* **Credit** AmEx, MC, V. **Map** p264 F6.

This is a helpful, efficient agency with some English-speaking staff. It will reserve and hold your tickets without payment for up to three days.

Mobile phones

Telcel

Parque Delta, Local L-202, Avenida Cuauhtémoc 462, Narvarte (www.telcel.com). Metro Etiopía L3 or Centro Médico L3, L9. **Open** *10am-8pm daily.* **Credit** MC, V. **Map** p265 I10.

Mobile phone rentals are now virtually obsolete. From MX$200, you can purchase an 'Amigo' pay-as-you-go phone and SIM card from Telcel agents. Low-cost options are available with Telefonica (Movistar), but Telcel coverage is more consistent. The cheapest phone packages are found along Calle Maeve, one block from the Plaza de Tecnología (*see p145*).

Other locations throughout the city.

Arts & Entertainments

Festivals & Events

Traditional flag-waving, modern culture – and the world's spookiest holiday.

A Holy Week hoe-down to mark **Semana Santa**.

Mexico City's left-leaning government has made it a priority to reclaim public spaces and enrich the capital's cultural life, and free film, art, music, literature and dance festivals are flourishing as a result. Under the city's Circuito de Festivales (festivals circuit), events are staged across the city's 16 *delegaciones* or boroughs, with the main square, the Zócalo, serving as a base.

Most Mexicans are patriotic, rejoicing in their traditional and contemporary culture. Labour reforms have cut the number of public holidays, but that doesn't stop *chilangos* from celebrating, and rarely a week goes by without some form of festivity. In a calendar still dominated by Roman Catholic events, other fiestas of national significance also figure, with the Day of the Dead and Independence celebrations among the most memorable. Whatever the occasion, special dishes are often associated with these festivals, underlining the importance of food in Mexican culture.

January-March

Día de los Santos Reyes

Monumento a la Revolución, Centro (www.cultura. df.gob.mx). Metro Revolución L2. **Date** 6 Jan. **Map** p266 I4.

Epiphany – the 'Day of the Holy Kings' – is arguably more important in Mexico than Christmas, with markets chaotic in early January as families stock up for the party. On this day, children customarily receive presents that recall the gifts bestowed upon Christ by the Santos Reyes; and though Santa and his sleigh full of booty have gained some traction in Mexico, it's still to Melchor, Gaspar and Baltasar that children write begging letters. Events aimed at young *chilangos* are organised downtown at the Monumento a la Revolución, where children queue to get their picture taken with the Reyes. The square is filled with stalls selling toys and food – don't miss the festive *rosca de reyes*, a crown-shaped dessert covered in sugared fruits.

Chinese New Year

Calle Dolores, Centro. Metro Juárez L3. **Date** late Jan to early Feb (2009: 26 Jan – Ox; 2010: 14 Feb – Tiger; 2011: 3 Feb – Rabbit). **Map** p267 L4.

New year celebrations centre on Mexico City's minuscule Barrio Chino – Chinatown. Chinese musicians and dancers lead a morning parade down Paseo de la Reforma that culminates in the community's compact, crowded neighbourhood. Calle Dolores, the sum total of Chinatown, is festooned with red and gold decorations; restaurants are packed with local families taking advantage of special menus, and street vendors sell charms depicting the coming year's animal.

Feria Internacional del Libro

Palacio de Minería, Tacuba 5, Centro (5623 2981/ 5623 2982/http://feria.mineria.unam.mx). Metro Allende L2 or Bellas Artes L2, L8. **Date** mid February-early Mar. **Map** p267 L4.

This vast international book fair is held annually in the UNAM's palatial engineering faculty. Authors and literary experts give talks and there are also music and dance productions staged by publishing houses from a different Mexican state each year, invite as guests of honour. Come along and soak up the atmosphere of the stunning late 18th-century palace. Constructed during colonial times, it was once the mining industry's administrative headquarters.

FICCO – Festival Internacional de Cine Contemporáneo

Hosted by the Cinemex chain at various venues across the city (www.ficco.com.mx). **Date** Feb-Mar.

Showing new movies every year since 2003, the International Contemporary Film Festival (FICCO) has become one of Mexico City's most important cultural events. Showcasing arthouse cinema from around the globe while also cultivating domestic talent, the festival has become increasingly influential on the Latin American circuit. Talk your way into one of FICCO's memorable parties, and you'll have the opportunity to rub shoulders with the international film set (along with some fellow resourceful gatecrashers).

I always take visitors to the Basílica de Nuestra Señora de Guadalupe. It's the heart of Mexico and the single most important expression of its soul. Without a visit to La Virgencita, the mystery of Mexico remains inexplicable.

Cristina Potters, food writer, Mexico Cooks website.

Semana Santa

Across Mexico. **Date** 6-12 Apr 2009; 29 Mar-4 Apr 2010.

For many *chilangos*, Holy Week is simply a chance to swap a crowded city for a crowded beach. Visitors wanting a taste of traditional religious practices within DF should head for the densely populated and poor neighbourhood of Iztapalapa, where religious street theatre starting on Palm Sunday culminates in the Good Friday procession (*see p163* **Thank God it's Friday**).

Festival de las Flores y Plantas

Paseo de la Reforma, between Ángel de la Independencia and the fountain of Diana La Cazadora, Juárez. Metro Insurgentes L1. **Date** mid Mar. **Map** p264 F6, G5, G6. .

All manner of blooms and greenery line the capital's most elegant avenue in this, the Festival of Flowers and Plants. Much of the flora is cultivated in Xochimilco, Mexico City's ancient garden *colonia*. Flowers and pot plants are sold alongside organic honey and coffee, and the general green vibe extends to the healthy snacks on offer. This makes for a particularly pleasant stroll on a Sunday morning, when Paseo de la Reforma is closed to traffic.

La Noche de Primavera

Zócalo, Centro (www.cultura df.gob.mx). Metro Zócalo L2. **Date** late Mar. **Map** p267 M4.

Every year, the city government runs the Spring Night festival, a line-up of free entertainment to help *chilangos* herald the arrival of spring, though it isn't always held on the actual spring equinox. Fledgling culture vultures are catered for early on, with performances aimed at kids, but concerts representing a mix of genres from opera to rock run on late into the night.

April-June

Festival del Centro Histórico

Zócalo, Centro (www.festival.org.mx). Metro Bellas Artes L2, L8 or Zócalo L2. **Date** mid to late Apr. **Map** p267 M4.

More than two weeks are devoted to dance, music, visual arts, multimedia, theatre and opera in this eclectic festival. The Zócalo square and Bellas Artes are the main focal points for the festival, but you can also catch street productions in plazas, churches and other venues across the Centro Histórico.

ZONAMACO

Centro Banamex, Avenida Conscripto 311, Lomas de Sotelo (5268 2000/www.centrobanamex.com). **Date** 22-26 Apr (2009).

Mingle with artists, collectors and art aficionados at Mexico's International Contemporary Art Fair, formerly called 'Femaco'. Local and overseas galleries exhibit in the immense Centro Banamex convention centre and the city's art scene, buzzing all year round, ratchets it up a notch with a profusion of parties and related events.

Arts & Entertainment

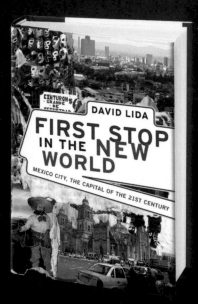

Ollin Kan Festival

Various venues in Tlalpan (www.ollinkan.tlalpan. gob.mx). **Date** mid Apr-mid May.
Organised and hosted by the *delegación* (borough) of Tlalpan, this multi-disciplinary festival has a political message – the celebration and diffusion of 'cultures in resistance' to globalisation. The four-week event features performers from Holland to Haiti.

Día de las Mulas

Zócalo, Centro and churches across the city. Metro Bellas Artes L2, L8 or Zócalo L2. **Date** May-June. **Map** p267 M4.
A colourful religious festival, the Day of the Mules or Corpus Christi Thursday has been observed in Mexico since the early 16th century. Children decked out in typical indigenous dress sell miniature wicker mules adorned with multi-coloured fabric, crepe paper, glitter, sweets and dried fruit. Visit the handicrafts fair in the Zócalo, which brings together artisans from across the country.

Fathers' Day Half Marathon

Bosque de Tlalpan, Parques del Pedregal (5666 5028/www.cbt.org.mx). **Date** 2nd Sun of June.
It seems a little unfair that in contrast with mothers, encouraged to put their feet up and eat chocolates on Mothers' Day, on their special day Mexican fathers are urged to don trainers for a half marathon through Bosque de Tlalpan woods in southern Mexico City. But thousands of them take part. There are categories for fathers of all ages, including over-75s, and many dads are joined by their offspring for the race.

Vive Latino

Foro Sol, Ciudad Deportiva (www.vivelatino. com.mx). Metro Velodromo L9. **Date** mid May. **Tickets** from MX$350.
Vive Latino – subtitled the 'Ibero-American Festival of Music and Culture' – is arguably the most *chido* (cool) event on offer in DF. Cool and happening – a kind of urban Glastonbury – it caters to both esoteric and mainstream tastes in a two-day event that brings together more than 60 bands from Mexico and around the world. It all takes place in Foro Sol, a modern sports and concert venue that is usually home to Mexico's Diablos Rojos baseball team. Families are welcome, and children under four get in free.

Gay Pride

Centro (www.marchalgbt.com). Metro Zócalo L2. **Date** last weekend in June. **Map** p264 G5.
Mexico's lesbian, gay, bisexual and transsexual community gets dressed up to parade down tree-lined Paseo de la Reforma every June. The procession struts on to Avenida Juárez and along Francisco de Madero before converging on the Zócalo. Not yet comparable with the gigantic parades of San Francisco and Berlin, Mexico's Marcha del Orgullo has nevertheless grown in strength and sass every year since it started in the mid-1970s.

Mexico City Marathon

Across the city (www.maraton.df.gob.mx). **Date** mid Aug.
Taking place at 2,300m (7,559ft) above sea level, Mexico City's marathon is one of the world's most gruelling. Starting and finishing in the Zócalo main square, the route is blessedly flat and decidedly scenic in parts, taking in Bosque de Chapultepec and Paseo de Reforma on the way.

Día de la Independencia

Zócalo, Centro. Metro Bellas Artes L2, L8. **Date** 15-16 Sept. **Map** p267 M4.
Fiestas Patrias – literally 'patriotic parties' – mark the anniversary of Mexico's declaration of independence from Spain in 1810. Catch a free concert in the Zócalo on 15 September, when thousands of Mexicans gather to witness the midnight *grito de independencia*. It commemorates liberator Miguel Hidalgo's 1810 'cry of independence', urging his compatriots to take up arms against the *gauchupines* or *peninsulares* (native Spaniards who enjoyed privileges in Mexico denied to those of Mexican birth). Mexico's president traditionally does the honours from a Palacio Nacional balcony.

Día de la Virgen de Guadalupe. *See p162.*

He rings the same bell Hidalgo rang and issues the *grito* – '¡Mexicanos, viva Mexico!' (Mexicans, long live Mexico!).

October-December

Día de los Muertos
El Panteón de San Fernando *Plaza de San Fernando 17, Centro. Metro Hidalgo L2, L3.* **Open** *Museum 9am-5pm Tue-Sun.* **Map** p266 K3.
El Panteón de San Andrés *Mixquic. Metro Taxqueña then RTP bus, route 149, to Mixquic.*
Both Date 1-2 Nov.
Revelries for the Day of the Dead, Mexico's answer to Hallowe'en, are world renowned. In 2003, UNESCO classified the festival as part of the world's 'intangible cultural heritage' and there's no doubt that being in Mexico during the All Saints' and All Souls' Day festivities is a unique opportunity to understand what makes the country tick. Even in the cosmopolitan capital, families create shrines with *ofrendas* (offerings) to late loved ones, and bakeries are piled high with sugared, anise-scented *pan de muertos* – 'bread of the dead', proving that some phrases are best left untranslated. Time-honoured customs centred on the cemetery are best observed at Mixquic, a former village now absorbed by the metropolis, where family vigils double as picnics. Within the city limits, commemorations for the dead take place at San Fernando and Tepeyac cemeteries, in Guerrero and Villa de Guadalupe respectively. Public access to the latter can be restricted, so check before making the trip; and note too that tremendous crowds descend on Mixquic, so you may spend hours on a bus just getting there.

Día de la Virgen de Guadalupe
Basílica de Santa María de Guadalupe, Plaza de las Américas 1, Villa de Guadalupe (5577 6022/www.virgendeguadalupe.org.mx). Metro Deportivo 18 de Marzo L3, L6. **Date** 12 Dec.
Mexico City is the focal point of celebrations on the public holiday commemorating the 16th-century 'appearance' of the *Virgen Morena* (the dark-skinned Virgin) to Juan Diego on Tepeyac hill. Expect enormous crowds if you visit the basilica between 9 and 12 December, and to see ritual Aztec-style dancing as well as penitents approaching the basilica on their knees. *Photo p161.*

Posadas and Christmas Eve
Across the city. **Date** 16-24 Dec.
Traditional advent parties or *posadas* have largely been replaced by a more contemporary party season, so it's time to start making friends if you'd like to be invited to a bash. Noche Buena – Christmas Eve – is the culmination of the *posadas*, when families enjoy dishes such as *lechón* (suckling pig) and *bacalao a la vizcaína* (salt cod slow-cooked in a tomato-based sauce). Christmas Day is largely devoted to nursing major hangovers and minor gastric complaints.

A feast day for all the family, dead or alive, on **Día de los Muertos**.

Arts & Entertainment

Thank God it's Friday

For many Mexicans, Maundy Thursday is just another day off work; for the faithful and their children, it is an opportunity to reflect before the prayers and hymns of Easter. But for one lucky hombre in Iztapalapa, a 1.8 million-strong suburb in eastern Mexico City, it's a long night of anticipation, apprehension and hope. Tomorrow will be one of the biggest days of his life. Because tomorrow, for one day only, he gets to play Jesus.

He has been stripped and searched, beaten and bullied, arrested and condemned to death. All in all, a night in a makeshift jail is a moment of relative peace. Chosen by the faithful to play the part of Christ in the Easter celebrations, he languishes in his lonely cell all through the night and into Friday morning. In the afternoon, he is pushed around some more, presented with a wooden cross weighing 90 kilos and told to walk three kilometres with it on his shoulders. Naturally, he wears a crown of thorns and a loincloth.

His zeal is matched by that of the audience. Other devout worshippers share his pain by grazing and spiking themselves with cactus burrs, carrying 100-kilo loads of thorny branches on their bare shoulders, or dragging yet more wooden crosses. As Jesus staggers past, those dressed as Romans call out insults and goad the doomed Messiah, while others call out for miracles and for help in general. Christ-for-a-day ignores the former and offers verbal succour to the latter as he moves towards the inevitable Calvary.

Iztapalapa's Good Friday events have their origins in real suffering. After a devastating cholera epidemic in the winter of 1833, the survivors decided to perform a Passion play to mark what they viewed as their miraculous survival. In his 2003 book, *Reliving Golgotha*, Richard C Trexler argues that, in the early years, the event was a means by which the indigenous groups of Mexico could incorporate some aspects of their own animistic traditions – for example, the wearing of masks – into a Christian festival. In the early 20th-century re-enactments, Nahuatl-speaking actors played the key roles, and the local congregation regarded the spectacle, unmediated by priests, as a protest against the conservative Church hierarchy.

By the 1950s, however, the authorities were encouraging the Passion as a tourist draw. Now a mainstream event complete with media coverage and government funding, it lacks much of its original raw drama. But as Christian street theatre goes, it's still pretty impressive, involving some 450 actors and as many as two million spectators. Up until 2002, Mexico's bishops maintained that the Passion was merely a theatrical event and undeserving of the Church's consent. Recently, however, the Mexican Church has woken up to the marketing potential of the Iztapalapa pageant, and priests have taken part in it.

Iztapalapa is not the only Mexican town to do Easter with a visceral commitment to realism. In the colonial town of Taxco, men in black hoods stagger barefoot along cobbled streets under the weight of thorny branches, while other penitents whip their bare backs with steel chains.

But though blood, sweat and tears are inevitable ingredients at Iztapalapa, nails are not used in the crucifixion. For that, you'll have to go to the Philippines, the former Spanish colony administered between 1565 and 1815 from New Spain – that is to say, Mexico.

Children

Interactive museums and cool, shady parks.

Mexico City is not all concrete and chaos – in fact, its many parks and museums make it a rather pleasant place for families to spend time with their children. History museums will satisfy older children's curiosity about the gore and lore of Mexico's pre-Hispanic civilisations, and the city's many markets are packed with strange sights and smells that will entice many kids. Mexicans tend to treat children warmly and to welcome them without question into most restaurants and cafés.

It's worth bearing in mind that adults and children alike can suffer from headaches and dehydration due to the high altitude, and that air pollution is worse during the dry season (November to April). The effect of smog, compounded by the altitude, can leave kids feeling a little out of breath or exhausted, so take it slowly and don't feel pressured to rush through the sights.

For up-to-date listings of films, puppet shows and children's theatre, take a look at the *niños* sections of the magazines **Tiempo Libre** (www.tiempolibre.com.mx) and **Dónde Ir** (www.donde-ir.com). Although most shows will inevitably be in Spanish, performances of familiar fairy tales and an emphasis on movement as opposed to dialogue often make it easy enough for little kids, bright sparks that they are, to catch on.

Parks & plazas

The vast green space that is Bosque de Chapultepec (*see p74*), with its many museums, lawns and little lakes, is an obvious choice for families visiting Mexico City; but it seems that everywhere you look there are pockets of greenery with something to capture a child's attention and imagination.

Both Roma's **Plaza Luis Cabrera** and Condesa's **Parque México** have bikes and pedal cars you can borrow if you leave a deposit and some ID. Also at the gorgeous, delightfully shady Parque México, a duck pond and a trampoline are designed to delight the younger generation. Condesa's **Parque España** has a relatively new playground, well lit in the evenings, where energetic kids can have a final and hopefully exhausting workout before bedtime. Keep an eye out for arts and crafts activities for children at weekends in parks and plazas, including in **Plaza Hidalgo** in Coyoacán.

Polanco's **Parque Lincoln** has an elaborate playground, and children will love the park's aviary, full of colourful budgies that swoop and flutter around visitors. At one end of the park is the Teatro Ángela Peralta, which often puts on shows at weekends. Kids can also race remote-controlled boats on one of the park's pools.

Kidding around at the highly regarded **Papalote Museo del Niño**.

Swinging, sailing and scaling at **Parque Lincoln**.

Parque Ecológico de Xochimilco

*Periférico Oriente 1 (5673 8139). Tren Ligero
Periférico, then a Cuamenco-bound bus to
park entrance.* **Open** 9am-6pm Mon-Sun.
Admission MX$20; MX$5 under-10s and
seniors. **No credit cards.**

Nature lovers are drawn to this park's shallow
lake and marsh for the wildlife: herons, cormorants
and ducks, as well as for the endangered axolotl
salamander – a strange amphibian that never
loses its gills and is native only to the Mexico City
area. *Trajineras* – Mexico's version of the gondola
– are available for rent at weekends, and mountain
bikes, paddleboats and four-seater pedal cars can
be hired throughout the week. In addition to the
walking and biking trails, there are several play-
grounds. The park should not be confused with
the canal area of Xochimilco, where *trajineras* can
also be rented.

Bosque de Chapultepec

As well as the places listed beneath, other
attractions in Bosque de Chapultepec that are
suitable for children include the **Botanical
Garden** (*see p76*), **El Museo de Historia
Natural y Cultura Ambiental** (Natural
History Museum) (*see p80*), and the **Museo
Tecnológico de la CFE** (*see p80*).

La Feria de Chapultepec

*Bosque de Chapultepec, 2nd section (5230 2121/
www.feriachapultepec.com.mx). Metro Constituyentes
L7.* **Open** 10am-6pm Tue-Fri; 10am-7pm Sat; 10am-
8pm Sun & public holidays. **Admission** MX$50-$150
depending on number of rides accessed. Additional
charge for go-karts & games of skill. **Credit** MC, V.
Map p262 B7.

La Feria is best known for its 1960s-era wooden roller
coaster along with a variety of other fairground-style
rides. Little kids will enjoy the bouncy castles and the
ball mazes, and love riding the carousels and trains.

Lago del Bosque de Chapultepec

*Bosque de Chapultepec, 1st section. Metro
Chapultepec L1.* **Open** 10am-4pm Tue-Sat.
Rates MX$40-$100 per hour. **No credit
cards. Map** p262 D6.

What better way to spend an afternoon than drift-
ing on a lake in the city's largest park? Different
sized kayaks, rowing boats and paddleboats are
available for rent by the hour. It's best to go during
the week when the park isn't too crowded.

Papalote Museo del Niño

*Avenida Constituyentes 268 (5237 1700/
www.papalote.org.mx). Metro Constituyentes
L7.* **Open** 9am-6pm Mon-Wed, Fri; 9am-11pm
Thur, 10am-7pm Sat, Sun & public holidays.
Admission MX$90; MX$85 under-12s and
seniors. Extra admission charges for IMAX,
Domo Digital Planetarium, Fantastic Bus and
temporary exhibitions. **Credit** AmEx, MC, V.
Map p262 B8.

At this multi-faceted museum kids can immerse
themselves in giant soap bubbles, experiment with
musical instruments and craft things from recycled
materials. Many staff members speak some English,
but children have a way of breaking through the language barrier and will have their fun either way,
pushing buttons and pulling handles on the displays.
Some of the themes visitors can delve into include the
human body, computers and the arts. The museum
is often crowded, but queues move quickly. Thursday
nights are geared towards adults, who can have dinner listening to live jazz bands.

Zoológico de Chapultepec

Bosque de Chapultepec, 1st section (5553 6263/ 5256 4104/www.chapultepec.df.gob.mx). Metro Chapultepec L1. **Open** 9am-4.30pm Tue-Sun. **Admission** free. Extra charge for butterfly & reptile houses. **Map** p262 C6.

Aztec Emperor Moctezuma's menagerie was located on this very spot in pre-Hispanic Tenochtitlán, the precursor to modern-day Mexico City. Chapultepec Zoo was founded in 1923 by a biologist who loosely modelled it on the zoo in Rome. Today's zoo has undergone major landscaping and renovations in order to provide more modern habitats for the animals, although some of the cages still seem rather small. There is a large open-air aviary, a reptile house, and a special area for the city's beloved giant pandas.

Museums

Museo Interactivo de Economía (MIDE)

Tacuba 17, Centro (5130 4600/www.mide.org.mx). Metro Allende L2 or Bellas Artes L2, L8. **Open** 9am-6pm Tue-Sun. **Admission** MX$55; MX$45 under-12s, students, teachers. **Credit** AmEx, MC, V. **Map** p267 L4.

Children can learn about the Mexican economy – which sounds like less fun than it actually is – in this high-tech, hands-on museum housed in a former monastery. Groups of kids can trade shares at a miniature stock exchange and create a banknote graced with their very own images at the mint. At the time of writing the museum was planning to translate the text for the different exhibits into English. As things stand, the content has a decidedly local focus, but the slick displays still make it a worthwhile trip.

Museo de la Luz

Calle del Carmen, corner of San Ildefonso, Centro (5702 3183/www.luz.unam.mx). Metro Zócalo L2. **Open** 9am-4pm Mon-Fri; 10am-5pm Sat, Sun and public holidays. **Admission** MX$20; MX$10 children, students, teachers; free seniors. **No credit cards**. **Map** p267 N4.

This museum is housed in an atmospheric 16th-century Jesuit temple, and its exhibits demonstrate the different properties of light. Although some understanding of Spanish will help immeasurably with the science part, even without it there are plenty of displays that make language irrelevant, such as the sculptures that create optical illusions, glowing plasma balls and the kaleidoscopes.

Universum Museo de las Ciencias

Insurgentes Sur 3000, UNAM (5622 7287/ www.universum.unam.mx). Metro Universidad L3. **Open** 9am-6pm Mon-Fri; 10am-6pm Sat, Sun. **Admission** MX$50; MX$40 children, students, teachers; free seniors. **Credit** V.

This interactive museum has an array of exhibits to pique kids' curiosity about science. Electricity, magnetism and the laws of gravity are all touched on in hands-on exhibits.

Other attractions

La Granja las Américas

Boulevard Pípila, Acceso 3, near Hipódromo de las Américas, Lomas de Sotelo (5387 0600/ www.granjalasamericas.com.mx). Metro Cuatro Caminos L2, then bus. **Open** 9am-5pm Tue-Thur; 9am-6pm Fri; 10am-6pm Sat, Sun. **Admission** MX$115 adults; MX$140 children over 2.6ft; free children under 2.6ft. **Credit** AmEx, MC, V.

Some of the activities here are a little bare bones but young children are mesmerised to see how milk comes from an actual cow and ends up in a chocolate drink box. Animal lovers will enjoy petting the sheep, calves and pigs, but may not like being reminded by the guides that some of them end up as sausages. The extreme sports area lets older kids run an obstacle course, scale a climbing wall and slide down a zip line; on weekends, parents can hang out in a bar that overlooks the nearby horse racing track. If you've had a long stay in the city and feel the need to stroke some fluffy bunnies, then this isn't a bad option — but it's pricey for what it is.

KidZania, Ciudad de los Niños

Santa Fe shopping mall, Avenida Vasco de Quiroga 3800, Antigua Mina la Totolapa (5261 1020/ www.laciudaddelosninos.com). Metro Auditorio L7/Metrobús La Piedad, then Centro Comercial Santa Fe-bound bus. **Open** 9am-7pm Mon-Thur; 9am-8pm Fri; 10am-3pm, 4-9pm Sat, Sun & public holidays. **Admission** MX$100 2-3s; MX$170 4-16s; MX$95 adults; MX$75 seniors; free under-2s and visitors with disabilities. **Credit** AmEx, MC, V.

After a simulated flight, kids visiting KidZania enter a miniature city where they can take on fun jobs in anything from detective work and newspaper reporting to dentistry and archaeology. Whichever they choose from the dozens of possible professions, they'll be paid in Kidzos, the local currency. Corporate logos dominate at every turn but don't take away the magic of this scaled-down city, where kids can make and gobble popsicles at an ice-cream factory, mix cocktails from fruit juices at a pool hall, and get gussied up for a walk down a fashion show runway.

Six Flags México

Carretera Picacho-Ajusco 1500, Tlalpan (5728 7200/www.sixflags.com.mx). Metro Tasqueña L2 or Universidad L3, then bus. **Admission** MX$315; MX$210 kids between 3 and 3.9ft; free kids under 3ft. **Open** varies – check website. **Credit** AmEx, MC, V.

Previously called Reino Aventura, this adventure park changed its name to Six Flags México in 1999 when it was bought by the US company of the same name. Now the largest amusement park in Latin America, it includes El Río Salvaje (a rafting ride), thrilling rollercoasters and plenty of rides for little ones.

Clubs

What DF's club scene lacks in sophistication, it makes up for in pure energy.

Though not on par with the ever-revelling cities of Berlin, London, New York, Madrid and Rio, Mexico City's nightlife can certainly hold its own. The city's party-loving residents adore letting loose and need little excuse to head out for a beer- or tequila-fuelled boogie session. And when it's closing time and partygoers spill out of a venue on to the sidewalk, *'Dónde está el afters?'* (Where's the after-party?) is an oft-echoed refrain, and a look of scorn may greet shirkers who decide to call it a night.

Boisterous cantinas, swinging tropical dance floors, jammin' reggae nights and gnarly punk and goth outposts await in the seemingly endless expanse of concrete and traffic that is Mexico City. There are squeaky-clean theme and cover-band bars, wee-hours electronica joints and too-cool-for-school hipster hangs and art events, plus a thriving gay and lesbian strip and the unmissable mariachi madness of Plaza Garibaldi (*see p167*). The fun generally gets rolling from Wednesday onwards, though in the bar-heavy Condesa neighbourhood, people often get started as early as Monday night.

The best Clubs

For killer electro
Pasaje América (*see p171*).

For vein-coursing techno
AM (*see p168*).

For mixing with the wealthy
Love Ixchel (*see p169*).

For 'am I really seeing this?'
Patrick Miller (*see p170*).

For rounding off an evening
El Jacalito (*see p169*).

Nightclubs

Sadly, many of Mexico City's nightclubs lack punch, originality and spontaneous excitement. One-off events, especially those associated with the city's thriving art scene, often offer more in

Pasaje América. *See p171.*

Digital dancehall

Many of Mexico City's best *reventones*, *pachangas*, fiestas and *pedas* – Mexicans have as many synonyms for 'party' as the English do for 'rain' – are one-off affairs that take place in roving locations. Consult **hellodf.com, syntheticrocks.blogspot.com, blog.turnthatshitoff.com, thecity lovesyou.com** and **colmilludo.com** to get yourself to the right place at the right time.

For electronic parties and to find out about visiting DJs, consult **kinetik.tv, comunidadelectronica.tv, myspace.com/imecamusic, myspace.com/discotecaonline** and **myspace.com/noiselab**.

Trance – as in progressive and psycho – is still big in Mexico. Raves occur monthly but most are poorly organised – better to stick to the big ones booking international names that take place around Christmas near Palenque, Acapulco and Playa del Carmen. Check **trance-it.org, dosisdigital.com, soundsofearth.net** and **kinetik.tv** for details. For the schedule of mainstream concerts in the city, check **warp.com.mx, sopitas.com, everythinglive.blogspot.com** and **prodigymsn.dixo.com**.

And when the party's over, you might spot your own debauched nighttime antics at **diariodefiestas.com**, or at the website of the city's premier over-the-top party photoblogger, Jesús León (**domesticfinearts. blogspot.com**), whose sexy images of DF's beautiful and damned grace the pages of this very chapter.

the way of fun and fabulousness; but there are still plenty of kicks to be had out in DF's clubland, and nights out always make for an interesting people-watching experience. Tables abound in most venues, reducing precious dance space, since Mexicans like to order bottles of tequila, rum, vodka or other spirits to share for the evening. Ladies should note that men usually outnumber women significantly, so be prepared to get hit on.

Cover charges vary widely depending on the type of place and who's playing, and more often than not, the dress code is informal. Bring some ID: the government has started cracking down on under-18s and you may be asked to show it. And when you've had your fun – and certainly if it's after, as it will be, 10pm – call a taxi from a *sitio* (fixed taxi rank) for a safe ride home.

Condesa

Chichi decor and dress-shirted yuppies and preppies (known as *fresas* in Mexican Spanish) pervade many of the establishments in the picturesque and upscale Condesa, though you'll find dressed-down, scuffed-shoed cooler kids in the more chilled-out venues.

AM
Nuevo León 67 (5286 8572/www.amlocal.com). Metro Sevilla L1. **Open** 11pm-5am Wed-Sat. **Admission** MX$150-$200. **Credit** AmEx, MC, V. **Map** p264 F8.

When it opened its doors in 2006, AM quickly established itself as one of the top electronic music venues, with a solid roster of local tech house, techno and progressive house DJs plus international guests like Germany's Kompakt Records crew. Its cosy, dimly lit, steel-beamed rectangle of a space packs in yuppies, hipsters, creative types and foreigners sharing a common love for artfully mixed, ear-assuaging electro. Men are advised to arrive with women to facilitate entry – and to check out the primping and preening in the semi-transparent bathroom area.

CFNA (Cafeína)
Nuevo León 73 (5212 0090). Metro Sevilla L1. **Open** 6pm-3am Mon-Sat. **Admission** MX$150 men, MX$100 women Mon; free Tue-Sat. **Credit** AmEx, MC, V. **Map** p264 F8.

Monday's 'Discopinha' is probably the busiest club night within a sizeable radius, with a talented Brazilian samba and pagode band playing from 10.30pm to 12.30am before a DJ steps in to spin electronica till the wee hours. Suits and silicon implants abound, with much of the same at weekends but without the live band and the cover charge. Check out the mid-week drinks promotions.

Imperial
Álvaro Obregón 293 (5525 1115/www.myspace. com/elimperialclub). Metro Sevilla L1. **Open** 10pm-3am Tue-Sat. **Admission** free-MX$100. **Credit** AmEx, MC, V. **Map** p264 G7.

Booking some of the city's best live rock, funk and jazz acts, Imperial has a pleasantly relaxed vibe. Hang out in the romantic Victorian-style downstairs area to hear bands, or head up to the red-tinted second floor to converse, take a whirl on the strippers' pole or lounge on one of the curved leather banquettes.

Move

Oaxaca 137 (no phone) Metro Sevilla L1.
Open 10pm-4am Fri, Sat **Admission** MX$100 men; free women. **Credit** MC, V. **Map** p264 G7.
Move is unpredictable and a little hit and miss – some nights hit the spot while others fall flat as two-day-old Coke. The line-up is not published, so the only way to see if it's happening on any given night is to take your chances and swing on by.

PM

Nuevo León 67 (5286 8456). Metro Sevilla L1.
Open 11pm-4am Wed-Sat. **Admission** MX$200 men; MX$100 women. **Credit** AmEx, MC, V. **Map** p264 F8.
Boogie here alongside twentysomethings from good families to music from the likes of Madonna, the Killers, Depeche Mode, as well as to hip hop and even *baile-funk* on an impressively kitsch Saturday Night Fever-esque flashing dancefloor. Wednesday night's Vuélvete Underground party, run by hot local DJ Damian Romero (www.myspace.com/imecamusic) lures in the hipsters and rocks them out to funky electro. *Photo p172.*

Rioma

Insurgentes Sur 377 (no phone). Metro Chilpancingo L9/Metrobús Campeche. **Open** 11pm-6am Wed-Sat. **Admission** MX$100-$200 Thur-Sat; free Wed, **Credit** AmEx, MC, V. **Map** p264 G9.
This intimate basement space has been a mainstay of the electronica scene for years, though the retro decor of its previous incarnation has given way to a rather more staid look. Techno and electro are what you'll hear, and preppies and electro-heads what you'll see. Things go on late, so it's not uncommon for party-lovin' folks to arrive at 4am and stumble out into early morning light.

Salón Pata Negra

Tamaulipas 30 (5211 5563/www.patanegra.com.mx). Metro Sevilla L1. **Open** 9pm-4am (no entry after 2.30am) Tue-Sat. **Admission** free. **Credit** AmEx, MC, V **Map** p264 F8.
Buoyed by the runaway success of their corner bar, the folks at Pata Negra (*see p137*) have opened this club-like counterpart upstairs. You can catch a live electro, funk or rock act on Tuesdays, while Wednesdays after midnight, the place jumps to a salsa/*son cubano* sound. Retreat to the calmer back bar to take a break from the morass of flirty office and creative types and Condesa-residing Argentinians and other foreigners.

Roma

This area has the advantage of being right next to Condesa, but it is rather less pretentious than that *colonia* – and it's home to an abundance of breathtaking art nouveau and earlier architecture.

Cream

Versalles 52 (5292 6114/www.myspace.com/creammexico). Metro Cuauhtémoc L1. **Open** 10pm-4am Thur-Sat. **Admission** MX$300-$500. **Credit** MC, V. **Map** p265 I5.
Cream took over this pretty two-storey house from the legendary Colmillo electronic club. Showcasing local techno, house, lounge and electro DJs alongside the occasional international act, there are several spaces to explore on the premises, from a small sunken dancefloor next to the DJ to an upstairs chill-out room.

El Jacalito

Medellín 143 (no phone). Metro Insurgentes L1/Metrobús Campeche. **Open** 10pm-7am Wed-Sat. **Admission** free. **No credit cards.** **Map** p264 H8.
The Jacalito's true decadent colours shine through after 3am, when the legendary outpost, which has been being shuttered up then reopened for years on end – check before you go – fills to overflow with a deliriously happy, beer-goggle-sporting crowd that runs the gamut from journalists and students to people of dubious profession. Cumbia, reggaeton, *norteño* and beer-by-the-bucket are its hallmarks, and girls should bring along at least one dude to fend off amorous glances and non-stop dance invitations.

Love Ixchel

Medellín 65 (3096 5010/www.liveinlove.com). Metro Sevilla L1/Metrobús Álvaro Obregón. **Open** *Restaurant* 8.30pm-midnight Wed-Sat. *Disco* midnight-6am Wed-Sat. **Admission** MX$200; women free. **Credit** AmEx, MC, V. **Map** p264 G7.
Located in an elegant former home, Love Ixchel is a hotspot for 25- to 40-year-old well-heeled yuppie and preppie patrons (dress code: pressed dress shirts, jeans and leather shoes for men; sexy minis, hip-hugging jeans and high heels for women). If you don't know door king Chepe or someone who does, your chances of gaining entry are slim, though arriving with a group of looker babes or making a dinner reservation might improve your odds. At midnight,

DF eye

Some of my favourite places to go out at night are the Río de la Plata cantina in the Centro Histórico, or Covadonga (*see p138*) in Roma for long evenings of eating, drinking and talking. Patrick Miller (*see p170*) is great for hi-NRG music, or AM in Condesa (*see above*) for electro – and then, in the early hours, El Jacalito (*see above*).

Fernando Montiel Klint, photographer, *Chilango* magazine.

the dining tables are whisked away, a curtain is drawn and the disco ball set spinning – expect to hear 1980s and '90s Spanish and English pop, and to groove elbow-to-elbow.

Malva
Durango 181 (no phone/www.myspace.com/malvadizco). Metro Sevilla L1. **Open** 10pm-4am Thur-Sat. **Admission** MX$30-$70. **No credit cards. Map** p264 G7.
Gay and straight club kids and fashion freaks grind enthusiastically to go-go, electronic and weird pop at Jun and Moli's nights at Malva, and to nu-electro, funky electro, glam and electro punk at Dave Rape's rocking parties. Check the website to see when they're on.

Mamá Rumba
Querétaro 230 (5564 6920). Metro Chilpancingo L9/Metrobús Sonora. **Open** 9pm-3am Wed-Sat. **Admission** MX$70 Wed, Thur; MX$80 Fri, Sat. **Credit** AmEx, MC, V. **Map** p264 H8.
For 17 years, this has been the place to hear Cuban timba, guaracha, rumba and son rhythms played by Cubans. Live acts kick off at round 11pm, and on Wednesdays, Thursdays and Saturdays there are dance classes when the doors open. Expect to mix with plenty of seriously snazzy salseros, Cubans and other foreigners as you manoeuvre around the two floors, trying not to get your drink knocked over.

Patrick Miller
Mérida 17 (5511 5406/www.patrickmiller.com.mx). Metro Cuauhtémoc L1. **Open** 8.30pm-3am Fri. **Admission** MX$30. **No credit cards. Map** p265 I6.
No, your cheap beer isn't tainted – those really are taxi drivers pirouetting to 1980s hi-NRG B-sides in the middle of controlled human circles. Dare to ask a circle chief for your five minutes of fame! High energy Fridays, when loads of young ad agency types pack the joint to watch the older regulars, are definitely more surreal and fun than the 1980s/90s nights, so be sure to click on the 'fiestas' tab on the website to find out the schedule. Arrive before 11pm and buy all your beer chips at once to avoid queues.

Rincón Cubano
Insurgentes Sur 300 (5584 0110). Metro Chilpancingo L9/Metrobús Sonora. **Open** 9pm-4am Fri, Sat; 2pm-3am Sunday. **Admission** MX$70 Fri, Sat; MX$50 Sun. **Credit** AmEx, MC, V. **Map** p264 G8.
The couples at the Rincón leave their tables to do their salsa thing when the Cuban tropical band takes to the stage at around 10.30pm or 11.30pm. On Thursdays, mojitos are two-for-one and on Sundays, there's a Cuban buffet. Look out for occasional guest appearances of tropical or reggaeton acts.

El Under
Monterrey 80 (5511 5475/www.theunder.org). Metro Insurgentes L1. **Open** 3-10pm Wed, Thur; 3pm-3am Fri, Sat. **Admission** free-MX$50. **No credit cards. Map** p264 H7.
There's no mistaking the entrance to El Under, where patrons with startling resemblances to Marilyn Manson or Edward Scissorhands peer out from the door and windows. You may want to leave that mango and pineapple Hawaiian shirt at home. DJs with names like Lady Palmolive and Herman Munster mix goth, 1980s synth pop, punk, new wave, industrial, EBM, surf and rockabilly.

Centro

Casa Blanca
Plaza de las Vizcaínas 3 (5521 8196). Metro Salto del Agua L1, L8. **Open** 8pm-4am Mon-Wed; 8pm-5am Thur-Sat. **Admission** free. **Credit** MC, V. **Map** p267 L5.
Set in a plaza opposite an 18th-century school, this 50-year-old dancehall has an intimate red hue, tables with white tablecloths, and two orchestras playing salsa and cumbia nightly.

Cultural Roots
Uruguay 70 (5737 4089/www.culturalroots.com.mx). Metro Isabel La Católica L1 or Zócalo L2. **Open** 4pm-2am Fri, Sun. **Admission** MX$20-$50; free women 4-5pm. **No credit cards. Map** p267 M5.
Lively up yourself at this authentic reggae and dub venue, where the stellar DJ collective known

as Hermandad Rasta keeps the mixed and, let us say, 'relaxed' crowd of red-eyed rasta boys in a permanent sway. The lovely colonial building that hosts the club also sees occasional guest appearances by Jamaican artists.

DadaX
Bolívar 31 (2454 4310/www.myspace.com/ dadax). Metro Isabel la Católica L1 or San Juan de Letrán L8. **Open** 9pm-3.30am Fri, Sat. **Admission** MX$30-$80. **No credit cards.** **Map** p267 L5.
Somewhat incongruously, wearers of serious fetish garb cruise the top floor of this striking colonial building. Goth, industrial and fetish scenesters are the in-crowd here, but they frequently lend their stage to trip-hop and alt-rock performers. *See also p193.*

Pasagüero
Motolinía 33 (5512 6624/www.myspace.com/ pasaguero). Metro Allende L2 or San Juan de Letrán L8. **Open** *Café* 2-11pm daily. *Club* 10pm-4am (no entry after 2am) Thur-Sat. **Admission** free-MX$180. **Credit** AmEx, MC, V. **Map** p267 M4.
The likes of Ratatat, Data Rock, Soulwax, Riot in Belgium and countless local bands and DJs have rattled the stone walls of this 19th-century former bank office, which is set on a cute cobblestoned pedestrian street. The lovely enclosed patio behind the building was once part of a 16th century monastery. Art openings and private parties also take place here – check the website for details. *See also p194.*

Pasaje América
5 de Mayo 7 (5521 0870). Metro Bellas Artes L2, L8. **Open** 10pm-7am Thur-Sat (no entry after 3.30am). **Admission** MX$100 $300. **Credit** AmEx, MC, V. **Map** p267 L4.
Located in a 19th-century commercial building, PA is considered by many to be hands-down the best club in the city –the best looking one, with the best line-up. Hot electro acts MIA, Adult, Apparat, Party Shank, Yuksek & Brodinski, Mr Flash, In Flagrant and Diplo have all taken to its patterned carpet, and a slew of opening and closing parties for film, music and fashion festivals are also thrown here. The interior is all plush furniture, red velvet, columns, marble, potted flora and large wood-framed windows, with at least three rooms to chill out in. *Photo p167.*

La Perla
República de Cuba 44 (1997 7695). Metro Bellas Artes L2, L8. **Open** 8pm-2am Thur; 8pm-3.30am Fri, Sat. **Admission** MX$40 Thur; MX$120 Fri, Sat. **No credit cards.** **Map** p267 L3.
At legendary La Perla, a DJ inside a giant sea shell broadcasts retro Spanish pop and popular cumbia from the 1980s and 90s, and drag queens emerge after midnight to lip-synch to Mexican and American oldies. Arrive by 10pm to ensure entry.

Pervert Lounge
Uruguay 70 (5510 4454). Metro Zócalo L2. **Open** 11pm-7am (no entry after 5.30am) Wed-Sat. **Admission** MX$70 men; free for women Thur; MX$100 Fri, Sat. **Credit** AmEx, MC, V. **Map** p267 M5.

Bumper-to-bumper boogying at **Pasagüero**.

Arts & Entertainment

Progressive house, tribal electro and tech house have been being pumped out here since 1994. The diminutive stone-walled space draws a sunglass-wearing, male-dominated regular crowd.

Other areas

Dobby Club
Vito Alessio Robles 138, Florida (5662 2154). Metrobús Altavista. **Open** from 3am Thur-Sat. **Admission** MX$100 men; MX$50 women. **Credit** AmEx, MC,V. **Map** p259 C2.
Don't be put off by Dobby Club's stone-faced door heavies, since just up the stairs lies a dark den of sofas, tawdry statues and a beaming bunch of self-confessed party addicts. An outdoor balcony provides a chance to smoke and a brutal reminder of the advancing day. Ideal attendance time: 7am to 10am.

Don Quintin
2nd floor, Avenida Presidente Masaryk 407, Polanco (5280 6986). Metro Polanco L7. **Open** 9pm-4.30am Thur-Sat. **Admission** MX$200 men; free Thur before 11pm. **Credit** AmEx, MC, V. **Map** p262 A4.
A rollicking cover band belting out 1980s and 1990s English and Spanish hits has the youthful preppie crowd singing at their tables. The drinks are reasonably priced and free flowing.

Pedro Infante Karaoke Bar
Insurgentes Sur 2351, San Angel (5616 4585/ www.elpeter.com.mx). Metrobús La Bombilla or Dr Gálvez. **Open** from 9pm Wed-Sat. **Admission** MX$30. **Credit** AmEx, MC, V. **Map** p259 B3.
Weekends after 2am are prime time at Pedro Infante, when very merry drunkards squeeze into its tiny

confines and belt out Spanish language hits from every era. As a welcome service to customers' eardrums and sanity, the management alternates each raw karaoke tune with one from the DJ, who sometimes throws in a few electronic tunes. Lest you despair, champing at the bit to take your turn, rest assured that at least five per cent of the song menu is in English, including gems by the likes of Barry Manilow, Roxette and the Rolling Stones.

Petra
Palmas 555, Lomas de Chapultepec (5095 6555). Metro Auditorio L7. **Open** 10pm-2am Wed-Sat. **Admission** free. **Credit** AmEx, MC, V.
Petra, in one of DF's fanciest 'hoods, caters to high-flying (and medium-level) execs and the models and bored, rich housewives who love them, so don't raise an eyebrow at the sight of sexily attired women of a certain age gyrating for seated suits. Bottle service and solid toe-tapping electro, pop and house are the norm.

Roots Magic Club
Rodolfo Gaona 3, Lomas de Sotelo (5580 6106/ www.rootsmagicclub.com.mx). Metro Cuatro Caminos L2. **Open** 10pm-3am Fri, Sat. **Admission** $150 men; free women; MX$200-$400 special events. **Credit** AmEx, MC, V.
With a 3,000-plus capacity, Roots Magic Club is the largest DJ club in the city and has hosted Adam Freeland, Paul Van Dyk, Justice, MANDY and many other world-renowned superstars. The sound system is top notch, the tables far too plentiful, the drinks horribly overpriced, and the pandemonium at the door when stars are on the bill a true headache. Arrive unfashionably early if a big name is playing.

PM. See p169.

Film

From DF to the world: Mexican talent reaches out beyond borders.

El Violín. See p175.

Mexican cinema is at an interesting point in its development, having reached beyond the country's geographical and cultural frontiers to coalesce into a truly global and indeed – given the relationships of its finest practitioners to Hollywood and beyond – a truly globalised cinema. The briefest run-down of just the biggest names in contemporary Mexican film would have to include directors Alfonso Cuarón (*Harry Potter and the Prisoner of Azkaban, Children of Men*), Alejandro Gonzalez Iñárritu (*Amores Perros, 21 Grams, Babel*) and Guillermo del Toro (*Pan's Labyrinth, Hellboy* and *Hellboy II*); the actor and producer Gael García Bernal (*Y Tu Mamá También, The Motorcycle Diaries*); the actress and producer Salma Hayek (*Desperado, Frida*) and the cinematographer Emmanuel Lubezki (*The New World, Children of Men*).

Despite their heavy dependence on Mexican talent, most of the aforementioned movies are, thanks to the economics of the movie business, gringo productions. But audiences and critics have, since the turn of the millennium, been rediscovering the Mexican film industry. The big shift came about with Iñárritu's 2000 film *Amores Perros* – an in-your-face urban triptych

of love and disillusion in Mexico City. The international recognition and awards it won put paid to the misconception that Mexico could only churn out burrito Westerns and feature-length *telenovelas* (soap operas).

THE GOLDEN AGE

Mexican film only really took off in the mid 1930s, heralding the so-called *época de oro del cine mexicano*: the golden age of Mexican cinema, which lasted until the 1950s. The film industry flourished during this period, winning national and international praise for its directors, actors and actresses. Notable films from the era include Ismael Rodriguez's *Nosostros los Pobres* (1947) starring the Mexican film idol, Pedro Infante, and *María Candelaria* by Emilio Fernández, which triumphed at the Cannes Film Festival in 1946, winning the Palme d'Or. Both films are pillars of the Golden Age. The first, an urban melodrama, recounts the tale of Pepe 'El Toro', a humble carpenter who lives a happy and dignified life, despite his poverty, with his daughter Chachita, his invalid mother and his girlfriend, La Chorreada. His life is ruined when he is wrongly accused and jailed for murder, but his family, friends and neighbours join forces to fight this social and judicial injustice. Fernández's film, *María Candelaria*, depicts quite a different Mexico. Set on the canals of Xochimilco in 1909, the year before the Mexican Revolution, the plot turns on the fortunes of the eponymous heroine and her lover, Lorenzo Rafael, who must fight discrimination and prejudice to be with the woman he loves. The film exposes the then commonplace maltreatment of indigenous Mexicans at the hands of whites and *mestizos* (those of mixed race), and explores the socioeconomic and race-determined tensions that disfigure Mexican society to this day. Viewed as social critique or as a simple romantic melodrama, the film is a firm Mexican favourite, and well worth the viewing.

At the peak of the golden age, in the mid-1940s, 70 Mexican films were being produced each year and the country's cinema dominated the Latin American market. A dip in the output of the US and European film industries during World War II was among a number of factors that contributed to the *época de oro,* leaving a local gap that Mexican cinema filled. In turn, the re-emergence of Hollywood in the mid-1940s brought on a decline in Mexican cinema, and eventually led to the end of the golden age.

MEXICAN WAVE

Mexican cinema began to enjoy a renaissance in the 1970s with the so-called *nuevo cine mexicano* or new wave. It was practically synonymous with the films of director Arturo Ripstein. Ripstein was immersed in the film world from the start – his father was producer Alfredo Ripstein, and he became Luis Buñuel's assistant in the early 1960s, forming a close friendship with him that lasted until Buñuel's death in 1983. He directed his first film, *Tiempo de Morir*, in 1965 and has continued to direct over the years since then. Ripstein's unnerving melodramas explore the themes of *l'amour fou*, solitude and the inability to change one's true nature. He has favoured independent films and collaborations with some of Latin America's most important novelists, including Gabriel García Márquez, who lives in Mexico City, and with whom he has worked on two adaptations. In the mid-1980s, Ripstein began a still-existing collaboration with his wife, Mexican scriptwriter Paz Alicia Garciadiego, and directed some of his finest works, including *Profundo Carmesí* (1996), about Mexico's 1940s 'lonely hearts murders', which won several awards at the Venice Film Festival.

Other notable names from the movement include Alfonso Auro, whose 1992 adaptation of Laura Esquivel's novel *Like Water for Chocolate* became the highest-grossing foreign film in the USA at the time, and María Novaro, whose *Danzón* – the story of Julia, a Mexico City telephone operator who goes in search for her missing dance partner –was presented at the Cannes International Film Festival in 1991, the first time a Mexican film had been screened at the festival in ten years.

But despite the plaudits and awards, the domestic distribution of Mexican films remains vulnerable. Domestic films are commonly pushed aside by the US-owned distribution companies in favour of Hollywood blockbusters; but there is a move by local

Tiempo de Morir.

producers to launch into distribution as well. Francisco Vargas's 2006 *El Violín*, a low-budget black-and-white feature about military repression of the 1970s peasant revolts in Mexico and its social implications to this day, struggled to find a distributor, despite being screened to wide acclaim at Cannes. Finally picked up by Canana, the production company of Mexican actors Gael García Bernal and Diego Luna and producer Pablo Cruz, *El Violín* went on to become a surprise box-office hit.

The Mexican film industry is currently the second largest in Latin America after Brazil, producing films that are presented and nominated in festivals worldwide. Since González Iñárritu's 2000 cinematic bombshell, *Amores Perros*, Mexican film has been generating world-wide interest; and thanks in part to the efforts of the Instituto Mexicano de Cinematografía, IMCINE (Mexican Film Institute), it has continued to flourish at a national level, with various festivals taking place around the country throughout the year, most notably the FICCO (*see p159*), Ambulante, Guadalajara and Morelia festivals.

Cinemas

Mexico City has an abundance of cinemas in which, as in most cities, the multiplex is king. These venues tend to show mainstream Hollywood blockbusters and high-profile European films. For arthouse cinema, smaller films and classics, both Mexican and foreign, your best bet is to check out the programmes at the few low-key, minor cinemas that are dotted around the city.

Information & tickets

Foreign films are released here almost immediately following their release in the USA or Europe, and are usually shown in their original language with Spanish-only subtitles, an exception to the rule being films for children. Most cinemas offer a weekly programme that changes on Thursdays. You can get complete cinema listings in *Primera Fila*, the Friday entertainment supplement of the Spanish-language daily newspaper *Reforma*. There are also listings in the English-language daily *The News* and in *Tiempo Libre*, the weekly social, cultural and entertainment listings magazine for Mexico City. You can also go to cinema websites to find out film information and showing times as well as to book tickets.

Ticket prices are not fixed by the name or type of the cinema but rather vary according to the location of the venue, irrespective of whether

Chinatown's **Palacio Chino**. *See p176.*

it is a multiplex or an independent. Tickets throughout the city cost between MX$30 and $50, with prices going up as you near the centre or stray into trendier, upscale *colonias*. Most cinemas have a two-for-one deal or a reduction on Wednesdays. In major cinemas, the first screenings start between 10.30am and 11am and the last ones are around 9pm, with a later 10pm show on Thursdays, Fridays and Saturdays. Smaller cinemas start their programmes in the early afternoon, at around 2pm.

Major cinemas

Cinemark Pedregal 70

Avenida San Jerónimo 263, Tizapán San Ángel (5550 3210/www.cinemark.com.mx). Metro Copilco L3 or Metrobus C.U. **Tickets** MX$52; MX$47 reductions; MX$32 Wed. **No credit cards**.
This US multiplex shows the latest Hollywood productions and a small selection of mainstream Mexican film. A good spot for a movie if you're in the south of the city visiting Coyoácan or San Ángel.

Cinemex Antara

Plaza Antara Polanco, Ejército Nacional 843-8, Granada (5280 2029/5280 2008/www.cinemex.com). Metro Polanco L7. **Tickets** MX$50; MX$45 reductions; MX$35 Wed; MX$100 Platino room. **No credit cards**. **Map** p262 A3.

In the high-end Antara shopping mall and entertainment centre, this Cinemex offers, in addition to its regular screens, an exclusive 'Platino' screening room, where you can recline in a lounge chair and enjoy waiter service throughout the movie.

Cinemex Casa de Arte
Plaza Masaryk, Anatole France 120, Polanco (5280 9156/www.cinemex.com). Metro Polanco L7. **Tickets** MX$50; MX$45 reductions; MX$35 Wed. **No credit cards. Map** p262 B4.
As its name suggests, this Cinemex screens Mexican and international arthouse films.

Cinemex Plaza Insurgentes
San Luis Potosí 214, Roma (5264 7079/ www.cinemex.com). Metro Insurgentes L1/ Metrobus Sonora. **Tickets** MX$50; MX$45 reductions; MX$30 Wed. **No credit cards. Map** p264 G8.
In a small shopping mall close to Avenida Insurgentes that includes a Sanborns and a Sears, this Cinemex is easily accessible from most areas, and just a five-minute walk from Condesa's Parque México and its restaurants and bars.

Cinemex Palacio Chino
Iturbide 21, Centro (5512 0348/www.cinemex.com). Metro Juárez L3. **Tickets** MX$46; MX$40 reductions; MX$30 Wed. **No credit cards. Map** p266 J4.
This 11-screen Cinemex owes its name to its pagoda-style building and the neighbourhood in which it is situated – Mexico City's minuscule Chinatown. One of the cheapest cinemas in the city, it's not in the safest of areas, so try not to go there alone, and watch your belongings. *Photo p175.*

Cinemex Polanco
Pabellón Polanco shopping mall, Avenida Ejército Nacional 980, Chapultepec Morales (5395 9045/ www.cinemex.com). Metro Polanco L7. **Tickets** MX$50; MX$45 reductions; MX$35 Wed. **No credit cards.**
In Polanco, the tree-lined retail heart of Mexico City, this cinema makes the perfect stopgap between an afternoon's shopping and dinner in one of the area's profusion of fine restaurants.

Cinemex Real
Avenida Colón 17, Centro (5512 7718/www. cinemex.com). Metro Hidalgo L2, L3. **Tickets** MX$46; MX$40 reductions; MX$30 Wed. **No credit cards. Map** p266 K4.
Opened in late 2001, the Real was the first multiplex to be built in the historic centre of Mexico City. Built to blend in with the surrounding architecture, it faces the Alameda park at the opposite end from the Palacio de Bellas Artes.

Cinemex WTC
World Trade Center, Montesito 38, Nápoles (9000 3388/www.cinemex.com). Metrobús Poliforum. **Tickets** MX$50; MX$45 reductions; MX$30 Wed. **No credit cards.**

A key building in terms of modern Mexican architecture, the World Trade Centre houses a mall, an exhibition area, restaurants and the 14-screen Cinemex in addition to its business space. Its central location, between Insurgentes and Circuito Interior and at an easy distance from Polanco, Condesa, Roma and the Centro, makes it a favourite with moviegoers. The downside is that it's nearly always crowded, and not as clean as other Cinemexes with a similar volume of visitors.

Cinepolis Diana
Reforma 423, Cuauhtémoc (5511 3236/www. cinepolis.com.mx). Metro Sevilla. **Tickets** MX$48; MX$40 reductions; MX$27 Wed. **Credit** AmEx, MC, V. **Map** p264 F6.
Located next to the fountain and statue of Diana the Huntress (*Diana Cazadora*), one of the main monuments along Avenida Paseo de la Reforma, this cinema always has a good selection of recent international and general releases, and also hosts the annual Tour de Cine Francés and the Festival de Cine Franco-Mexicano.

Other venues

Cineteca Nacional
Avenida México-Coyoacán 389, Xoco (4155 1200 /www.cinetecanacional.net). Metro Coyoacán L3. **Tickets** MX$40; MX$25 reductions; MX$25 Tue, Wed. **No credit cards. Map** p259 F1.
The Cineteca Nacional, opened in 1974, is also the National Film Archive, with library and research facilities open to the public. It has eight modern screening rooms, each showing a different film every day including an extensive selection of new releases as well as older Mexican and foreign films. It offers two-for-one tickets for specific films – see the website for details, as the films change frequently – and regularly presents film cycles.

Lumiere Reforma
Río Guadalquivir 104, Cuauhtémoc (5514 0000/ www.cinemaslumiere.com). Metro Insurgentes L1. **Tickets** MX$42 Fri-Sun; MX$40 Mon, Tue, Thur; MX$23 Weds; MX$30 reductions. **Credit** MC, V. **Map** p264 G5.
The Lumiere screens blockbusters as well as foreign and arthouse films. Near the Angel of Independence statue by the Zona Rosa, this is a good cinema to pick for a sightseeing/movie-night-out combo.

Papalote Museo del Niño
Avenida Constituyentes 268, Daniel Garza (5237 1773/www.papalote.org.mx). Metro Constituyentes L7. **Map** p262 B8.
In the Bosque de Chapultepec, this interactive children's museum has two 3D Imax screens showing the latest G-rated animations and documentaries – most definitely a worthwhile stop for those with kids. Admission to the Imax is $65 for under-12s and $75 for others, or you can get combo deals covering various parts of the museum.

Mexico City in the movies

Here are a few things you probably won't see during your time in Mexico City: an organised dog fight, a contract killing, a bad case of gangrene and – crossing our fingers – a multiple traffic pile-up. But in the movies, anything can happen; and in Alejandro González Iñarritu's brilliant debut feature, **Amores Perros** (2000), all of the above takes place in the course of the film's intricate, gritty trajectory. It depicts an almost unflaggingly dysfunctional city – a systematically nasty society, punctuated by random acts of even greater nastiness.

Is it the whole story? Of course not. Iñarritu is a stylist, not a sociologist, and **Amores Perros** is no more a complete portrait of Mexico City than **Annie Hall** is of New York. To build up a more complete, complex picture of DF – or at least, a broader sense of the way it is perceived by writers and filmmakers – you need to see as many DF films as possible. Here are some contemporary suggestions.

Amar te Duele (Love Hurts, 2002)
This love story is set amid the shopping malls of upscale Santa Fe. Upper class racism, in which dark skin is often equated to poverty, is portrayed as being second nature to many of the characters, with their disdain for those worse off than them exemplified when the protagonist's younger sister writes off her sibling's love interest, gesturing to their (darker-skinned) driver and saying, in English: 'I mean look, he could be this guy's brother'.

Man on Fire (2004)
This critically acclaimed Denzel Washington film depicts a Mexico City in which the rich, white elite live in fortress-like homes, terrified of being kidnapped. A series of recent real life, high-profile kidnappings has given the lie to the line that this is merely a Hollywoodian riff on the problem. In the film, burnt-out CIA operative John Creasy takes on what seems like a cushy job: protecting the child of a Mexican businessman. When the kid gets 'napped, Creasy sets out to get even with the perps in a film that develops from pure action thriller into a surprisingly clinical dissection of DF's dark heart.

**Nadie te Oye:
Perfume de Violetas** (2000)
A bleak look at the lot of the lower classes and specifically that of women in DF, Perfume de Violetas tells the story of 15-year-old Yessica, subjected to the taunts of her stepbrother and expected to iron his shirts when she gets home from school. Meanwhile, he is busy renting her out to a workmate in order to buy himself a pair of trainers. The adults are too busy worrying about appearances or scraping together enough pesos to pay the rent to find out what lies beneath the surface of this troubled girl.

Temporado de Patos
(Duck Season, 2004)
This no-budget gem follows two teenage boys as they while away a Sunday afternoon with their parents away. A power failure prevents them from playing videogames, but triggers more interesting interactions. Vividly set in the Tlatelolco apartment complexes, which went from deluxe to ghetto after the 1985 earthquake, the film is full of street scenes that will be achingly familiar to anyone who's ever spent time in the city — vochos (taxis) crossing low-hanging overpasses; the pizza delivery guy on his junky scooter. A raw, witty, cliché-free slice of modern Mexicana.

Y Tu Mamá También (2001)
From the opening sequence of two handsome young chilangos ejaculating into a family swimming pool to the shocking ending, this is a rites-of-passage flick with a difference. The aforementioned teens take lessons in life and love from Ana, an older woman, in this candid, hilarious and ultimately heartbreaking road movie. The film is, amongst other things, an unsparing but controlled tirade against Mexico's fractured society, and the salty, slang-filled banter of Tenoch and Julio – played by Diego Luna and Gael García Bernal respectively – couldn't be more authentic.

Galleries

Welcome to the modern art capital of Latin America.

If you thought Mexican art was all Diego Rivera and Frida Kahlo, think again. True, the epic murals and tortured canvasses of the iconic couple are imperishable landmarks in the country's cultural history; but with a thriving art scene to rival that of Kahlo and Rivera's 1930s heyday, Mexico City is busy cementing its status as the contemporary art capital of Latin America. New exhibition spaces have sprung up in colonial-era mansions and cavernous warehouses showing fresh and often daringly experimental work, while more established galleries continue to shift pieces by the big names of Latin American modernism, as well as the international superstars of contemporary art.

In the last decade, art production in Mexico City has noticeably picked up the pace, with young artists and new collectors invigorating an already lively scene and showing abroad to some acclaim. Local galleries such as **Enrique Guerrero**, **OMR** and **Kurimanzutto** have become regulars at some of the world's most important art fairs, and each spring Mexico City's art scene – and partyscene – is invigorated by **ZONAMACO** (*see p159*), the international contemporary art fair.

While the upscale Polanco neighbourhood has many of the city's big name galleries, it can be hard to traverse on foot. Trendy Roma is easier to get around, with several galleries loctaed just a few blocks from one another. Since most galleries are a short taxi ride from the city centre, it's perfectly possible to spend an evening hopping from one opening to another, brushing elbows with artists and their patrons, sipping free tequila and taking in shows that can include everything from digital animation to kinetic sculpture.

TIPS
Although many galleries keep regular hours, it doesn't hurt to give them a call before dropping in as lunches can be at odd times. Check *Tiempo Libre* – a weekly Spanish language entertainment magazine – for information on openings. Another good resource is the website www.arte-mexico.com which, if you can look past its oddly garish design, lists decent

Rock'n'roll lite: *Untitled* (2006) by Artemio, at **Galería Enrique Guerrero**.

information (in Spanish) about upcoming exhibitions at museums and galleries. Keep an eye out for its monthly Mapa de Galerías (gallery map) which lists openings and addresses. These maps are free and can be picked up at many galleries and museums in the city.

Polanco

Alfredo Ginocchio Arte Internacional

Arquímedes 175 (5254 8813/www.ginocchiogaleria. com). Metro Polanco L7. **Open** 10am 7.30pm Mon-Fri; 10am-3pm Sat. **Map** p262 C4.

Duck down into this gallery (previously called Praxis México) just below street level to take a look at the work of contemporary artists – mostly painters – from all over the globe. Founded in 1988 by Alfredo Ginocchio, the gallery shows hyper-real canvasses by Santiago Carbonell, subdued urban landscapes by Trini, and lush paintings of waterfalls and jungles by Carlos Ríos.

Galería Enrique Guerrero

Horacio 1549 (5280 2941/5280 5183/www.galeria enriqueguerrero.com). Metro Polanco L7. **Open** 10am-3pm, 4-7pm Mon-Fri; 11am-2pm Sat.

You'll find the Enrique Guerrero gallery in an unmarked building in a residential area close to Polanco's cluster of other galleries. Although the space itself is unremarkable – just a simple white cube – it has been showing some of the hottest contemporary Mexican art since 1997. Step inside to see Artemio's cheeky video montages, Ricardo Rendón's tool-obsessed constructions, or Fernanda Brunet's massive day-glo animal paintings. The gallery also hosts shows by well-known foreigner artists such as provocative photographer Robert Mapplethorpe and abstract expressionist sculptor Louise Nevelson.

Galería López Quiroga

Aristóteles 169 (5280 1710/5280 3710/www.lopez quiroga.com). Metro Polanco L7. **Open** 10am-7pm Mon-Fri; 10am-2pm Sat. **Map** p262 B4.

One of the city's older galleries, López Quiroga has been showing work by some of Mexico and Latin America's best-known painters since 1972. Step into the gallery at any time and you're likely to see Rufino Tamayo's unmistakeable figures and fruits, or Francisco Toledo's weird configurations of skeletons and insects. Other celebrated painters on the roster include José Luis Cuevas, Manuel Felguérez and Gunther Gerszo, and there's also work by some of the great Mexican photographers (among them Manuel Álvarez Bravo, Enrique Metinides and Graciela Iturbide) who have documented the country's often harsh social conditions.

Galería Juan Martín

Dickens 33, Unit B (5280 0277). Metro Polanco L7. **Open** 10.30am-2.30pm, 4-7pm Mon-Fri; 10.30am-2.30pm Sat. **Map** p262 A5.

The best Galleries

For up and coming artists
Proyectos Monclova (*see p182*).

For international stars
Galería Hilario Galguera (*see p82*).

For longevity
Galería de Arte Mexicano (*see p180*).

For inauguration bashes
Garash Galería (*see p181*).

For large-scale installations
KBK Arte Contemporáneo (*see below*).

For modern art
Lourdes Sosa Galería (*see p180*).

Juan Martín is largely devoted to showing Mexico's most important artists of the 1960s and 1970s. Look out for group shows featuring photographers Manuel Álvarez Bravo, Lola Álvarez Bravo and Graciela Iturbide; painters Manuel Felguérez, Mario Martín del Campo, Roger Von Gunten and Irma Palacios; printmaker Francisco Toledo, and sculptors such as Alba Rojo and Sebastián.

Galería Oscar Román

Julio Verne 14 (5280 0436/www.galeriaoscarroman. com.mx). Metro Auditorio L7. **Open** 10am-3pm, 5-7pm Mon-Fri; 11am-2.30pm Sat. **Map** p262 B5.

This gallery sells a range of indigenous Mexican art, dating from the colonial era to the present, including naive abstract painting and colonial and contemporary ex-votos.

KBK Arte Contemporáneo

Privada Miguel Cervantes de Cevedra 42, Ampliación Granada (2624 1291/5203 2965/www.kbkart.com). Metro San Joaquín L7. **Open** 10.30am-7.30pm Mon-Fri; 11am-2pm Sat. **Map** p262 A3.

Housed in what used to be a chocolate factory, KBK is one of the city's premier spaces for large-scale installations, which means its wares are more geared toward big buyers like museums and foundations than smaller collectors. The enormous exhibition hall is perfect for big, sweeping pieces like Mexican artist Ale de la Puente's installation, which involved dumping half a ton of coloured confetti on the gallery floor. Colombian artist Mateo López created a shoebox as big as a room filled with the items you might find in a shoemaker's workshop – glue, scissors, coffee cup, mattress all constructed out of paper.

Myto

Temístocles 23, Unit 2 (5282 2131/5282 0980/ www.mytogallery.com). Metro Polanco L7. **Open** 9am-2.30pm, 4-7pm Mon-Fri. **Map** p262 C2.

Young contemporary Cuban artists dominate the wall space at this gallery packed with fresh ideas. Yunior Mariño distorts landscapes with his kaleidoscopic photo collages, while Ariel Orozco uses film and photography to document his encounters with the denizens of Mexico City – including one project in which he convinces different people over the course of several days to exchange clothes with him. Reverse rags-to-riches, he starts out in a designer suit and ends up dressed in tatters.

Lourdes Sosa Galería

Ibsen 33, Unit A (5280 6857/52822452/www.lourdessosagaleria.com). Metro Auditorio L7. **Open** 10am-6pm Mon-Fri. **Map** p262 A5.

As someone who has been involved in the Mexican art scene since the early 1980s, Lourdes Sosa knows her stuff, and has handled the work of artists from Diego Rivera and Rufino Tamayo to Rafael Colonel and Arnaldo Coen. While the gallery does sell work by young artists new to the scene, much of what is on display is painting rather than installation or new media, in keeping with Sosa's charming idea of her space as 'modern, but not contemporary'.

Chapultepec

Cien Metros Cúbicos

General Antonio León 70, Unit A, San Miguel Chapultepec (5276 4287/www.originalmultiple.com). Metro Juanacatlán L1. **Open** 11am-6pm Mon-Fri; 10am-1pm Sat. **Map** p262 D8.

The premises are a little off the beaten track, but this place is well worth checking out. Most of the work is by young photographers and graphic artists, and the gallery also offers arts classes and workshops.

Galería de Arte Mexicano

Gobernador Rafael Rebollar 43 (5272 5529/www.artegam.com). Metro Juanacatlán L1. **Open** 10am-7pm Mon-Fri. **Map** p262 D8.

The Galería de Arte Mexicano, or GAM, is the oldest gallery in Mexico City. Opened in 1935, it helped shift the focus of local art collectors from European art to Mexico's home-grown talent. Nowadays, contemporary sculptures adorn the atrium, and the immensely high ceilings lend a sense of grandeur to whatever art is on display. Although the gallery still deals in the works of modernists like the British-born grande dame of Mexican art, Leonora Carrington, the brothers Pedro and Rafael Colonel, José Luis Cuevas and Rufino Tamayo, there are also neon sculptures by Stefan Brüggemann and intense photographs by Graciela Iturbide.

Condesa

Kurimanzutto

Mazatlán 5, Unit T6, Condesa (5256 2408/www.kurimanzutto.com). Metro Chapultepec L1. **Open** 10am-2.30pm, 4-6pm Mon-Fri. **Map** p264 F7.

José Kuri and Mónica Manzutto opened Kurimanzutto in 1999 as an itinerant gallery, dedicated to nurturing up-and-coming Mexican artists on a shoestring budge in exhibitions that roamed from space to space. That was then. These days, it'sone of the city's leading galleries, mixing hot international names with local talent, and firmly established in a warehouse-cum-gallery that's best described as peculiar. Past exhibits include an enormous Thomas Hirschhorn installation in which the Swiss artist transformed ten clapped-out old bangers into 'race

Contemporary art bursts into life at the springtime **ZONAMACO** fair. *See p159.*

cars' using foil, duct tape and magic marker slogans. The gallery also represents art stars such as Gabriel Orozco and Miguel Calderón.

Ricardo Reyes Arte Contemporáneo

Campeche 362, No.2 (5211 8711/www.ricardo reyesarte.com). Metro Patriotismo L9 or Chapultepec L1. **Open** 11am-7pm (private viewings only; call in advance). **Map** p264 F9.

Ricardo Reyes lives and breathes art. His funky Condesa apartment doubles as a warehouse, and is crammed with hundreds of works by dozens of contemporary artists, Mexican and international. Realising that renting a space just to display work can often be more of a burden than anything else, Reyes organises exhibitions with other galleries in the city and concentrates on networking through art fairs and promoting his artists abroad. Amongst them, Vik Muniz photographs celebrities' portraits created from materials ranging from dust to chocolate syrup, Gabriel de la Mora fashions human hairs into figurative 'drawings', and Italian artist Massimo Vitali captures hordes of tourists on beaches or parks in his massive photographs.

Roma

Casa Lamm

Álvaro Obregón 99 (5511 0899/5525 0019/www. galeriacasalamm.com.mx). Metro Insurgentes L1. **Open** 9am-midnight daily. **Map** p265 I7.

The gallery part of this early-20th-century mansion is a bit hit and miss, with many of the works for sale the sort of bland, non-figurative paintings found in corporate waiting rooms. There are always a few gems, though, notably the vivid and sometimes politically charged canvases of Oaxaca artist Demián Flores.

Gaga Arte Contemporáneo

Durango 204 (5525 1435/www.houseofgaga.com). Metro Insurgentes L1. **Open** noon-6pm Tue-Sat. **Map** p264 G7.

Relatively new on the scene, this storefront space showcases newbies, wannabes and the occasional big name. The gallery represents artists such as Adriana Lara, Diego Berruecos, Claire Fontaine and Guillermo Santamarina. Expect installations, mixed media works and, on selected evenings, performance artists and weird 'happenings'.

Galería el Estudio

Álvaro Obregón 73 (5525 1339/5208 8205/www. galeriaelestudio.com). Metro Insurgentes L1. **Open** 11am-3pm, 4-6.30pm Mon-Fri. **Map** p264 H7.

Don't visit the Casa del Poeta Ramón López Velarde (*see p59*) without also checking out Galería el Estudio. Since Rita Alazraki and Eva Marcovich founded the gallery in 1995, they have made it their mission to show innovative new art in both group and individual exhibitions. They also curate works by some of Mexico's greats such as Leonora Carrington, Irma Palacios and Juan Soriano.

DF eye

Diego Rivera's illustrations and some of his murals tell you everything you need to know about Mexico City culture and political life in his period. His work may fall in and out of fashion but once seen, it never gets out of your brain.

Daniel Hernández, Intersections blog.

Galería OMR

Plaza Río de Janeiro 54 (5511 1179/5207 1080/ www.galeriaomr.com). Metro Insurgentes L1. **Open** 10am-3pm; 4-7pm Mon-Fri; 10am-3pm Sat. **Map** p264 H6.

You might find your steps beginning to turn to a stagger as you survey the artwork in this gallery, but never fear: it's only the heavily inclined floors in the handsome art deco building that are playing tricks on you. Founded in 1983, Galería OMR is best known for showing Thomas Glassford's works in neon, Gabriel Acevedo Velarde's hand-drawn animation, and Daniel Lezama's massive allegorical oil paintings.

Garash Galería

Álvaro Obregón 49 (5207 9838/www.garash galeria.com). Metro Insurgentes L1. **Open** 10am-7pm Mon-Fri. **Map** p264 H7.

What started out as gallery director Rodrigo Espinoza's university thesis project in 2002 has blossomed into a hub for art exhibitions and cultural events for Mexico City's young artists and trendsetters. Parties with experimental music sometimes rage on into the night on the upstairs patio, so if the idea of artscene schmoozing appeals, here's a good place to try it. You might catch a performance artist in the act or even a fashion show, while sipping some fine mescal. *Photo p182.*

Galería Pecanins

Durango 186 (5514 0621/5207 5661). Metro Insurgentes L1 or Sevilla L1. **Open** 11am-2.30pm, 4pm-7pm Mon-Fri. **Map** p264 H7.

The three Pecanins sisters, famous art scenesters in the 1960s who hobnobbed with the likes of Spanish filmmaker Luis Buñuel, launched their gallery in 1964 to exhibit works by artists such as José Luis Cuevas, Brian Nissan, Sebastián, Chucho Reyes and Vlady. Their work went beyond Mexico, with a branch of Galería Pecanins in their native Barcelona in the 1970s.

Nina Menocal

Zacatecas 93 (5564 7209/5564 7443/www. ninamenocal.com). Metro Insurgentes. **Open** 10am-6pm Mon-Fri; 10am-3pm Sat. **Map** p265 I7.

Since 1990, Nina Menocal has staked out a reputation for promoting the cream of the crop in Mexican

Garash Galería. *See p181.*

contemporary art, with strong showings by artists from Cuba and other parts of Latin America as well. You'll find the likes of Carlos Aguirre, Miguel Ventura and Oscar Cueto among the artists represented here.

Terreno Baldío Arte

Orizaba 87 (2454 4013/2454 4014/www.terreno baldioarte.com). Metro Insurgentes L1. **Open** 10am-6pm Mon-Fri (by appointment only; call ahead). **Map** p264 H7.

Only two shows are held here each year, though they often last several months. The gallery's small group of artists includes Javier Marín, who creates sculptures and bas-relief panels of contorted bodies in clay, bronze and resin. Fellow sculptor Héctor Velázquez bases his cast body parts wrapped in coloured thread on an ancient Aztec ritual of human sacrifice, in which priests would wear a garment made of human skin until it eventually disintegrated. Other artists on the roster include Eva Gerd, Annette Kuhn and Luis Ruiz.

Other areas

Galería Hilario Galguera

Francisco Pimentel 3, San Rafael (5546 6703/ www.galeriahilariogalguera.com). Metro Revolución L2. **Open** 10am-6pm Mon-Fri; on weekends by appointment. **Map** p263 H3.

In 2006, owner Hilario Galguera opened up this space with a flourish – with a show of new work British superstar artist Damian Hirst. The exhibition featured Hirst's iconic animals in formaldehyde, paintings of cows' heads, and collages made from butterflies. A second show nearly a year later featured Demián Flores' paintings, some commenting

on a 2006 teachers' strike in Oaxaca in which several people were killed. Since then, the body count has mounted by way of English photographer David Bailey's photos of skulls perforated by gunshot wounds, and Omar Rodríguez Graham's broad-stroked oil paintings of cadavers.

Proyectos Monclova

Goya 6, Mixcoac (5514 2624/5563 7156/ www.proyectosmonclova.com). Metro Mixcoac L7. **Open** 11am-6pm Tue-Sat.

Call before you set out for this edgy gallery showcasing works by young artists, as opening hours can be as creative as the works on display. Marcos Castro inks surreal tableaux of animals and accidents. Former graffiti artist Marco Rountree Cruz now works with just about any media he can get his hands on to create odd installations; while Napoleon Habeica's photos of scantily clad girls will leave you thinking, 'Is this fashion, porn or art?'

La Refaccionaria Galería

Bucareli 128, Unit E40, Juárez. Metro Juárez L3 (5512 0012/5512 5080/www.galerialarefaccionaria. com). **Open** 10am-3pm, 4-6pm Mon-Fri; 10am-2pm Sat. **Map** p266 J5.

Tucked back from the street in a belle époque-style townhouse, La Refaccionaria is a short walk from downtown and displays funky work by more than a dozen contemporary artists. Fabián Ugalde uses liquid vinyl on plastic to create cartoon-like paintings of fantastic machines, and Betsabeé Romero carves Aztec-inspired designs into all kinds of materials, including car tires. Canadian Richard Moszka's light boxes showing photos of colourful moulds growing on tortillas as they decompose are not recommended for the pre-lunch crowd.

Painted prayers

One day I was walking along the Alameda when I saw a dark young man sitting on a bench eating a pineapple. I sat down beside him and he offered me a bite of his tasty pineapple. Then I invited him back to my apartment for a drink and now he is my boyfriend. And this is why I would like to give thanks.

This text, accompanied by a clumsy painting of two men enjoying a glass of wine together, is one example of a popular Mexican religious art form know as the *ex-voto*. Essentially thank-you letters to God or a variety of saints, official and otherwise, *ex-votos* date back 500 years and are accounts painted on metal and tin sheets with an accompanying picture illustrating the disaster averted, the illness cured, the lost child recovered, and so on.

The paintings are crude and colourful, often featuring angels, devils, bloody scenes or sexual mishaps. Stories range from the touching – thanks for how I met my husband – to the near tragic – thanks for not letting my child drown when he fell in the river – to the comical – thanks for not letting my brother discover me when I was in bed with his wife.

Although the paintings were initially a private gesture, often offered by people on the fringes of society, they later started to draw recognition as a popular art form. Mexican artists Frida Kahlo and Diego Rivera were famously prolific collectors of *ex-votos*, and in Frida's childhood home, the **Casa Azul**, which is now a museum (*see p70*), their original collection is on display.

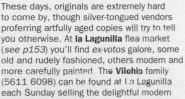

These days, originals are extremely hard to come by, though silver-tongued vendors proferring artfully aged copies will try to tell you otherwise. At **la Lagunilla** flea market (*see p153*) you'll find *ex-votos* galore, some old and rudely fashioned, others modern and more carefully painted. The **Vilchis** family (5611 6098) can be found at La Lagunilla each Sunday selling the delightful modern *ex-votos* in which they specialise – these days they often pick stories out of newspapers and magazines to use in their pieces. Examples of their work can be seen in the book *Infinitas Gracias: Contemporary Mexican Votive Painting*.

At kitsch haven **El Milagrito** (Mazatlan 152A, Condesa, 5553 5334), you can buy well-crafted and pricier *ex-votos* (pictured). You can also design and commission your own themes – what more original gift could there be than a personalised, hand-painted prayer on tin? Sex, and in the comparatively more open climate of modern-day Mexico, homosexuality are prevalent themes in these 21st century *ex-votos*. One depicts a man on the beach and another man swimming; the author gives thanks that when he and his boyfriend went on holiday to the coast, nobody stared or made a big deal about them being a gay couple.

So if your partner didn't find you in bed with that hot holiday fling, then perhaps it's time to commission – or paint – a little *ex-voto* of your own. If they did, it's going to take a little more than a painting to fix.

Gay & Lesbian

Dynamic, eclectic and a bit different: DF's gay scene is jumping.

Buenos Aires, Rio and even Puerto Vallarta have bigger reputations as gay destinations in Latin America, but the Mexico City scene is as varied and ebullient as the city itself, and is without question the most dynamic in the country. This metropolis of palaces and hovels has a similarly eclectic gay scene covering everything from posh – and costly – clubs and hotels; disco infernos and rotating dance parties that don't let up till dawn; all the way through to flirty, friendly dive cantinas for twinks, bears, grrrlz and everyone in between. And for those who like it *picante*, there are even wilder watering holes and trysting spots, with strippers, fantastic drag and all manner of immodesty, on and off stage. You could spend weeks exploring all the different scenes. And no, you won't get bored.

Outside the 'official' gay ghetto, the **Zona Rosa**, you won't see too many places that explicitly promote themselves as gay-friendly. On one level, DF is one of the most gay-friendly places in the world. Same-sex civil unions were legalised in 2007, as were conjugal visits for gay prisoners, all amid a notable lack of controversy. However, couples from the US or Europe should not be lulled into assuming

too much licence from this. For instance, hand-holding and public displays of affection among gay couples are not accepted in most areas of Mexico City, outside certain areas (principally the Zona Rosa and Centro Historico). There is a huge amount of gay activity here, but much – if not most – of it falls somewhere between 'discreet' and closeted.

On the other hand, even if Mexicans had an interest in judging the way you live, most would probably be far too courteous to say so. Overwhelmingly, hoteliers, restaurant employees, bartenders, shopkeepers and the people you meet throughout the city are happy to welcome a visitor or customer, and to treat them with charm, kindness and respect. If you demonstrate similar live-and-let-live attitudes, the chances are you'll have no problems anywhere. So don't be afraid to explore the city's off-gaydar delights – and talk to the locals . The Mexicans you meet may be shy at first, but usually a simple greeting (even just a smile) is all it takes to strike up a conversation, or to start flirting.

As in the gay world almost everywhere, venues open and close with head-spinning alacrity, and there's more to see and do here than would be possible in one trip. Finding a like-minded local guide to help you pick and choose is one of the best ways to get exactly what you want from gay DF.

THE LESBIAN SCENE

Lesbian life in Mexico City is still notably low-key, with nightlife organised informally and often via word of mouth. Thursday nights in the Zona Rosa are reckoned to be *para las chavas* (for the girls), with ground zero being **Lipstick** which attracts well-heeled groups of sapphic sisters. There's considerable spillover to **Blackout** on Thursday nights too. Many of the larger gay discos such as Spartacu's and Buttergold get plenty of girls, especially at weekends, and lately **Marrakech** and **El Oasis** in the Centro are attracting their share too.

MEDIA AND PUBLICATIONS

Gay and lesbian publications and websites seem to exist more in theory than in practice here – they can be hard to find, incomplete and frustratingly devoid of descriptive information. Those you do get your hands on, however, will

Gay Pride Mexico. See p161.

In the pink: Mexico City's **Zona Rosa** neighbourhood.

help you find your way around the city and keep tabs on the ever-changing party scene, though some grasp of Spanish will help. Look out for **Homópolis** magazine (www.homopolis.com.mx) – ostensibly available in bars and cafés though often frustratingly elusive, it's the most complete of all the mags, with fairly exhaustive listings but almost zero description of what you'll find in a venue once you get there. Other publications include **ZG: Zona Gay la Guía** (www.zona gayonline.com.mx), which is very similar to *Homópolis*, and **SerGay**, a pulpy, second-tier rag available at most of the establishments advertised inside it. Currently no gay/lesbian website covers the entire city. If you stumble across a guide, great; if not, save yourself the hassle and get your information from a friendly local or bar employee.

ACCOMMODATION
As noted above, Mexico City's gay/lesbian scene is more live-and-let-live than rainbow-flag waving, so it doesn't boast the gay guesthouse scene of other cities its size. The good news is that negative attitudes toward gay and lesbian travellers in the city's hotels are virtually unheard of, as long as guests are reasonably orderly and respectful of others' privacy.

The Red Tree House (*see p49*) and Condesa Haus (*see p49*), while not exclusively gay-oriented, have a loyal gay following. Both are located in beautiful townhouses with tasteful

appointments and friendly, informal service. Additionally, traditional hotels like the Marco Polo (*see p43*) and the Calinda Geneve (*see p43*), both in the Zona Rosa, as well as Condesa DF (*see p49*) and Polanco's Habita (*see p46*), enjoy reputations as gay-friendly establishments.

6M9
Marsella 69, Zona Rosa (5208 8347/www.6m9 guesthouse.com.mx). Metro Insurgentes L1.
Rates MX$500-$950 double. **No credit cards.**
Map p264 H6.
6M9 specifically describes itself as a gay guesthouse (for men only) and is located in a charming part of the Zona Rosa just a short stroll from the area's bars and clubs. Rooms in the restored, late 19th-century townhouse are clean and modest while aspiring to a bit of style. The pool and jacuzzi scenes are popular.

Bars & clubs

Unless otherwise indicated, all the bars and clubs listed here are open to both gay men and lesbians.

El Almacén
Florencia 37, Zona Rosa (5525 3030/www.eltaller-elalmacen.com.mx). Metro Insurgentes L1. **Open** 6pm-4am daily. **Admission** free Mon-Thur; MX$50 Fri-Sun. **No credit cards. Map** p264 G6.
Upstairs from El Taller (*see p188*) and indeed, connected through the men's room, is El Almacén, a

Total drag

When asked what the hardest part of the drag life is, the 'girls' of Les Femmes – a four-shows a week troupe at **Buttergold** – keep it simple: 'It's pushing out what you don't have and pushing down what you do'. There's no complaining about a world that doesn't understand, or family member rejection. So one wonders: have the performances already begun backstage, or are 'Eros', 'Michael', 'Moss' (short for 'Mozambique') and 'Luci' just tireless troupers who do it all for the love of showbiz? Drag is heightened in Mexico City. There's an emphasis on impersonating divas and on turgid, torchy numbers, but the shows are as equally influenced by old-style Latin nightclub revues, presented on as grand a scale as budgets will allow. Feature songs are jazzed up with dancing boys, feathered and sequinned 'showgirls', props, stunts, lighting effects and impressive precision choreography – and sometimes even mariachi singers. Revues open and close with ambitious full-cast numbers, and every act demands a complete costume change.

But behind the glitter and stardust, the pay is miserable – easily blown in post-performance cocktails; 'curtain' is no earlier than 1am, including Monday morning; and there are jobs to go to just hours later, plus two long rehearsals each week and new numbers every weekend. Added to that, costumes this elaborate are hardly cheap, and the girls shoulder almost all of the expense. So is it sheer youthful exuberance that keeps them going? Not exactly: maquillage and limelight can work wonders, but backstage you discover that these girls (and the boys, too) have got some mileage on them. When you ask why they do it, the responses are pretty matter-of-fact: 'It's your trade,' says Moss, 'a way to make a living, like if you were in a union'.

Inevitably, there's more. The joy and glamour they offer the club's largely working-class public – 'and most of all, the applause' – have motivated Luci and the other girls to hold their falsies high for up to 13 years at Buttergold alone. A conventional reason, yes; but it's convincing. The girls' perfectly made-up façades crack only once. Eros admits they all have their troubles: 'With most, it's money; for others, it's men. I've seen lots of girls go down, too, because of drugs or diseases, or trouble with the cops...' There's a second's melancholy in the dressing room; and then, as the number that signals the imminent start of the show strikes up, a sudden frenzy of pad insertion, wig shaking, drink slamming – and not a little bitchiness.

As she flies out the dressing room door, stunning Michael looks back. 'But listen, *papi*: you've got to put that all behind you the second your foot hits that stage. You can't do this work with a frown on your face. The people come here to be entertained, and the show must go on.'

casual bar and lounge with a low-rent honky-tonk feel. You'll find mixed after-work groups or friends chilling on weekdays, with the El Taller crowd spilling in on weekends to revel beneath video screens featuring Madonna, Cher, Shakira and other international pop divas. Lately, a Star Wars-themed drag show has been pleasing crowds on Thursdays. Women are welcome, albeit hardly in the majority.

Blackout

Amberes 11, Zona Rosa (5511 9973/www.black-out.com.mx). Metro Insurgentes L1. **Open** 6pm-1am Wed; 6pm-3.30am Thur, Fri; 8pm-3.30am Sat. **Admission** free. **Credit** AmEx, MC, V. **Map** p264 G5.

This stylish space, painted in its eponymous colour and dominated by a dramatic 20-foot bar, sits in the middle of the Amberes Street strip, packing in a pre-disco crew of young, well-scrubbed queers and queer friendlies. There's no dance floor per se, but the DJ gives the kids what they want, so dancing ensues in every possible space. Most popular Thursdays, but still crowded at weekends. Don't forget your ID.

Bota's Bar

Niza 45, Zona Rosa (5514 4608/5649 8393/ www.botasbar.blogspot.com). Metro Insurgentes L1. **Open** 8pm-4am Wed-Sun. **Admission** MX$80 Fri Sat (includes 1 drink). **Credit** MC, V (MX$320 minimum spend Fri, Sat). **Map** p264 H5.

Get over the sports bar/airport lounge aesthetic: this is the grandmamma of all Mexico City lesbian bars, still going strong after more than 20 years under various names, and attracting 'real women' with little interest in showboating at Lipstick. Subdued and friendly during the week, at weekends the place comes alive with two dancefloors, a drag review and thongalicious showgirls (note: actual women). Music is a good mix of pop, Latin and disco, and make no mistake: though guys are admitted, this is absolutely girl country.

Buttergold

José María Izazaga 9, Centro (5761 1861). Metro Salto del Agua L1, L8. **Open** 9pm-4am Wed, Thur, Sun; 9pm-7am Sat **Admission** free Wed, Thur, Sun; MX$100 Fri; MX$120 Sat (includes 2 drinks). **Credit** MC, V. **Map** p267 L5.

A champagne club on a *cerveza* budget, this hangar-like space hosts one of the liveliest and most inclusive DF scenes around, packed with men and women, old, young, straight, gay, whatever. Arrive at around 11pm and snag a table, then watch as the pageant unfolds: electronica, salsa, cumbia and *norteña* music, dance contests, pop-idol imitators… Starting at 1am on Thursday to Sunday nights is a drag extravaganza whose Vegas ambitions and dedicated cast will amaze you. Tawdry tinsel will look like stardust by the time you leave – just before dawn. *See left* **Total drag.** *Photo p189.*

Hysteria

Avenida Oceania (no number) at the corner of Norte 25, Moctezuma (5785 1521/www.hysteria disco.com). Metro Ricardo Flores Magón L8. **Open** 9pm-4am Fri, Sat. **Admission** MX$50. **Credit** AmEx, MC, V.

At once fabulous, dazzling and squalid, this legendary two-level disco on a nondescript corner east of downtown is considered by many to be the wildest, most colourful party in the whole of Mexico City, the last resort of fierce and extravagant trannies as well as a haven for practically all other planetary life forms. Nightly floor shows are elaborate and varied; dancing is frenetic. Along with Spartacu's, one of the off-the-beaten-track joints well worth the trip. Don't lose your bearings in all that dry ice.

Lipstick

Amberes 1, Zona Rosa (5514 4920/www.lipstickbar. com). Metro Insurgentes L1. **Open** 10pm-5am Wed-Sat. **Admission** $70-$150. **Credit** AmEx, MC, V. **Map** p264 G5.

This is probably the most elegant dance club in the Zona Rosa, with various layers and spaces for dancing, flirting and hanging out. The creative kitsch decor adds drama to the proceedings, and attendees of both genders are overwhelmingly easy on the eyes. The dancefloor stays packed until the wee hours, with Wednesdays best for loungeish chilling, Thursdays for girls who like girls, and weekends attracting the straight and gay *jeunesse dorée* (as well as wannabes) from all over the city.

Marrakech

República de Cuba 18, Centro (04455 3901 8745 mobile). Metro Bellas Artes L2, L8. **Open** 5pm-midnight Tue, Wed; 5pm-1.30am Thur; 5pm-3am Fri, Sat. **Admission** free. **No credit cards.** **Map** p267 L3.

A newcomer to the Centro, Marrakech has a stylish, artsy vibe, with hipsters of both sexes (and all persuasions) hanging out in its campy, gaily-coloured bar. Performance artists – some decidedly more riveting than others – appear on weekends. Ordering a snack, freshly made on the premises, comes with the bonus of interaction with the comely, friendly staff.

The New Queen

Londres 182, Zona Rosa (1380 7359). Metro Sevilla L1. **Open** 8pm-3am Thurs-Sat. **Admission** free. **No credit cards.** **Map** p264 G6.

It ain't the Ritz – who wants the Ritz? – but it's a room of one's own for the elusive DF lesbian scene, with comfy banquettes, an inviting back bar and lots of tables in a warm, dare we say womb-like atmosphere. Come on weekends if you're looking for action – weekdays are decidedly *tranquilo*. Men admitted as well.

Nicho Bears and Bar

Basement, Londres 179, Zona Rosa (no phone/ www.bearmex.com). Metro Sevilla L1. **Open** 8pm-3am Thur-Sat. **Admission** free. **Credit** MC, V. **Map** p264 G6.

DF's haven for guys who like 'em manly, hirsute and otherwise ursine, Nicho seems tamer – but friendlier – than other bear watering-holes around the world. Apart from some naughty art, the place could be a neighbourhood pub. Fridays are the big night, with matchmaking games and karaoke. Bring ID since, unlike many places in Mexico City, you will be carded. A photocopy of your passport suffices. Men only.

El Oasis

República de Cuba 2G, Centro (5521 9740). Metro Bellas Artes L2, L8. **Open** 3pm-3.30am daily. **Admission** free. **Credit** MC, V. **Map** p267 L3.

One of four gay joints along the gritty but fun República de Cuba strip, El Oasis is the largest and perhaps liveliest of them all, with table service and

Arts & Entertainment

an ample dance floor that attracts working-class *chulos* (cuties), slummers of both genders and a fair number of Daddy types. Flirty but not dirty, it's a fun place to take your steady. And even if you don't know those fancy Latin dance moves, your efforts will attract favourable attention. Neighbourhood-y during the week, they come from all over the city on weekends. Women welcome.

Papi FunBar

Amberes 18, Zona Rosa (5208 3755/www.papifun bar.com). Metro Insurgentes L1. **Open** 1pm-1am Mon-Wed; 1pm-2am Thur; 1pm-3.30am Fri, Sat; 4pm-2am Sun. **Admission** free. **Credit** AmEx, MC, V. **Map** p264 G5.

This compact cocktail bar fills up with a mixed crowd of twinks, girlfriends and admirers, starting after work and going until it's time to hit the discos after midnight. Be prepared for loud Mexican pop – and note how the kids know all they lyrics. There's lots of eye candy, and many a deal later closed at nearby dance venues is discreetly initiated here; but if you're in heavy cruise mode, this is probably

not the place. Come with your posse for pre-smut fun, and relax – the night is young. *Photo p285.*

La Perla

República de Cuba 45, Centro (1997 7695). Metro Bellas Artes L2, L8. **Open** 8pm-3.30am Fri, Sat. **Admission** $MX40 Thur; MX$120 Fri, Sat. **No credit cards. Map** p267 L3.

An extraordinary drag cabaret and dance bar frequented by the lavender crowd as well as by slummers, swingers and the just plain fun. No one knows for sure if the elegant/sleazy vintage lounge scene is original or not, but drag queens begin chewing the scenery after 11. While the door policy is not restrictive, you may have to wait for a table due to low seating capacity. Highly recommended.

Spartacu's

Cuauhtémoc 8, Maravillas, Estado de México (5763 8028/5701 0204). Take a taxi. **Open** 8pm-8am Fri, Sat. **Admission** MX$40-$80. **Credit** MC, V.

Ever wondered how the Hooters waitress uniform looks on men? Located in a rough, out-of-the-way DF neighbourhood east of the airport (we recommend you get the management to call you a taxi for your journey home), Spartacu's brings together a great mix of cuties, couples, boys and girls (including plenty of lesbians), and some of the biggest (in all senses) trannies you'll ever meet – plus the guys who love them – in a cavernous, black-lit, multi-storyed space (upper deck for adults only). Weekends feature seemingly innumerable go-go boys, drag divas and headlining strippers who leave nothing to the imagination. A walk on the wild side and a bit of a hike, but good, sleazy fun.

Switch

Niza 73, Zona Rosa (5207 1792). Metro Insurgentes L1. **Open** 9pm-4am Fri, Sat. **Admission** MX$170-$300. **No credit cards. Map** p264 H5.

At time of writing, Switch is *the* place for Mexico City's 'A-Gays'; the young(ish), buffed and expensively turned-out set. Expect the elect to remove their clingy Abercrombie & Fitch T-shirts just as soon as they can. The focus here is on the dancing, with rotating popular DJs, crème de la crème strippers, a ravey atmosphere with all the excesses that implies, and beautiful, if not especially approachable young men. Scenesters insist it's merely a flavour-of-the-month, so take advice before committing – the party may have moved on by the time you read this.

El Taller

Florencia 37, Zona Rosa (5525-3030/www.eltaller-elalmacen.com.mx). Metro Insurgentes L1. **Open** 6pm-4am Tue-Sat. **Admission** free-MX$50. **No credit cards. Map** p264 G6.

Though showing its age, this subterranean *boîte* (with small dancefloor) has been reliably cruisey for going on 30 years. Strippers, porn and a heavy-industry aesthetic to go with the name – '*taller*' means 'workshop' – are the backdrop for making friends of all ages and types here, or for dancing. Don't be surprised to discover late-night trysting in dark corners. Note:

girlfriends are welcome upstairs at El Almacén (*see p185*), but it's boys only below decks at El Taller.

Tom's Leather Bar

Insurgentes 357, Condesa (5564 0728/www.toms-mexico.com). Metro Chilpancingo L9 or Insurgentes L1/Metrobús Campeche. **Open** 9.30pm-3.30am Tue-Sun. **Admission** MX$120. **Credit** AmEx, MC, V. **Map** p264 C9.

The only leather you'll find at Tom's are shoes and unbuckled belts: it's arguably the city's most insistently libidinous scene, with blue movies, and the most immodest strippers west of Bangkok and a lively back room (mind your valuables). The decor (Prince Valiant meets Castle von Dracula) and eclectic music mix keep the proceedings from growing too heavy. The semi-steep cover means a slightly older crowd, or the young ones with cash. No women admitted.

El Viena

República de Cuba 2-A, Centro (5512 0929). Metro Bellas Artes L2, L8. **Open** 2pm-3am Mon-Fri, Sat; 2pm-5am Sun. **Admission** free. **No credit cards.**

Appealingly renovated and expanded, Viena still maintains the down-home charm that reputedly made it Almodóvar's favorite watering hole when visiting Mexico City. The new annex features loungey banquettes and lots of eye contact; the old space (originally a bare bones cantina) is for dancing and tête-a-têtes. During the week expect fluorescent lighting (you'll get used to it), career waiters and few frills. At weekends, the lights are turned down and the music turned up, drawing a younger, hipper clientele.

Saunas & bathhouses

Baños San Juan

López 120, Centro Histórico (5521 2959). Metro Salto del Agua L1, L8. **Open** 6.30am-8.30pm daily. **Admission** $70. **No credit cards.**

Though hardly elegant, Baños San Juan is inexpensive and wide open, attracting cute working-class dudes and wedding-ringless husbands, along with the requisite trolls and some hotties. Late afternoons – especially weekends – are the time to go.

Red Hot Party

Havre 68, Zona Rosa (04455 3226 1039 mobile). Metro Insurgentes L1. **Open** 7pm-midnight Tue; 7pm-midnight Thur; 10pm-6am Sat; 7pm-midnight Sun. **Admission** MX$100-$120. **No credit cards.**

Look for the candle burning on the porch of this early 20th-century townhouse, indicating that its popular underwear party is on. You can have a drink, chill out or put on a public performance upstairs, and below stairs it's no holds barred with this young, uninhibited crowd.

Sodomé

Mariano Escobedo 716, Polanco (5250 6653/www.sodome.com mx). Metro Chapultepec L1. **Open** 4pm-midnight Tue, Wed; 4pm-4am Thur; 4pm Fri-midnight Sun. **Admission** MX$200. **Credit** MC, V.

This classy joint provides clients with clean towels, a sarong and flip-flops, plus a full bar and lounging areas, a video room, sauna, steamroom, twin hot tubs and a maze.

At **Buttergold**, the show's not over till the drag lady sings. *See p187.*

Arts & Entertainment

Music

Much more than mariachis.

Mexico City is a vibrant, noisy, sometimes cacophonous place, but it moves to the sound of music, day and night. From the sing-song cry of a street vendor to the amp-busting power chords of a rock band grinding out Led Zeppelin covers in a local bar, more often than not there'll be something to stimulate your ears, no matter what your tastes.

As the nation's cultural capital, Mexico City pulls in artists from all over the country, with a constant rotation of big acts with established fan bases mixed up with new kids trying to make names for themselves. And as the largest city in Latin America, DF is a key stop on the tour schedules of many international acts, as well as being home to some of the continent's best classical ensembles. Naturally, it has a wide array of excellent concert spaces. In addition to the venues listed below, several clubs host live music, among them the fabulous **Pasaje América** (*see p171*), whose DJ nights are interspersed with live sets by the likes of MIA and hip local electronica outfits, and **Pata Negra** (*see p169*) which hosts jazz nights in its original downstairs space on Mondays and a mix of live acts and DJs the rest of the week.

FESTIVALS

There are a number of venues around the city that regularly host outdoor concerts and festivals. In the Centro, the Zócalo main square is often the setting for A-list rock en español bands performing as part of festivals and events put on by the city government (check www.cultura.df.gob.mx for listings). Big arena rock acts, Latino and gringo, also play at sports venues around the city including at its three football stadiums: the 120,000-plus capacity Estadio Azteca, the Diego Rivera-decorated Estadio Olimpico, and the Estadio Azul (*see p198*). Other venues include the Palacio de los Deportes, the Autódromo Hermanos Rodríguez and Foro Sol (*see p197*) – all part of the Ciudad Deportivo (sports city) complex near the airport.

Big music festivals are also frequently held in towns outside the city such as Toluca in Estado de México and Tepoztlán in Morelos. Festival organisers sometimes arrange transport from locations in Mexico City, but cheap bus rides are also usually available. To check who's coming to town and when, and to purchase tickets online, go to www.ticketmaster.com.mx.

Jazz it up at **Zinco Jazz Club**. *See p195*.

Major venues

Along with the **Auditorio Nacional** (*see below*), these are the most important music venues in the city.

The **Teatro de la Ciudad** (*see p205*), built in 1918 and recently renovated, has capacity for 1,300 spectators. It's one of the architectural gems of the historic downtown, with a glorious history that includes performances by the likes of Enrico Caruso. Also located in the city centre is the **Teatro Metropólitan** (*see p206*). This venue (capacity 3,700) puts on a mix of musicals, children's shows and concerts – everything from 'Lazy Town' to 'Laser Floyd'. The **Centro de Convenciones Tlatelolco** (Manuel González 75, Guerrero, 5782 3761, www.convencionestlatelolco.com) primarily plays host to *norteña* acts (country music from the north of Mexico). Its website doesn't do a particularly good job of keeping listings up to date, so call ahead, or better yet keep an eye out for posters advertising performances.

Auditorio Nacional

Paseo de la Reforma 50, Chapultepec (9138 1350/ www.auditorio.com.mx). Metro Auditorio L7. **Box office** 10am-7pm Mon-Sat; 11am-6pm Sun. **Tickets** varies. **Credit** AmEx, MC, V. **Map** p262 B6.

Built in 1952 and redesigned in 1990, this modern structure is Mexico City's flagship music venue. It has a capacity of close to 20,000 and has played host to the biggest national and international acts and events. Within the same complex is the Lunario (www.lunario.com.mx), an intimate 500-seat venue that typically features the likes of singer-songwriters and jazz artists.

Traditional cantinas & bars

Mexico is perhaps most famous for mariachi – the word can refer either to the kind of music or to the musicians who play it – which originated in Jalisco state in the 19th century. In Mexico City, the best place to go to hear mariachi bands playing and singing their hearts out is Plaza Garibaldi in all its seedy, chaotic glory (*see p192* **Cry me a río**). They can also be found performing at private parties, in the city's traditional cantinas and at the more touristy restaurants, often in the form of trios – three-part vocal and guitar bands – which are more manageable size-wise than a full ten-piece mariachi band.

Norteña music, heavily influenced by the polka brought over by late 19th- and early 20th-century immigrants from central Europe, remains a popular dance genre and has many adherents in the capital – as well as a wildly

popular alter ego in the form of *narcocorridos*. In what might best be described as gangsta polka, these ballads celebrate the derring do exploits of drug traffickers to an oompah beat. Originating in the cartel heartland of Mexico's northern states, it's one of the most popular musical forms in the country, rivalling salsa and other Latin music sales in the USA, and it can be heard pounding out of open-windowed pickups along dusty streets all over Mexico. Like all the best popular music genres, it comes with its own look – snakeskin boots and tight pants with shiny belt buckles – a typical *norteña* style that's sported as far south as the streets of Mexico City.

Las Bohemias

Londres 142, Zona Rosa (5514 0790/5207 4384). Metro Insurgentes L1/Metrobus Insurgentes. **Open** 1.30pm-midnight Mon-Sat. **Admission** free. **Credit** AmEx, MC, V. **Map** p264 G6.

This cantina-style neighbourhood bar is a relaxing alternative to the Zona Rosa's nightclub scene – catch *norteña* and trio bands here at weekends.

Cantina El Centenario

Vicente Suárez 42, Condesa (no phone). Metro Chapultepec L1. **Open** 1pm-midnight daily. **Admission** free. **No credit cards.** **Map** p264 F8.

Surrounded by trendy bars and restaurants, El Centenario attracts a mix of old-timers and hipsters to its unostentatious premises. The lights are bright, the beer is cheap and everyone seems to know the words to all the songs.

El Lugar del Mariachi

Hamburgo 86, Zona Rosa (5207 4841/5207 4864/ www.ellugardelmariachi.com). Metro Insurgentes L1/Metrobús Hamburgo. **Open** noon-3am daily. **Admission** free. **Credit** MC, V. **Map** p264 H5.

This large restaurant and bar hosts full mariachi bands and folk dancers, with shows twice nightly from Tuesday to Saturday. Conveniently located in the Reforma–Zona Rosa hotel district, it's a good choice for those without the time or the inclination to make the pilgrimage to Plaza Garibaldi.

Cry me a río

On a typical evening at Plaza Garibaldi, just north of the Centro Histórico, mariachi musicians strut like peacocks in their finery among stray dogs, homeless men high on tequila, electric shock vendors, groups of merry friends out to purchase a song or two, and bewildered tourists. If that sounds like a fair description of the last place on earth you'd like to spend an evening, then so be it. But if your interest is piqued and you're a little curious, then don't miss one of Mexico City's all-time classic nights out.

For best results, start the evening at a Centro cantina for a spot of dinner and a drink or two, then head to the Plaza in the company of friends, be they old-time buddies or the brand-new, instant best friends you picked up at the cantina. You'll be needing them later for embracing to the *ranchera* tunes as you weep along to the music, or to cheer you on as you take on the challenge of the electric shock machine.

Famous the world over, not least as a result of the success of the 1993 Robert Rodríguez film *El Mariachi*, the iconic musicians are hired by Mexicans for weddings, parties and serenades.

For around MX$50, the musicians, kitted out in *charro* suits with skin-tight trousers and waist-level jackets dotted with gold and silver studs, will gather round and serenade you with a song of your choice. If you're not familiar with their range of *sones* or *rancheras*, they'll pick one out for you.

It's not just tourists who come to the square – amorous Mexican couples can always be found here too, enjoying the melancholy, romantic music. And in much the same way as prospective clients kerb-crawl for prostitutes, cars cruise by the square looking for mariachi bands to pick up, whisking them off to entertain guests at birthday and funeral parties held in private houses.

The rich cocktail of glory and destitution on show at Plaza de Garibaldi can be a heady one for the uninitiated visitor. The square, flanked by brothels and seedy cantinas, represents both sides of the Mexico City coin – the glamour and the poverty, the joy and the suffering, the beautiful and the grotesque.

Salón Tenampa (*see p130*), on the left-hand side of the square, opened its doors in 1925 and is the perfect place to enjoy music over a meal or a drink. The walls are adorned with soft-focus paintings of old greats such as José Alfredo Jiménez, Juan Gabriel and Pedro Infante, and if you're not yet ready to buy your own song and find yourself surrounded by an eight-strong band, trumpets and all, playing for and at you, you can still enjoy watching the Mexican visitors doing it. They dance and twirl around to the *ranchera* beat, often joining in the singing themselves, while in another corner of the bar, a toothless old man fires up a Heath Robinsonesque shock machine and cranks up the voltage for a grimacing customer keen to prove his mettle. The key, with the shocker as with the Plaza itself? Hold tight and never scream.

Rodeo Santa Fe

Avenida de los Maestros 6, San Andrés Atenco, Tlanepantla (5361 6491/www.rodeosantafe.com.mx). Metro Rosario L7, then a San Pedro Bodegas Progreso-bound bus from platform D or F. **Open** 9pm-4am Thur-Sat; 4pm-3am Sun. **Admission** free-MX$250. **Credit** MC, V.

Strap on your spurs and head out to this huge *charro* (cowboy, Mexican-style) palace in the north of the city. In addition to dance exhibitions and live country music – the country's top *norteño*, *duranguense* and *banda* acts play live here – there are also rodeo demonstrations in an on-site arena. Ticket prices vary according to who's playing and on what day, so check the website in advance.

Rock, pop & reggae

In a heartening counterpunch to cultural globalisation, Mexican rock continues to reclaim space on charts once dominated by acts from the US, Spain and elsewhere in Latin America. Originating in the 1950s as artists covered and adapted hits from US radio into a genre dubbed *refritos* (refried), the musical cross-pollination cut both ways, with Richie Valens's monster hit, 'La Bamba', originating as a standard of *son jarocho* music from Veracruz state.

The Mexican rock scene suffered a setback in 1971 when images of open drug use and casual sex at a large festival were widely disseminated, fuelling a backlash that led to restrictions being placed on future events of this type. Populist governments of the period viewed rock as a foreign influence that undermined *la Mexicanidad* – Mexicanness; but the rock genie couldn't be kept in its bottle for long and as the London/New York new wave rolled into Mexico in the early 1980s, the Mexican rock renaissance began. *Nueva onda* (new wave, also known as *guacarock*) bands like Botellita de Jeréz and Maldita Vecindad fused punk, rock, and ska – and up to the present day, new influences continue to be added to the mix. Mexican bands like Molotov show the influence of socially-conscious US hardcore and hip-hop in songs that excoriate injustice on both sides of the border and generally rage against the machine.

Other groups such as Café Tacuba (named after the venerable restaurant; *see p129*) draw influences from closer to home. Often described as the U2 of Mexico, the band incorporates indigenous sounds and Latin jazz into its rock anthems. Popular legend has it that the band was catapulted to fame after bootlegged concert recordings were distributed around the Chopo Market (*see p153*) – Mexico City's ground zero for rock 'n' roll subcultures.

Black Horse

Mexicali 85, Condesa (5211 8740/www.caballonegro. com). Metro Patriotismo L9/Metrobús Campeche. **Open** 6pm-2am daily. **Admission** free. **Credit** AmEx, MC, V. **Map** p264 F9.

This venue attracts lots of expats as well as the Condesa cool crowd. On Wednesdays and Thursdays, the focus is on jazz and funk acts, with punk or indie bands taking over the joint from DJs on Saturdays.

Bulldog Café

Rubens 6, Mixcoac (5611 8818/5598 1614/www. bulldogcafe.com). Metro Mixcoac L7. **Open** 10pm-4am Fri, Sat. **Tickets** MX$350-$400 men; MX$100-$200 women. **Credit** AmEx, MC, V.

This club close to San Ángel features a very strong line-up of gigs by Mexican indie rock acts like Los Dynamite and Motel.

Centro Cultural de España

Guatemala 18, Centro (5521 1925/www.ccemx.org). Metro Zócalo L2. **Open** 10am-8pm Tue; 10am-1am Wed; 10am-2am Thur-Sat; 10am-4pm Sun. **Admission** free. **Credit** MC, V. **Map** p267 M4.

The top floor of this downtown cultural centre is a chic patio space that hosts an eclectic variety of musical acts most evenings, ranging from alternative and electronic music to jazz.

Dada X

Bolívar 31, Centro (2454 4310/www.myspace.com/ dadax). Metro Allende L2 or San Juan de Letrán L8. **Open** 9pm-3.30am Thur-Sat. **Admission** MX$40-$60. **No credit cards. Map** p267 L4.

The best Venues

For catching the next big thing
Multiforo Alicia (*see p194*), **Pasagüero** (*see p194*).

For grooving with other gringos
Black Horse (*see right*); **Irish Winds Pub** (*see p194*).

For cheesy tunes
Don Quintin (*see p194*); **St Elmo's Bar** (*see p194*).

For crying into your tequila
Cantina El Centenario (*see p191*); **El Lugar del Mariachi** (*see p191*).

For impressing a date
Zinco Jazz Club (*see p195*).

For pretending you're in Cuba
Rincón Cubano (*see p196*); **Salón Los Ángeles** (*see p196*).

For pretending you're in Jamaica
Kaya (*see p194*).

This temple to electronic and goth music features regular live performances by local and national artists. The regulars here tend to rock an iconoclastic, nonconformist look, so it's best to save your polo-shirt and loafers for another night and another place.

Don Quintin
2nd floor, Avenida Presidente Masaryk 407, Polanco (5280 6986/5280 6797). Metro Polanco L7. **Open** 9pm-4.30am Thur-Sat. **Admission** MX$200 men (free Thur before 11pm). **Credit** AmEx, MC, V. **Map** p262 A4.
Come to hear the latest *pop en español* hits without waiting (and shelling out) for huge concerts in the Auditorio Nacional. Pitch-perfect cover bands get the stylish Polanco crowd dancing.

Hard Rock Live
Campos Elíseos 290, Polanco (5327 7101/www. hardrock.com/live2/mexicocity.asp). Metro Auditorio L7. **Open** 1pm-2am daily. **Admission** MX$150-350. **Credit** AmEx, MC, V. **Map** p262 B5.
The Mexico City branch of this global institution has a 1000-person auditorium in which you can catch a mix of established and new Mexican rockers and international bands.

Irish Winds Pub
Río Tiber 71, Cuauhtémoc Cuauhtémoc (5208 0929, 5208 0513). Metro Insurgentes L1/Metrobus Insurgentes. **Open** 2-10pm Mon-Wed; 1pm-1am Thur; 2pm-3am Fri; 5pm-3am Sat. **Admission** free. **Credit** AmEx, MC, V. **Map** p264 G5.

The best Music

Café Tacuba
One of the country's most popular acts since its formation in 1989, CT draws on a variety of styles and influences.

Molotov
These veteran rap-rockers recently reformed after a hiatus and have returned with a new album full of socially conscious anthems.

Los Dynamite
Recently named by *Rolling Stone Mexico* as one of the nation's best new bands.

Chikita Violenta
This much-talked-about indie band worked with the producer of alt-rock icons Broken Social Scene on their latest album.

Julieta Venegas
The former lead singer of political punk band ¡Tijuana No!, Venegas has branched out to become a Grammy and Latin Grammy-winning singer-songwriter.

This Irish-style pub is popular with staff from the nearby British and US embassies. On Thursdays and Fridays the small stage hosts acts singing in both English and Spanish, many of which crank out a Celtic-punk sound that fits the atmosphere.

Kaya
Tamaulipas 223, Condesa (5272 0709/www. kaya-rr.com). Metro Patriotismo L9/ Metrobús Chilpancingo. **Open** 6.30pm-2.30am Tue-Sat. **Admission** free. **Credit** MC, V. **Map** p264 E9.
A new entry on la Condesa's night-time dance card, Kaya offers live reggae acts from all over Latin America and the Caribbean – check the website for a calendar of gigs.

Multiforo Alicia
Cuauhtémoc 91, Roma (5511 2100/www.myspace. com/foroalicia). Metro Cuauhtémoc L1. **Open** from 8pm on show nights; check website for schedule. **Admission** MX$30-$100. **No credit cards.** **Map** p265 J6.
Raw and grungey, long-running Alicia – Mexico's answer to the defunct New York City legend CBGBs – is one of the few centrally located spots in which underground rock, ska, reggae, hardcore, hip-hop, death metal, punk rock, surf, garage, blues and political folk bands can express themselves. And they do. Three to five bands jam nightly, making it a bit of a bargain cover-wise.

Pasagüero
Motolinia 33, Centro (5512 6624/www.myspace. com/pasaguero). Metro Allende L2 or San Juan de Letrán L8. **Open** *Café* 2-11pm daily. *Club* 10pm-4am Thur-Sat. **Admission** MX$50-$180. **Credit** MC, V. **Map** p267 M4.
This popular downtown spot hosts hip international and local acts like Nouvelle Vague, Peaches and Monterrey's Plastilina Mosh. It's also a good (and safe) place to try *pulque*, a traditional drink made from fermented maguey cactus. *See also p171.*

St Elmo's Bar
Bosque de Ciruelos 187, Bosques (5596 4999). Metro Auditorio L7, then Bosques-bound bus. **Open** 1-8pm Mon; 1-10pm Tue, Wed; 1pm-2.30am Thur-Sat. **Admission** free. **Credit** AmEx, MC, V.
Children of the 1980s can safely break out their Vuarnet and Frankie Says Relax T-shirts here, teaming them with shoulder-padded jackets for best effect. Live bands play the decade's hits (some in Spanish) while the upscale crowd dances along with varying degrees of ironic detachment.

Vive Cuervo Salón
Lago Andromaco 17, Ampliación Granada (5255 1496, 5255 5322). Metro San Joaquín L7. **Box office** 10am-3pm, 5-7pm Mon-Fri. **Tickets** MX$200-$380. **Credit** AmEx, MC, V.
The 3,500 capacity (1,700 seated) Salón is a venue for shows by anyone from classic acts like KC and the Sunshine Band to up-to-the-minute buzz bands like Metric, the Go! Team and Klaxons.

Zydeco

Tamaulipas 30, Condesa (5553 3329/www.zydecobar.com). Metro Patriotismo L9 or Sevilla L1/Metrobús Sonora. **Open** 2pm-1.30am Mon-Sat; 3pm-1am Sun. **Admission** free. **Credit** AmEx, MC, V. **Map** p264 F8.

Promising a taste of New Orleans in Mexico, Zydeco hosts live rock and funk bands – and of course Zydeco Cajun acts – on Tuesdays and Wednesdays.

Folk & jazz clubs

One of the most important musical genres to emerge from Latin America in the latter half of the 20th century is *trova*, sometimes known as *nueva canción*. Influenced by everything from traditional folk to 1960s British-invasion rock, and freighted with politically radical messages, *trova* remains very popular in Mexico City's coffeehouses.

La Bodega

Popocatépetl 25, Condesa (5511 7390/www.labodega.com.mx). Metro Insurgentes L1/Metrobús Sonora . **Open** 1pm-1am Mon-Sat. **Admission** MX$60. **Credit** AmEx, MC, V. **Map** p264 G8.

Incorporating a restaurant, a cantina and a cabaret stage, La Bodega books an array of bands in Latin and Caribbean genres like *son*, rumba and Cuban jazz.

Grammy-award winning **Julieta Venegas**.

El Breve Espacio

Alvaro Obregón 275, Roma (5533 5197/3096 9571/www.elbreveespacio.com). Metro Sevilla L1. **Open** 8pm-1am Tue-Thur; 8pm-3am Sat, Sun. **Admission** free-MX$200. **Credit** MC, V. **Map** p264 G7.

This classic coffeehouse venue hosts some of the top *trova* and folk singers on the circuit. **Other locations** Arequipa 734, Lindavista (5781 9356).

Foro Del Tejedor

Hamburgo 126, Zona Rosa (5208 2327). Metro Insurgentes L1/Metrobús Hamburgo. **Open** perfomances at 8.30pm or 9.30pm. **Admission** MX$35-$100. **Credit** AmEx, MC. V. **Map** p264 G6.

This Zona Rosa branch of excellent bookshop cum café chain El Péndulo (*see p143*) hosts regular concerts by *nueva canción* singers.

T Gallery

Saltillo 39, Condesa (5211 1222/www.tgallery design.com). Metro Chilpancingo L9 or Patriotismo L9/Metrobús Chilpancingo. **Open** 5pm-2am Mon-Sat. **Admission** free. **Credit** AmEx. MC, V. **Map** p264 F9.

This funky space offers a great selection of teas and coffees as well as nightly live music ranging from bossanova to the blues.

Zinco Jazz Club

Motolinia 20, Centro (5512 3369/www.zincojazz.com). Metro Allende L2 or San Juan de Letrán L8. **Open** 7pm-2am Wed-Sat. **Tickets** MX$150-$300; free Wed. **Credit** AmEx, MC, V. **Map** p267 M4.

Arguably DF's best jazz venue, this converted bank vault has a sophisticated atmosphere and a superb roster of performers. The food and drinks are excellent, but they don't come cheap. *Photo p190.*

Salsa & Caribbean

Mexicans young and old love to dance, whether it's grooving to up-to-the-minute DJ tunes or tearing up the floor at hot salsa clubs – or channelling the rhythms of *danzón*, a style similar to rumba with European ballroom influences, at a traditional *salón de baile*. The popularity of this and other strains of Cuban-style music reflects the influence the island nation has had on music in Mexico for well over a century, and the cultural exchange continues today as Cuban musicians visit regularly, and frequently settle in Mexico City. The venues listed below represent some of the best places in the city to catch live bands playing Caribbean and related rhythms.

Barfly

Avenida Presidente Masaryk 393, Polanco (5282 2906/www.bar-fly.com.mx). Metro Polanco L7. **Open** 9.30pm-4am Tue-Sat. **Admission** MX$250. **Credit** AmEx. MC, V. **Map** p262 A4.

Arts & Entertainment

Attracting the chic Polanco set, Barfly's mall location may lack atmosphere, but the excellent line up of bands and the sheer enthusiasm of the dancers more than compensate.

La Bodeguita del Medio
Cozumel 37, Roma (5553 0246/www.labodeguita delmedio.com.mx). Metro Sevilla L1. **Open** 1.30pm-2am daily. **Credit** MC, V. **Map** p264 F7.
DF is home to two locations of 'La B del M', both of which capture the atmosphere of the Havana original where Hemingway famously drank (and drank) his mojitos. In addition to this classic cocktail and the excellent food, patrons come for Buena Vista Social Club-style *son* music performed by strolling musicians who charge by the song. Great for Americans who long to hear Cuban classics like 'Chan Chan' and 'Guantanamera' but can't make the trip to Havana.
Other locations Insurgentes Sur 1798, San Ángel (5661 4400).

Embajada Jarocha
Zacatecas 138, Roma (5584 2570). Metro Hospital General L3/Metrobús Sonora or Álvaro Obregón. **Open** noon-7pm Mon-Wed; noon-midnight Thur; noon-2am Fri, Sat; noon-9pm Sun. **Admission** free, but MX$100 minimum spend Fri, Sat. **Credit** MC, V. **Map** p265 I7.
Jarocho is a nickname for anything from Veracruz, and this small cantina delivers exactly the right vibe, with live bands from Thursday to Sunday that give a taste of the Caribbean rhythms of that state.

Mojito Room
Circuito Novelista 2, Satélite (5374 0081/www.mojito room.com). Metro Auditorio L7, then Satélite-bound bus or taxi. **Open** 8pm-3am Wed-Sat. **Admission** MX$70-$100. **Credit** AmEx, MC, V.
This Miami-style club in a northern suburb offers a large dance floor and live music. A new branch is set to open soon at Nuevo León 81 in Condesa.

Rincón Cubano
Insurgentes Sur 300, Roma (5264 0549). Metro Chilpancingo L9/Metrobús Sonora. **Open** 9pm-3.30am Thur-Sat; 2pm-3am Sun. **Admission** MX$50-$100. **Credit** AmEx, MC, V. **Map** p264 G8.
Another Havana-style dancehall – not as stylish as Mama Rumba, but with a bustling charm nonetheless. Look out for their two-for-one drink specials and dance shows on Sundays.

Salón La Maraka
Mitla 410, Narvarte (5682 0636/www.lamaraka. com.mx). Metro Eugenia L3. **Open** varies by event. **Admission** MX$50-$500. **Credit** MC, V (cash only for tickets).
A popular spot for serious salsa and merengue dancers, with regular live bands and dance shows.

Salón Los Ángeles
Lerdo 206, Guerrero (5597 5181/5597 8847). Metro Tlatelolco L3. **Open** 6-11pm Tue, Sun. **Admission** MX$40. **No credit cards.**

This institution – slogan: 'if you haven't been here, you don't know Mexico' – is the best spot to enjoy dancing to a traditional *danzón* orchestra. Expect to meet people at least twice your age – many have been coming here for decades – and probably ten times as funky; but lessons are available so you can try to catch up.

Classical music

Mexico has a long tradition of excellence in classical music dating back to the colonial era; and befitting its status as one of Latin America's cultural capitals, Mexico City is home to a number of important orchestras and chamber groups.

The downtown **Teatro de la Ciudad de México** (*see p205*), renowned for its excellent acoustics, frequently boasts performances of classical music on its historic stage. The spectacular **Palacio de Bellas Artes** (*see p204*) is a landmark in its own right, both for its stunning architecture and for its murals by Diego Rivera, David Alfaro Siquieros and others. Home to the National Symphony Orchestra, the Bellas Artes Chamber Orchestra and the National Opera Company, the stage has also hosted the world's top philharmonic orchestras and ballet companies, as well as soloists from Callas to Pavarotti. The three-tier concert hall seats up to 2,000 patrons, and tickets to performances generally cost between MX$240 and MX$400.

The **Centro Cultural Universitario** (*see p205*) at the National Autonomous University (UNAM) is home to a number of excellent ensembles who perform in a variety of venues. Chief among the latter is the acoustically innovative Sala Nezahualcóyotl (capacity 2,376), with its 'vineyard' seating arrangement enabling some listeners to get a musician's-eye view of the conductor. Headquartered here is the world-class UNAM Philharmonic Orchestra, which performs Saturday evenings and Sunday matinees, and the Orquesta Sinfónica de Minería, composed of top musicians from around the world, which gives concerts throughout July and August. Touring orchestras pay frequent visits, and chamber groups often feature in the nearby **Sala Carlos Chávez** (capacity 163). Tickets for these concerts go for between MX$90 and MX$350.

Mexico City's fourth major orchestra, the Mexico City Philharmonic, is based at the Centro Cultural Ollin Yoliztli (Periférico Sur 5141, Tlalpan, 5606 0016, www.cultura.df. gob.mx), where it performs every weekend. Tickets usually cost MX$100.

Sports & Fitness

DF's sporting scene is popular with everyone except bulls.

The hands-down favourite sport in Mexico City is football. No other game even comes close. You can join the raucous crowd at one of three stadiums – **Estadio Azteca**, the country's largest and team America's home ground; **Estadio Olympico**, home of the ever-popular Pumas and location of the 1968 Olympic Games; or **Estadio Azul** for Cruz Azul matches.

Mexicans are also locos for *lucha libre*, a highly entertaining, costumed, macho ballet with slapping and body slams involved (*see pp32-4* **Viva la lucha**). For those who can stomach it, a bullfight at **Plaza México**, the world's largest bullring, is a spectacle worth attending.

Spectator Sports

Baseball

Foro Sol
Avenida Río Churubusco, Ciudad Deportiva, Puerta 5 entrance, Granjas México (5237 9999/ www.diablos.com.mx). Metro Ciudad Deportiva L9. **Ticket office** 10am-10pm game days or through Ticketmaster (5325 9000). **Credit** AmEx, MC, V

Mexico's major baseball league consists of 16 teams, and the regular season runs from March through the end of July with playoffs in August. Mexico City's team, Diablos Rojos, plays home games at Foro Sol, which is part of the huge Magdalena Mixiuhca sports complex and the only ball field in the world that sits inside a Grand Prix racetrack. Games start at 7pm on weekdays, 4pm on Saturdays and at noon on Sundays. Ticket prices range from MX$10 to $70 and are almost always available at the gate.

Bullfighting

Plaza México
Augusto Rodin 241, Ciudad de los Deportes (5563 3961/www.lamexico.com). Metrobús Ciudad de los Deportes. **Ticket office** 9.30am-2pm, 4-7pm Sat; 9.30am-4pm Sun. **No credit cards.**
With seating for more than 41,000 fans, the enormous soup bowl that is Plaza México presents a spectacle of blood and pageantry every Sunday at 4pm from November to March. You'll pay more to sit in the shady side than in the sunny side, with ticket prices ranging from MX$60 to $700 during the regular season. In the off-season you can see a *novillada* pitting younger bulls against less experienced bullfighters who haven't graduated to full matador status.

Three colours *chilango*

Chilangos love football almost as much as they loathe the city's interminable traffic jams that make it a mission to get to a match. Weekends wouldn't be the same without putting your feet up with a group of friends or family to watch *el fut* on TV. Part of the ritual involves munching your way through a massive piece of *chicharrón* (pork scratchings) and sinking a few *chelas* (beers).

Fans congregate in bars for big European and domestic matches, much like their fellow obsessives in the Old World. For the most authentic sports bar atmosphere, try the Black Horse (*see p134*), Condesa's surprisingly stylish English pub. Even better, get off your backside and go straight to the source. It's the only way to learn the lingo and share the city's obsession with the beautiful game.

Resident fans rarely book ahead, tending to turn up and buy a ticket on the day. Reserve your seat in advance if you plan to catch a popular club match or one involving the national team, called *el Tri* after the tricolor Mexican flag. *Clásicos* are *chilango* versions of a British 'derby' – matches between rivals from the same city or clashes of titans like Liverpool versus Chelsea. América participates in every DF *clásico*, attracting hatred and adoration in equal measure. They contend with Guadalajara's Chivas in the original *clásico* and challenges Cruz Azul in the *clásico jóven*, a term coined in the 1970s when competition between that pair of *chilango* teams was at its peak.

DF has bid farewell to other teams along the way. Atlante now plays in Cancún and Necaxa in Aguascalientes. The capital also loses promising footballers to foreign clubs with their deeper pockets. Still, Mexico City remains a top training ground for some of the nation's most promising players, like youthful striker César Villaluz, who earned his studs at Cruz Azul, and goalie Francisco 'Memo' Ochoa who has saved América's skin on countless occasions.

Football rivalry runs deep in DF, but generally, it's all good fun. Teams have playful nicknames for each other. The Águilas (América) are known as the *pollos* or *gallinas* (chickens or hens) while the Pumas (Club Universidad Nacional) are reduced to *gatitos* (pussy-cats). Crowds are boisterous, invariably vocal but rarely violent. Games are family friendly – if you're the kind of family that swears at one another. Insults range from *¡Pinche árbitro!* ('bloody ref!') to the usual interplay about players' lack of ability in the bedroom, and conversely, their mothers' unbridled carnality.

Charrería

Rancho del Charro

Constituyentes 500, Puerta 4, Bosques de Chapultepec, third section, Chapultepec (5277 8706/www.nacional decharros.com). Metro Observatorio L1, then bus or taxi. **Admission** free.

The official national sport is *charrería*, and Rancho del Charro at the far west end of Chapultepec park is the site for *charreadas* – competitions featuring intricate manoeuvres on horseback by men, women and children. The men – *charros* – wear ornate som-breros and dazzling skin-tight suits as they compete in roping and riding events, while the *charras* wear long, flouncy dresses and perform their precision movements riding side-saddle.

Football

The Mexican football league has two seasons per year, one running from August to December, the other from January to May. The debate rages about which team is the town favourite, though plenty of *chilangos* thumb their noses at all three and support Chivas of Guadalajara instead. Advance tickets, recommended for derby matches between DF teams or when Chivas are playing, can be purchased through Ticketmaster (5325 9000, www.ticketmaster.com.mx). Ticketmaster is your only option if you want to pay by credit card (AmEx, MC, V).

Estadio Azteca

Calzada De Tlalpan 3465, Santa Ursula Coapa (5617 8080/www.esmas.com/estadioazteca). Metro Tasqueña L2, then tren ligero to Estadio Azteca. **Ticket office** 10am-5pm Sun. **No credit cards.**
With capacity for 120,000 screaming fans, Estadio Azteca is the largest football arena in the country and home to Águilas del America, Mexico City's most successful team, with ten national titles to its name. The stadium also hosted the World Cup finals in 1970 and 1986. Games take place at 4pm on Sundays, with tickets costing from MX$50 to $680 depending on the game and seat location. Tickets are available through Ticketmaster or at the stadium box office one or two days prior to match days and on the day itself.

Estadio Azul

Indiana 225, Ciudad de los Deportes (no phone/ www.cruz-azul.com.mx). Metro San Antonio L7/Metrobús Ciudad Deportivo **Ticket office** 10am-6pm Sat. **No credit cards.**
Cruz Azul, winner of eight league championships, play at Estadio Azul, next door to the Plaza México bullring. Matches kick off on Saturdays at 5pm. Tickets cost around MX$250 during the regular season and are available in advance from Ticketmaster or on game days at the stadium box office.

Estadio Olímpico

Insurgentes Sur south of Avenida Copilco, Ciudad Universitaria campus (no phone/ www.pumas unam.com.mx). Metro Copilco L3. **Ticket office** 9am-2pm Sun. **No credit cards.**
Estadio Olympico on UNAM's Ciudad Universitaria campus is home to five-time title-winning Pumas, and while not really a college football team, Pumas does represent the university to a certain degree. Fans have a reputation for being rowdy, but plenty of families pack the stadium as well. Games kick off at noon on Sundays. Tickets, which cost MX$70 and upwards during the regular season, are available in advance from Ticketmaster or on game days at the stadium box office, which opens three hours before kick off.

Equestrian events

Hipódromo de las Américas

Avenida Industria Militar just south of Ejército Nacional, Lomas de Sotelo (5387 0600/www. hipodromo.com.mx). Metro Tacuba L2, L7, then Tecamachalco-bound bus. **Ticket office** 2-6pm Fri-Sun. **No credit cards.**

Horse racing takes place at the Hipódromo de las Américas, north-west of Chapultepec park. The first race starts at 4pm on Fridays, 3.30pm on Saturdays, and 3pm on Sundays with subsequent races every half hour. Your MX$10 entry ticket is good for any of the general admission areas, and lower-level table seating is MX$15. The minimum bet is MX$3, and a racing programme (MX$16) is essential. *Photo p200.*

Lucha libre

This 'free wrestling' involves masked and caped characters competing in a highly choreographed affair of acrobatics, body slams, limb-twisting and tossing from the ring. Despite the testosterone-infused atmosphere and scantily clad women presenting each round's wrestlers, families flock to Arena México and Arena Coliseo to cheer on their favourites.

Arena México

Dr Lavista 197, Doctores (5588 0266/www.arena mexico.com.mx). Metro Cuauhtémoc L1 **Ticket office** 5.30-10pm Fri. **No credit cards. Map p265 J6.**
Arena México plays at 8.30pm on Fridays. Tickets for regular matches are MX$40 and up, available in advance through Ticketmaster or at the ticket office on the night. For some matches, called 'Cabello vs Cabello' (in which the loser's hair gets cut off) or 'Máscara vs Máscara' (the loser is unmasked), prices jump considerably and seats can be hard to come by except for the general admission section. The Doctores neighbourhood is sketchy at night, so exercise caution walking to the metro station after the match, or call a taxi rather than hailing one on the street.

Arena Coliseo

República de Perú 77, Centro (5526 1687). Metro Allende L2. **Ticket office** from 4.30pm Tue; from 2pm Sun. **No credit cards. Map p267 M3.**
Matches at this scruffier venue take place at 7.30pm on Tuesdays and at 5pm on Sundays. Tickets are only available at the arena ticket office, which opens three hours before each event. Touts tend to buy up the good seats, so get there early.

Participation sports

While *chilangos* are enthusiastic spectators, there's a slowly growing fitness culture as well. The city's 2,250-metre (7,380-foot) elevation may leave you short of breath and the air quality can be less than desirable at times, but there are plenty of recreational activities available to prevent the tamales and tequila from packing on the pounds. Runners have numerous options including Bosque de Chapultepec, the Magdalena Mixuhca sports complex and Bosque de Tlalpan. To stretch your legs and lungs even more, head west to Desierto de los Leones for hiking, horse-riding or a mountain biking session.

Arts & Entertainment

Take a breather

If you'd flown in to Mexico City 20 years ago, a glance out of your aeroplane window might have had you reaching for a gas mask. However, thanks largely to newer, cleaner vehicles and factory relocations, pollution levels have fallen considerably since then. The smog layer, dubbed *la nata* (cream) by locals, is still visible nearly every day, but its effects in terms of breathing and eye irritation are minimal. Nevertheless, there are days when ozone and airborne particulates rise to an unhealthy level and the city government suggests curbing outdoor exercise.

In the year 2000 the city issued 24 health alerts, but they are now a rarity, with only two or three a year since 2003; an extreme smog alert hasn't taken place since 2005.

For small children, the elderly and those with respiratory ailments such as asthma, these alerts are nothing to sneeze at, but healthy adults are less vulnerable. Pollution is usually at its worst from late February to early May, and even on the smoggiest days, exercising before noon will reduce your exposure.

Alerts are issued to the local news media, or visit the city's Atmospheric Monitoring System website at **www.sma.df.gob.mx/simat** to check out the current day's ozone, particulate and UV ratings.

Cycling

To get *chilangos* out of their cars, the city's environment secretary has turned Avenida Paseo de la Reforma into a cyclists' paradise every Sunday from 7am to 2pm, closing it to motor vehicles. They even loan bikes at no cost on a limited basis when you leave ID, with an early start increasing your chances of snagging a freebie. Bike loan and rental stands move around but generally can be found in front of the Museo de Antropología (Metro Auditorio), at the Zócalo (Metro Zócalo) and at Alameda Park across from the Sheraton Centro Historico (Metro Bellas Artes). The Gran Meliá, Sheraton María Isabel and Sevilla Palace hotels, all situated on Reforma, have joined in the effort and provide free bikes to their guests. The principal ten-kilometre (six-mile) round-trip route connects the Zócalo to Chapultepec Park, and additional routes are closed to cars once a month in sections of Coyoacán, Xochimilco and other neighbourhoods. And on the last Sunday of every month, families

Have a day of fun and frustration at the **Hipódromo de las Américas**. *See p199.*

are encouraged to bike, skate, walk or run together in a *ciclotón*, a longer 32-kilometre (20-mile) route that circles the city.

Gyms

If your hotel doesn't have a gym but you belong to an IHRSA (International Health, Racquet & Sportclub Association) gym at home, you can work out at Sport City, but you'll need to request an IHRSA passport from your home gym's general manager first. Be sure to call Sport City in advance to verify guest fees and programme availability.

Sport City Coyoacan
Miguel Ángel de Quevedo 279, Romero de Terreros (5339 0180/www.sportcity.com.mx). Metro Miguel Ángel de Quevedo L3. **Open** 6am-11pm Mon-Thur; 6am-10pm Fri; 8am-6pm Sat; 9am-4pm Sun. **Map** p259 D3.

Sport City Polanco
Miguel de Cervantes Saavedra 397, Irrigación (5580 0442/5580 0161/www.sportcity.com.mx). Metro Polanco L7. **Open** 5.30am-11pm Mon-Thur; 5.30am-10pm Fri; 8am-6pm Sat; 9am-4pm Sun.

Hiking

Desierto de los Leones is neither a desert nor a lion reservation but a lovely park laced with forested trails that provides a much-needed dose of nature and tranquillity for stressed-out city dwellers. Back in the early 1600s it was the site of a Carmelite convent and remained so for 200-odd years before being declared a national park and forest reserve. Today, hiking, mountain biking and horseback riding are popular activities. One path ascends to the lookout tower on the 3,780-metre- (12,400-foot-) high Cerro San Miguel (plan on at least five hours get to the summit and back). Reaching the park using public transit can be confusing, so a taxi from your hotel is best. Admission is MX$10 and the park is open from 6am to 5pm daily.

The large **Parque San Nicolás Totolapan** (5630 8935) near Ajusco in the southern part of town makes for another pleasant day trip with hiking, mountain biking and horse-back riding trails, as well as rock climbing, a zip line, trout fishing and camping/cabins with 24-hour security. At weekends, bicycles and motorbikes can be rented onsite. Admission is MX$10 for hikers and MX$20 for bikers, and the park is open 8am to 4pm Monday to Friday and 7am to 5pm at weekends. To get there, take the Route 39 Santo Tomás Ajusco bus from the Tren Ligero Huipulco station and ask to be dropped off at Parque San Nicolás (the 11.5

kilometre point on Carretera Picacho Ajusco), or take a taxi from your hotel or Metro Universidad.

Ice skating

If you're in town over the Christmas season, lace up your skates for a spin on the world's largest outdoor ice skating rink in the Zócalo. Despite Mexico City's high elevation, ice doesn't naturally form here even on the coldest of winter days, but in 2007 city officials created a 3,000 square metre artificial rink that some residents adored, and others called a waste of taxpayers' pesos. The city considered it a smashing success and plans to make it an annual attraction from early December to early January. Admission was free during the inaugural season; check with your hotel for current hours and prices.

Mountain biking

Mountain biking is much more popular than hiking among *chilangos*, and weekends bring out downhillers to the mountain parks surrounding the city (see Hiking). If you've brought your own bike, an excellent online resource for trail maps and links is www.bicimapas.com.mx. Otherwise, you can rent bikes at **Parque San Nicolás Totolapan**, and outfitters can arrange day trips to parks and other nearby points of interest.

Factor Bike (04455 2709 8236 or 04455 3467 6953, www.factorbike.com) offers group trips to

Don't try this at home: *lucha libre*.

A great way to see the city is to rent a bike and ride along Paseo de la Reforma and through the Centro on a Sunday. When you get to the Zócalo, go stand in the middle, turn slowly in a circle and just try to take it all in. Don't miss the Rivera murals or going to Coyoacan for a lazy walkabout – and a tip to the *lucha libre* is a must.

Aran Shetterly, editor, *Inside Mexico* magazine.

several destinations each month. Day trips cost from MX$980 to $1,250 depending on location, and weekend excursions vary from MX$1200 to $1500 per day. Packages include round-trip transport from the Condesa neighbourhood, meals, instructors and a support vehicle for bike repairs and first aid. Overnight trips include three- or four-star hotel stays or camping facilities in remote locales without adequate hotels. Bike rental packages include helmet and

Cycling on **Paseo de la Reforma**. *See p200.*

gloves and cost MX$300 per day or MX$500 per weekend, and the outfitter also rents camping equipment and arranges trekking, skydiving and motocross excursions.

Running

You can go for a jog along sections of Paseo de la Reforma, throughout Chapultepec and in numerous parks around town, but the two most appealing and popular places with soft tracks are El Sope and Bosque de Tlalpan. **El Sope** is a popular two kilometre wooded track winding through Bosque de Chapultepec's second section, with several workout stations along the path. The entrance is near Fuente Las Ninfas. **Bosque de Tlalpan** in the south of the city has four kilometres of running and hiking paths and is a nice picnic spot if the altitude has you huffing and puffing. You can get there by taking the Metrobús to Villa Olimpica.

Tennis

Club Deportivo Mixcoac

Jeréz 32, Insurgentes Mixcoac (5598 87932/ www.clubmixcoac.com). Metro Mixcoac L7. **Open** 7am-9.30pm daily. **No credit cards.** This club opens its five clay courts (all with lights) to non-members. Rates for visitors on weekdays are MX$170 per hour; on weekends and public holidays this rises to MX$220 per hour with an extra charge for after-sunset play. Call to confirm exact fees and to reserve a court in advance.

Yoga

The **Mexican Yoga Institute** is the umbrella organisation for yoga in the country. Check out its website (www.yoga.com.mx) for recommended schools and centres.

Namaste Yoga & Pilates

Nápoles 39, Juárez (52071349/www.namaste. com.mx). Metrobús Hamburgo. **Open** 9am-9pm daily. **Credit** MC, V. **Map** p264 H5. This studio has a robust schedule of yoga and pilates classes with prices ranging from MX$85 to $170 for group classes and MX$500 for private sessions.

Sahaja Yoga Studio

5th floor, Avenida México 99, Condesa (5574 2907/ www.sahaja.com.mx). Metro Chilpancingo L9. **Open** 8.30am-9pm Mon-Sat. **No credit cards**. **Map** p264 G8. In addition to yoga and meditation, this studio offers Thai massage and Yogazcal, a combination of yoga and *temazcal* – a pre-Hispanic steam ritual employing hot volcanic rocks and herbs to cleanse and relax the body. Individual 90-minute classes cost MX$130.

Theatre & Dance

Shakespeare, slapstick and all that jazz

Mexican theatre tends to be more commercial than avant-garde, with farcical comedies proving eternally popular. There's a strong chance that the humour won't translate even for Spanish-speakers, unless slapstick antics à la Benny Hill are your thing. But with over 1,800 cultural and arts centres in the capital alone, there are plenty of high-quality productions to be found; and if language is a limitation, you're in luck: DF excels in contemporary, classical and traditional dance. The **Palacio de Bellas Artes**, the **Centro Nacional de las Artes**, the **Centro Cultural del Bosque** and UNAM's cultural spaces are good bets for catching the best of the genre.

Spanish speakers should try the **Foro Shakespeare** for creative revivals of classic plays and new writing in Spanish, while theatre-bars are appealing options for cabaret-style sketches and live music. For occasional plays in English, consult the Anglo Mexican Foundation (3067 8800, www.tamf.org.mx), the British Council (5263 1900, www.britishcouncil.org/Mexico.htm) and the embassies of English-speaking countries (*see p241*).

Tickets and information

Shows usually start between 8pm and 8.30pm, with matinées rare except on the occasional Sunday. Consult www.teatro.com.mx or www.interescena.com for comprehensive information on upcoming theatre and dance events. Also useful is the Primera Fila supplement in Friday's edition of *Reforma*. Local government venues are featured in the free sheet *Chilanguía*. The online version can be viewed at www.cultura.df.gob.mx.

Major venues

Centro Nacional de las Artes
Río Churubusco 79, Country Club (4155 0000, ext 1035/box office 4155 0109/http://espacios. cenart.gob.mx). Metro General Anaya L2. **Box office** 2.30-7pm Tue-Fri. **Tickets** MX$100-$120. **No credit cards**.

The National Arts Centre comprises several performance venues that attract artists from across the globe. The Teatro Raúl Flores Canelo devotes itself to contemporary drama while the Teatro de las

Palacio de Bellas Artes.
See p204.

Dancing in the sunlight

You don't have to find a salsa club to practise your dance moves in Mexico City. On Saturday afternoons at the plaza in front of the **Ciudadela market** (*see p66*), dancing devotees gather to strut their stuff in the open air. But this is no informal affair.

Mostly older couples come a-courting in their Saturday best and take their dancing very seriously. The men are often decked out in *guayaberas* (traditional short-sleeved shirts, often embroidered) or three-piece suits, accessorised with trilbies or cowboy hats and two-tone shoes, while the ladies don evening dresses, beads and heels.

A full band – keyboards, drums, maracas, guitar and trombone – keeps the dancers on their toes and occasionally runs competitions for the sprightliest twosome. If you fear your salsa moves aren't up to the challenge, watch out for dancers giving classes or, if you stand around long enough (women, that is), some *galán* is sure to offer to show you his moves. You can also buy amateur salsa DVDs if you prefer to try out your steps at home first, but the crowd is very forgiving here.

On Sundays at the **Alameda** (*see p64*) there is more outdoor dancing, but this tends to be a bigger, rowdier affair. Regarded as more popular ('for the people'), it is where many household servants (male and female) gather on their one day off for free entertainment, walks in the park and perhaps the chance to meet that special someone.

Fewer suits and dresses and more jeans and hair gel are in evidence here, and

there is definitely flirtation in the air. The groups that play are often quite well known and are installed above the crowd on a bandstand. Salsa and *cumbia* are still the order of the day, but be prepared for a bit of a crush if you want to get in there and dance. Compared to the Ciudadela's ballroom vibe, this is more like a packed disco.

Artes presents dance and music in a light and airy auditorium. It's a real schlep to reach this place, in the city's deep south, so book tickets in advance to avoid disappointment.

Palacio de Bellas Artes

Avenida Hidalgo 1, Centro (5521 9251/ www.bellasartes.gob.mx). Metro Bellas Artes L2, L8. **Box office** 11am-7pm daily. **Tickets** MX$20-$700. **Credit** MC, V. **Map** p267 L4.

The Palace of Fine Arts, a spectacular public building blending art deco and art nouveau styles, is the jewel in Mexico's cultural crown. One of its showstopping elements is in place even before the show starts: a stunning stained-glass safety curtain portraying Mexico City's Ixtaccihuatl and Popocatépetl volcanoes. Designed by local artist Gerardo Murillo, it was created by New York's celebrated Tiffany Studios. Bellas Artes stages regular classical concerts and opera, but its heart lies in

dance. The house troupe is the Compañía Nacional de la Danza (National Dance Company), Mexico's answer to the Royal Ballet. The Company also presents outdoor productions in Bosque de Chapultepec. If you'd prefer to catch a less Eurocentric production, look out for one of the regular performances of the Ballet Folklórico de México de Amalia Hernández, founded in the early 1950s by legendary choreographer Hernández and celebrated for its dramatic, jewel-coloured costumes and spellbinding music inspired by indigenous traditions. *Photo p203.*

Teatro Benito Juárez

Villalongín 15, Cuauhtémoc (5592 7389/www. cultura.df.gob.mx). Metro Revolución L2/Metrobús Reforma. **Box office** 5-8pm Fri-Sun. **Tickets** around MX$100. **No credit cards**.

Located close to the Monumento a la Madre, Teatro Benito Juárez presents diverse genres, with a special emphasis on children's theatre. Plays aimed at kids are staged on Sundays, usually in July and August, and the theatre is also home to the International Puppet Theatre Festival, held in March.

Teatro de la Ciudad

Donceles 36, Centro (5518 4926/box office 5510 2197/http://tcm.cultura.df.gob.mx). Metro Bellas Artes L2, L8. **Box office** 10am-3pm, 4-6pm daily. **Tickets** MX$150-$450. **No credit cards. Map** p267 M4.

This beautifully restored 1918 building houses one of Mexico's most celebrated venues, with most performances in its Italian-inspired auditorium being of the refined variety, whether dance, theatre, music – often by international artists – or film premieres.

Cultural centres

Centro Cultural del Bosque

Paseo de la Reforma, behind Auditorio Nacional, Chapultepec (5280 8771/www.bellasartes.gob.mx). Metro Auditorio L7. **Box office** noon-3pm, 5-7pm Mon-Sat; 11am-2pm, 4-6pm Sun. **Tickets** MX$150; MX$30 Thur. **Credit** AmEx, MC, V. **Map** p262 B6.

This expansive arts centre inside Bosque de Chapultepec is part of the country's Institute of Fine Arts. With seven auditoria, the Centre is renowned for its thought-provoking productions.

Centro Cultural Universitario

Insurgentes Sur 3000, Tlalpan (5622 7125/ www.danza.nam.mx/www.teatro.unam.mx).

Metro Universidad L3. **Box office** 10am-2pm Tue; 10am-2pm, 4.30-8.30pm Wed-Sat. **Tickets** MX$80-$200. **Credit** MC, V.

This, UNAM university's principal cultural centre, is at the cutting edge of performing arts. Sala Miguel Covarrubias specialises in dance, with a series of diverse workshops ranging from Afro-Antillean dance to Zumba open to the public. You can catch classical concerts and opera at the Sala Nezahualcóyotl, while the Teatro Juan Ruiz de Alarcón and Foro Sor Juana Inés de la Cruz are dedicated to drama.

Teatro Casa de la Paz

Cozumel 33, Roma (5286 5315/www.uam.mx/ difusion). Metro Sevilla L1. **Box office** from 5pm on performance days. **Tickets** MX$80. **No credit cards. Map** p264 F7.

Serious drama, rehearsed readings and free film screenings are on offer at this, the flagship cultural venue of the Universidad Autónoma Metropolitana (UAM). Wednesday nights are dedicated to live jazz.

Mainstream and musicals

Centro Cultural Telmex I & II

Avenida Chapultepec 19, Roma (5514 2300). Metro Cuauhtémoc L1. **Box office** 10am-8pm Mon-Wed; 10am-showtime Thur-Sun. **Tickets** MX$200-$650. **Credit** MC, V. **Map** p265 J6.

This is Mexico City's principal venue for musical theatre, with Spanish language adaptations of Broadway shows a speciality. *El Fantasma de la Opera*, anyone?

Dance, music, theatre and film shows are on the menu at **Teatro de la Ciudad.**

Teatro Blanquita

Eje Central Lázaro Cárdenas 16, Centro (5510 1581). Metro Bellas Artes L2, L8. **Box office** 11am-7pm daily. **Tickets** MX$275-$450. **Credit** AmEx, MC, V. **Map** p267 L4.

This once important vaudeville house has had trouble redefining its identity over the past ten years. Anything goes, from straight commercial theatre to pop concerts to variety shows.

Teatro Insurgentes

Insurgentes Sur 1587, San José Insurgentes (5611 4253/http://teatroinsurgentes.com.mx). Metrobús Teatro Insurgentes. **Box office** 10am-6pm daily. **Tickets** MX$150-$600. **Credit** MC, V.

The theatrical delights on offer here tend towards popular culture, with an emphasis on Spanish-language adaptations of West End and Broadway hit shows. Most interesting of all is the building itself. Its circular exterior is adorned with a Diego Rivera mosaic that depicts the history of Mexican performing arts.

Teatro Metropólitan

Independencia 90, Centro (5510 1035/5510 3964). Metro Hidalgo L2, L3 or Juárez L3. **Box office** 10am-6pm daily. **Tickets** MX$80-$490 pesos. **Credit** MC, V. **Map** p266 K4.

Mainstream musical theatre productions are periodically held here, but the venue is becoming increasingly important for gigs too. Musicals aimed at children are common in July and August.

Fringe & arthouse venues

Centro Cultural Helénico

Avenida Revolución 1500, Guadalupe Inn (4155 0900/www.helenico.gob.mx). Metro Barranca del Muerto L7, then San Ángel-bound bus. **Box office** noon-8.30pm daily. **Tickets** MX$90-$400. **Credit** MC, V. **Map** p259 B2.

Award-winning new writing is *de rigueur* at Teatro Helénico. Its Foro la Gruta specialises in original works, mostly using young casts, and in a cycle reminiscent of the Elizabethan theatre, a different production is staged here every day of the week, with plays for children on Sundays.

Foro Shakespeare

Zamora 7, Condesa (5553 4642/5553 5244/www.foroshakespeare.com). **Box office** 11am-6pm daily. **Tickets** free-MX$200. **No credit cards. Map** p264 E7.

The Foro is right at the forefront of Mexico City's theatre scene, with a strong line in new writing and fresh interpretations of established works.

Teatro Santa Catarina

Jardín Santa Catarina 10, Coyoacán (5658 0560/ www.teatro.unam.mx). Metro Coyoacán L3, then taxi. **Box office** 7-8.30pm Fri; 6-7.30pm Sat; 5-6.30pm Sun. **Tickets** MX$100. **No credit cards. Map** p259 E3.

Part of the UNAM's cultural network, this intimate space, located off-campus in Coyoacán, is celebrated for its experimental theatre.

Theatre bars

La Casa del Poeta

Álvaro Obregón 73, Roma Norte (5533 5456/5207 9336). Metro Insurgentes L1. **Tickets** free. **Open** 2-9pm daily. **No credit cards. Map** p265 I7.

Regular poetry readings take place at the Café-Bar Las Hormigas here, on the first floor of what was once the home of Mexican bard Ramón López Velarde (1888-1921). The venue also contains a large literary library, making it a pleasant spot for a drink and, with a bit of luck, a visit from your muse as you gaze out of the French-style windows onto Álvaro Obregón – that's if you can filter out the traffic noise.

Centro Cultural Mora/ El Café del Teatro

Tonalá 261, Roma Sur (5574 2170/http://hexen cafe.blogspot.com). Metro Centro Médico L3, L9. **Open** 10am-midnight daily. **Tickets** MX$60-$150. **No credit cards. Map** p264 H8.

This arts centre is a bohemian mix of entertainment and eating spaces under one roof. El Café del Teatro specialises in informal theatre and live jazz. It also serves light meals and sells second-hand 'experienced' books. Through the large wrought-iron gate towards the back, Hexen Café presents three performance areas: the intimate Casa de Tespis; the concert-friendly Gran Carpa, and the Sala de Cine, which screens arthouse films. It also hosts poetry readings on Tuesdays. Most performances kick off at 8pm across all venues.

Teatro-Bar El Bataclán de La Bodega

Popocatépetl 25, Condesa (5511 7390/www.labodega. com.mx). Metro Insurgentes L1. **Open** 1pm-1am Mon-Sat. **Tickets** MX$60-$300 **Credit** AmEx, MC, V. **Map** p264 G8.

Mainly a music venue, this theatre bar in a grand Condesa townhouse also presents works of drama. The house also contains an art gallery, a contemporary cantina, and an upscale restaurant serving gourmet Mexican cuisine.

Teatro Bar El Vicio

Madrid 13, Coyoacán (5659 1139/www.lasreinas chulas.com). Metro Coyoacán L3, then taxi. **Open** varies – check website. **Tickets** MX$150-MX$200. **Credit** AmEx, MC, V. **Map** p259 E1.

El Vicio is home to Las Reinas Chulas, the queens of the DF cabaret comedy circuit. This is a great place for testing your Spanish amid peals of laughter at the Reinas' edgy political and social satire. Live bands keep things up-tempo after the show and inexpensive drinks flow freely, while in June, this becomes the venue for the International Festival of Cabaret.

Best of Mexico

Mexico

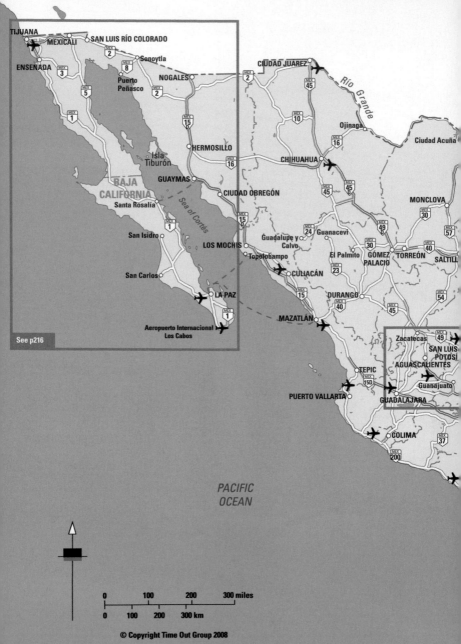

TIJUANA
San Luis Río Colorado
MEXICALI
ENSENADA
Sonoytla
MEX 2
MEX 8
CIUDAD JUÁREZ
MEX 3
NOGALES
Puerto Peñasco
MEX 5
MEX 2
MEX 2
MEX 45
MEX 1
MEX 15
Río Grande
MEX 10
Ojinaga
Ciudad Acuña
HERMOSILLO
MEX 16
CHIHUAHUA
MEX 16
Isla Tiburón
BAJA CALIFORNIA
GUAYMAS
CIUDAD OBREGÓN
MEX 45
MONCLOVA
MEX 45
Santa Rosalía
Sea of Cortés
MEX 30
MEX 57
MEX 49
MEX 24
Guanaceví
MEX 30
San Isidro
MEX 1
Guadalupe y Calvo
LOS MOCHIS
Topolobampo
El Palmito
GÓMEZ PALACIO
TORREÓN
SALTILL
San Carlos
MEX 23
CULIACÁN
LA PAZ
MEX 15
DURANGO
MEX 54
MEX 1
MEX 40
MEX 45
Aeropuerto Internacional Los Cabos
MAZATLÁN
Zacatecas
MEX 49
SAN LUIS POTOSÍ
AGUASCALIENTES
TEPIC
Guanajuato
MEX 15D
PUERTO VALLARTA
GUADALAJARA
See p216
COLIMA
MEX 37
MEX 200

PACIFIC OCEAN

0   100   200   300 miles
0   100   200   300 km

© Copyright Time Out Group 2008

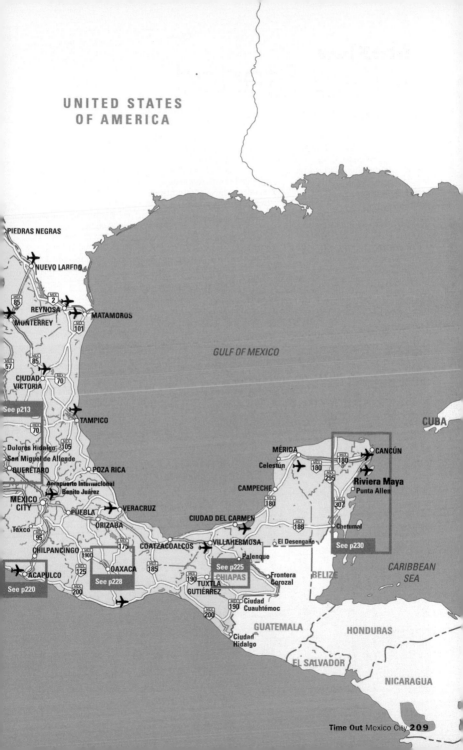

UNITED STATES
OF AMERICA

PIEDRAS NEGRAS

NUEVO LAREDO

MEX 85
MEX 2
REYNOSA
MATAMOROS
MONTERREY
MEX 101

MEX 57
MEX 85

GULF OF MEXICO

CIUDAD
VICTORIA
MEX 70

See p213
MEX 70

TAMPICO

CUBA

Dolores Hidalgo
San Miguel de Allende
QUERÉTARO
MEX 105
POZA RICA

MÉRIDA
CANCÚN
MEX 180
Celestún
MEX 180
Riviera Maya
Punta Allen

Aeropuerto Internacional
Benito Juárez
CAMPECHE
MEX 295
MEX 307

MEXICO
CITY
VERACRUZ
PUEBLA
MEX 180

Taxco
ORIZABA
CIUDAD DEL CARMEN

MEX 95
COATZACOALCOS
CIUDAD
MEX 186
Chetumal

CHILPANCINGO
MEX 190
MEX 175
VILLAHERMOSA
El Desengaño
See p230

MEX 125
OAXACA
MEX 185
Palenque
See p225
CARIBBEAN
SEA

ACAPULCO
See p228
CHIAPAS
Frontera
Corozal

See p220
MEX 200
TUXTLA
GUTIÉRREZ
BELIZE

MEX 190
Ciudad
Cuauhtémoc

MEX 200
GUATEMALA
HONDURAS

Ciudad
Hidalgo

EL SALVADOR

NICARAGUA

Getting Started

Take a trip out of town for a flavour of Mexico's rich, wildly diverse terrain.

As wonderful and vibrant a place as Mexico City is, to go on tourism statistics alone, you'd hardly think so. For every gringo who dives headlong in to the rich, colourful, cultural life of the capital, many thousands more come in to land slap-bang in the holiday zone – that is, Cancún, where vacationing Americans, who make up the bulk of foreign visitors here and throughout Mexico, come to take their pleasure.

For decades, too, they have been travelling to and buying homes in colonial gems such as San Miguel de Allende. Indeed this pretty – some might say prettified – pueblo in the Bajio mountains 170 miles north-west of Mexico City has become such a consummate gringolandia that George W Bush once mentioned it in a speech he gave to voters at a Republican rally. Included in UNESCO's World Heritage list

in July 2008, the town looks set to attract even more tourists and rich residents in the future.

Oaxaca has attracted Americans for slightly different reasons. The mix of native cultures, fascinating fusion cuisines and the nearby Monte Albán ruins combine to give the town obvious appeal to anyone seeking the 'real Mexico'. But a standoff in 2006 between striking teachers, their supporters and the local government turned the city's handsome central plaza into a battleground, and only now are Americans beginning to trickle back.

INTERIOR MOTIVES

Mexico City is big, but Mexico the country is huge, and if you have time to spare after or during a visit to DF, you'd be wise to explore at least some of it. With coasts on the Pacific

Teatro Macedonio Alcalá, part of Oaxaca's flourishing cultural scene.

Ocean and Caribbean Sea, a dozen major mountain ranges, a vast range of terrains, from desert to tropical rainforest to mangrove swamp, and some of the most impressive volcanoes on earth, it can be all things to all travellers. This applies to those on a budget too – while the Cabos in Baja California, for example, are crammed with pricey US-style resorts, there are also mid-range boutique hotels, surf shacks, hostels and campsites.

Generally speaking, provincial Mexico is safer than the capital, though some of the border towns are best avoided. The pace is slower, traffic is not a nightmare, and you can balance the obvious pleasures of town life with trips to national parks, small villages or the beach. But going out into the hinterlands is also a chance to take some of the cultural, social and culinary pleasures of DF a step further. Eating out in Condesa or Polanco, in many cases you'll be served excellent Mexican food, but in Oaxaca or San Cristóbal de las Casas, you can also see the market where the produce is sold, chat to the *mestizo* farmers who work the land, and then, in a local cantina, taste the dishes made from that same produce. The same goes for local parades, religious festivals, weddings, folk music concerts and indigenous rituals. In Mexico City, many of these are filtered, modified or simply erased by the sheer momentum of the melting pot, not to mention the diluting impact of cosmopolitan urban culture. With its many expats, American-Mexicans and well-travelled *chilangos*, DF belongs to the world as much as it does to Mexico. In far-flung provincial towns – in particular in Chiapas, Oaxaca and the less developed corners of the Yucatán – there are strong ties with pre-Columbian times, visible not least in the survival of several Maya languages.

Not that the interior is one big, beautiful rustic haven untainted by modern life. In many of the towns featured in this section you'll see, just blocks from perfectly preserved colonial quarters, expanses of run-down apartment blocks and slums. In Tijuana you'll get a taste of borderland Mexico, the enduring illusion of riches and security across the Rio Grande, and the damage it inflicts on local communities. On drives between towns, you'll see instances of extreme poverty and the marginalised realities of rural life: the violence in Chiapas in the 1990s and the more recent unrest in Oaxaca sprang partly from hardships resulting from divisions between town and country life.

But sober sociology aside, there's a lot of pleasure to be had. Much of it will be a simpler, more authentic version of the experiences you have sampled in DF; but you can also surf, whalewatch, hike and bike, eat ants and sip mescal with cowboys. At the end of each day,

instead of taxi-ing back to your boutique hotel, you'll stroll down cobbled streets or sit gazing out of a cave, with or without a peyote nightcap, gazing at landscapes that would be iconic if they were in the USA – or in other words, filmed, marketed and visited by zillions – but are still relatively unexplored in Mexico.

PRACTICALITIES

Getting around overland can be time-consuming. Mexican buses are generally good though – shell out for the *directo* or *primera clase* option if available, as the buses stop less and are much more comfortable. Visiting the Silver Cities, close to DF, a car is by far the most useful way of getting round (for car hire, *see p239*) – though be warned: toll roads can be very expensive. Nevertheless, to visit Chiapas, Oaxaca and Yucatán, flying from DF (for airlines, *see p236*) and hiring a car locally is probably the ideal option. Alternatively buses, or even taxis, can take you around. Baja California is best enjoyed as a road trip – most people fly in at the top, bottom or middle or, indeed, drive in from Tijuana; or from the mainland, ferries ply the Sea of Cortés.

Be alert to safety while driving in Mexico: driving styles are different to those you may be used to and other motorists can behave unpredictably. Women driving alone, or even in pairs, should be particularly cautious, planning ahead to avoid desolate areas, particularly at night. The UK Foreign Office has up-to-date advice on areas in which particular care should be exercised, and they currently include the highlands around San Cristóbal de las Casas, and the northern border areas, where drug-related violence has been a problem in recent years.

Silver Cities

Mexico's historic mining towns haven't lost their lustre.

For many Mexicans there is only one silver city – **Taxco**, an unspoilt colonial town 160 kilometres (100 miles) to the south-west of the capital. But there are also many beautiful cities associated with the exploitation of silver to the north of DF. The best known are **Guanajuato**, **San Miguel de Allende** and **Zacatecas** – all three UNESCO World Heritage Sites – and at the top of the second division come **Querétaro**, **Dolores Hidalgo** and **San Luis Potosí**. All may seem to have the same mix of beautiful architecture, quaint hotels, alfresco restaurants and museums, but each has its own identity.

Hernán Cortés first saw the flash of silver within months of arriving in central Mexico. Between the 16th and 18th centuries, the colonial authorities in New Spain mined thousands of tons of high-grade silver, a fifth of it coming from Zacatecas alone. Cities sprang up around the mines, and while the bulk of the precious metal was exported to fill the coffers of the Spanish crown and its creditors, including the Vatican, there was still enough left to build handsome cathedrals and mansions for the ruling class and the peasant-turned-aristocrat class of *conquistador extremeños* that had settled in New Spain. The human cost of extracting the silver was huge, in terms of truly horrific conditions for native and imported slave labourers. This cost is rarely mentioned except by the more politicised tour guides who take groups into abandoned mines. It is ironic that such cruelty produced some of the quaintest towns in the Americas.

Taxco

Taxco (pronounced Tas-ko) is easy to reach from DF and its spectacular location, on a rugged slope 1,800 metres (5,900 feet) above sea-level, makes it a popular day trip or weekend escape.

The Spanish came here in 1522 after being told by the Aztecs of mineral deposits. For a century, the mines provided a constant flow of high-quality silver and the town, largely unspoilt, is evidence of the great riches that have come and gone. Taxco was lucky, however, in that later booms – in the 18th century when a new lode was found, and in 1932, when it became a centre for silversmiths – have meant that it was generally wealthier than the other silver cities.

To get an overview, ride on the cable-car at the west end of Calle Juan Ruiz de Alarcón.

Guanajuato.

Down below, the Plaza Borda – named after José de la Borda, who discovered the second major lode in 1717 – is the centre of town life. There are silver shops around the edges, some lively restaurants and bars, and the **Casa Borda** (762 622 6617), built by the Borda family to house the parish priest in 1759. Nowadays it is a cultural centre and a good place to see painting and sculpture by local artists.

On the same plaza, the **Iglesia Santa Prisca**, and, a block away, the **Museo del Arte Virreinal Casa Humboldt** (Calle Juan Ruiz de Alarcon 12, 762 622 5501) are the town's most impressive buildings. The former, built between 1751 and 1758, is a Churrigueresque masterpiece and an exuberant homage to Mammon as well as Jesus and Mary; the latter, a handsome Moorish-meets-baroque building, is now a museum of colonial art.

Where to eat & stay

You don't have to sleep over in Taxco, as it's an easy day trip from DF. But if you do, check into **Los Arcos** (Juan Ruiz de Alarcón 4, 762 622 1836, www.hotellosarcos.net, doubles from MX$500), an arched, Saltillo-tiled beauty conjured up from the vestiges of a 17th-century monastery.

For a dinner of excellent grilled meats with classic Mexican sides – green enchiladas, stuffed avocado, spinach and palm-heart salad – book a table at the **Del Ángel Inn** (Celso Muñoz 4, 762 622 5525 ext 2, mains MX$85-$205).

Tourist information

Oficina de Convenciones y Visitantes de Taxco

Avenida de los Plateros 1 (762 622 5073/www. taxco.com.mx). **Open** 10am-noon, 4-8pm Mon-Sat.

Guanajuato

Guanajuato is a UNESCO World Heritage Site, and on a sunny day its narrow streets heave with (mostly Mexican) tourists sightseeing, snapping photos and shopping.

The town is a draw for architecture buffs who can't get enough of the colonial buildings and elegant plazas. Outstanding among these are the **Templo de la Compañía** (corner of Lascurain Retana and calle Del Sol), with its neo-classical dome and Churrigueresque façade, the lavish Doric-columned Teatro Juárez (Sopeña s/n, Jardín de la Unión, 473 732 0183), and the Casa Rul y Valencia (Plaza de la Paz), an 18th-century mansion now used as a courthouse. If the pace on the pedestrianised main streets gets a bit much, find a tree to sit

beneath on the Jardín de la Unión, a laurel shaded plaza built in 1861 where students hang out and brass bands play oom-pah tunes several times a week.

Diego Rivera was born in Guanajuato and if you've not murralled yourself into misery while on a Frida-Diego tour of DF (*see p88* **Got the Frida fever?**) go to the **Casa Diego Rivera** (Pocitos 7, 473 732 1197). More than 100 works are on display upstairs, including some important sketches for the best-known murals, while the ground floor still contains the furniture that was here when he was born in 1886.

On the south-west edge of town is the **Museo de las Momias** (Esplanada del Panteon s/n, 473 732 0639), where dozens of mummies, with gaping mouths and rigor mortis poses, provide a mock-zombie nightmare. Their display is not related to some earnest ethnological pursuit; they are there simply because Mexicans like a bit of death on their tourist rounds. Pasted up between the cabinets are grim cartoons about the afterlife, one showing a smiley skeleton warning '*Como te ves me vi, como me ves te verás*' or 'As you see yourself I saw myself, as you see me you shall see yourself'. Another features a young girl coyly eyeing a handsome youth and telling her mother, 'Mama, I'd die for him'. She is, of course, already a corpse.

Now run by a co-op, with guided tours by request (8am-7pm), the **La Valenciana mine** (five kilometres north of the town, 473 732 0570) is a dark window into the wealth of Guanajuato. It was opened in 1557, and huge quantities of silver and gold were found in the 16th and 18th centuries. Also take time to visit the nearby Templo La Valenciana church (aka San Cayetano), one of the town's most spectacular. The pink limestone façade glows gorgeously at dusk, while the interior – featuring a tortoiseshell-and-ivory pulpit and three gold and polychrome altars – is lavish to the point of sinfulness. Also on the outskirts is the **Hacienda San Gabriel de Barrera** (Camino Antiguo a Marfil km 2.5, 473 732 0619), where you can see how a 17th-century Spanish silver baron lived, with heavy wooden furniture from Spain, France and England, and vast reception rooms.

Where to eat & stay

Lots of the restaurants around the Plaza de la Paz have a touristy feel, but **El Truco Siete** (473 732 8374, mains MX$40-$80) is a popular arty café serving delicious salads, pies and cakes. Its name is its address: 7 *calle* Truco.

There are many lovely places to stay in Guanajuato. The **Hotel Quinta Las Acacias** (Paseo de la Presa 168, 473 731 1517, www. quintalasacacias.com.mx, doubles from

MX$2,400) is an elegant, 19th-century summer residence. The **Posada Santa Fe** (Jardín de la Unión 12, 473 732 0084, www.posadasantafe. com, doubles from MX$1,400 incl breakfast), an enchanting house built in 1862, is on the Plaza Principal. The six luxury suites of the **Hotel Refugio Casa Colorada** (Cerro de San Miguel 13, Lomas de Pozuelos, 473 732 3993, www. hotelesrefugio.com, doubles from MX$2,520) command spectacular views of the valley.

Tourist Information

Oficina de Turismo

Avenida Embajadoras 41 (473 732 1070/www. guanajuato.gob.mx). **Open** 9am-4pm Mon-Fri.

Dolores Hidalgo

The birthplace of modern Mexico is a humdrum town 210 kilometres (130 miles) north of Mexico City, and 54 kilometres (33 miles) from Guanajuato. It was just called Dolores until 16 September 1810, when a local priest, Miguel Hidalgo y Costillo, performed the famous *grito* – or cry – of *Independencia*. It has been Dolores Hidalgo, the 'Cradle of Independence', ever since. On the main plaza a handsome mansion is kept permanently empty, solely to accommodate the president when he arrives on the night of 15 September, ready to reenact the *grito*.

Dolores is a place of secular pilgrimage for Mexicans. The main shrine is the **Museo Casa de Hidalgo** (Hidalgo & Morelos, 418 182 0171), which exhibits the bill of rights signed by all the revolutionaries, as well as Hidalgo's pen,

his chair and dog-collar. With its priestly furniture and genteel façade, the house seems an unlikely revolutionary headquarters. But Hidalgo and his comrades were middle-class liberals and, as in other independence movements in Latin America, it was these bourgeois creoles who led the way.

It's a short walk round the corner to visit the Parroquia de Nuestra Señora de Dolores, on the main plaza; Hidalgo spoke to the massed crowds from the pulpit here.

Where to eat & stay

El Carruaje (Plaza Principal 8, 418 182 047, mains MX$85-MX$210) is a friendly, ranch-style restaurant, themed in the green and red of the national colours. It serves excellent rib-eye steaks and nopal-based dishes.

Also on the central square is **Posada Cocomacan** (Plaza Principal 4, 418 102 6086, www.posadacocomacan.com.mx, doubles from US$50), with 37 well-appointed rooms.

San Miguel de Allende

All Mexico's silver cities glimmer with the sheen of old money, but it is in San Miguel de Allende that contemporary gringo barons prefer to live out their Hispanic fantasies. To Americans, this is one of the best-known towns in Latin America; it is viewed in the US as authentic Mexico without the hassles.

The town lends itself to this idealised view. Its ochre and rose façades are artfully distressed, its streets are tweely cobbled and

Zacatecas.

flowerpotted, and it manages to be both chic and traditional. Aromas of coriander and lime ooze from cool restaurants, and shops selling organic coffee from Chiapas share the pavements with emporia piled with religious artefacts. After dark, bars stage jazz and mariachi concerts, and you can dine out on sushi and pizza as well as Tex-Mex standards.

There is always a danger that San Miguel could become an American theme park, but luckily it has a beatnik heart. Artists came to study with the likes of David Alfaro Siqueiros, a leading muralist and friend of Diego Rivera and Frida Kahlo. The Instituto Allende (Ancha de San Antonio 22, 415 152 0190, www.instituto-allende.edu.mx), with its muralled galleries, is still a centre of learning for aspiring artists. Then came the Beats. Both groups were fascinated by the magical, chaotic, Catholic soul of the place, and the period gave rise to a mutual empathy and admiration between local people and gringo intellectuals. Neal Cassady – Jack Kerouac's co-driver and the inspiration for Dean Moriarty in *On the Road* – died in San Miguel in 1968; he walked outside stoned on a cold night, slept by the railway tracks and fell into a coma, dying in hospital the following day.

The Beats had also come to explore the spirit-freeing potions and guidance provided by local healers. Nowadays, going to a *curandero* (healer) is as normal as popping to the dentist, and this applies to middle-class urbanites as well as to the peasant classes. But don't expect a hirsute warlock, as modern healers are more likely to be well-groomed fortysomethings.

Where to eat & stay

There are dozens of slick bars, expensive restaurants and even a few cantinas in San Miguel. **Bugambilia** (Hidalgo 42, 415 152 0127, mains MX$75-MX$180) is the oldest eaterie in town, serving traditional favourites. If you're tiring of tacos, **Mama Mía** (Umarán 8, 415 152 2063, mains MX$160-MX$195) is great for lasagne and pizza. **Tío Lucas** (Mesones 103, 415 152 4996, mains MX$60-MX$270) is equally good for big, tender steaks and Mexican meat-based dishes, with live jazz every night.

San Miguel's hotels are beautiful. The **Casa de Sierra Nevada** (Hospicio 42, www.casadesierranevada.com, 415 152 7040, doubles from MX$3,715) is a colonial property built in 1580, with 33 suites spread over five mansions, two smart restaurants and an art gallery. The **Posada Corazón** (Aldama 9, 415 152 0182, www.posadacorazon.com.mx, doubles from MX$1,200) is a leafy refuge occupying a whole block, hidden behind thick walls that cut out the rumble of the SUVs.

Zacatecas

Zacatecas is yet another well-preserved UNESCO site, but it is the only 'silver city' that actually feels like a city – big, bold and full of smart shops and restaurants. It was here that the first seam of silver north of Mexico City was discovered, in 1546. The vast mine, El Edén, is open to visitors: you put on a hard hat and are led down to explore the veins in the mountain. The dank, cold pit is a potent reminder of the brutality that powered Spain's imperial machine.

Back above ground, watch the sun set on the baroque façade of the cathedral. Other civic landmarks include: the whitewashed, noble-looking **Palacio de Gobierno** on the Plaza de Armas; the baroque **Ex-Templo de San Agustín** (Plazuela de Miguel Auza, 492 922 8063), which was stripped of many adornments by Presbyterian missionaries from the US during the 1880s but still retains a splendid Plateresque entrance; and the **Cerro de la Bufa**, a hill just northeast of the city where Pancho Villa won a famous victory in 1914. A cable car takes you from here to the top of the Cerro Grillo, 650 metres away.

Where to eat & stay

The cool and the rich mix at the **Cantina Las Quince Letras** (Mártires de Chicago 309, 492 922 0178), one of Zacateca's livelier bars. A five-minute taxi ride from the centre, the **Hacienda del Cobre** (Boulevard López Portillo y Orquídeas, 492 923 1364, mains MX$75-$170), serves trad classics.

Sleep at the **Quinta Real** (Avenida Ignacio Rayón 434, 492 922 9104, doubles from MX$470). With its lovely Andalusian decor, cobbled floors, and pots of flowers everywhere, you won't realise you are in a onetime bull-ring – it's an absolute one-off.

Tourist Information

Oficina de Turismo

2nd floor, Avenida Hidalgo 403 (492 924 0552/ www.turismozacatecas.gob.mx). **Open** 9am-1pm, 3-7pm Mon-Fri.

Getting there

By bus

To Taxco, Estrella de Oro buses (5549 8520, www.autobus.com.mx/edo) leave from Terminal Centro del Sur bus station. Buses to the northern towns leave from Terminal Centro del Norte. ETN (5089 9200, www.etn.com.mx) will take you to Guanajuato, San Miguel de Allende and Zacatecas. Regular buses run to Dolores Hidalgo from San Miguel de Allende.

Baja California

This desert peninsula offers perfect terrain for a road trip.

The 1,300-kilometre (800-mile) leg of land that dangles down from the US state of California is, unsurprisingly, a rather different Mexico from the mainland. Its main road – Carretera 1, or the Transpeninsular – leads naturally to San Diego and Los Angeles rather than to DF, and, as a result, US influence on the region has been strong and complex. In the north, in the state of Baja California, are the marks of cultural invasion, illegal immigration and low-cost tourism. Around Tijuana and Ensenada, pharmacies sell cut-price prescription drugs, catering for gringo daytrippers; prostitutes ply their trade and radio broadcasts warn Mexicans not to try to walk to the USA through the Arizona desert. The northern part of Baja California is known as '*la frontera*'.

Beyond the 28th parallel is the state of Baja California Sur. This attracts wealthier American tourists, most of whom come down by plane to fish, dive, or eat lobsters and drink litres of margarita in and around the resort towns of the Cabos, La Paz and Mulegé.

Baja California – a term commonly used to refer to the two states combined – has considerable natural riches. One coast runs along the inland Sea of Cortés (also known as the Golfo de California); the other is exposed to the pounding Pacific Ocean. In summer, the former can be a sickly, hot pool of semi-stagnant, turquoise water – beautiful on the eye but sluggish on the body.

The following is a south-to-north road trip that takes you from the beach to the border (or from heaven to hell). Listings are given only for the towns we recommend you stay in. Allow at least five days to drive the route, with stopovers in each direction, and although it's fairly smooth tarmac all the way, the *carretera* passes through towns, villages and farming areas. Avoid night driving, or you might hit a cow.

Cabo San Lucas (km 0)

This is '*kilometro cero*' on the long haul north, and not a place you'll be particularly sorry to leave behind. But look around and you'll see frigate birds wheeling overhead, cormorants gliding on the surf, and courting manta rays leaping up vertically and falling back into the sea with a slap – an extraordinary sight.

San José del Cabo (km 23)

A so-called 'tourist corridor' connects Cabo San Lucas with San José del Cabo. This 30-kilometre (20-mile) road follows the southern coast and is bordered, on its south side, by a string of high-end hotels, many of them refuges for LA-based VIPs and entertainment industry types. But for travellers, the road is a transition from the very American town of San Lucas to the charming cobblestone streets and ramshackle sprawl of San José.

The latter's centre is such a harmonious ensemble of Spanish-style buildings, leafy plazas and a colonial church, the church of San José, that it sets you wondering why the holiday resorts didn't take inspiration from the indigenous architecture.

Pirates raided galleons anchored off San José in the 18th century, and their hiding place is now a protected wildlife area irrigated by a freshwater spring where more than 100 species of bird come to wade in the pristine waters of the estuary.

The posh boutique hotel **Casa Natalia** (624 146 7100, www.casanatalia.com, doubles from MX$3,625) is the place to stay. It pitches itself as a 'European-style' property, which translates into understated chic, cosy rooms, a plunge pool and healthy breakfasts. Alfresco restaurant Mi Cocina serves 'Mexicarranean' dishes like salmon marinated in tequila, and crispy lamb with charred chile poblano.

Tourist information

Oficina de Turismo
Plaza San José (624 142 3310). **Open** 9am-5pm Mon-Fri.

La Paz (km 156)

The road north out of San José fords countless dry river beds, then climbs and winds and doubles back on itself. In the middle of a particularly barren nowhere, you cross the Tropic of Cancer and roll into a wide valley. Stop for a swim at Rancho Buena Vista (km 105, 805 928 1719, www.ranchobuenavista.com, doubles from MX$3000 including meals), a fishing hotel for aficionados that's also your first opportunity to bask in the warm, placid waters of the Sea of Cortés (the Gulf of California). The sea here is good for mahi-mahi and marlin fishing, and also for diving.

After Buena Vista, the landscape gets lusher, the low hills carpeted with dense foliage that seems to be strangling the cactuses. Road signs warn of '*caminos sinuosos*' (sudden bends), and these last for long stretches. You pass through small towns, including shabby San Antonio, tiny Agua Blanca and surprising El Triunfo, which is serene and clean and perfect: an impressive old-style Spanish town of single-storey houses with plain, austere, colonial-style façades, a cream-and-chocolate church and rough cobbled streets.

Hernán Cortés arrived in La Paz in May 1535, after conquering central Mexico. He couldn't be bothered to do any colonising here because of its relative isolation from the rest of the country. It's the kind of place where not bothering comes naturally. The promenade is a stunner, and at dusk becomes a perfect strip for strolling, drinking cold Dos Equis beers and gawping at the sunset. There are swaying palms, shacks selling fish tacos and cruising vintage cars. Stay right on the prom at the colonial style **Posada de las Flores** (Álvaro Obregón 440, 612 125 5871, www.posadadelasflores.com, doubles from MX$1,700), or at cosy B&B **El Ángel Azul** (Independencia 518, 612 125 5130, www.elangelazul.com, doubles from MX$1000) just behind the cathedral.

This will let you go diving and kayaking out in the bay, around Isla Espíritu Santo. There are a dozen grumpy sea lions, a few shy turtles and hundreds of leaping dolphins. Day-long excursions, which most hotels will arrange, take you to secret beaches and beautiful bays.

Tourist information

Secretario de Turismo del Estado

Edificio Fidepaz, Carretera Transpeninsular km 5.5, 612 124 0199. **Open** 8am-3pm Mon-Fri.

Loreto (km 513)

Loreto is flanked by castellated, dirt-coloured mountains, the road winding down to the beach through a series of switchbacks. This well-preserved colonial town was founded in 1679 by Milan-born Jesuit padre Juan María Salvatierra, who established the Misión Nuestra Señora de Loreto. The pediment of the original church reminds visitors that Loreto was once 'Head and mother of the Mission of Lower and Higher California'; the town was the capital of the Californias until 1777, and its historic centre

is low-slung, elegantly lined with topiary and paved with huge cobblestones.

The **Posada de las Flores** hotel (613 135 1162, doubles from US$170) – run by the same small chain that owns the lodging in La Paz (*see above*) – occupies a former indoor market on the main plaza, and the clever refurbishment has made use of every open space and alcove to show off Mexican fabrics, old tequila bottles and talavera ceramics. There's a small swimming pool on the roof, with views of several churches, the Giganta mountain range, and the Coronado and Del Carmen islands in the Sea of Cortés. Loreto is pretty enough, but it can be sleepy midweek. It's best to arrive late, stroll along the front where the restaurants and funk

bars are, see the **Museo de las Misiones** (Corner, Loreto and Misioneros, 613 135 0441) next morning, and roll on north.

Tourist information

Oficina de Turismo

Corner of calles Francisco Madero and Salvatierra (613 135 0411). **Open** 8am-3pm Mon-Fri.

Santa Rosalia (km 708)

There's nothing spectacular about this town, but you should at least pull over to see its metal church, the Iglesia de Santa Barbara, designed by Gustave Eiffel and shown at the 1889 Exposition Universelle in Paris. It was meant to go to Africa, but was left in pieces in Belgium. Frenchman Charles La Forgue bought it and had it placed in Santa Rosalia, possibly to cheer up the French mining engineers who lived here.

Mulegé (km 847)

Requesón and the other beaches of Mulejé look amazing, but they are meltingly hot, and the seawater seems stagnant. Mulejé town is, however, a great and gritty little town. Dine at the celebrated restaurant **Los Equipales** (2nd floor, Calle Moctezum, no number, 615 153 0330), which serves Mexican standards on tables laid with colourful tablecloths. A typical lunch might comprise lentil soup, prawns, chicken strips, beef, tortillas, rice, brown beans, chillies, stuffed burritos, tamales and a fried taco – and beers.

Punta Chivato (km 888)

You won't find Punta Chivato in many travel guides or maps. It is reached by a dirt road: turn right off Carretera 1 at Palo Verde (km 871), then drive for 18 kilometres (11 miles) to what is possibly the most tranquil, romantic spot in the whole of Baja California. Occupying a lovely stretch of beach at the very tip of the *punta* are a few hotels and a hacienda-style mansion owned by the Campbell soup family.

Guerrero Negro (km 934)

Named after a whaling ship that ran aground in the mid 19th century, Guerrero Negro ('black warrior') is a humdrum town wrapped around a lagoon, the Ojo de Liebre, main breeding ground of the Californian grey whale. The whale travels almost 10,000 kilometres (6,200 miles) from the Bering Strait to calve in the warm lagoons off Mexico's Pacific Coast. Eight kilometres south of Guerrero Negro, a dirt road off Carretera 1 takes you to a low bluff from which you can see the whales breaching and blowing. Better still, take a ride on a dinghy with one of Guerrero Negro's many specialist tour agencies; **Malarrimo Eco Tours** (www.malarrimo.com) is a responsible and accredited firm. You'll also see elephant seals, sea turtles and lots of pelicans.

There are just a few decent hotels in Guerrero Negro. The rustic **Cabañas Don Miguelito** (615 157 0250, www.malarrimo.com, doubles from MX$450) has ten basic rooms with bathrooms and eight smarter suites with traditional decor, as well as a good restaurant and bar. Owned by one of the best whalewatching firms, it's ideal if you want to arrange everything in one place.

Cataviña (km 1167)

Just after Guerrero Negro, you cross the 28th parallel out of Baja California Sur and into Baja California proper. This region is known as *la frontera* for obvious reasons, and is (at least from the road) scruffier and more barren than the southern portion.

Now you have to drive and drive to get to Cataviña. The name suggests drunken delight, but it's a real middle-of-nowhere place that serves only to break up the journey. The single motel, **La Pinta** (km 178, San Quintín-Punta Prieta section of Carretera 1, 1 800 262 4500, US toll-free number, www.lapintahotels.com, doubles from MX$800) is cheap and cheerless, with cockroaches, dysfunctional air-conditioning and scowling staff.

Ensenada (km 1438)

At km 1200, the road became tortuous and tedious, winding slowly through a series of steep mountain ranges. As you approach Ensenada, you effectively leave the peninsula and enter that little corner of mainland Mexico between the US border and the Gulf of California.

Stop at La Bufadora, a noisy tidewater blowhole at the base of some dramatic craggy cliffs, for your first collision with *frontera* culture: tacky souvenir shops (for unfunny T-shirts, jumping beans and wrestling masks) and shacks selling cheap antibiotics, analgesics and Viagra.

Ensenada has lovely beaches fringed by public spaces and pedestrian spaces, and a town centre that hints at its eventful history: gold was discovered in 1870, and Ensenada was capital of Baja territory between 1882 and 1915. During the revolution the power base shifted to Mexicali.

There are dozens of bars and restaurants, but **Hussong's Cantina** (Avenida Ruiz 113, 646 178 3210) is one of the nicest joints in Mexico: in business since 1892, it's an old-style wooden cantina with shoeshines working the stools and sunlight slanting through the shutters.

Sleep here rather than in Tijuana. The **Baja Inn Hotel Cortéz** (Avenida López Mateos 1089, 646 178 2307, www.bajainn.com, doubles from MX$1070) is a pleasant small hotel with wrought-iron window grills; rooms surround a small pool, and the boardwalk is little more than a block away. Or for a sea view, pick the **Estero Beach Hotel** (Playa del Estero, Ejido Chapultepec, 646 176 6225, www.hotelestero beach.com, doubles from MX$790).

Tourist Information

Oficina de Turismo
Boulevard Costero 540 (646 178 2411/www.enjoy ensenada.com). **Open** 8am-8pm daily.

Tijuana (km 1559)

Mexico's frontier towns get an awful press. If it's not immigration strife and angst-ridden vigilantes in Arizona, it's drug-running and freakish murders. Tijuana is no exception. Drop off your hire car here, then make a bolt for California or DF.

Tourist information

Oficina de Asistencia Turística
Calle via de la Juventud 8800, Centro Comercial Viva Tijuana (664 973 0430, www.seetijuana.com). **Open** 8am-8pm Mon-Fri; 9am 1pm Sun.

Getting there & around

By air

Mexicana flies direct between Tijuana International and Mexico City (twice a day) and between San José Cabo and Mexico City (twice a day). **Aeroméxico** flies once daily between Tijuana and Morelia, and four times daily between La Paz and Mexico City. There are also flights between San José Cabo and Los Angeles.

By bus & ferry

There are regular buses between Mexico City and Mazatlán, from where there's a daily ferry to La Paz: the crossing takes at least 15 hours.

Car hire

Avis
San José airport (624 146 0046/www.avis.com.mx.

Budget
www.budget.com.mx. Locations at San José airport (624 146 5333) & Carretera Transpeninsular km 19 (624 144 2000).

Acapulco

The magic down there is still strong.

Acapulco is one of the oldest beach resort destinations in North America. Located on Mexico's southwestern Pacific coast and featured in countless films, songs, ads and soap operas, it's a living legend of sun, stars, sex, fun and glamour, in a setting of golden sandy beaches, palm-fringed bays and a sparkling sapphire ocean teeming with dolphins, porpoises and the occasional stately whale.

Its name a byword for sunny holidays and happy days, Acapulco is one of the few tourist destinations with the power to thrill three generations, from grandparents gone misty-eyed the Hotel Pierre Marques, built by Jean Paul Getty in the 1950s; to twenty- and thirty-something paragliders, waterskiers and disco kings and queens; to thrilled kids swimming with dolphins, banana-boat riding, or on a glass-bottomed boat to La Roqueta.

And that goes double for Mexicans. '*Como Acapulco no hay dos*', they say round here – there's only one Acapulco; and the resort's many Mexican visitors help the port maintain its authenticity – and keep prices down.

Attractions like Fuerte de San Diego, the archaeological site of Palma Sola in Veladero National Park, cascading Jardín Botánico and the colourful Museo de la Mascara are also beginning to draw visitors who demand a higher cultural content to their holidays. But be warned: Acapulco is Mexico's most lascivious city. Author Harold Robbins and others of the free-love persuasion staged, it is said, orgies here that could have been rivalled only by the Romans. A famous Mexican ad shows a row of plump babies in every colour and size, with the tagline 'Made in Acapulco' and you'll see that the reproduction thing is only the tip of the iceberg.

Acapulco is divided into three parts. Along the main bay, Acapulco Dorado (Golden Acapulco) has all the zany joints, from Mangos, Barba Azul and Disco Beach to the quaint Hotel Malibu. Acapulco Tradicional is where it all began, and includes Caleta Beach, La Quebrada, where the world-famous cliff divers still plunge five times a day; the Mirador and Flamingos hotels; plus the Zócalo, the shady town square complete with cathedral, shoeshine guys, mangos and raucous crows. The hot new Acapulco is Acapulco Diamante, named after Punta Diamante. Home to the Quinta Real Hotel,

it's close to the Hotel Fairmont Pierre Márquez and the Hotel Princess, the town's best golf courses, a brand new convention centre, Mundo Imperial, and a zone of huge new gated condos, mostly serving *chilangos*.

Sightseeing

Acapulco's great landmark, in addition to its splendid horseshoe-shaped bay, is the jagged cliff of **La Quebrada** in Acapulco Tradicional, where valiant cliff divers perform one of the world's most famous dive shows. Since 1934, local men (and the occasional woman) have plunged anything from 18 to 30 metres into a narrow, rock-studded channel only four metres deep. They also scale the cliff at night, delighting spectators by diving with torches. The performance can be seen from the layered steps administered by the divers, or from La Perla restaurant in adjacent El Mirador hotel.

Acapulco's other classic sightseeing activity is more popular with Mexicans than foreigners, but provides a raucous glimpse into popular culture and is great family fun. The trip to **La Roqueta** island on a glass-bottomed boat (it leaves every half hour from Caletilla and costs MX$80) includes all the beer you can drink and scandalous jokes that only those with excellent Spanish will get; but the mood is upbeat and indeed, downright silly. You'll watch a scuba diver (without tank) play with coral and tropical fish under the boat, see the sunken Virgin (a statue reputedly from a shipwreck), and be deposited for a day of beaches and swimming at verdant La Roqueta, a beacon of environmental preservation in a town too busy drinking to think of ecology until recently. Bay tours are another excellent watery sightseeing option, especially the **Acarey Sunset Cruise** that includes free drinks, live music and games.

Although Acapulco is not known for its culture, one visit well worth making is to the beautifully restored 18th-century **Fuerte de San Diego**. Well-preserved exhibits evoke ancient civilisations, all documented in entertainingly poor English. And don't miss the **Casa de la Máscara**, which houses masks, including the classic jaguar masks typical of Guerrero state, two-faced devils with long lolling tongues, and colourful wooden faces that are half human, half animal or insect.

Divers scaling the cliffs to reach the diving spot at **La Quebrada.**

A stroll around the Zócalo is a must. The old town square is pretty and busy with local activity. Peruse summery dresses and handicrafts in the open-front shops, and nose around the religious icon shops with their near life-size saints with soulful eyes - but not between 1pm and 5pm, when it's too hot

The cathedral is cool, tall and a museum of local characters, including a blind beggar, hand outstretched, who will sing beautifully for you for a few pesos. Towards the back of the cathedral on the right-hand side, there's a square with a fountain devoted to the nun Sor Juana Inés de la Cruz, the 'the Phoenix of the Americas' and the region's first feminist.

In Calcta, jump in a taxi and off to see the **Casa Dolores Olmedo**, one of the city's most important cultural treasures, with mosaic murals on its outside walls by Diego Rivera.

Acarey Sunset Cruise

Departures opposite the Zócalo (744 482 3763/4/5).
Sunset cruise 4.30-7pm daily; moonlight cruise
10.30pm-1am daily. **Tickets** MX$250. **Credit** MC, V.

Casa Dolores Olmedo

Calle Inalámbrica 6, Cerro de la Pinzona, Acapulco Tradicional (744 84 7046). **Open** 9am-5pm Mon-Fri. **No credit cards.**

Casa de la Máscara

Hornitos y Morelos, no number (744 485 3404).
Open 10am-4.30pm Tue-Sun. **Admission** free.

Fuerte de San Diego

On a hill on calle Hornitos, opposite cruise ship terminal (744 482 3828/www.acapulco.com/es/tours/ fuerte). **Open** 9.30am-6.30pm Tue-Sat. **Admission** MX$30; free reductions; free Sun. **No credit cards.**

La Quebrada

Plazoleta La Quebrada, Acapulco Tradicional.
Open Dive shows 12.45pm, 7.30pm, 8.30pm, 9.30pm, 10.30pm daily. **Admission** MX$35; MX$10 reductions. **No credit cards.**

Beaches

Caleta and (next door) Caletilla are where it all began in the 1940s. They were secluded and safe from undercurrents, and foreigners and Mexicans would come to swim, leaving their watches and valuables on their towels. In those days there were no hotels, and local women would cook at home, bringing tamales and steamed fish wrapped in cloth to sell to the sunbathers. Now these beaches are packed during the Mexican holiday season, when they are perhaps best enjoyed in the early morning.

The best place to hang out while the Hotel Boca Chica is being refurbished is La Cabaña de Caleta, a family restaurant in business since the 1950s. Children will enjoy Magico Mundo Marino, a cheap and cheerful, not to say tacky sort of seaworld, but memorable for little ones.

Hornos and Las Hamacas are beaches on the great Acapulco Bay between Acapulco Tradicional and Acapulco Dorado, and include great seafood restaurants like Mi Amigo Miguel and Sirocco. It's a hub of activity as the fishing boats leave (while you're still asleep, in fact) and come back with the catch in the middle of the morning. Opposite Las Hamacas, a venerable hotel with a great pool, is the most pleasant branch of the successful chain 100% Natural – one of the best lunch (and supper, and breakfast) places for grease-averse foreigners.

Not everyone recommends Condesa beach (Acapulco Dorado), also on the main bay, because the undertow can be ferocious. But it's beautiful for sitting and sipping *micheladas* (beer with lime juice and salt), and is a very good sandcastle-building spot. Only very strong swimmers should give the sea a go – children most definitely excluded. The trick here is to swan into El Cano hotel, whose beach area is on Condesa, enjoy a leisurely lunch at the restaurant, try the beach if it appeals to you, and if not, make the most of the pool and excellent service at your fingertips.

Revolcadero beach in Acapulco Diamante faces open sea, and is a magnet for surfers. It goes on for ever and gets very hot, so plan an early morning or late evening visit. A great way to enjoy this beach is at the heavenly Pierre Marques hotel or the huge Princess hotel – worth a visit for its huge lobby alone.

Where to eat & drink

Dining in Acapulco is varied and fun, with great seafood and authentic cuisine – but it's also about seeing and being seen. Currently the best and hippest restaurant in town for food, atmosphere and setting (it overlooks Puerto Marqués bay) is **Zibu** (Avenida Escénica s/n, 744 433 3058, www.zibu.com.mx, mains MX$250-$400, closed lunch), a swish Mexican-Thai seafood restaurant and bar. The town's latest sophisticated newcomer, **El Pámpano** (Avenida Escénica 33, 744 446 6536, www.modernmexican.com, mains MX$190-$275, closed lunch) serves modern coastal Mexican cuisine with delicately balanced dishes full of traditional ingredients such as *chayote*, *chipotle*, *huazontle* and *huitlacoche*. Signature drinks include the traditional Cuban mojito; you could also try the novel mix with cucumber or mango.

A few steps down the road from the cliff divers, **Paco's** (Quebrada 36, 744 483 3117, mains MX$150-$250) is a lunch-only seafood restaurant serving a delicious *pescado huérfano* ('orphaned fish', just a tad spicy) and tasty langoustines with garlic. On the Costera at the start of Acapulco Dorado, lunch or supper at **Sirocco** (Costera Miguel Alemán, no number, 744 485 2386, mains MX$250-$400) is a chance to delight in great *arroz negro* (rice steamed in octopus ink) and paella, as well as fresh scallops. **La Mansión** (Costera, near the Hotel Calinda, 744 481 0796, mains MX$250-MX$400) in Acapulco Dorado is the best steakhouse in town, and its salads, chips and everything else are perfect too. **La Cabaña de Caleta** (Playa Caleta, no number, 744 482 5007, mains MX$70-$180) is one of the oldest and best restaurants,

by the sea in Acapulco Tradicional. Try *tamales de cazón* (baby shark) or the octopus salad.

A number of branches of the successful health food restaurant **100% Natural** are dotted around Acapulco Dorado and Acapulco Diamante, with the most scenic branch on the little pier opposite the Hamacas hotel (Avenida Costera Miguel Alemán, 744 484 2624, mains MX$100-$300). Many locals, at least in the Costa Azul neighbourhood of Acapulco, consider La Jaiba Loca (Rivadavia 402, Costa Azul, 744 481 0407, mains MX$135-$300) the best seafood joint in town. Try the *perceves* (gooseneck barnacles) and *almejas* (clams).

For well-priced seafood and plenty of authentic local charm, including a one-man band who struts in at lunchtime, the original branch of **Mi Amigo Miguel** (Teniente José Azueta s/n, 744 482 5195) is in the centre of Acapulco Tradicional; or at the beach, go to the branch on Costera at Benito Juárez 31 (744 483 6981, mains MX$70-$200).

Siboney (at Club Mandara; see below) is the only piano bar in Acapulco, and is popular with the 30-plus crowd. **La Perla** (at Hotel Mirador; see below) is the place to drink and applaud cliff divers at the same time. Or for a really classy treat, disappear into the posh **Tequila Bar** in Tabachines, the fine dining restaurant at the Hotel Fairmont Pierre Marques (*see below*).

Nightlife

Ninety per cent of activity in Acapulco goes on after dark, and it's worth making sure you rest in the late afternoon and resurface in the wee hours to catch some of the action. There's no point arriving before 11pm at any of the following clubs – after 1am is most fashionable.

Known for its great floor shows, **Palladium** (Carretera Escénica Las Brisas, no number, 744 466 5490, www.palladium.com.mx) is probably the hottest disco in town. **Mandara** (Calle Escénica Las Brisas s/n, 744 446 5711, www.acapulcomandara.com) draws a younger crowd, and **Baby O** (Costera Miguel Alemán, Costa Azul, 744 484 7474, www.babyo.com.mx) has been a favourite for decades. **Alebrije** (Costera Miguel Alemán 3308, 744 484 5902, www.elalebrije.net) is another flashy, enormous disco on the Costera, and **Disco Beach**, on the main bay in Acapulco Dorado (Playa Costera, no number, 744 484 8230) is more of a giggle, with foam parties and paddling around in the sand. **Salón Q** (Costera Miguel Alemán 23, 744 481 0114) is the current favourite for tropical music (salsa), along with the new **Mojito** on Condesa beach (Costera Miguel Alemán, no number, 744 484 8274, www.mojitoacapulco.com).

Where to stay

The **Malibu** in Golden Acapulco (Costera 79, 744 484 1070, www.acapulcomalibu.com, doubles MX$1,200-$2,700) is a good family hotel, with a great location. It's not flashy, but very friendly. John Wayne and Johnny 'Tarzan' Weissmuller used to live in what is now the **Hotel Los Flamingos** (Avenida Adolfo López Mateos, no number, Las Playas, 744 482 0690, www.hotellosflamingos.com, doubles MX$700-$1,150); and you can even stay in Tarzan's 'Round Room'. The service is a little slow, but the views of the open ocean are superb, the pool great and food very good. A favourite among the well-heeled are the **Fairmont Pierre Marques** (Playa Revolcadero, Granjas Marques, 744 435 2600, www.fairmont.com/pierremarques, doubles MX$2,345-$4,125). All the accommodation at this grande dame of Acapulco hotels, built by Jean Paul Getty in the 1950s, is in villas. Humble, friendly and with a super location, the **Hotel Las Hamacas** (Costera Miguel Aleman 239, Playa Hornos, 744 483 7006, www.hamacas.com.mx, doubles MX$700-$1,400) has a couple of large pools, is walking distance from supermarkets, and ideal for families.

The celebrated **El Mirador** (Plazoleta La Quebrada 74, Acapulco Tradicional, 744 483 1155, www.hotelelmiradoracapulco.com.mx, doubles MX$995-$1,230) started as a few cliff-top shacks in 1934. Spectacular flights of steps jut off at all angles. It's the setting for the famous dives and huge, varied buffet breakfasts. **Brisas** (Carretera Escénica 5255, Zona Diamante, 744 469 6900, www.brisas.com.mx, doubles MX$2,810-$9,840) is the pink-and-white fort on a hill where the stars stay. Breakfast (included) is delivered to your room every morning. **Casa Yalma Kaan** (on the way to Barra Vieja, km 29, 744 444 6389, www.casayalmakaan.com, doubles MX$3,200) is a tiny retreat an hour's drive from Acapulco towards Barra Vieja. This ecological paradise is perfect for lovers and weddings, with trips on the canals of the Tres Palos lagoons. The **Hotel Elcano** (Costera Miguel Alemán 75, Zona Dorada, 744 435 1500, www.hotel-elcano.com, doubles MX$1,465-$1,700) has an excellent restaurant known for its Sunday paellas, a clean child-friendly pool, beachside views, and a baby-blue, retro lobby.

Tourist information

OCVA

Acapulco Convention and Visitors Bureau, Costera 38-A, above HSBC bank (744 484 8554/8555 /info@visitacapulco.com.mx).

Getting there

By air

Flights with Aeroméxico or Mexicana from Mexico City cost around MX$2500 and take 40 minutes. It's cheaper to fly from Toluca airport, but if you factor in the time to get to Santa Fe in the west of Mexico City and take the shuttle bus from Santa Fe to Toluca, you'll probably have saved neither money nor time.

By bus

Buses leave roughly every half hour from the Terminal Sur (Terminal de Autobuses Taxqueña) bus station in the south of Mexico City with the clean, new Costa Line/Estrella Blanca, and more or less on the hour with Estrella de Oro. The price is around MX$350 one way. Both lines offer a luxury service at around noon, midnight and 4pm for an extra MX$150. The journey takes about five hours, unless you get caught in traffic returning on a Sunday afternoon. The buses have air-conditioning and play DVD movies, often loud – ask the driver to turn it down.

By car

Acapulco is four hours along the Autopista del Sol. Toll booths make this prohibitive unless you are very wealthy or fill your car with three other people; it costs about MX$850 one way.

There are many Mexicos.
Discover yours!

MÉXICO

There is a tailored Mexico waiting for all of us. Yours could be found deep in one of the Sacred Wells located in the Yucatan Peninsula, where you can encounter amazing natural treasures entwined with the man made treasures and history of the Mayan culture.

Balankanchen Caves | Rio Lagartos | Celestun | **Come and discover it.**

00 800 11 11 22 66

Chiapas

The breathtakingly beautiful Maya heartland.

Hip for a blip in the 1990s, Chiapas has drifted back into relative obscurity. Only readers of the *New Internationalist* and of books by Tariq Ali really care what the poet and rebel leader Subcomandante Marcos is up to these days, and his message – along with his balaclava – has been thoroughly co-opted by purveyors of tourism and tourist tack.

But Chiapas is one of Mexico's most entrancing states, both for its dramatically rugged landscapes and for its vibrant indigenous cultures. Several important pre-Columbian ruins, including the Maya citadel at Palenque, are dotted around the region, while **San Cristóbal de las Casas** is like a grittier Oaxaca, with pretty, 'colonial' colours, but peeling paint.

The Spanish *encomienda* system, under which local people were forced by the Spanish invaders to work the land, has left Chiapas with a legacy of tension between the landowners and patrician city fathers on one side, and native subsistence farmers on the other. Despite this, indigenous culture, with its roots in the Maya legacy, has prospered independently of governments and guerrillas, and a trip to San Cristóbal's neighbour, San Juan Chamula, provides an opportunity to peek into an alternative, syncretistic vision of modern life in the Americas.

San Cristóbal de las Casas

Since its foundation in 1528, San Cristóbal de las Casas has been a crossroads for indigenous traders, as well as a hotbed for rebellion. The city, one of the best preserved in Latin America, has a combined *mestizo* and indigenous population of 150,000. Aptly, it is named after Bishop Bartolomé de las Casas, a fervent defender of indigenous rights.

It remains a junction to this day: most travellers use the city as a stopover between visits to Maya ruins and nature reserves, only to find themselves wishing they could stay put a few days, even weeks. At 2,200 metres (7,200 feet) above sea level, it has a refreshing climate, and – the Zapatista uprising notwithstanding – is wonderfully laid back and convivial.

To get here, you'll most probably land at Tuxtla Gutiérrez and be taken down the winding road from the lowlands, passing through a series of *cañadas* – corrugated seismic folds that form canyons swathed in subtropical rainforest. Amid the mahogany trees and wild figs lining the roadside are gleaming coffee plants.

Wedged as they are between the Pacific and the Gulf, the highlands of Chiapas are often shrouded in mist, but sooner or later you will

Cathedral, Sán Cristobal de las Casas.

emerge into the open and arrive at colourful, sprawling San Cristóbal. To get a feel for the city's , take a walk on the main thoroughfare, Calle Hidalgo, where people from a variety of indigenous settlements outside of the city move among the mainly *mestizo* population.

San Cristóbal is full of markets, roadside stalls and impromptu showcases for high-end textiles run by cooperatives. The sprawling food market on Calle General Urdilla is a joy, with hundreds of stalls selling chocolate, tropical fruits, maize of every shade, fried ants, cheeses, and chillies of every size and potency.

The main plaza is the communal epicentre. Particularly worth a visit is the cathedral – work on which began in the 16th century, but which wasn't completed until the 19th – and, just next door, the San Nicolás parish church, built for African slaves (insofar as it kept them out of the cathedral). A few blocks north is the Templo de Santo Domingo, a pink walled building with a gilded baroque interior and a pulpit carved from a single trunk of oak.

San Cristóbal is more of a strolling and coffee-drinking town than a museum and gallery hub, but **Na Bolom** (Avenida Vicente Guerrero 33, 967 678 1418, www.nabolom.org, tours daily), founded in 1951, is a worthy campaigning museum. Dedicated to preserving the culture of the Lacandón people and their rainforest homelands, it is considered to have played a key role in preventing the complete eradication of the tribe.

Excursions

Ten kilometres north-west of San Cristóbal de las Casas lies San Juan Chamula, a small village in which indigenous culture is still the norm. The Mayan language, Tzotzil, dominates the street banter, while motifs from an ancient belief system – flowers, maize, ceiba trees – decorate the pavements, monuments and the façade of San Juan Bautista, the most important local church. (John the Baptist is more revered than Jesus in this fiercely independent town.)

Inside the church, which has neither priests nor pews, the spirituality of the Maya is on show. Pungent incense whirls around an interior lit only by thousands of candles. Men stand around smoking, and drinking from bottles of cola or high-grade firewater called *pox* (pronounced 'posh') as they make appeals to assorted Christian saints. The sculptures of the more highly valued saints and disciples are adorned with mirrors; the Maya used polished obsidian to create reflective surfaces, which they believed could be used to divine the future.

The stone floor is covered with pine needles, transforming the nave into something resembling a sacred forest. Women kneel, pouring out enigmatic, incessant prayers, holding live cockerels by the legs and waving them first over the flames of the candles and

Members of the Tzetzal community, one of Chiapas's indigenous groups.

Maya monument

The collapse of the Maya kingdom was, it is thought, probably due to a disease that ravaged the close-knit tribal network. In any case, the rise of the Aztecs in the 14th century was a watershed, and the arrival of the conquistadores marked a definite end to the ancient Maya world.

Palenque (www.inah.gob.mx), in the lowlands of Chiapas, was built during the Classic period, which lasted from the third to the ninth century, and it is an enduring reminder of the greatness of Maya culture. The Maya were innovators in astronomy, writing, mathematics and architecture; here in Palenque, the remains of that architecture are spectacularly visible.

The main burial pyramids and ceremonial buildings – Temple XIV, the Temple of the Cross, the Palace and the Temple of the Inscriptions – are constructed from limestone slabs that, despite the lichen and mosses, glow against a backdrop of dense vegetation bursting out of the steep hills all around. Apart from the toucans and parrots, the only sound in many corners is that of the streams that trickle through the underground aqueduct the Maya built to beautify their environment. The fringes of the site are dotted with partially excavated residences and workplaces, in which ruins compete with a tangle of lianas and orchids. Humidity seems to sweat from every knotted trunk and curved leaf, and the jungle is always reclaiming its stolen territory.

Bishop Diego de Landa Calderón of Yucatán was told of the site in the 16th century; and it was he who had many of the Maya codices and texts destroyed. Archaeologists have used his records of what he demolished and destroyed in order to salvage as much knowledge of the past as possible.

The site is open from 8am to 4.45pm daily, and admission costs MX$45.

---

then over a member of their private circle or congregation. The key moment of worship involves a sudden pause, in which the woman – the shaman of the group – violently twists the neck of the confused bird and so puts to death any evil spirits that had been drawn out.

The only other thing to 'do' in San Juan is to visit people's homes, where the locals will show off their weaving, potting and jewellery-making, for a fee. There are also numerous markets. But ultimately, this is a place in which to simply wander and soak up the mood.

Where to eat & stay

An abundance of colonial mansions-turned-hotels makes San Cristóbal a choice destination for budget holidaymakers craving a touch of class. The three-storey **Palacio de Moctezuma** (Juárez 16, 967 678 0352, doubles from MX$400) has large and airy rooms, open courtyards, and tile fountains surrounded by flowers. The **Casa Mexicana** (28 de Agosto 1, 967 678 0698, www.hotelcasamexicana.com, doubles from MX$1175) is a colonial mansion with 52 spacious, comfortable rooms, flower-filled patios and corridors hung with Mexican art.

Dining out, **El Fogón de Jovel** (Avenida 16 de Septiembre 11, 967 678 1153, www.fogondejovel.com) is a converted family home decked out with textiles and attended by waiters in local garb. Try the scrumptious tamales, stuffed chillies and *mole* enchiladas. A cheaper option is

Madre Tierra (Avenida Insurgentes 19, 967 678 4297), which does simple Mexican dishes, and does them well.

Tourist Information

Dirección de Turismo Municipal de San Cristóbal

Plaza 31 de Marzo s/n (967 678 0665, www.turismochiapas.gob.mx). **Open** 8am-8pm daily.

Getting there & around

By air

There are frequent flights between Mexico City and Tuxtla Gutierrez Airport (961 615 5060) with **Click Mexicana** (01 800 112 5425, www.click.com.mx) and **Interjet** (01 800 011 2345, www.interjet.com.mx). Alternatively, you can fly between Mexico City and Tapachula Airport (Carretera Puerto Madero km 18.5, 962 626 4189, www.asur.com.mx), in the south-east of the state, on **Aeroméxico** (962 626 2532, www.aeromexico.com) and **Volaris** (01 800 7VOLARIS, www.volaris.com.mx).**Aviacsa** (01 800 AVIACSA, www.aviacsa.com) serves both destinations from DF.

By bus

There are regular buses between San Cristóbal de las Casas and Palenque (journey time 4-5 hours, approx MX$130), and between Tuxtla Gutierrez and San Cristobal (journey time 1hr 15mins, approx MX$35).Tickets can be reserved at www.ticketbus.com.mx.

Best of Mexico

Oaxaca

Civic charm, glorious churches and leafy and lovely plazas.

Fly or drive into the state of Oaxaca (pronounced wa-HA-ka) and you'll notice how rugged the land is, riven by countless narrow valleys, the reason for the great diversity of native cultures and languages around these parts. In around 2500 BC, the most fertile area in the region, the Oaxaca valley, was occupied by the Zapotecs, who became the dominant force in the region as they domesticated animals and grew beans, chillis, squash, agave and many varieties of fruit. Between 600 and 900 AD, when the culture was at its apogee, they built the magnificent city of Monte Albán on a flattened mountain top to the west of present-day Oaxaca city.

The Mixtecs invaded three centuries later, and a hybrid culture evolved. Many Zapotec traditions persisted, but the combined peoples spread their influence into many small highland villages. The Aztecs demanded tribute in the mid-15th century, and strong ties grew up between Tenochtitlán and the Oaxaca valley. When the Spanish came in 1521, conquistador Francisco de Orozco claimed the region on behalf of Cortés, who took the title Marqués del Valle de Oaxaca. Wheat was planted, sugar cane and silkworms were introduced, and gold mines were bored into the mountains.

Oaxaca City

Between May and October 2006, the city of Oaxaca was under siege, occupied by the Popular Assembly of the Peoples of Oaxaca, a loose-knit confederation of teachers, left-wing cooperatives and NGOs demanding higher salaries for teachers and protesting against the corruption of state governor Ulises Ruiz Ortiz. The dispute spiralled out of control when the protesters occupied the Zócalo and public buildings; at least 18 people died in clashes between protesters and police, and barricades turned the old centre into a battleground.

Tourists stayed away in 2006 and well into 2007, and many hotels, restaurants and language schools – Oaxaca has long been a preferred destination for would-be Spanish speakers – were closed. By 2008, the city's tourism industry was tentatively reviving.

Oaxaca is famous for three things: the predominance of native cultures, its art scene, and its food. Oaxaca's *centro histórico* is a UNESCO World Heritage site, and has the requisite grandiose churches, crumbling palaces, leafy patios and plazas, plus flower-laden royal poinciana trees on every corner and a human face to the city that's as exuberant as the civic one. From dawn to dusk, everyone seems to be out and about, shopping, eating, strolling, chatting, watching open-air concerts, so that the place feels like an idyll of community life.

If you're lucky enough to be in Oaxaca for July's Guelaguetza cultural festival or for saints' days, look out for the Monos de Calenda, huge papier-maché puppets, and the *marmota* lanterns that are carried through the streets.

Art-lovers can pop into a number of private galleries to see impressive paintings, all by local artists. The best contemporary work at **Arte Mexicano** (Alcalá 407, 951 514 3815, Alcalá 407), **La Mano Mágica** (Alcalá 203, 951 516 4275, www.lamanomagica.com) and at the **Galería Gráfica Soruco** on the Plazuela Labastida (Pino Suarez 304, 951 514 886 3938) is full of mexicana, but not clichéd or aimed strategically at tourists. Away from the commercial galleries are a couple of socially minded arts centres. To see and buy contemporary woodcuts, satirical cartoons and hand-made papers, go to the **Instituto de Artes Gráficas de Oaxaca** (Alcalá 507, 951 516 2045). Nearby is an excellent little cinema, the **Cine Pochote** (García Vigil 817, 951 514 1194), run by the same organisation.

But the must-see gallery – and here 'museo' most definitely means gallery – is the **Museo Rufino Tamayo de Arte Prehispánico de México** (Avenida Morelos 503, 951 516 4750). Its collection of pre-Columbian artefacts has been arranged according to aesthetic principles, rather than by periods, by famed muralist Tamayo. Late 2007 brought the opening of the new **Museo Textil de Oaxaca** (Hidalgo 917, 951 501 1617, www.museotextildeoaxaca.org.mx), a showcase for regional and international tapestries, shawls, ponchos and dresses.

The town has a profusion of grandiose basilicas, their cream stone façades cleaned up and gleaming like new. If you only see one, see the **Santo Domingo** – behind its plain façade on Alcalá (six blocks north of the Zócalo) lurks a breathtaking gilded interior.

Once the greatest of all Zapotec cities, **Monte Albán** (Ruta 190, 8km west of Oaxaca, 8am-6pm daily, admission MX\$45, 951 516 1215),

Gilt baroque treasure lurks behind the plain façade of **Templo de Santo Domingo de Guzmán**.

high on a hill on Oaxaca's western flank, is a remarkable feat of engineering. A citadel was founded here as early as 500 BC by the Olmecs, but at a later stage the mountain top was levelled off and the ceremonial site was laid out. Outstanding features include an observatory, ball court, sunken patio and several pyramidal platforms where temples were built, and a huge open space called the Grand Plaza.

Where to stay & eat

A variety of microclimates makes for a huge range of produce and Oaxacan food is very special. Hit the Mercado de Abastos on the corner of Periférico and Las Casas to see and smell every kind of chilli, vegetable, fruit or meat imaginable, raw, cooked – and rancid.

You'll want to eat some of this bounty, so go along to **Casa Oaxaca** (Constitución 104-A, 951 516 8889, www.casaoaxaca.com.mx; dinner for two, with drinks, from MX$800). Chef Alejandro Ruiz Olmedo's wholly original menu includes such treats as grilled Oaxaca string cheese with grasshoppers in a green *tomatillo* sauce, a soup of nopal, fava bean and sun-dried shrimp, and guava tart with rose petals. Cheaper but very cheerful is **La Farola** (20 de Noviembre 3, 951 516 5353, dinner for two with drinks MX$200). Opened in 1916, this cantina serves throat-scorching mescal with tapas of shrimp, cheeses, nachos and ants.

There are dozens of pretty, small hotels. **La Provincia** (Porfirio Díaz 108, 951 514 0999, www.hotellaprovincia.com.mx, doubles from MX$1800) has just 14 rooms, arranged around a small patio. The hotel's excellent restaurant does a spectacular dish of burritos drenched in subtly

spiced chocolate *mole*. The **Casa del Sótano** (Palacios 414, 951 501 1827 doubles from MX$680) is a cosy two-storey inn with a terrace restaurant and art gallery, and rooms with tiled floors and muted decor in the local style.

Tourist information

Secretaría de Desarrollo Turístico

Zócalo government building, corner Avenida Independencia Juárez/Garcia Vigil (951 502 1200/ 516 0123, www.aoaxaca.com. **Open** 9am-3pm, 6pm-8pm Mon-Fri; 10am-1pm Sat.

Getting there

By air

Mexicana (951 144 7652, www.mexicana.com), **Aeroméxico** (951 511 5044/5055, www.aero mexico.com) and **Aviacsa** (01 800 AVIACSA, www.aviacsa.com.mx) fly to **Oaxaca airport** (951 511 5088, www.asur.com.mx), an hour's flight from Mexico City's Benito Juárez airport. **Volaris** (01 800 7VOLARIS, www.volaris. com.mx) flies from Toluca, just outside Mexico City. Mexicana's budget airline, **Click** (01 800 112 5425, www.clickmx.com), operates direct flights between Mexico City and Oaxaca or Puerto Escondido.

By road

There are more than 50 buses daily between Oaxaca's bus terminal (Calzada Niños Héroes de Chapultepec 1036, 951 515 9920, www.ticket bus.com.mx) and Mexico City; the journey time is five to six hours.

Riviera Maya

Ancient culture, cutting-edge hotels – and did we mention the pristine beaches?

With its warm sea a palette of blues from aquamarine to high-res turquoise, powdery white sand and the sort of benevolent climate (hurricanes aside) of which millions dream, the Caribbean coast of Mexico's Yucatán peninsula is one of the world's most beautiful holiday spots. It's green, tropical and bustling with plants and flowers on land, with a similarly multicoloured universe just below the water's surface, where the world's second largest coral reef runs alongside the beach all the way to Belize, Guatemala and Honduras, attracting scuba divers and snorkelists from far and wide.

Almost as colourful and teeming with life, Cancún, the area's main point of arrival and a tourist magnet since its late-1960s evolution from a sleepy and unsuspecting coastal village, has earned a reputation as a gaudy, cocktail-fuelled holiday destination from hell. And yet there are good reasons why Cancún draws two and a half million visitors every year. Yes, it has a slick tourism infrastructure that includes the sweep of the Zona Hotelera – a slim, 22 kilometre-long spit of sand, actually an island, on which a legion of grand hotels and all-inclusive resorts cram shoulder to shoulder, facing the sea. Yes, it has an abundance of noisy, beery bars and restaurants catering to US holidaymakers, most of them on a main drag festooned with haiku-like banners that take a moment to process: 'Girls no cover'; 'Ladies drink free'; 'Crazy tattoos'. But walk around a little, duck into the hotels, stroll the paths between their lavish, navy-blue pools, and the people you'll see will be happy, relaxed and delighted to be basking in the bounty of Cancún.

South of Cancún is the Riviera Maya, a 200 kilometre stretch of coastline in the process of becoming a key holiday destination in its own right. The 'Riviera Maya' tag is as much a tourism industry gimmick as the two-for-one margaritas at Cancún's Hooters bar, but from the simultaneously hip and tacky fabulousness of Playa del Carmen's coast resorts – some of them exceptionally luxurious – to the exquisite *cabañas* of Tulúm and on into the wild Sian Ka'an Biosphere Reserve, all the beauty is real.

Soak up the sun in sight of the ruins at **Tulúm**. *See p233.*

Cancún

With a population of more than a million all year
round, Cancún has way more to offer than its
most obvious assets – though its obvious assets
and its well-executed tourist industry make it a
great place to enjoy a mass market holiday. If it's
unspoiled nature you're after then keep moving
on down the coast, but if you have even a couple
of days to spare – or perhaps just a night on the
way in or out – then you could do worse than
making a stop in Cancún.

There's little in the way of high culture here –
that's really not the point of Cancún – but if you
must, the **Casa de Arte Popular Mexicano**
is brimming over with an excellent collection of
folk art from across the country and is located
right in the Zona Hotelera. First, though, head
for a gaze at the big blue and the soft sand –
millennia worth of calcium deposits washed up
from the coral reefs. The R1 bus will take you
from the main terminal all the way along the
Zona Hotelera for a flat fare of MX$6.50. Ride
through spring break ground zero – around the
Forum by the Sea shopping mall – and once you
start passing dozens of hotels, their backs to
you and their faces to the sea, pick a stop and
hop off. It's unlikely you'll have seen the sea by
now – to call the seafront 'built up' would be an
understatement – but nip through a hotel lobby
and out on to the beach to understand in an
instant why Cancún is so popular

Evening is a good time to visit downtown
Cancún, where most of the action revolves
around Avenida Yaxchilán; if it's a weekend,
don't miss a stroll in Parque la Palapas, where
live music and dance on the large stage draw
smartly dressed Cancunians, many of them
grazing at the row of food stalls to one side.

Casa de Arte Popular Mexicano

*El Embarcadero, Boulevard Kukulcán km 4 (998 849
4332/www.museoartepopularmexicano.org).* **Open**
9am-6pm Mon-Fri; 11am-6pm Sat, Sun. **Admission**
MX$50; MX$33 reductions. **No credit cards**.

Excursions

Take the ferry from Puerto Juárez to tranquil
Isla de Mujeres (MX$35), just four kilometres
north of Cancún, or head for the astonishing
Maya ruins at **Chichén Itzá**. At its peak –
between AD 850 and 1150 – the city's population
reached around 50,000, and it became a place of
pilgrimage before being abandoned for reasons
unknown around 1200. Take the 9am Mayab
Line bus from the terminal, returning at 4.30pm
(998 884 5542, MX$150 each way); alternatively,
you can join an excursion through a tour
company (though be aware that most tours

make other stops along the way whether you
like it or not). Best of all, you can rent a car (try
Hertz at Plaza Forum, Avenida Tulum 260, 800
405 7000), making an early start to beat the heat
and driving 217 kilometres (135 miles) inland
towards Mérida, taking the toll road for speed.

Where to eat & drink

Right on Parque las Palapas, **La Habichuela**
(Margaritas 25, 998 884 3158, mains MX$145-
$500) is a local institution with a beautiful
terrace garden. Giant prawns in tamarind
sauce are the way to go, with a little tequila
first to whet the appetite accompanied by one
of the best sangritas – a tiny tomato-juice
chaser – in town. Louder, brasher and lots
of fun, **La Parrilla** (Avenida Yaxchilán 51,
998 287 8118, mains MX$75-$600) has a
Tex-Mex menu, roaming mariachis and a jolly
atmosphere that local families adore. If you're
in search of the real Cancún, head for the Zona
and **Jimmy Buffet's Margaritaville**

(Boulevard Kukulcán km 11.5, 998 885 2376, mains MX$180-$350), or **Ruth's Chris Steakhouse** (Boulevard Kukulcán km 13.5, 998 885 3301, mains MX$290-$500).

Where to stay

El Rey del Caribe (Avenida Uxmal 24, 998 884 2028, www.reycaribe.com, doubles from MX$835), despite an unpromising location on the far side of the downtown bus terminal, is a gem of a hotel thanks to the lush tropical garden around which it is set. **Hostel Haina** (Orquídeas 13, 998 898 2081, www.hainahostel.com, rates MX$390 double, MX$110 dorm bed) is a nice budget option near Parque las Palapas, while down among the hotel megaliths, the **Gran Meliá** (Boulevard Kukulcán km 16.5, 998 193 0090, www.granmeliacancun.com, doubles from MX$1,400) is gorgeous, with a stunning ivy-draped lobby recalling the lush mangroves that once lined this shore.

Tourist information

Oficina de Turismo

Palacio Municipal, Avenida Tulúm 5 (998 881 2800/ www.cancun.gob.mx). Open 9am-4pm Mon-Fri.

Getting there

By air

Aeroméxico (998 287 1822, www.aero mexico.com) and **Aviacsa** (998 886 0093, www.aviacsa.com) are two of the airlines that serve the DF-Cancún route, flying into Cancún International Airport. From the airport, take the ADO bus into town (MX$35) – buy a ticket at the booth inside the terminal – or, at the same booth, a ticket for a taxi collective at MX$120. Private taxis cost around MX$500.

Playa del Carmen

Playa, as those in the know call it, isn't half so hip as it thinks it is. If you come expecting to find a chic and fashionable beach resort, you'll be sorely disappointed at first glance. Looking a lot like Benidorm these days, much of the main drag, 5ta Avenida, is so crammed with shops, bars, restaurants and cafés that after a few blocks it becomes a bit of a visual blare. But if hipness matters, look a little closer and you will find what you seek: **at Mamita's Beach Club** on Playa Tukán near Calle 28 (www.mamitasbeachclub.com); with a cucumber martini by the pool at **Hotel Deseo** (*see below*); at **Diablito Chachacha** (1a Avenida near Calle 12, 984 803 3695); or at hot-as-hell bar

Santanera (Calle 12 between 5ta Avenida and Calle 10, 984 803 2294), where you must never arrive before 1.30am if you want to fit in. When you're partied out, take the Ultramar Ferry (998 843 2011) to the island of Cozumel, from the pier at the southernmost end of 5ta Avenida.

Where to eat

Shrimp tacos by the pool – read: 'immersion tanks' – at Hotel Básico (*see below*) are a house speciality, and for good reason. **Babe's Noodles & Bar** (10th Street, 984 120 2592, www.babesnoodlesandbar.com, mains MX$63-$110), opposite Básico, serves quality Pad Thai noodles along with ice-cold lemon and mint smoothies that are *una delicia*. Near the end of 5ta Avenida, **La Cueva del Chango** (Calle 38, 984 147 0271, mains MX$86-$136) does authentic Mexican food brilliantly.

Where to stay

Hotel Básico (5ta Avenida & Calle 10, 984 879 4448, www.basico.com.mx, doubles from MX$2,000) is a hymn of praise to industrial chic. It's a great hotel in many ways, and a Habita hotel to the core (*see p40* **Habita forming**), reflective of the group's willingness to experiment with delightfully theatrical styles. Exposed pipes and large hospital beds set the tone for the rooms, where you get the feeling your presence might be messing up the design; and since, in their stripped-down frenzy, the designers neglected to add furniture except for odd modernist tables and deep drawers beneath the beds, your cluttered piles of bags, clothes and books most certainly will. The rooms at **Hotel Deseo** (5ta Avenida & Calle 12, 984 879 3620, www.hoteldeseo.com, doubles from MX$2000), round the corner, are similarly minimalist but simpler and prettier. **Hotel Lunata** (5ta Avenida between Calles 6 & 8, 984 873 0884, www.lunata.com, doubles from MX$1,500) is at the other end of the scale: a tranquil, peaceful, classically lovely hotel in the colonial style.

Tourist information

Playa del Carmen

Avenida Juárez at 15a Avenida (984 873 0242). Open 9am-9pm Mon-Sat; 9am-5pm Sun.

Getting there

By car

Highway 307 runs from Cancún all the way south along the Riviera Maya.

Hotel Básico.

By bus

Take one of the frequent buses from Cancún bus terminal (MX$35); take a *combi* minibus (from MX$30) from Calle 2 near Calle 20 to continue south along the Riviera Maya.

Tulúm

After the hustle and bustle of Cancún, Tulúm is the tranquil jewel in the crown of the Riviera Maya. It's beautiful, with a chocolate-box set of Maya ruins and wider beaches than you'll see further north. At Tulúm, attractive couples walk hand-in-hand along the beach, and with no mains electricity along the beachfront, resorts and *cabañas* eke their way with generators, plus lots of solar- and wind-generated power. Which isn't to say that the area is cheap and undiscovered – it's not. Accommodation along the beach is expensive and there's little available these days for less than MX$1000.

The area is particularly well endowed with *cenotes* (pronounced 'se-NO-tays'), part of the enormous network of underground rivers and lakes that honeycomb the whole of the Yucatán peninsula (*see p234* **Cavediver**). The Cenote Dive Center offers well-run *cenote* tours that can include snorkel or scuba diving, as well as ocean dives and various certification courses. The Tulúm Maya Ruins, on a spectacular seaside setting above a charming little beach, make for a short, very pleasant excursion; and a trip into the magnificent **Sian Ka'an Biosphere Reserve** (984 871 2499, www.cesiak.org) is another very rewarding experience.

Cenote Dive Center

Carretera Cancún-Tulúm, opposite HSBC bank (984 871 2232/www.cenotedive.com). **Open** Call or email ahead to make a booking. **Rates** MX$500-$16,000.

Tulúm Ruins

Carretera 307 km 232. **Open** *Summer* 8am-7pm daily. *Winter* 7am-6pm daily. **Admission** MX$45.

Where to eat, drink & stay

In town, try **Posada Luna del Sur** (Luna Sur 5, 984 871 2984, doubles from MX$700) for reasonably priced, clean and pleasant lodgings. At the beach, the *cabañas* at **Diamante K** (Carretera Ruinas Tulúm km 2.5, near Carretera Boca Paila , 998 185 8300, www.diamantek.com, rates MX$500-$3000) are in an exquisite setting with their own tiny sand beach at this, the rockier end of the shoreline. **Casa de Miel** (Carretera Boca Paila km 5, 998 185 7428, www.casademiel.com, doubles from MX$1,900) offers eco-chic *cabañas* that are well located on a particularly wide and gorgeous stretch of beach between rickety Hemingway's restaurant and the Posada Margherita resort, which also has an exceptional Italian restaurant (Carretera Tulúm Boca Paila km 4.5, 984 801 8493, www.posada margherita.com, doubles from MX$1,785, mains MX$150-$250). Casa de Miel's sister property, **Amansala** (Carretera Boca Paila km 8, 998 185 7428, www.amansala.com, rates from MX$1100), much further down the beach, is also home to Bikini Boot Camp, where squads of high-achieving New York girls power-walk, practise yoga and glow healthily. In town, good restaurants include La Nave (Avenida Tulúm 570, 984 87 12592, mains MX$45-$180) for excellent pizza and home made bread, and **El Pequeño Buenos Aires** (Avenida Tulúm and Calle Beta, 984 871 2708, mains MX$70-$400) for great steaks. Friday night parties at the sophisticated **Mezzanine** (998 112 2845, www.mezzanine.com.mx) are legendary – you can either pay MX$100 admission or try to wheedle passes from staff at your hotel.

Best of Mexico

Going underground

Cenotes comprise a unique system of fresh-water sinkholes found throughout the Yucatán peninsula. Deeply associated with the area's ancient Maya culture, they served as the main source of water and as a place of ritual ceremony for the Maya, and artefacts and human remains dating back thousands of years have been discovered within many of them.

Modern divers have explored around 350 miles of the peninsula's interconnected passageways, and cenotes have become a popular tourist attraction for obvious reasons. Where else can you swim, snorkel or dive through crystal waters in limestone halls of stalactites and stalagmites; glide underground with bats sleeping overhead; or press through open-air mangrove channels with eerie roots reaching into the turquoise water?

Sadly, increased tourism is taking its toll, with pollutants detected in the waters and linked to seepage from developed areas. Swimmers wearing sunscreens, repellents and lotions also affect pH levels, so it's essential to refrain from applying such products before diving, or from touching the delicate, exquisite rock formations.

The **Cenote Dive Center** (see p233) runs tours that take you deep inside the geological marvel.

Best of Mexico

Getting there & around

By bus
Inexpensive *combis* run from Playa del Carmen to Tulúm and all the way back to Cancún.

By car
Renting a car is a very good idea on the Riviera Maya, since it opens up the possibility of side trips – the colonial town of Valladolid, for example, or the ruins at Coba. In Tulúm, Executive (Carretera 307 km 232, 984 802 5371, www.executive.com.mx) rent jeeps from around MX$650 per day, and scooters from MX$300.

Along the Riviera Maya

The coast between Cancún and Tulúm is studded with a growing number of plush all-inclusive beach resorts and deluxe hotels. If you're good for the lavish rates they charge, some of the standouts are the **Mandarin Oriental Riviera Maya** (Carretera 307 km 299, 984 877 3888, www.mandarinoriental.com, doubles from MX$5,270) and **Esencia** (Carretera 307, 20min south of Playa del Carmen,

984 873 4835, www.hotelesencia.com, doubles from MX$5,775). The latter is a chic white dream of a beachside spa hotel in a 50-acre estate at Xpu-Ha. It specialises in deluxe organic facial and body treatments and the science of deluxe restfulness – there's nothing to do here but soak up the flawless surroundings.

Xel-Ha and **Xcaret** are a pair of water-themed adventure parks that celebrate the rich flora and fauna of the peninsula in a very hands-on way. Excellent fun for children and adults, Xcaret is the larger and more action-packed, while Xel-Ha has a more natural feel.

Xcaret
Carretera 307, 6km south of Playa del Carmen (998 883 0470/www.xcaret.com). **Open** *Summer* 8.30am-10pm. *Winter* 8.30am-9pm. **Admission** MX$730; MX$365 children; 10% discount when booking online. **Credit** AmEx, MC, V.

Xel-Ha
Chetumal-Cancún highway km 240 (998 884 7165/ www.xelha.com). **Open** 8.30am-6pm. **Admission** MX$795; MX$530 children. **Credit** MC, V.

Directory

Directory

Getting There & Around

Arriving & leaving

The Metro (underground train) system serves **Benito Juárez International Airport** (Terminal Aérea L5) and major bus stations, but it's best avoided if you are laden with luggage or passing through late at night. Take an authorised taxi from your arrival airport or bus station for a safe and relaxing start to your trip to DF (Distrito Federal), as Mexico City proper is also called.

By air

Aeropuerto Internacional Benito Juárez

Capitán Carlos León s/n, Peñon de los Baños (Terminal 1 2482 2424/ Terminal 2 2598 7000/www.aicm. com.mx). Metro Terminal Aérea L5. Mexico City's airport, known by the acronym AICM and located close to the highway exit to Puebla, comprises two terminals, both of which serve international and domestic flights. The new Terminal 2, opened in 2008, is connected to Terminal 1 by an Airtram. Check your arrival terminal in advance to avoid possible mishaps if you are arranging for someone to meet you there. A phalanx of keen porters gathers round each exit ready to assist you with your luggage; consider contracting their services if you have lots of bags, since travellers are required to leave trolleys at the exit to customs. The service is free of charge, but you are expected to give a tip: between MX$10 and MX$20 per bag is the norm. Getting to and from the city's central *colonias* (neighbourhoods) can take as little as 20 minutes, but give yourself plenty of time as traffic is unpredictable. At rush hour (7.30-9.30am and 5.30-8pm), the same trip can take 60 minutes or more. Budget travellers are using Toluca airport, located in the eponymous neighbouring city, in increasing numbers. Most low-cost flights operate from Toluca, with

airlines providing buses to and from Mexico City. For advice on coping with lost or mislaid baggage, *see p244.*

Airlines

Aeroméxico *01800 021 4010/ www.aeromexico.com.*
Air Canada *5208 1883/ www.aircanada.com.*
Air France *01800 123 46 60/ www.airfrance.com.mx.*
American Airlines *5209 1400/ www.aa.com.*
British Airways *5387 0300/ www.ba.com.*
Continental *5283 5500/ www.continental.com.*
Delta Air Lines *5279 0909/ www.delta.com.*
Iberia *1101 1515/ www.iberia.com/mx.*
KLM *5279 5390/www.klm.com.*
Lufthansa *5230 0000/ www.lufthansa.com.*
Mexicana *5448 0909/ www.mexicana.com.*
Northwest Airlines *5202 4444/ www.nwa.com.*
United Airlines *5627 0222/ www.united.com.*
US Airways *001 800 428 4322/ www.usairlines.com.*

By road

Heavy traffic and other drivers' often cavalier attitudes towards the rules of the road make driving in Mexico an intimidating option. If you decide to drive from the airport, car rental companies can help you navigate to your destination. The airport is located just off the **Circuito Interior** ring road. In most cases, Viaducto will be your best bet to get into the city centre, and it is reached by heading south on the Circuito and taking a left-hand turn.

Public transport

Like Los Angeles, DF is a drivers' city – at least for

those who can afford a car. Deep-seated snobbery means that most affluent *chilangos* – Mexico City natives – wouldn't be seen dead on the Metro, let alone on a *pesero* or *micro*, the green-and-grey minibuses shuttling students, workers and other low-income residents around the metropolis. Contrary to what well-heeled locals would have you believe, however, DF's public transport is mostly reliable, efficient and safe, provided you take basic precautions. The local government is expanding the network, with extensions of the Metro, Metrobús and tram services in progress.

Buses

The bendy buses of the **Metrobús** system run along a central stretch of Avenida Insurgentes in a dedicated lane connecting far-flung neighbourhoods with the Metro network. Tickets cost MX$4.50 per journey and can be bought from smartcard machines inside the station stops. A second line under construction in 2008 on Eje 4 Sur will connect Metro Tacubaya with Metrobús Nuevo León. Another eight routes are scheduled to criss-cross DF by 2012.

Minibuses (*peseros* or *micros*) cover all corners of the capital, but the system – operated by private drivers – is byzantine. There is no central information service to explain routes or timetables. Check the front of the bus or ask your hotel for advice (although staff may be reluctant to let tourists

Directory

loose on the network). Single trips cost MX$2.5 to MX$5 depending on the distance. Government-run RTP bus services (www.rtp.gob.mx/red_rutas.htm) are less confusing, but it is still easier and quicker to travel by Metro or Metrobús for *colonias* featured in this book. Route taxis, known as *colectivos*, operate from the same Metro station and charge MX$25 for the same trip. In 2008 the DF government launched women-only RTP routes running along Reforma (Santa Fe–La Villa) and Eje Central Lázaro Cárdenas (Salto del Agua–Reclusorio del Norte) during peak hours (6-9am and 6-9pm). Single journeys on RTP buses cost MX$2. Pay the driver, ideally with coins as drivers are often short of change. For lost property, see p244.

Coaches

Inter-city *camiones* (coaches) are a cheap, convenient and comfortable way to travel. Four main bus terminals, served by private bus companies, connect the capital with the rest of the country. Luxury and first-class *(primera clase)* services offer reclining seats and lots of leg-room. A *primera clase* return ticket from DF to Oaxaca will cost around MX$770. Good companies include luxury line **ETN** (5089 9200/www.etn.com.mx); **Estrella Blanca** (5729 0725/www.estrella blanca.com.mx); **Flecha Amarilla** (5587 5200/www.flecha-amarilla.com); **ADO** (5785 9659/www.ado.com.mx) and **Ómnibus de México** (5567 6756/www.odm.com.mx).

Terminal Central del Norte
Eje Central Lázaro Cárdenas 4907, Magdalena de las Salinas (5587 1552/www.centraldelnorte.com.mx). Metro Autobuses del Norte L5.

Catch a bus from DF's northern terminal for Teotihuacán, Querétaro, Guanajuato, Zacatecas, San Miguel de Allende and northern cities.

Terminal Central del Sur
Avenida Tasqueña 1320, Campestre Churubusco (5336 2321). Metro Tasqueña L2.
Colloquially known as Terminal Tasqueña, this station offers south-bound services taking holidaymakers to Acapulco and Taxco.

Terminal Oriente (TAPO)
Calzada Ignacio Zaragoza 200, 10 de Mayo (5784 3077). Metro San Lázaro L1, LB.
TAPO is your eastern Mexico City departure point for travel to Oaxaca and the Yucatán peninsula.

Terminal Poniente
Avenida Sur 122, Real del Monte (5212 8816). Metro Observatorio L1.
Terminal with coach services to western destinations.

Ticketbus – Zócalo
Local CM-25, Zócalo Metro station, Centro (5133 2424/www.ticketbus.com.mx). Metro Zócalo L2.
Map p267 M4.
Tickets for the main coach operators can be booked through Ticketbus over the phone (you'll need some Spanish), online, or via agents distributed around DF. This central agency is located inside the Zócalo Metro station, close to the exit for Palacio Nacional.

Metro

The Metro network is rapid, clean, easy to navigate and extensive enough to reach most places of interest. People tend to refer to the different lines by their colours rather than their numbers, so it's handy to note that there are two lines in slightly differing shades of green. Single journeys cost MX$2, available as either paper tickets or rechargeable smartcards. Expect buskers to provide a salsa soundtrack to your journey, and to be approached by *ambulantes* (hawkers peddling anything from pirate CDs and confectionery to pens and kitchen utensils).

A new line – Line 12 – is scheduled to open before the end of 2010. Running between Mixcoac and Tláhuac, it will link Buenavista with the second Metrobús route being constructed on Eje 4 Sur (Xola).

Trams

Electric trams – *trolebuses* – operate on other central avenues, carrying commuters from the capital's poorer areas and state university campuses to the Metro's main hubs (www.ste.df.gob.mx). Pay the driver between MX$2.5 and MX$5 depending on distance. A modern tram network – *tranvía* – is planned for the Centro Histórico. Its 32 stations will connect Buenavista with Pino Suárez.

Rail

Passenger trains are extremely rare in Mexico: the last inter-city services stopped running in 1997. A light railway connects southern DF with the floating neighbourhood of Xochimilco. The new **Tren Suburbano de la Zona Metropolitana del Valle de México** opened in June 2008, linking Estado de México's Cuatitlán (Edomex) to the north with central Buenavista. Tickets for the Tren Suburbano cost MX$5.50 for journeys between three stations, and MX$12.50 for four or more. Plans are in place for two additional suburban services.

Driving

Driving in Mexico City can be a hair-raising experience. Stick to public transport or taxis if you are a nervous or easily rattled driver. Road surfaces are generally good in the capital's main *colonias*, but tarmac takes a battering during the rainy season, producing potholes. The drivers' bible in Mexico is the *Guia Roji*, an A-Z available from newsstands and branches of Sanborns. It can also be consulted online (www.guiaroji.com.mx).

Speed limits are generally 40 kilometres per hour (25 miles per hour) within cities and 110 kilometres per hour (68 miles per hour) on highways – but these are rarely observed. Local drivers change lanes without indicating and regularly ignore traffic lights, particularly at weekends when traffic is lighter. During rush hour, brigades of police randomly direct traffic, adding to congestion instead of facilitating the flow of DF's automobiles. Since September 2008, local authorities have banned private vehicles with foreign plates from driving in the Zona Metropolitana (DF and part of Edomex) between 5am and 11am on weekdays as part of broader efforts to cut congestion and pollution (www.sma.df.gob.mx). Avoid driving on Friday afternoons when *chilangos* head out of the city en masse. Roads are even more congested on *viernes quincenas*, Mexico's fortnightly paydays.

Corruption is endemic within Mexico's transit police, so don't be surprised if you are pulled over for a bogus offence. Make sure you carry a valid driving licence and photocopies of your passport, tourist card or visa, and other important documents with you at all times. Keep the originals in a safe place. Drink driving is illegal but socially acceptable in some circles, adding to risks on the roads. Police pulling over individuals found to be driving under the influence have been known to accept small bribes in exchange for letting the suspect off.

Taxi tips

Cabs are cheap and ubiquitous, but visitors should take taxis from registered ranks or *sitios* instead of hailing cars on the street. Serious crimes, including kidnappings, have been linked to 'pirate' (*pirata*) taxis, and even to some registered roaming ones. Street taxis are usually either green Volkswagen beetles or white saloon cars with red side-bars, although some *sitio* taxis look the same. A gold-and-wine livery is the latest colour code for authorised taxis. To avoid confusion and associated risks, catch or call a cab from one of the official bases that are widely distributed around the city. Official taxi number plates start with 'A –' or 'B –' followed by the usual six characters.

Always carry the telephone number of a reputable radio taxi firm with you. Most *sitio* taxis charge using a meter, plus an initial MX$20 hire fee to *bajar la bandera* or 'take down the flag'. Some taxi drivers speak English (mainly those who have lived in the US), but few telephone operators do. Your hotel should happily order you a car even if you call the reception from elsewhere to ask for help. Insist that they ring one of the companies listed below instead of a hideously overpriced tourist taxi or private car. Ask the concierge to make a note of the taxi's *número de la unidad*, usually a two-digit number that you can subsequently check for on the front windscreen. It's a good way to be sure of getting into the right vehicle.

Chilangos have learned to be security conscious, and they take the safety of foreign visitors very seriously. If you do decide to take a street taxi, make sure you check for official plates and ensure that they match the licence numbers displayed on the side of the car and on both windscreens. You should also ask to see the driver's *tarjetón*, which is his or her official registration with the local government. Carry small notes and coins as taxis usually provide minimal change. Taxi drivers don't have 'the knowledge' of all DF's streets; even addresses in touristy areas sometimes elicit a furrowed brow. Street taxi drivers will usually rely on their passenger to give them directions – another reason why they should be avoided. *Sitio* cabs tend to carry a *Guia Roji* streetmap to help you get to your destination even if the driver doesn't know the way. It's worth carrying a map with your hotel marked on it just in case.

Taxi Radio Unión *5514 8124*
Taxi Sitio Durango *5514 2700*
PROEM (run by women, for female passengers only) *5597 2573*
Servitaxi *5516 6020*

Omega Cars *5714 1919*
Servicio Ejecutivo Ciudad Santa Fe *2167 4280/2167 4281*
These are executive – unmarked – cars charging by distance instead of by meter. You can save yourself a lot of cash if you get stuck in traffic, but make sure you agree on a rate before you set off. Ask for the vehicle model and the name of the driver when booking so you know who to expect.

Directory

Lock the car doors as soon as you get in and avoid opening windows, particularly when passing through poorer neighbourhoods. Car-jacking isn't common, but it happens. Try to leave a gap behind other vehicles when waiting in traffic to facilitate a getaway. Use toll (*cuota*) instead of free (*libre*) roads when driving further afield as the former tend to be safer. It's a pricey way to travel, however: each booth (*caseta*) charges between MX$25 and MX$150. A round-trip to Acapulco from DF by car would set you back MX$900 in tolls alone (2008 rates). Toll charges must be paid in cash (Mexican pesos only).

Australian, Canadian, US and UK driving licences are all valid. You can also use international driving permits (IDP – www.international-license.com). Mexican authorities strictly regulate the entry of vehicles into the country. Don't be tempted to borrow a friend's car unless the owner is going to be inside the vehicle with you at all times, or you'll run the risk of the car being impounded by customs. If you are driving across the border, you'll need to purchase the prerequisite insurance locally. Neither US nor Canadian policies are valid. That said, many Mexican drivers are uninsured, escaping detection with the habitual *mordida* (bribe). This merely increases your need for comprehensive cover.

Breakdown services

SECTUR's Corporación Ángeles Verdes

Information 3002 6300 ext 8987 or 8989/24hr toll-free 01800 987 8224. **Open** service available between 8am-8pm; 24hr in case of emergency. Mexico's Tourism Secretariat (SECTUR) provides the Angeles Verdes (Green Angels) free highway patrol service on all major toll

highways for trips outside or on the outskirts of the capital. Mechanics speak English and Spanish and can fix your car for a small fee. It is customary to tip the driver (MX$50-$100 is about right).

Vehicle hire

Most international car rental companies have a presence in DF. Mexican insurance *must* be purchased. Take out the most comprehensive policy available. You must be 21 to hire a vehicle, and rates are higher for under-25s. Rentals can be reserved in advance via your travel agent, with online agents offering the most competitive rates (www.holidayautos.co.uk or www.expedia.com). All hire firms listed below have offices at the international airport.

Alamo

Unit 19-B, International Arrivals, AICM (5786 9214/5786 8099/ www.alamo-mexico.com.mx). Metro Terminal Aérea L5. **Open** 24hrs daily. **Credit** AmEx, MC, V. Ubiquitous international rental agency with a good range of well-maintained vehicles. Book online with a travel agency for the best rates or check the Alamo website for special offers.

AVIS

Hotel Presidente Intercontinental, Campos Elíseos 218, Polanco (5327 7700 ext 2847/US international reservations 1 800 331 1084/Mexico 01800 288 8888 /www.avis.com.mx). Metro Auditorio L7. **Open** 7am-10pm Mon-Fri; 8am-4pm Sat, Sun. **Credit** AmEx, MC, V. **Map** p262 B5. Large fleet with a good range of pricing options. English-language operators available on Mexican reservation line. Additional services available include GPS, and car-seat rental for babies and infants. Offices across the country with eight outlets in DF alone.

Budget

Hotel Nikko, Campos Elíseos 204, Polanco (5280 8974/www. budget.com.mx). Metro Auditorio L7. **Open** 7am-9pm Mon-Fri; 8am-4pm Sat, Sun. **Credit** AmEx, MC, V. **Map** p262 C5. With branches across the country, including in smaller cities like

Zacatecas, Budget offers good-value rentals and an efficient service for drivers.

Hertz

AICM, Avenida 602 (5784 7400/ www.hertz.com). Metro Terminal Aérea L5. **Open** 24hrs daily. **Credit** AmEx, MC, V. One of the cheapest rental options in Mexico. Car seats are available for babies and young children.

Parking

Car crime is common in DF. To reduce risks, try to use official car parks (*pensiones* or *estacionamientos*) or the valet service provided by most bars and restaurants.

Cycling

Terrifying traffic, fear of crime and the tyranny of the car have traditionally stopped *chilangos* from getting on their bikes. Yet cycle-friendly policies are gradually coming into force – an essential development in light of DF's pollution problems. Paseo de la Reforma is closed to motor transport on Sunday mornings to encourage outdoor activity. Cycle paths are starting to cut across central *colonias* – an encouraging sign. Buses on 15 local routes now boast cycle racks. Metro passengers are permitted to travel with their bikes on Sundays and bank holidays (between 7am and noon).

Walking

Walking is not in the lexicon of most *chilangos*. Massive thoroughfares and horrendous traffic can make meandering between *colonias* stressful, not to mention unhealthy. The Centro, tree-lined Roma and Condesa and San Ángel and Coyoacán are best for committed pedestrians. Central DF is largely flat, but the altitude and pollution can tire you out. For maps, *see pp257-268*.

Directory

Resources A-Z

Addresses

Addresses are written with the street name first, followed by the building number, sometimes the floor (*piso*) and either the flat (*departamento*) or office (*oficina*) number. For ease of reference, we have rendered all addresses in this guidebook in standard English style.

Age restrictions

You must be over 18 to drive or buy cigarettes or alcohol. An individual stops being a minor at 18, the age at which there are no restrictions on consensual sexual activity. In some states, marriage is legal from age 12 and sex is classed as consensual for heterosexuals of this age, if married. The homosexual age of consent varies by state law, which tends to override federal law, but it is never lower than 18.

Attitude & etiquette

Mexicans are characteristically courteous: saying 'please' (*por favor*) and 'thank you' (*gracias*) goes a long way.

Leave expectations of punctuality at the airport: arrival 30 minutes late for an appointment is considered no big deal. Even a one-hour delay is perfectly acceptable provided it is accompanied by a flurry of apologies and (always plausible) excuses about the traffic.

Business

Conventions & conferences

Hotels are the best venues for conferences and other large-scale business events. Most of the international and domestic chains offer excellent, modern facilities. *See pp35-50.*

Couriers & shippers

Ciclos Mensajeros
(5516 3984/www.ciclosmensajeros. com). **Open** 8am-7pm Mon-Fri (Sat service available if booked on Fri). **No credit cards.**
Rapid courier service within DF and the metropolitan area.

Toda la Mensajería
Ground floor, Mártires de la Conquista 111, Escandón (5276 4600/5276 4601/www.todala mensajeria.com.mx).

Local, national and international courier and postal service. Collection available from anywhere in DF.

Office services

Big Office
Aniceto Ortega 817, Del Valle (5575 6204/www.bigoffice.com.mx). Metro División del Norte L3/Metrobús Parque Hundido. **Open** 24hrs daily. **Credit** MC, V.
Professional pay-as-you-go office rental, with secretarial and IT assistance available (9am-7pm).

Regus International Offices Worldwide
1st floor, Avenida Presidente Masaryk 111, Polanco (3300 5800/ 3300 5999/www.regus.com). Metro Polanco L7. **Open** 8.30am-7pm Mon-Fri. **Credit** AmEx, MC, V. **Map** p262 D4.
Business facilities and executive suites from this global supplier of serviced offices.

Translators

Servitrans
Fuente Bella 79, Rincón del Pedregal (5135 1763/www.servitrans.com.mx). Metro Barranca del Muerto L7. **Open** 9am-6pm Mon-Fri. **Credit** AmEx, MC, V.
Full-service translation agency offering interpreters for conferences.

Useful organisations

American Chamber of Commerce, Mexico (AmCham)
Lucerna 78, Cuauhtémoc (5141 3800/www.amcham.com.mx). Metro Insurgentes L1/Metrobús Insurgentes. **Open** by appointment only 9am-6pm. **Map** p265 I5.
Mexico's largest bilateral business organisation.

British–Mexican Chamber of Commerce
Río de la Plata 30, Cuauhtémoc (5256 0901/www.britchamexico. com). Metro Chapultepec L1 or Sevilla L1/Metrobús Reforma. **Open** by appointment only 9am-6pm. **Map** p264 F5.
Promotes trade and investment between the UK and Mexico through business breakfasts and other networking events.

Travel advice

Contact your home country's foreign affairs department for current travel advice and information on safety, security and health issues as well as information on local customs and legal requirements. They also track weather systems – useful if you are planning a trip to the Gulf of Mexico or nearby areas during hurricane season.

Australia
www.smartraveller.gov.au

Canada
www.voyage.gc.ca

New Zealand
www.safetravel.govt.nz

Republic of Ireland
http://foreignaffairs.gov.ie

UK
www.fco.gov.uk/travel

USA
www.state.gov/travel

Consumer

The Procuraduría Federal del Consumidor (PROFECO) is dedicated to addressing consumer complaints. Foreigners are better off seeking assistance from SECTUR (*see p243*).

Customs

Visitors can only bring in personal items of clothing, shoes and toiletries in quantities proportionate to the length of their stay in Mexico. A computerised random search system at the airport determines whether your bags will be checked. An individual is only permitted to bring in US$1,000 worth of personal effects – any more and they must pay duties. An additional US$300 goods allowance is granted to those entering by sea or air (US$50 for those arriving overland).

Disabled

Mexico's capital is not yet disabled friendly: higgledy-piggledy pavements and potholes are the norm. Wheelchair ramps are randomly distributed, but 100,000 more were planned for completion on DF's streets in 2008.

The airport is fitted with ramps and lifts. Wheelchairs are available from airlines, which should be advised of any other special requirements before travel. Metro carriages include seats reserved for travellers with disabilities, and guide dogs are allowed. The Metrobús is accessible for those with disabilities.

Drugs

Mexico's Felipe Calderón government is cracking down hard on the illegal drug trade. This is fuelling an upsurge in drug-related gang and cartel violence which occasionally touches Mexico City but, contained for the most part between *narcos* and the authorities, rarely has any impact on tourists. Drug offences of all kinds carry severe penalties, including jail terms of up to 25 years.

Electricity

DF's standard current is 110v, although this varies elsewhere in Mexico. Power cuts occur periodically, mainly in the rainy season, so pack a torch (flashlight).

Embassies & consulates

Australian Embassy *Rubén Darío 55, Polanco (1101 2200/ www.mexico.embassy.gov.au). Metro Auditorio L7.* **Open** 8.30am-5.15pm Mon-Fri. **Map** p262 D5.

British Embassy *Río Lerma 71, Cuauhtémoc (5242 8500/www.embajadabritanica.com.mx). Metro Sevilla L1/Metrobús Reforma.* **Open** 8.30am-1pm Mon-Thur, 8.30am-11.30pm Fri. Collection of documents 3-4pm Mon-Thur. **Map** p264 G6.

Canadian Embassy *Schiller 529, Polanco (5724 7900/consular service for Canadians 5724 7900/www.canadainternational.gc.ca/mexico-mexique). Metro Polanco L7.* **Open** *General* 8.45am-5.15pm Mon-Fri. *Consular services* 9am-12.30pm, 2-4pm Mon-Fri. *Notarial services* 9-10.30am Mon-Fri. **Map** p262 D5.

Irish Embassy *3rd floor, Boulevard Ávila Camacho 76, Lomas de Chapultepec (5520 5803/ 5520 5892). Metro Auditorio L7 then taxi.* **Open** 8.30am-1pm, 2.30-4pm Mon-Fri.

New Zealand Embassy *4th floor, Jaime Balmes 8, Polanco (5283 9460/www.nzembassy.com/mexico). Metro Polanco L7.* **Open** 8.30am-2pm, 3-5.30pm Mon-Thur; 8.30am-2pm Fri.

US Embassy *Paseo de la Reforma 305, Cuauhtémoc (5080 2000/ext 4326 for US citizens/http://mexico.usembassy.gov/eng/main.html). Metro Sevilla L1/Metrobús Reforma.* **Open** *US Citizens Passport, Citizenship and Notaries Unit* 8-10.30am Mon-Fri. *Consular Services* 8.30am-5pm. *Non-US citizens* by appointment only; make appointment at visa call centre 7am-9pm Mon-Fri; 9am-3pm Sat, Sun. **Map** p264 G5.

Emergencies

Emergency services

060 is Mexico's version of 999 or 911. It functions on a national level. Local numbers (*see below*) can get you in touch with the necessary service more swiftly.

24-hour emergency services in DF

Police
066.

Judicial police/ Emergency line for tourists in DF
061 (for reporting a crime).

Fire service
068/5768 3477.

Red Cross
065/5395 1111 (Cruz Roja – free ambulance service).

Gay & lesbian

Same-sex civil partnerships are legal in Mexico City, but attitudes towards homosexuality run the gamut from extremely conservative to unabashedly liberal. Unless you are walking the gay-friendly streets of Zona Rosa, it is safest to avoid public displays of affection. For information on HIV/AIDS services, *see p243*.

Fundación de Ayuda a la Diversidad Sexual

2nd floor, Avenida Insurgentes Sur 771, Roma (1450 9511). Metro Insurgentes L1. **Open** 2-10pm Mon-Fri; 2-8pm Sat, Sun.
An NGO providing comprehensive advice to lesbian, gay, bisexual and transgender (LGBT) people in Mexico. Legal counsel available. English-speaking advisors can be made available, but you may have to wait or call back at an agreed time.

Gay Mexico

www.gaymexico.com.mx
Bilingual resource with up-to-date tips on where to find fun in DF – and beyond – as well as how to avoid unnecessary risks.

Directory

Gay Pride Committee

www.marchalgbt.com
News and events for LGBT community across Mexico (Spanish only) from an organisation that has grown around the annual Gay Pride March (see p161).

Health

General tips

Contact your doctor or travel clinic at least six weeks in advance of travelling in case vaccinations are required. GPs usually recommend jabs against hepatitis A, tetanus and typhoid. Immunisation against blood-borne hepatitis B is optional for tourists but a prerequisite for health workers. Travellers visiting rural areas should consider getting a rabies shot. Avoid drinking tap water. Pharmacy staff are not qualified to give medical advice.

Air quality & altitude sickness

Air pollution, combined with the dry atmosphere and high altitude (2,240 metres), can contribute to breathing problems and is a particular issue for asthma sufferers. It can also cause minor eye irritation and dryness. Mild altitude sickness occasionally strikes visitors to DF. Symptoms include headache, nausea, shortness of breath and lethargy. Give yourself a few days before attempting to ascend to higher elevations in the surrounding mountains or volcanoes. Above 3,000 metres, acute mountain sickness (AMS) is possible. Physical warning signs are similar but more severe, and include insomnia and lack of appetite. Risks can be diminished by a gradual ascent; by avoiding dehydration; and by eating light, carbohydrate-rich meals.

You'll need to drink more water than you'd probably imagine at these heights, despite the cool temperatures. The air is dry and your body will have to work harder to compensate for lower oxygen levels. If you suspect AMS, descend at least 600 to 900 metres and you should start to feel better. Seek medical attention if you are in any doubt.

Accident & emergency

Go directly to the **Urgencias** department of your nearest hospital. If an ambulance is required, call the **Cruz Roja** (065). Its paramedics know all of DF's hospitals and can take you to the closest facilities free of charge. Private hospitals offer their own emergency services (charges apply).

Angeles Clínica Londres *Durango 50, Roma (5229 8400, emergency ext 4). Metro Cuauhtémoc L1 or Insurgentes L1/Metrobús Insurgentes.* **Map** p265 I6.

Centro Médico ABC *Avenida Carlos Graef Fernández 154, Santa Fe (emergency 1103 1666/ information 1103 1600/www. abchospital.com). No public transport; take a taxi.*

Hospital Español *Ejército Nacional 613, Granada (emergency 5255 9645/information 5255 9600/www.hespanol.com). Metro Auditorio L7 or Polanco L7, then taxi.* **Map** p262 B3.

Hospital Metropolitano *Tlacotalpan 51, Roma (5265 1900/emergency ext 1801 or 1802). Metro Chilpancingo L9/Metrobús Chilpancingo.* **Map** p264 G9.

Hospital Santa Fé *San Luis Potosí 143, Roma (switchboard 1084 4733, emergency ext 1/www.hospitalsantafe.com.mx/ www.starmedica.com). Metro Insurgentes L1/Metrobús Alvaro Obregón or Sonora.* **Map** p264 H8.

Complementary medicine

For some recommended multi-disciplinary clinics, see p151.

Contraception & abortion

Mexican pharmacies stock condoms (*condones*). The contraceptive pill (*la píldora*) can also be purchased if you mislay your own packet: consult a doctor to identify a compatible local brand. Emergency contraception (*la píldora del día siguiente* or *anticoncepción de emergencia*) is also sold legally. Available brands include Glanique, Postday, Neogynon and Ovral. It is important to seek medical advice before taking any of the above to avoid possible complications and incorrect dosage. Early-term abortion is permitted in DF alone. On-request terminations are available during the first 12 weeks of pregnancy.

Dentists

Dentists tend to work from their own surgeries rather than in larger clinics. Health tourism has led to a boom in English-speaking dentists. These are more common along the US border and in coastal resorts, but you'll still find high-quality, cost-effective services in DF.

Drs Saul and Roberto Rotberg *Consultorio 104, Ejército Nacional 650, Polanco (5531 8839). Metro Polanco L7.* **Open** 4-7pm Mon-Fri. **No credit cards.** **Map** p262 B3.

Dr Victor Zfaz *Consultorio 101, Paseo de las Palmas 830, Lomas de Chapultepec (5540 6767/ 5540 6655). Metro Auditorio L7, then taxi.* **Open** 9am-2pm, 4-7pm Mon-Thur; 9am-5pm Fri. **No credit cards.**

Doctors/hospitals

Hospital Santa Fé has a consultancy tower where general practitioners (*medicina general* or *medicina interna*) conduct out-patient appointments. GPs' surgeries are often located within larger health clinics such as Clínica

Londres. Your hotel, embassy or the SECTUR helpline (*see below*) can recommend specific practitioners. Some large hotels offer access to an on-call doctor.

Opticians

See p152.

Pharmacies

See p152.

STDs, HIV & AIDS

In 2006, a UN/WHO working group estimated that around 180,000 Mexicans aged 15 and over were living with HIV. The prevalence of the virus within the adult population (0.3 per cent) is marginally higher than that of the UK (0.2 per cent).

AMSAVIH

4th floor, Río Nazas 135, Cuauhtémoc (5525 7417/www. amsavih.org). Metro Sevilla L1 or Insurgentes L1. **Open** appointments 10am-1pm Tue, Thu, Sat; 5-8pm Mon-Fri. **Map** p263 G5.
Sexual-health information and related medical and psychological support to help avoid and detect HIV infections. Staff includes English speakers.

Helplines

Acercatel

Freephone 24hr helpline 01800 110 1010/www.casa-alianzamexico.org.
A 24-hour telephone hotline providing information and emotional support for young people in crisis. English-language speakers can be made available, although you may have to arrange a time to call back.

Alcoholics Anonymous

5662 2225/044 55 5431 6706/ www.aamexico.org. **Open** 5-6pm Sun (Roma branch). Call for details of other locations.
Regular English-language meetings take place at venues across the city.

Mexico City Tourism Secretariat

01800 0089090/www.mexicocity. gob.mx.
Comprehensive services from DF's tourism ministry include medical and legal advice.

SECTUR

078/01800 987 8224/www.sectur. gob.mx.
Mexico's federal tourist agency offers a 24-hour helpline, 365 days a year. Aside from comprehensive travel information, it can put you in contact with hospitals and the Red Cross (Cruz Roja) and give advice on immigration services and legal issues.

ID

Mexicans are required by law to carry their national photo identification (*credencial*) with them at all times. Visitors should follow suit, preferably sporting a photo driving licence and a photocopy of their passport. DF's bars and clubs are under pressure to stop under-age drinking and businesses face severe fines if found to be breaking these laws. Very occasionally bars will demand to see the official document, but it's not worth carrying around your original passport on the off chance. Official ID is required to enter public buildings.

Insurance

Do not travel to Mexico without a comprehensive travel insurance policy. It makes sense to protect your possessions from the capital's high crime rates and save your body from a stay in a public hospital.

Internet

Mexico City is replete with places to surf the web. Internet cafés are abundant and many coffee shops and bars offer free wireless access. Online connections and local websites are generally reliable except in the event of periodic power cuts.

Language

Spanish is Mexico's official language. English is widely spoken in hotels, shops and restaurants, but a basic grasp of Spanish will be a big help, particularly if you plan to stray from the typical tourist circuit. Only two per cent of *chilangos* can communicate in indigenous dialects. For language tips and vocabulary, *see p250.*

Left luggage

Mexico City's airport and main bus terminals offer left-luggage facilities. Most hotels will look after your bags for you after check-out if you aren't moving on until later that day.

Legal help

If you get in trouble with the law, the SECTUR helpline (*see above*) can also help with emergency legal matters. Local authorities are obliged to contact your consulate or embassy (*see p241*) in the event that you are taken into custody. Your diplomatic representative can furnish you with a list of approved English-speaking lawyers.

Libraries

Benjamin Franklin Library

Liverpool 31, Juárez (5080 2089/ http://mexico.usembassy.gov/eng/ library.html). Metro Cuauhtémoc L1. **Open** 11am-7pm Mon-Fri. **Map** p265 I5.
The mission of the Benjamin Franklin Library, inaugurated in 1942, is 'to promote friendship and understanding between Mexico and the United States by providing access to information on their bilateral relationship'.

Biblioteca Nacional de México

Centro Cultural Universitario, Coyoacán (5622 6800/http:// biblional.bibliog.unam.mx/bib/ biblioteca.html). Metro Universidad L3. **Open** 9am-8pm Mon-Fri.
Mexico's largest library, the Biblioteca Nacional, holds over 1,250,000 books and documents. The reference library, housed in an iconic building within the UNAM's

Directory

main campus, is open to the public. The collection includes books in English, French and Italian.

British Public Library at the Anglo Mexican Foundation (TAMF)

Antonio Caso 127, San Rafael (3067 8817). Metro San Cosme L2. **Open** 8.30am-7.30pm Mon-Fri; 10am-4pm Sat. **Map** p263 G4.

The TAMF library is doubly special: Mexico's only lending library also boasts the biggest selection of English-language books available for reference anywhere in the country. The library includes a pleasant children's collection and reading area.

Lost property

The airport's lost property department (Oficina de Objetos Perdidos, 2482 2289) is found in the lobby area of Terminal 1. To reclaim luggage you must describe its contents and where it was misplaced – you must also show your ID and boarding pass. Contact Metrobús customer services if you have mislaid an object on their network (5th floor, Avenida Cuauhtémoc 16, Doctores, 5761 6870 ext 121). The Metro's Oficina de Objetos Extraviados (5627 4643) is located on the ground floor at Metro Candelaria. Assistance in locating property left behind on the *trolebús* or Tren Ligero (5539 2800) is provided by their respective customer service offices. If you leave something in a cab, call the main number for the taxi firm. The operator will then send a radio message to all drivers with the aim of locating your property.

Media

Magazines

Inside Mexico *www.insidemex.com* This is a colourful monthly magazine enlightening English-speaking expats and visitors about the marvels and challenges of living in Mexico.

Vista *www.mexperience.com* E-magazine available from Mexperience which covers real estate and travel.

Newspapers

Excélsior *www.exonline.com.mx* Serious yet ailing newspaper with falling distribution. Still good for international and political coverage. **La Jornada** *www.jornada. unam.mx/ultimas* Mexico's leading leftist paper is a good choice for arts and entertainment reviews and the other side of the political debate. **The News** *www.thenews.com.mx* Daily newspaper in English re-launched in 2008. Interesting columns and lifestyle stories, but it still relies heavily on wire services. **Reforma** *www.reforma.com* Conservative daily publishing a mix of strong investigative journalism and high-society stories. Website is subscription only. **El Universal** *www.eluniversal. com.mx* Centrist, hard-hitting paper with good all-round coverage.

Radio

Try **Ke-Buena** (92.9 FM/www.kebuena.com.mx) or **La Mejor** (102.5 FM/www.lamejor.com.mx) for top Latin tunes including salsa, *bandas norteñas* and *cumbia*. Classical music is best discovered at the Instituto Mexicano de la Radio (IMER)'s dedicated **Opus** station (94.5 FM/www.opus.imer.com.mx), or **Radio UNAM** (96.1 FM/www.radiounam.unam.mx) which also features programmes dedicated to traditional Mexican melodies. **Universal** fulfils your guilty penchant for soft-rock power ballads plus golden oldies in English from the 1960s, 70s and 80s (92.1 FM/www.universalstereo.com.mx).

Television

Canal 11 *www.oncetv.ipn.mx* Mexico's state-owned channel is the best for documentaries, political and educational coverage and foreign – often arthouse – films, shown with subtitles. You might get lucky and catch a classic movie in English.

Canal 22 *www.canal22.org.mx* Televisión Metropolitana is DF's state-owned cultural network, with high-brow programming. **CNN en Español** *www.cnn. com/espanol* The cable news channel's Spanish-language version is strong on national, regional and international coverage. Award-winning Mexican reporter Carmen Aristegui anchors the channel's weekday hard news programme. **Televisa** *www.televisa.com* Mexican media giant that runs four TV networks. Tune into Canal 2 – the channel of the stars (*canal de las estrellas*) – for news, low-brow entertainment, sport and *telenovelas* (Latin American soap operas). Mexico City's 4TV channel broadcasts local news and feature pieces plus dubbed foreign (mainly American) TV series. For domestic programming – child and youth friendly by day, adult oriented by night – try Canal 5. Spanish-language and dubbed films, *telenovelas* and sport, including *lucha libre* wrestling bouts, can be found on Canal 9. **TV Azteca** *www.tvazteca.com* This network competes with Televisa in the cheesy stakes. Azteca 7 and Azteca 13 both show a mix of news, sport, game shows and the essential *telenovelas*.

Cable & satellite

Comprehensive cable service is provided by Cablevisión (www.cablevision.net.mx), and satellite TV by Sky. Both offer a wide selection of domestic and international channels.

Money

After decades of monetary turbulence, the Mexican peso is now relatively stable. The main note denominations in circulation are the following: MX$20, MX$50, MX$100, MX$200 and MX$500. Try to use MX$500 bills in shops or restaurants when paying for relatively large sums. Stall holders and taxi drivers will rarely change anything greater than a MX$100 note. Coins come in denominations of 50 centavos, MX$1, MX$2, MX$5 and MX$10. Visa and MasterCard are accepted in most shops, bars and restaurants. Paying with AmEx is possible in most upmarket places. Very few shops accept travellers' cheques.

Banks & ATMs

The main banks in Mexico City are BBVA Bancomer, Scotiabank, Banamex, Banorte, HSBC and Ixe. There's an immense network of ATMs, with one found every few blocks. You'll be charged a handling fee (usually MX$7.5) by the dispensing bank in addition to charges at home (usually GBP2.50 in the UK and US$2 in the US). Unless you are with a local, avoid using ATMs late at night for security reasons.

Bureaux de change

Mexican currency exchange houses are known as *casas de cambio*. They generally offer better deals than banks. Official money changers at the airport offer some of the city's best rates. There are several on-site, so look for the most competitive offer.

Lost/stolen credit cards

American Express 5326 2522
MasterCard 001 800 307 7309
Visa 001 800 847 2911

Tax

Value-added tax (VAT – known in Spanish as IVA) is charged at 15 per cent on most goods in Mexico with the exception of food products and medicine. Tax is included in the ticket price, not added on at the point of sale. You'll pay IVA on drinks and meals in restaurants and bars. Hotels levy an additional two per cent state tax on top of the IVA, which is usually included in the quoted rate.

Natural hazards

Earthquakes

Seismic activity is an unavoidable reality in DF. Over 20,000 people died in the 1985 earthquake that measured 8.0 on the Richter scale. Since then, many buildings in well-heeled *colonias* have been reinforced to withstand tremors. The US Federal Emergency Management Agency (FEMA/ www.fema.gov/hazard/earthqu ake/eq_during.shtm) issues detailed advice on how to reduce risks in the event of an earthquake.

Mosquitoes

Mexico City is malaria free but dengue fever is a threat. Use insect repellent and, in the absence of bug screens, keep windows closed at night.

Rainy season

Torrential rains (most likely from May to October) can create hazardous driving conditions on roads that are treacherous enough at the best of times. Try to stay put until the downpour stops. Flooding occurs periodically. Few hotels are affected, although older buildings are more vulnerable to leaks.

Opening hours

Department stores tend to welcome customers from 11am to 9pm, sometimes with an extra hour either side. Hours are slightly reduced on Sundays. Most branches of Sanborns, however, open their doors at 7.30am every day and are still serving as late as 1am. Offices in the private sector are usually staffed on weekdays from 9am to 7pm (sometimes until 8pm or 9pm), with a two hour lunch taken from 2pm to 4pm or from 3pm to 5pm.

Local government workers are similarly available from 9am to 7pm (weekdays) with an equivalent lunch break. Most banks operate on a nine-to-five timetable on weekdays. HSBC opens on weekdays from 9am to 7pm. Post offices normally serve customers between 8.30am and 5pm on weekdays, and some branches are open at weekends.

Police

Security reforms approved in 2008 introduced sweeping changes to the criminal justice system. This could eventually change procedures for reporting a crime, but progress is expected to be slow. For now, you'll need to contact the **Ministerio Público** to file a police report on a crime that took place in the capital. Don't delay, especially in the case of ID theft: you'll need a Mexican police report to protect you from further repercussions should your identification be misused. There are three designated Ministerios Públicos in Mexico City (listed below) whose purpose is to assist tourists; they are known as Agencias del Ministerio Público Especializadas en Atención al Turista. Go to the Agencia closest to where the incident occurred and talk to an English-speaking official. Access to assistance in French, German, Italian and Japanese can also be arranged.

Centro Histórico

Calle Victoria 76, Centro (5346 8720/5346 8724, ext 16520). Metro Balderas L1, L3 or San Juan de Letrán L8. **Open** 24hrs daily. **Map** p266 K4

Reforma

Ground floor, Cámara Nacional de Comercio de la Ciudad de México (CANACO – Mexico City Chamber of Commerce), Paseo de la Reforma 42, Centro (3685 2269, ext 1009). Metro Juárez L3/Metrobús Reforma. **Open** 9am-5pm Mon-Fri. **Map** p266 J4.

Zona Rosa

Amberes 54, Zona Rosa (5345 5382). Metro Insurgentes/Metrobús Reforma. **Open** 9am-5pm Mon-Fri. **Map** p264 G6.

Postal services

It's easiest to purchase stamps and send postcards from international hotels unless you are in the Centro and can stop by the stunning Correos de México building. Use shipping companies (*see p240*) to send bigger items, since the Servicio Postal Mexicano is notoriously unreliable.

Stamps for postcards and letters sent to a Mexican destination cost MX$6.50 to MX$27.50, depending on weight. To the US (and Belize), the range is MX$9.50 to MX$92. Other parts of the globe are organised into zones and costs are calculated accordingly (A: MX$10.50-$197 Canada, Central America and the Caribbean; B: MX$13-$275 South America and Europe; C: MX$14.50-$357.50 Rest of the World). The lower price is the norm for average-weight correspondence.

Post offices

Palacio Postal (Correos de México HQ) *Tacuba 1, Centro (5521 1408). Metro Bellas Artes L2, L8.* **Open** 8am-7.30pm Mon-Fri; 8am-4pm Sat; 8am-2pm Sun (sale of stamps only). **No credit cards**. **Map** p267 L4.

San Ángel *Dr Gálvez 16, San Ángel (5550 2840). Metro Viveros L3.* **Open** 8am-5pm Mon-Fri; 8am-3.30pm Sat. **No credit cards**. **Map** p259 B3.

Zona Rosa *Cámara Nacional de Comercio de la Ciudad de México, Londres 208, Zona Rosa (5514 3029/5207 6072). Metro Insurgentes L1 or Sevilla L1/Metrobús Insurgentes or Reforma.* **Open** 8.30am-5pm Mon-Fri; 8.30am-3pm Sat. **No credit cards**. **Map** p264 G6.

Religion

Mexico is overwhelmingly Roman Catholic. Over 90 per cent of *chilangos* described

themselves as Catholic in the last census (2005). Mass at the Metropolitan Cathedral or the Basilica (*see p84*) is a memorable experience even if you aren't among the faithful.

Anglican

Christ Church *Montes Escandinavos 405, Chapultepec (5202 0949/ www.christchurchmexico.org). Metro Auditorio L7, then taxi.* **Services** 8.30am Sun (English); 10am Sun (Spanish).

Jewish

Bet El De México *Horacio 1722, Polanco (5281 2124/www. comunidad-betel.org). Metro Polanco L7.* **Services** 7.30am, 7.45am daily. *Friday* Minjá 7.30pm; Kabalat Shabat 7.45pm. *Saturday* Shajarit 8.30am; Minjá 7.45pm. *Sunday* Shajarit 9am; Minjá Arvit 7.45pm.

Muslim

Centro Salafí de México *Sur 77 32, Lorenzo Boturini (5541 8583/ information in English from Musa Abdullah Reyes 2615 6008/www. islammexico.net). Metro Fray Servando L4.* **Services** phone ahead or check website.

Safety & security

Mexico City has a reputation for crime that deters many a would-be visitor. But security, most notably in the Centro and other tourist-friendly areas, has improved in recent years despite the occasional incursion of north Mexico's drug-related violence into the capital, and a recent spate of high-profile kidnappings for ransom. Foreigners are rarely involved in such violence or kidnappings, and indeed, crimes against tourists fell by 18 per cent in the first half of 2008 compared to the same period in the previous year. Most crime against tourists is of the petty variety, but even so, a few precautions could help you avoid an unpleasant experience. For essential information on taking taxis safely, *see p238* **Taxi tips**.

● Avoid being a tempting target for street crime: leave expensive jewellery at home and dress discreetly.

● Keep tabs on your possessions in public places, staying aware of your surroundings and alert to anyone taking undue interest in you.

● Be particularly alert in places such as bus stations, at tourist sites and on public transport, particularly long-distance buses.

● Use cashpoints in well frequented locations in daylight hours, withdraw small amounts, and be vigilant when leaving bureaux de change.

● If you are approached by strangers for no apparent reason, be wary. Ask for identification from police officers.

● Don't leave your food or drink unattended in public places, and be cautious in accepting it from strangers.

Smoking

Once a city in which every night out led to a new load of laundry, streaming eyes and a hacking cough, DF took the unlikely step of banning smoking in public areas in 2008. Even more incredibly, the anti-tobacco law is being strictly enforced, so smokers have to congregate outside cantinas and bars to top up their nicotine levels.

Study

Mexico City has many universities, of varying standards. To register for university-based study you will need to show evidence of the appropriate student visa. Commercial language schools are more flexible and it is possible to take courses on a tourist card. The selected institutions outlined below have high standards in their areas of expertise. The largest – and the cheapest – is the government's **Universidad Nacional Autónoma de México** (UNAM – Oficina de la Dirección, Circuito Escolar S/N, Ciudad Universitaria, Coyoacán, www.cepe. unam.mx). Particularly strong on arts, humanities, political science and languages, UNAM's southern campus – Ciudad Universitaria (CU) – is recognised by UNESCO as a World Heritage Site. **The Instituto Tecnológico Autónomo de México** (Río Hondo 1, Progreso Tizapán, 5628 4000 ext 1600, www.itam.mx) is best for economics, business studies and politics, but courses are pricey. **La Universidad de la Salle** (ULSA), an international institution with a campus in Condesa, is a good option for language courses (Centro de Idiomas, Benjamín Franklin 47, Condesa, 01800 527 2553, www.ulsa.edu.mx). Other campuses are located in Cuernavaca, Playa del Carmen and Cancún. There is also the mid-range private **Universidad del Valle de México** with its well-located campus in Roma (01800 000 0886, www.uvmnet.edu).

Language classes

Berlitz Mexico City

First floor, Nisa 5, Zona Rosa (5525 4780/5525 4782/www. berlitz.com.mx). Metro Insurgentes L1/Metrobús Reforma or Insurgentes. **Open** 7am-9pm Mon-Fri. **Credit** AmEx, MC, V. **Map** p264 H5.
Berlitz dominates English-language teaching in Mexico with nine campuses in Mexico City alone.

Centro Educativo Multidisciplinario Polanco (CEM Polanco)

Hipólito Taine 246, Polanco (5254 0313/5203 3926, ext 108/www.cempolanco.unam.mx) Metro Polanco L7. **Open** 10am-8.30pm Mon-Fri during term time. **Credit** MC, V. **Map** p262 D4.
The UNAM's School for Foreign Students (CEPE) has a conveniently located campus in Polanco. Classes available in Spanish language and Mexican culture. You'll need to give evidence of a student visa to register

for courses. You can take the globally recognised Spanish Language Proficiency Exam. Courses count towards university credits. A term of conversation classes starts at MX$2,000.

International House

Alfonso Reyes 224, Hipódromo Condesa (5211 6500/www.ihmexico. com). Metro Chilpancingo L9 or Patriotismo L9/Metrobús Chilpancingo. **Open** 7am-9pm Mon-Fri, 9am-1pm Sat. **Credit** MC, V. **Map** p264 F9.
Tailor-made Spanish tuition in a gorgeous listed building. Intensive group and individual courses available. The school can also organise home-stay accommodation with a local family to increase your exposure to the language.

Telephones

Dialling & codes

The international access code for Mexico is +52, while DF's city code is 55. Landline numbers in the capital consist of eight digits. You don't need to dial 55 to call a fixed-line phone within DF from either a mobile or another landline. To call a Mexican landline outside of the capital (from DF) you dial 01 followed by the city code. Dial 01 55 followed by the local number to ring Mexico City from elsewhere in the country.

Mobile phone codes change according to the city in which the service was registered. Mexico City mobiles start with 04455 followed by an eight-digit number. To call the same from abroad, the code changes to +52 155. When calling from a landline to a mobile registered to another city, you must replace the 044 with 045. Mobile-to-mobile calls are made by dropping the 044 and just dialling the area code (55 for Mexico City) and the eight-digit number. To phone abroad from Mexico, dial 00 followed by the relevant country code (eg 0044 for the UK). Useful country codes are as follows.

Australia 61
Canada 1
Ireland 353
New Zealand 64
South Africa 27
United Kingdom 44
United States 1

Mobile phones

GSM 1900 mobile networks cover the capital and most of Mexico. There is a strong 3G network in Mexico. Leading cellphone providers – Telcel (www.telcel.com) and Movistar (www.movistar.com) – both supply iPhones at a high price. Check with your service provider about roaming services before leaving home. Most Mexicans use pay-as-you-go mobiles. These are cheap and readily available. Call charges are high by European standards but still much cheaper than using a roaming service. Top-up cards of MX$100 to MX$500 can be purchased from supermarkets and most convenience stores.

Operator services

National long distance service and operator 020
Wake-up call 031
Speaking clock 030
National directory enquiries 040
International long distance operator 090

Public phones

Public phones are still commonplace in Mexico, with one on practically every street corner. **Telmex** (the near-monopoly in the Mexican telecommunications market) runs almost all payphones through Ladatel. Some phone boxes accept coins while others can only be used with a prepaid Ladatel card (MX$30, MX$50 and MX$100), available from grocery shops and supermarkets. Local calls (to a landline) are MX$3 with no time limit. National calls to a fixed line cost MX$4 per minute. Calls to local mobile phones will set you back

Directory

MX$3 per minute. Calls to mobiles registered outside DF will cost double. Calls to US, Canadian or EU landlines are charged at MX$5 per minute. To make a local reverse-charge (collect) call, dial 020 and ask the operator for assistance (call 090 for an international equivalent).

Time

Mexico is spread across three time zones. The capital – along with most of the country – is located in Central Standard Time (CST), which is six hours behind GMT. The states of Chihuahua, Nayarit, Sonora, Sinaloa and Baja California Sur apply Mountain Standard Time (MST), while Baja California Norte uses Pacific Standard Time (PST). Daylight Saving Time (CDT) comes into effect from 2am on the first Sunday in April until 2am on the last Sunday in October. Sonora does not observe DST, keeping in line with the neighbouring US state of Arizona.

Tipping

Tipping is customary, but not obligatory. In restaurants, ten per cent is perfectly acceptable and 12 to 15 per cent not excessive if you've received excellent service. Check your credit card slip carefully to see if a space has been left for the *propina* (tip). Put a line through the box if you plan to tip in cash or ask for a *cuenta cerrada* (literally closing your tab). This will stop you from accidentally tipping twice and prevent the quantity charged to your card from being altered subsequently by an unscrupulous waiter. Hotel maids will be glad of a tip, while bellboys expect them. Parking, toilet and petrol pump attendants rely on gratuities for their livelihoods. Be sure to tip those helping to pack your shopping at the supermarket. They often receive only a token

salary, if that. Taxi drivers don't expect to receive gratuities but it's a nice gesture if they've given you a pleasant ride.

Toilets

There is a dearth of public toilets in Mexico City. In theory, you should purchase something before attempting to use bathrooms in bars or cafés, but if you ask nicely and look desperate enough, the staff might let you pop in.

Tourist information

SECTUR and DF's Secretaría de Turismo will both oblige (*see p243*). Most hotels also offer a wealth of information for tourists.

Visas & immigration

Citizens of the US, Canada, Australia, New Zealand and almost all Western European countries including the UK and Ireland can enter Mexico without obtaining a tourist visa in advance. Non-Mexican single parents entering the country with their child (under 18) must present a notarised

document giving the consent of the non-travelling parent to enter Mexico. Check with your nearest Mexican consulate for further information.

Airline flight attendants distribute tourist cards (FMTs) to fill out before landing. Mexican passport control will normally issue visitors with a 90-day tourist visa.

Non-US nationals travelling to Mexico via the United States, even in transit, must meet US entry requirements.

Weights & measures

Mexico uses the metric system across the board. Weights are measured in grams and kilograms and distances in metres and kilometres.

When to go

Climate

The high altitude makes for nippy mornings and evenings in DF, and visitors might forget that they are technically in the tropics. The capital's rainy period coincides with the hurricane season suffered in the south-west and along the

Weather report

Average daytime temperatures and rainfall in Mexico City.

Month	Max temp (°C/°F)	Min temp (°C/°F)	Rainfall (mm/in)
Jan	21/70	6/43	7/0.3
Feb	23/73	7/45	5/0.2
Mar	26/79	9/48	10/0.4
Apr	27/81	11/52	24/0.9
May	27/81	12/54	57/2.2
June	25/77	12/54	136/5.4
July	23/73	12/54	173/6.8
Aug	24/75	12/54	164/6.5
Sep	23/73	12/54	142/5.6
Oct	23/73	10/50	59/2.3
Nov	22/72	8/46	14/0.6
Dec	21/70	6/43	6/0.2

Caribbean coast. Rains may start around April and May, the hottest months, continuing throughout the summer and into October. The heavens usually open in mid afternoon, sometimes for a matter of minutes, and at other times rain pours down long into the night. DF usually feels the effects of any hostile weather system lashing the country's hurricane belt. In these cases, be prepared for endless rainy days. July, August and September are usually the soggiest. *Chilangos* claim that the weather is becoming '*aún más loco*' (even more crazy and unpredictable) due to the effects of climate change.

Air quality & pollution

The relocation of a large portion of DF's industry to Toluca has helped reduce pollution levels. Similarly, initiatives to restrict the movement of older vehicles within the city limits – such as the *No circula hoy* or 'Don't drive today' programme – are improving air quality. Yet the sheer quantity of cars on the roads and the geography of the city complicate matters. There is no hard and fast rule, but conditions are generally worse in the winter (dry season), when there is little or no rain to wash pollutants away and windy days are rarer.

Air pollution levels are monitored and published daily via the Índice Metropolitano de la Calidad del Aire (IMECA). DF's Sistema de Monitoreo Atmosférico (SIMAT) is charged with measuring and forecasting levels of air contamination (ozone, sulphur dioxide, nitrogen dioxide, and so on). Occasionally the index shows an increase above levels safe for vulnerable groups (101-150) such as children, and adults with cardiovascular or

respiratory problems. You can consult the monitoring service daily (www.sma.df.gob.mx).

Public holidays

Gone are the days when a mid-week saint's day or other national holiday would allow employees to take off half the week. Mexico now observes a reduced *puente* system – literally a 'bridge' that groups days off together. Most special commemorations – *días festivos* – are observed on a designated Monday to grant workers a long weekend. Other traditional holidays are no longer obligatory and tend to be observed only by the public sector and sometimes by banks, if at all. We've marked these with asterisks.

New Years Day/Año Nuevo
1 Jan.
Constitution Day/Día de la Constitución *5 Feb (observed 1st Mon of Feb).*
Birthday of Benito Juárez/ Natalicio de Benito Juárez *21 Mar (observed 3rd Mon of Mar).*
Maundy Thursday/Jueves Santo *Mar/Apr. Thur of Holy Week/Semana Santa.*
Good Friday/Viernes Santo *Mar/Apr. Fri of Holy Week/ Semana Santa.*
Labour Day/Día Internacional de los Trabajadores *1 May.*
Anniversary of Battle of Puebla/Anniversario de la Batalla de Puebla o 5 de Mayo *5 May*.
Mothers' Day/Día de la Madre *10 May*.
Independence Day/Día de la Independencia *16 Sept.*
Columbus Day/Día de la Raza *12 Oct*.
Day of the Dead/Día de los Muertos *2 Nov.*
Anniversary of the Mexican Revolution/Aniversario de la Revolución Mexicana *20 Nov (observed 3rd Mon of Nov).*
Presidential Inauguration Day/Transmisión de Poder *1 Dec every 6 years (2012 is the next observation).*
Day of Our Lady of Guadalupe/Día de la Virgen de Guadalupe *12 Dec*.
Christmas Day/Día de Navidad *25 Dec.*

Women

Women travelling alone can expect overt male attention. If you are lucky enough to be accompanied by a male Mexican friend, potential suitors tend to back off. Sometimes you'll hear a strange hissing noise – like someone doing an impression of a snake – designed to attract your attention, preceding the usual advances. 'Suitors' are often forward but not overly persistent unless you show an interest.

Owing to the frequency of the mostly low-level harassment that many women tend to suffer while using the city's overcrowded public transport system, a number of measures have been put in place to help lessen the pain. On the city's underground system, or Metro, carriages are set aside at one end of the train during peak hours for women and children only. Look out for the *mujeres y niños* sign and a barrier at the end of the platform, usually manned by a bored-looking policeman who is meant to stop men from riding those carriages. There often *are* men in there, but they are grossly outnumbered by women and the dedicated space provides a welcome respite from the rest of the train.

Working in Mexico

Visitors entering on a tourist card (FMT) are not permitted to carry out paid or voluntary work. In reality, many tourists do so in the knowledge that detection rates are low. It is recommendable to apply for a working visa (FM3) before entering the country, but you can change your migration status (*estado migratorio*) at the **Instituto Nacional de Migración** (Homero 1832, Polanco, 5387 2400) if you are subsequently offered a job.

Vocabulary

Mexicans refer to their Spanish as *español*. *Chilangos* use a lot of slang but generally tone it down when speaking to *extranjeros* (foreigners).

The informal subject pronoun *tú* (you) is used more regularly in DF than in the rest of the country, where it is frowned upon for being over familiar. Hotel and restaurant staff will usually use the formal subject pronoun *usted* when addressing customers. Stick to *usted* in any kind of formal or business environment, and when addressing older people.

Pronunciation

c before an **i** or an **e** is like the **c** in city or **s** in sinner.
c in all other cases is as in catalogue.
g before an **i** or **e** is pronounced like a guttural **h** (think of a Spanish person saying hhhamster).
g in all other cases is as in goal.
h at the start of a word is usually silent unless it is a proper noun borrowed from another language (eg Calle Herschel).
ll is similar to a **y** (*llegar* – to arrive – is pronounced like 'yay-GAR'.
ñ sounds like the **ny** in canyon.
r is rolled at the beginning of a word and spectacularly so if it's a double **rr** elsewhere.

Stress rules

Mexicans stress the penultimate syllable in words concluding with a vowel, **n** or **s** – chil-AN-go, CRE-ma, vent-AN-as. The last syllable is stressed in words ending with any other consonant – ciu-DAD, ball-ET. Words that deviate from the rules are given an accent (*tilde*) to clarify matters – *habitación, lámpara*.

Basics

hello *hola*
hello (when answering the phone) *bueno*
good morning, good day *buenos días*
good afternoon, good evening *buenas tardes*
good evening (after approximately 7pm),
good night *buenas noches*
goodbye/see you later *adiós/hasta luego*
please *por favor*
thank you *gracias*
you're welcome *de nada*
do you speak English? *¿habla usted inglés?*
I don't speak Spanish *no hablo español*
I don't understand *no entiendo*
what's your name? *¿cómo te llamas?* (informal); *¿cómo se llama usted?* (formal)
speak more slowly, please *habla más lento, por favor*
Sir/Mr *señor*
Madam/Mrs *señora*
excuse me, please (to get attention) *disculpe*
excuse me please (to squeeze past someone) *con permiso*
sorry/excuse me *perdón* or *lo siento*
where is…? *¿dónde está…?*
how much is it? *¿cuánto es?*

Getting around

airport *aeropuerto*
bus station *terminal de autobuses/camiones*
metro station *estación del metro*
entrance *entrada*
exit *salida*
car *coche/auto/carro*
bus *autobús/camion*
minibus *pesero/micro*
train *tren*
a ticket *un boleto/ticket*
return *ida y vuelta*
bus stop *parada de autobús*
left *izquierda*
right *derecha*
here *aquí/acá*
there *ahí/allá*
straight on *todo derecho*

near *cerca*
far *lejos*

Accommodation

do you have a double/ single room for tonight/ one week? *¿tiene una habitación doble/sencilla/ para esta noche/una semana?*
we have a reservation *tenemos una reservación*
with/without bathroom *con/sin baño*
double bed *cama matrimonial*
breakfast included *desayuno incluído*

Time

now *ahora*
later *más tarde*
yesterday *ayer*
tomorrow *mañana*

Numbers

0 *cero*; **1** *uno*; **2** *dos*; **3** *tres*; **4** *cuatro*; **5** *cinco*; **6** *seis*; **7** *siete*; **8** *ocho*; **9** *nueve*; **10** *diez*; **11** *once*; **12** *doce*; **13** *trece*; **14** *catorce*; **15** *quince*; **16** *dieciséis*; **17** *diecisiete*; **18** *dieciocho*; **19** *diecinueve*; **20** *veinte*; **21** *veintiuno*; **22** *veintidós*; **30** *treinta*; **40** *cuarenta*; **50** *cincuenta*; **60** *sesenta*; **70** *setenta*; **80** *ochenta*; **90** *noventa*; **100** *cien*; **200** *doscientos*; **1,000** *mil*; **1,000,000** *un millón*.

Days & dates

Monday *lunes*; **Tuesday** *martes*; **Wednesday** *miércoles*; **Thursday** *jueves*; **Friday** *viernes*; **Saturday** *sábado*; **Sunday** *domingo*.

January *enero*; **February** *febrero*; **March** *marzo*; **April** *abril*; **May** *mayo*; **June** *junio*; **July** *julio*; **August** *agosto*; **September** *septiembre*; **October** *octubre*; **November** *noviembre*; **December** *diciembre*.

Further Reference

Books

Fiction & literature

Jessica Abel *La Perdida* A young American woman's adventures in DF, told in graphic-novel form.
Carlos Fuentes *Where the Air Is Clear* This unsparingly brutal depiction of Mexico's stratified society put both Fuentes and Mexico City on the literary map.
Jack Kerouac *Tristessa* Kerouac's short but definitive Mexico City novel. It tells the gritty tale of an American poet and his obsessive love for a DF drug addict, Tristessa. The pre-eminent writer of the Beat movement also published his seminal 'jazz poem', *Mexico City Blues*, inspired by his sojourn in DF.
DH Lawrence *The Plumed Serpent* Lawrence wrote this novel, originally entitled *Quetzalcoatl* (the Aztec name for the Mesoamerican deity), during his stay at Mexico's immense lake Chapala. The novel opens in the capital, where a group of foreigners are spectators at a bullfight.
Malcolm Lowry *Under the Volcano* A semi-autobiographical novel telling the story of an alcoholic British diplomat drinking himself to death on the Day of the Dead in 1939 in a small Mexican town believed to be Cuernavaca.
Paco Ignacio Taibo II *An Easy Thing* A classic creation by the premier *chilango* crime writer. Cruel yet captivating DF is the backdrop to super sleuth Héctor Belascoarán Shayne's triple investigation. Part of a series starring Mexico City's answer to Inspector Morse, the first of which, *Días de Combate*, has yet to be translated into English.

Non-fiction

Nicholas Gilman *Good Food in Mexico City: A Guide to Food Stalls, Fondas and Fine Dining.* A wide-ranging culinary tour of DF from a food-obsessed resident.
Richard Grabman *Gods, Gachupines and Gringos* The first general history of Mexico to have been published in English in almost 30 years, by the writer of our History chapter.
David Lida *First Stop in the New World: Mexico City, the Capital of the 21st Century.* A street-level panorama of contemporary Mexico City. A work of literary journalism, it's told through the eyes of the people who live there, from sex workers and street kids to socialites

and multinational executives. Critically acclaimed in the US press and around the world.
Octavio Paz *The Labyrinth of Solitude and Other Writings* A seminal study of Mexico's national character including insights into the deeper meanings of traditional religious and cultural festivals.
Alan Riding *Distant Neighbors: A Portrait of the Mexicans* The musings of a former *New York Times* correspondent on Mexican politics, culture and the country's complex relationship with the USA.

Film

Ahí Está el Detalle (Juan Bustillo Oro, 1940) Satirical comedy from Cantinflas – Mexico's answer to Charlie Chaplin – involving a classic case of mistaken identity and the conflict between rich and poor.
Amores Perros (Alejandro González Iñárritu, 2000) The lives of three *chilangos* become linked after a horrendous car accident. A hugely influential indie hit which explores the capital's social polarisation.
La Ley de Hérodes (*Herod's Law*, Luis Estrada, 1999) A well meaning politician is unable to resist Mexico's corruption in this controversial film that was originally banned in Mexico.
Los Olvidados (Luis Buñuel, 1950) Iconic film documenting the lives of a juvenile gang in the slums of DF.
Nosotros los Pobres (*We the Poor*, Ismael Rodríguez, 1947) Celebrated epic from 1940s actor and singer-songwriter Pedro Infante. It's the first in the trilogy about 'Pepe el Toro' (Pepe the Bull), a carpenter, wrongly accused of murder, who later triumphs as a boxer.
Temporada de Patos (*Duck Season*, Fernando Eimbcke, 2004) Whimsical indie film set entirely in a DF apartment. With the intimacy of a stage play, it mixes humour with emotionally revealing dialogue between two teenage friends on a day that the power goes out.
Y Tu Mamá También (Alfonso Cuarón, 2001) A fun, filthy but thought-provoking road movie kicking off in Mexico City that, combined with *Amores Perros*, put modern *chilango* cinema on the map.

Music

Los Ángeles Azules Deliciously cheesy, brass-heavy Mexican *cumbia* that will put a smile on your face.
Austin TV *Fontana Bella* Instrumental indie tunes with a touch of Mogwai from local boys made

good, whose music features in the soundtrack of *Temporada de Patos*.
Café Tacuba *Cuatro Caminos* Alternative rock band with a knack for catchy tunes. They are one of Mexico City's most successful musical exports, named after the classic eaterie in the Centro Histórico.
Oscar Chávez *20 Exitos* Popular selection of songs from the undisputed saviour of Mexico's fading traditional music.
Salvador 'Chava' Flores *Su Antología* The best of DF's musical storyteller (1920-87) whose folkloric songs are part of the fabric of local popular culture.
Jaime López 'Chilanga Banda' Seminal song from rebel-rocker, activist and adopted son of DF, which was later covered by Café Tacuba. Stuffed with *chilango* slang.
El TRI 35 *Años y lo que falta todavía* Greatest hits from DF's acoustic rock and blues band – an institution across Latin America since the late 1960s.

Websites

www.theanglo.org.mx/www.tamf.org.mx The Anglo-Mexican Foundation builds cultural links between Mexico and the UK.
www.cenapred.unam.mx/popo/UltimalmagenVolcanl.html Real-time images of Mexico City's magnificent volcano, Popocatépetl.
www.geocities.com/Athens/Academy/3088/nahuatl.html Basic instruction in Náhuatl, one of Mexico's most important indigenous languages, including links to an English-Náhuatl dictionary.
www.goodfoodmexico.blogspot.com Blog from food-writer Gilman on Mexico City's tastiest culinary options.
www.davidlida.com Wide-ranging and cliché-free online journal from one of DF's most perceptive commentators.
http://mexicoreporter.com Multimedia news blog by talented reporter Deborah Bonello.
www.mexicocooks.typepad.com The essential Mexican foodie blog – highly recommended
www.mexpat.com Website of expat community organisation.
http://mexfiles.wordpress.com Chilango-born blog by an expat pair musing on life in Mexico. A great selection of links for further research.
www.mexicotodayblog.com Current affairs blog by broadcaster and former US government advisor
www.mexperience.com Well-informed resource for lovers of Mexico, with advice on doing business plus travel and real estate.

Directory

Index

Note: entries in **bold** are key sights, places and topics; page numbers in **bold** indicate section(s) giving key information on an entry; page numbers in *italics* indicate photographs.

Area name	ROMA
National park/protected area	
Place of interest and/or entertainment	
Railway station	
International boundary	
Regional/provincial boundary	
Highway	
Dual carriageway	
Main road	
Important other road	
Railway	
Town or village	○
Mountain/volcano	▲
Hospital	✚
Church/cathedral	✚
Tourist information	ℹ
Metro station	Ⓜ
Metrobús station	ⅯⒷ

Maps

Greater Mexico City & Around

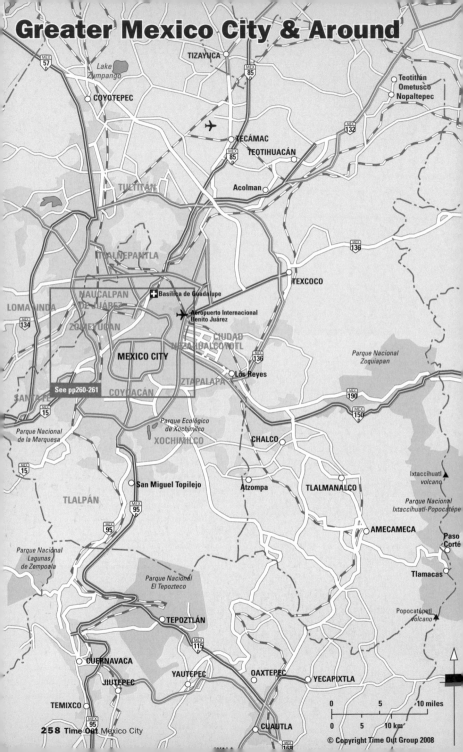

MEX 57
Lake Zumpango
TIZAYUCA
MEX 85
COYOTEPEC
Teotitlán
Ometusco
Nopaltepec
MEX 132
TECÁMAC
MEX 85
TEOTIHUACÁN
Acolman
TULTITLÁN
MEX 136
TLALNEPANTLA
TEXCOCO
Basílica de Guadalupe
NAUCALPAN DE JUÁREZ
LOMA LINDA
MEX 134
Aeropuerto Internacional Benito Juárez
ZONTECÓN
CIUDAD NAZAHUALCOYOTL
Parque Nacional Zoquiapan
MEXICO CITY
MEX 136
See pp260-261
Los Reyes
MEX 190
IZTAPALAPA
COYOACÁN
MEX 15
SAN FE
MEX 150
Parque Ecológico de Xochimilco
Parque Nacional de la Marquesa
CHALCO
XOCHIMILCO
Ixtaccíhuatl volcano
MEX 15
San Miguel Topilejo
Atzompa
TLALMANALCO
Parque Nacional Ixtaccíhuatl-Popocatépe
TLALPÁN
MEX 95
AMECAMECA
Paso Corté
MEX 95
Parque Nacional Lagunas de Zempoala
Parque Nacional El Tepozteco
Tlamacas
Popocatépetl volcano
TEPOZTLÁN
MEX 115
CUERNAVACA
YAUTEPEC
OAXTEPEC
YECAPIXTLA
JIUTEPEC
TEMIXCO
MEX 95
CUAUTLA
MEX 168

0   5   10 miles
0   5   10 km

San Ángel & Coyoacán

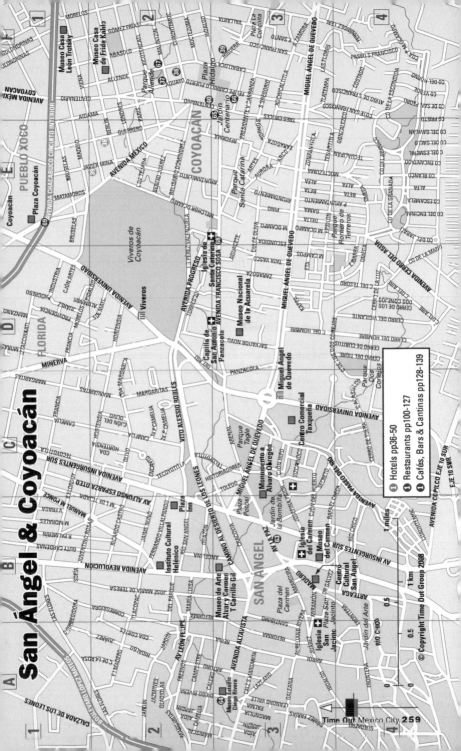

Museo Casa León Trotsky
Museo Casa de Frida Kahlo

MORELOS
GÓMEZ FARÍAS
VALLARTA
MALINTZIN
XICOTÉNCATL
ABASOLO
ALLENDE
Parque Xicoténcatl
Plaza Hidalgo
Jardín Centenario
AGUAYO
CENTENARIO
PRESIDENTE CARRANZA
Plaza La Conchita
SAN FRANCISCO
CORINA
TRES CRUCES
MIGUEL ÁNGEL DE QUEVEDO

COYOACÁN

AVENIDA MÉXICO

Viveros de Coyoacán

AVENIDA PROGRESO
Capilla de San Antonio Panzacola
Iglesia de Santa Catarina
AVENIDA FRANCISCO SOSA
Museo Nacional de la Acuarela
Parque Santa Catarina
PANZACOLA

FLORIDA
MINERVA

Parque Tagle
Centro Comercial Taxqueña
Miguel Ángel de Quevedo

Monumento a Alvaro Obregón
Jardín de la Bombilla
HISTORIADORES

Plaza Inn
Instituto Cultural Helénico
AVENIDA REVOLUCIÓN
AVENIDA INSURGENTES SUR

SAN ANGEL

Museo de Arte Alvar y Carmen T Carrillo Gil
Iglesia del Carmen
Museo del Carmen
Centro Cultural San Ángel
Plaza del Carmen
Iglesia San Jacinto
Plaza San Jacinto
Jardín del Arte

Museo Estudio Diego Rivera

CALZADA DE LOS LEONES
BOULEVARD ADOLFO LÓPEZ MATEOS

AVENIDA CHACABUCO CIRCUITO INTERIOR

PUEBLO XOCO
Coyoacán
Plaza Coyoacán

AVENIDA UNIVERSIDAD

AVENIDA CERRO DEL AGUA

AVENIDA PASEO DEL RÍO

AVENIDA INSURGENTES SUR

AVENIDA CEPILCO EJE 10 SUR

EJE 10 SUR

1 Hotels pp36-50
2 Restaurants pp100-127
3 Cafés, Bars & Cantinas pp128-139

1 miles
0.5

1 km
0.5

© Copyright Time Out Group 2008

Mexico City by Area

EJE 2 NORTE

INSTITUTO TECNOLÓGICO Y DE INDUST.

SAN ESTEBAN

CALZADA MÉXICO TACUBA

CALZADA LEGARIA

CALZADA MÉXICO TACUBA

MIGUEL
HIDALGO

AV MARINA NACIONAL

LOMAS DE
SOTELO

RÍO SAN JOAQUIN

AMPLIACIÓN
GRANADA

AV DEL CONSCRIPTO

Hipódromo

INDUSTRIA MILITAR

BOULEVARD ÁVILA CAMACHO

See pp262-263

AV EJÉRCITO NACIONAL

SAN MIGUEL
CHAPULTEPEC

SAN RAFA

HORACIO

POLANCO

CUAUHTÉMOC

PRESIDENTE MASARYK

AV DE LOS BOSQUES

PASEO DE LA REFORMA

PASEO DE LA REFORMA

ZONA
ROSA

AV CHAPULTEPEC

BOSQUE DE
CHAPULTEPEC
(1st Section)

CHAPULTEPEC

BOSQUE DE
CHAPULTEPEC
(2nd Section)

JOSÉ VASCONCELOS

AV MAZATLAN

CONDESA

ROM

AV INSURGENTES CENTRO

DANIEL
GARZA

BENJAMIN FRANKLIN

AV INSURGENTES

AV CONSTITUYENTES

PERIFÉRICO

JALISCO

BOSQUE DE
CHAPULTEPEC
(3RD SECTION)

OBSERVATORIO

VIADUCTO MIGUEL ALEMA

XOL

Terminal Central Poniente
(Bus Terminal)

AV LAS TORRES

DEL VALLE

Presa de
Tacubaya

VASCO DE QUIROGA

AV PATRIOTISMO

PENNSYLVANIA

AV EUGENIA

SANTA FE

AV COYOACAN

ALTA TENSIÓN

BOULEVARD ADOLFO LÓPEZ MATEOS

FÉLIX CUEVAS

AV SANTA LUCÍA

MIXCOAC

RÍO MIXCOAC

JOSÉ MARÍA RICO

AV CENTENARIO

Presa Mixcoac

FLORIDA

REVOLUCIÓN

AV INSURGENTES SUR

AV UNIVERSIDAD

CALZADA DE LAS ÁGUILAS

SAN
ÁNGEL

Viveros de
Coyoacán

COYOACÁN

MIGUEL ÁNGEL DE QUEVEDO

See p259

to Terminal Central Norte
(Bus Terminal)

GUADALUPE

AV 506

AV INSURGENTES NORTE

MANUEL GONZÁLEZ

FERROCARRIL DEL NORTE

RÍO CONSULADO

AV RICARDO FLORES MAGÓN

AV CANAL DEL NORTE

OCEANÍA

AV 602

OCEANÍA

Antigua Estación de
Ferrocarriles Buenavista

See pp266-267

AV DEL TRABAJO

AV CONGRESO DE LA UNIÓN

AV ING E MOLINA

EJE 1 NORTE

RAYÓN

SAN COSME

CENTRO

ALBAÑILES

OCEANÍA

AV HIDALGO

ANILLO DE CIRCUNVALACIÓN

EJE 1 ORIENTE

Terminal de Oriente
(Bus Terminal)

EJE 1 NORTE

BOULEVARD PUERTO AÉREO

Aeropuerto Internacional
Benito Juárez

PASEO DE LA REFORMA

BUCARELI

BALDERAS

I ZARAGOZA

IZTACCÍHUATL

See pp264-265

JUÁREZ

ALAMEDA

Jardín Chiapas

FRAY SERVANDO TERESA DE MIER

DOCTORES

AV CUAUHTÉMOC

EJE CENTRAL LÁZARO CÁRDENAS

N HÉROES

EJE 1 PONIENTE

EJE 2 SUR

SAN ANTONIO ABAD

AV DEL TALLER

AV MORELOS

VIADUCTO RÍO DE LA PIEDAD

AV BAJA CALIFORNIA

Ciudad Deportiva
Magdalena Mixhuca

RÍO CHURUBUSCO

SAN ANTONIO

NARVARTE

DIAGONAL SAN ANTONIO

FRANCISCO DEL PASO Y TRONCOSO

AV RÍO CHURUBUSCO

SAN RAFAEL ATLIXCO

XOLA

CALZADA DE TLALPAN

CALZADA DE LA VIGA

AV C DE TEZONTLE

CHURUBUSCO

AV UNIVERSIDAD

AV ANDRÉS MOLINA ENRÍQUEZ

AV RAMOS MILLÁN

LEYES DE REFORMA

ANGEL URRAZA

RÍO CHURUBUSCO

PURÍSIMA

EJE CENTRAL LÁZARO CÁRDENAS

MORELOS

PLAYA PIE DE LA CUESTA

AV DIVISIÓN DEL NORTE

AV PRESIDENTE PLUTARCO ELÍAS CALLES

MUNICIPIO LIBRE

AGUSTÍN YAÑEZ

IZTAPALAPA

PUEBLO
XOCO

AV POPOCATÉPETL

AV 5 DE MAYO

AV RÍO CHURUBUSCO

CAL E IZTAPALAPA

EL CARMEN

0   1   2 miles

0   1   2 km

© Copyright Time Out Group 2008

Terminal de Sur
(Bus Terminal)

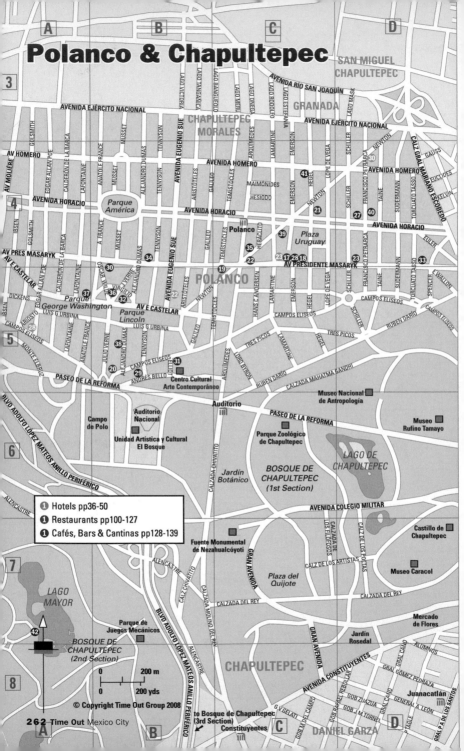

Polanco & Chapultepec

A | B | C | D

3

SAN MIGUEL CHAPULTEPEC

AVENIDA EJÉRCITO NACIONAL

GRANADA

CHAPULTEPEC MORALES

AVENIDA RÍO SAN JOAQUÍN

AVENIDA EJÉRCITO NACIONAL

AVENIDA HOMERO

AV HOMERO

AV MOLIERE

4

AVENIDA HORACIO

Parque América

AVENIDA HORACIO

AVENIDA HORACIO

41

AVENIDA HOMERO

MAIMÓNIDES

HESIODO

21

27 40

AV PRES MASARYK

Polanco

39 Plaza Uruguay

35

POLANCO

22

19

23

23 17 28 18

AV PRESIDENTE MASARYK

23

33

AV E CASTELAR

30

34

Parque George Washington

37 36

38 32

Parque Lincoln

AV E CASTELAR

CAMPOS ELISEOS

5

28

PASEO DE LA REFORMA

20

38

29

31

Centro Cultural Arte Contemporáneo

TRES PICOS

TRES PICOS

CAMPOS ELISEOS

Museo Nacional de Antropología

Auditorio

PASEO DE LA REFORMA

Campo de Polo

Auditorio Nacional

Unidad Artística y Cultural El Bosque

Parque Zoológico de Chapultepec

Museo Rufino Tamayo

6

Jardín Botánico

BOSQUE DE CHAPULTEPEC (1st Section)

LAGO DE CHAPULTEPEC

AVENIDA COLEGIO MILITAR

Castillo de Chapultepec

① Hotels pp36-50
① Restaurants pp100-127
① Cafés, Bars & Cantinas pp128-139

Fuente Monumental de Nezahualcóyoti

Plaza del Quijote

Museo Caracol

7

LAGO MAYOR

42

BOSQUE DE CHAPULTEPEC (2nd Section)

Parque de Juegos Mecánicos

Jardín Rosedal

Mercado de Flores

Juanacatlán

0   200 m
0   200 yds

CHAPULTEPEC

AVENIDA CONSTITUYENTES

DANIEL GARZA

© Copyright Time Out Group 2008

to Bosque de Chapultepec (3rd Section) Constituyentes

A | B | C | D

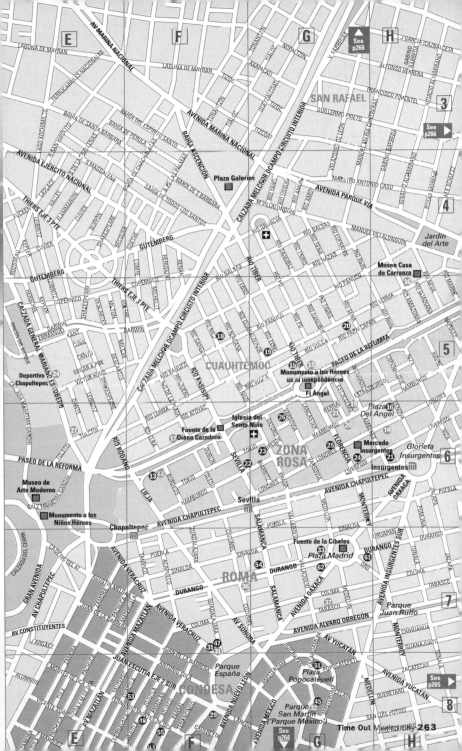

Centro

- **1** Hotels pp36-50
- **1** Restaurants pp100-127
- **1** Cafés, Bars & Cantinas pp128-139

Street Index

Advertisers' Index

Inside covers

Where to Stay

Sightseeing

Eat Drink Shop

Restaurants

Bars

Shops

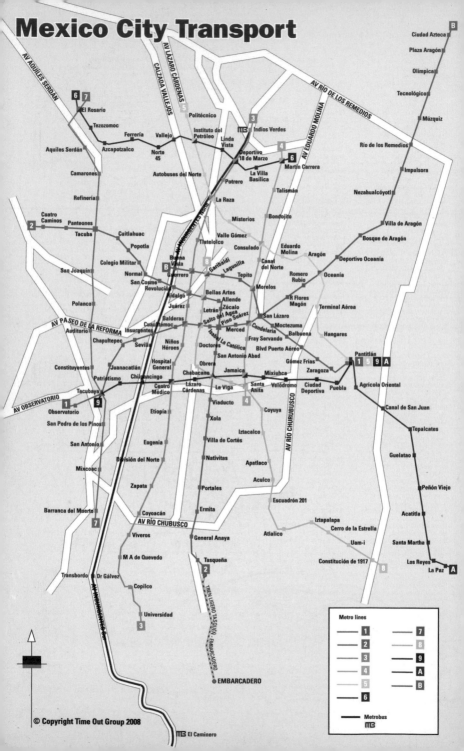

Mexico City Transport